# RELIGION

## in Indian History

# RELIGION

## in Indian History

Edited with an Introduction by

**Irfan Habib**

Aligarh Historians Society

Tulika Books

Published by **Tulika Books**
35A/1 (ground floor), Shahpur Jat, New Delhi 110 049, India



First edition (hardback) 2007
Second edition (paperback) 2007
Third edition (paperback) 2010
Fourth edition (paperback) 2012

Fifth edition (paperback) 2015

ISBN: 978-93-82381-54-9

Typeset in Minion and Univers at Tulika Print Communication Services, New Delhi; printed at Chaman Enterprises, 1603 Pataudi House, Daryaganj, Delhi 110 006

'He [the Mughal Emperor Akbar] cared little that in allowing everyone to follow his own religion he was in reality violating all religions.'

Fr. A. Monserrate, *Commentary on his Journey to the Court of Akbar* [1580–82], translated by J.S. Joyland, Cuttack, 1922, p. 142

'Religion is the sigh of the oppressed creature, the heart of a heartless world, just as it is the spirit of a spiritless situation. It is the opium of the people.'

Karl Marx, 'Contribution to the Critique of Hegel's *Philosophy of Right*' (1844)

# Contents

# Preface

The Aligarh Historians Society organized, with the assistance of the Indian Council of Social Science Research, New Delhi, and the Project of History of Indian Science, Philosophy and Culture, a panel on Religion and Material Life at Mysore on 29–30 December 2003, alongside the 64th session of the Indian History Congress. Most of the chapters in this volume were, in their initial versions, presented as papers at that panel. I am most grateful to the contributors who came to Mysore and threw open their papers to lively discussions. In addition, I am grateful to Mrs Feroza Athar Ali, who has permitted us to reprint the article on the Islamic Background to Indian History by the late Professor M. Athar Ali; to Professor Osamu Kondu for permission to include his paper on the Theologians' Declaration of 1579; and to Professor D.N. Jha for permission to reprint a large part of his address to the Indian History Congress (January 2006) on Constructing the Hindu Identity. Professor Kamlesh Mohan let us have her paper on Sikhism and women, after our panel had been held. My own paper on Kabir is a much revised version of what I had earlier published in *Social Scientist.*

The subject of Religion in Indian History is so vast that a volume like ours can hope to cover only bits and pieces of it, especially when our contributors wish to take up specifically defined themes in order to study them in some depth. The Introduction picks out four themes across our past (including prehistory), but it is intended more to raise questions or offer tentative hypotheses than to present an overarching survey of the field. I should mention that for Section 4 of the Introduction I have drawn heavily on certain drafts I had prepared for my chapters in UNESCO *History of Humanity*, Vol. 4, and *History of the Civilizations of Central Asia*, Vol. 5.

As to transliteration, different contributors have generally followed their own systems, mostly using, in the case of Sanskrit, the standard one, and in the case of Persian, that of Steingass's *Persian–English Dictionary*. But in the Introduction as well as in Professor Shrimali's chapter, 'ch' and 'chh' in Sanskrit words stand for 'c' and 'ch'; 'sh' and 'sh' for 'ś' and 'ṣ'; and 'ri' for 'ṛ' of the standard system.

The text has been processed at the office of the Aligarh Historians Society by Mr Muneeruddin Khan. Much other work including the keeping of accounts and xeroxing has been carried out by Mr Arshad Ali and Mr Idris Beg. Professor Shireen Moosvi, Secretary of the Society, is chiefly responsible for the fact that the papers in the volume could at last be brought together and made ready for publication.

On the side of Tulika Books, Dr Rajendra Prasad, Ms Indira Chandrasekhar and Mr Shad Naved have borne patiently with my delays, and made every effort to produce a volume that can hopefully be put alongside their other publications.

IRFAN HABIB

# Introduction

*Irfan Habib*

## I
## Religion and History

Any work dealing with religion (that is, religions in plural, rather than a particular religion) must grapple with the problem of definition. The massive *Oxford English Dictionary* (*OED*) gives a number of distinct senses of the word 'religion', but the most relevant for us are the following two senses:

(i) 'Action or conduct indicating a belief in, reverence for, and desire to please a divine ruling power; the exercise or practice of rites or observances implying this.'

(ii) 'Recognition on the part of man of some higher unseen power as having control of his destiny, and as being entitled to obedience, reverence and worship; the general mental and moral attitude resulting from this belief, with reference to its effect upon the individual or the community; personal or general acceptance of this feeling as a standard of spiritual or practical life.'

Looking closely at these definitions it is obvious that the *OED* editors' citations have references only to theistic religions, based on the worship of God or gods. A broader definition should cover all modes of human thought or action designed to cause or cajole a natural, or supernatural being, or force, or mechanism, to confer some benefit on, or ward off some harm from, the individual or group in this life or the conjectured existence beyond. Such a definition, while not confining religion to merely God/god-worshipping faiths would include nature-worship, cults of human gods (like the pharaohs) and 'philosophical' religions like Buddhism and Jainism with their *karma* doctrine. So enlarged in its meaning, the term 'religion' would include practically all forms of 'superstition' which the *OED*, *s.v.*, defines as 'unreasoning awe or fear of something unknown, mysterious or imaginary, especially in connexion with religion' or 'an irrational religious belief or practice; a tenet, scruple, habit, etc. founded on fear or ignorance'. Since all religion is founded on basic premises that are ultimately not subject to the scrutiny of reason, 'superstition' can usually do duty for any religion which is different from the one to which the speaker belongs, or is familiar with.

With religion as a distinct factor guiding human conduct, human actions become divisible into two kinds: one, where, knowing the inevitable or likely consequences from his own observation or practical experience, an individual acts in a particular way; or, secondly, where, by a belief communicated by custom or instruction he feels he has to act in a certain way, for otherwise by some supernatural action, he would suffer or fail to receive a benefit he could have received in this life or beyond. The fear of death often creates or fortifies a belief in afterlife where only a supernatural force can provide one with either some comfort or some form of existence. Religion seems, therefore, to meet a vital psychological need.

The following words come from Karl Marx, during an early phase in his intellectual life (1844), precisely to this effect: 'Religion is the sigh of the oppressed creature, the heart of a heart-less world, just as it is the spirit of a spiritless situation. It is the opium of the people.'[1]

These remarks are prefaced by the statement that 'man makes religion, religion does not make man'.[2] Marx calls this formula the basis of 'irreligious criticism'; it also necessarily represents the standpoint of the critical historian, except, perhaps, with the qualification that once made by man, religion also influences human conduct, and, to that extent, makes man.

Man-made, existing purely in human minds, religion is subject to change in the same manner as are all other mental constructs. Marx had been greatly affected by Ludwig Feuerbach's work *The Essence of Christianity* (1841) in which that philosopher had argued that man makes God in his own image, but producing a reverse kind of image – 'God is what man is not.' This being so,[3] as human rational knowledge grows, the realm of the supernatural contracts. 'The course of religious development', Feuerbach wrote, 'consists specifically in this that man abstracts more and more from God and attributes it to himself.'[4] It is inherent in this process that isolated cults, which we today regard as superstitious beliefs and rituals, give way in time to widely spread religious systems, or, as in China, to ethical codes.

In Chapter 1 of our volume Professor D.P. Chattopadhyaya discusses in great depth the theoretical and historical issues involved in our search of the roots of religion; and the ways religions develop are most carefully and clinically explored there. I need here only deal with two points.

Religions, by and large, tend to accommodate their ethical codes to existing social circumstances. (This matter will be discussed, particularly with reference to the growth of the caste system, in Section 3 of this Introduction.) It may, then, happen that a religion, or certain aspects of a religion, become popular as they adjust better to the changes in the economic or social order. This is what Marx said in 1867 with respect to Christianity, but especially, its 'bourgeois developments, Protestantism, Deism, & c.', as being more suited to the conditions of rising capitalism.[5] Max Weber in 1904–05 presented a contrary view where 'Protestant ethic' was seen not merely as a consequence or complement of capitalism, but as the very source of 'the spirit of capitalism'.[6] The historical part of Weber's thesis was weak and unconvincing.[7] But surely when a religion suits a particular form of social order, it also helps to sustain and reinforce it; and to this extent, as we have affirmed, religion also 'makes man', of whatever kind. Professor Barun De in Chapter 5 in this volume takes stock of how two leading historians of ancient India, D.D. Kosambi and Niharranjan Ray, dealt in different ways with the relationship between religion and the changes in social history.

The second point I wish to take up concerns the spheres of religion and reason. Implicit in Feuerbach's formula of man 'abstracting' more and more from God, is the notion that the realm of reason advances as religion retreats. The general truth of the proposition may be conceded, but complexities cannot be ignored. Religions build up from their irrational fundamental premises a superstructure of theology or philosophy, which follows the methods of rational logic; on the other hand, many premises prevail in the realm of reason, like the current love of market and awe of globalization, which have, to say the least, questionable credentials from the point of view of the interests of large numbers of people. Dr Farhat Hasan in his essay (Chapter 14) takes up the issue of the post-modernist critique of rationalism offered by Foucault, who himself was quite firmly on the side of those resisting contemporary neo-imperialism. It happens, then, that the US assertions of supremacy in West Asia impart to the resistance the colour of practically a religious war, so that 2007 in Iraq, Palestine and Lebanon may remind us quite forcefully of our own 1857.[8]

Marx said that for religion to be abolished, the conditions of society, 'the vale of woe', must be abolished first.[9] This recognition of the roots of religion is constantly impressed upon us, in a myriad of ways, as we read our daily newspapers.

## II

## Religion in Prehistory

The moment when hominids began to think in some logical sequence, relating cause and effect, was probably also the moment when they began to entertain fears of the unknown and the unforeseen and look for rescue and protection from supernatural forces, which they hoped could be pacified or won over by gifts and ritual. Death being the supreme disaster to be afraid of, a netherworld or some other world had to be invented. Human burial is, therefore, one of the earliest indications of the arrival of religion. Such a development did not wait for the evolution of our own species, the *Homo sapiens.* With the Neanderthal man, living 230,000 to 30,000 years ago, burial was already a common practice. At the Teshik Tash cave, in Uzbekistan, was found, with the characteristic 'Mousterian' stone tools of the Neanderthal, 'the burial of a Neanderthal child surrounded by six pairs of horns of a Siberian mountain goat'.[10] Our own, being a younger species, is, therefore, likely to have been already affected by religious superstitions when it originated by hominid evolution in Africa some 150,000 years ago.

The earliest evidence of our species' recourse to religion in India seemingly comes from the Upper Palaeolithic settlement at Baghor I (Sidhi district, Jharkhand), datable to between 25,500 and 10,500 years ago. Here a sandstone rubble platform has been unearthed, at the centre of which was found embedded a piece of ferruginous sandstone, brought from a considerable distance. It must have had some cultic significance, as a charm or even as a representation of a deity.[11] By 10,000 years ago or 8,000 BC as the Mesolithic hunter-gatherers in the Central Gangetic Plains began to gather wild grains, the signs of religious practices and beliefs become more visible. There were regular burials, with bone ornaments and slaughtered animals also buried apparently to serve for food in the afterworld. The bone ornaments were worn by men, apparently not only as decorations, but also as charms.[12] A bone figurine has been recovered from the Belan valley south of Allahabad, and engraved ostrich egg shells from Patne in Maharashtra and Rojde in Madhya Pradesh in Mesolithic contexts. These, again, probably had some cultic significance. There could also have been some religious motive behind many of the famous Bhimbetka rock paintings near Bhopal, which could date back to 6000 BC, and have Mesolithic associations.[13]

The physical remains that point to the existence of beliefs in the supernatural or extra-human forces controlling events do not directly indicate how the cults represented by these beliefs were organized or institutionalized within human groups. A distinguished prehistorian writes with confidence that already in the Upper Palaeolithic (preceding the Mesolithic) phase:

> Another person, apart from the chief, dominated the social group, namely, the 'witch doctor' or 'shaman', to whom was attributed the power of communicating with spirits. This individual had to secure the group's survival through magical practices, by ensuring the success of hunt, for example.[14]

These are, it must be insisted, mere guesses. Practices found among 'primitive' tribes of recent times cannot be invoked with any real degree of certainty as evidence for what prevailed in early human communities where the reserve food available for maintaining any specialists in religion or magic must have been small.[15] In any case, it is very likely that immense variations in beliefs and ritual prevailed among the widely-spaced hunting and gathering communities, using a possibly ever increasing multiplicity of tongues.[16]

Archaeological evidence for religion increases considerably in the aftermath of the Neolithic Revolution, which ushered in agriculture and cattle domestication.[17] In the Indian subcontinent the crucial site where it can be studied is Mehrgarh, near Quetta in Pakistan. Here one sees, from *c.* 7000 BC to *c.* 4000 BC how agriculture and cattle-domestication took root, and how correspondingly we have evidence of class differentiation, which leaves its traces in religion and ritual. The inhabitants were buried, with much use of ochre, and with their tools and slaughtered animals – apparently to take care of their subsistence in the afterlife. Those who were richer had ornaments like beads of turquoise, lapis lazuli and cornelian, besides shells, accompanying them. These could also have been regarded as charms.[18] Clay figurines, foot-shaped and violin-shaped, coloured with ochre, could, again, have been charms or representatives of deities. A distinct development can be traced in the female figurines in their reproductive aspects.[19] This appears to conform to the hypothesis of a 'Mother Goddess' arising in early agricultural societies, based on analogies between sexual and plant reproduction, the goddess becoming a guarantor, when suitably appeased, of successful crop-raising.[20]

There also arises, with the appearance of surplus-producing, internally differentiated societies, a new function of religion, that is, the complex of various beliefs, rites and charms that prevailed in society. In pre-Neolithic societies, religious ritual was resorted to in order to assure the community safety or success against natural forces or external human enemies. As the community itself broke into differently placed segments, in terms of wealth and power, faith and ritual became, additionally, the instruments for sanctifying this division. If so, religion could become a powerful force for maintaining a given social order.

D.D. Kosambi, indeed, saw in religion the crucial factor in maintaining the Indus civilization, which marked an important advance with its towns and the use of plough, ox-cart, bronze and writing, during the period *c.* 2500–2000 BC.[21] While there should be little objection to the supposition that religion occupied an important place in the make-up of the Indus civilization, it is difficult to accept the assertion that the Indus state had only a weak command over force, or that religion was the 'powerful adjunct that reduced the need for violence to a minimum'.[22] Kosambi sustains his argument by an assumption that the entire citadel of Mohenjodaro, and not simply its famous tank, was a religious complex, corresponding 'to the temple-*zikhurat* structures in Mesopotamia'.[23] It must be said that this, given the physical remains as they stand, is a rather far-fetched interpretation;[24] and one may retort that if the number of weapons found in the Indus cities is not so impressive, nor is the number of structures that can, with any confidence, be identified as temples or sites of ritual.

There is a further question about the Indus civilization, which has provoked much debate – the extent to which elements of its religion survived its end and continued into later 'Aryan' times. Noticing heaps of broken small clay cups around public wells at Mohenjodaro,

Piggott found in these an evidence of the sensitivity to pollution, by which the clay cup was immediately discarded on first use, 'as in contemporary Hinduism'.[25] The Great Bath at Mohenjodaro was held by its excavators to suggest a ritual regard for water, as in the Hindu tradition; and Kosambi has even identified the tank as a *pushkara* pool, 'a prototype of such tirthas', where men consorted ritually with human nymphs (*apsaras*).[26] Mahadevan has suggested that the 'cult object' placed in front of the unicorn on Indus seals is actually a *soma*-filter, so that the sacred drink of *soma/hoama* of the Aryans (Indo–Iranians) must have been derived from the Indus civilization.[27] A deity is represented on seals sitting in a 'Yogic' posture: in one broken seal, this deity sits surrounded by a tiger, elephant, rhinoceros and water-buffalo – prompting from Marshall its identification with 'Proto-Shiva' in his aspect as Pashupati – except that the animals the deity lords over are not cattle, but wild beasts![28] Then, there have been clay-plaster lined pits found at some Indus sites (Kalibangan, Lothal, Banawali and Nageshwar, all in India), described as fire altars; a 'sacrificial pit' at Kalibangan reportedly contained ox bones. These are sought to be linked with the Vedic ritual of sacrifices, though, except for Kalibangan, all descriptions of the pits or platforms as fire altars have been deemed to stand on very weak grounds.[29]

Individually, each part of the above evidence adduced for links with the subsequent Vedic culture involves much speculation, and in each case there are alternative interpretations possible. But even collectively, the features touched upon do not represent what we may call the mainstream of the Indus religion. Though the Indus script mainly carried on seals has not been deciphered, it is clear from the figures and scenes represented on these seals that the deities which, at least, the seal owners, and therefore the wealthy and the powerful in the Indus civilization, worshipped, were in bulk zoomorphic, and not, like the Vedic deities, anthropomorphic.

Mahadevan counts 1521 seals showing single animal figures. Of these seals as many as 1164 depict a unicorn (single-horned humpless bull), 154 a bull, 56 an elephant (one of them, horned), 16 a tiger, 5 a horned tiger, 39 a rhinoceros, 36 a goat/antelope, and 10 a hare. As against these, Mahadevan lists only 43 seals which contain anthropomorphic depictions of single beings.[30] Not only is the anthropomorphic element so small in relative terms, there has been, except for the dubious Proto-Shiva, no other figure that recalls any

Aryan deity. There is, for example, no woman with a tiger's body, depicted on an Indus cylinder-seal, paralleled in the Vedic pantheon. On the other hand, there is a seal which recalls the Mesopotamian hero Gilgamesh fighting off two tigers.[31] What places the Indus religion still farther away from the Vedic, is the practice of burial of the dead, laid supine, north–south, found in cemeteries at Harappa, Kalibangan and Lothal. The positive evidence for cremation is small and debatable. In funeral rites too, then, any association with Vedic practices is hard to establish.

By and large, therefore, the balance of evidence seems to favour the supposition that the Indus civilization had a religious tradition, or traditions, which mainly disappeared with its demise; and that what possibly survived of it to be adopted in the later Vedic belief or ritual, only comprised elements that were at best marginal to the Indus religion in its heyday.

## III
## Religion and Caste

The most characteristic social institution of India is caste. Most visibly, 'caste' is a community that maintains its separate identity by a strict practice of endogamy (and hypergamy), and by a reputed, professed or actual obligation to undertake an occupation or perform a particular kind of duty. It is further assumed that all castes stand in an hierarchical order, though the exact position of a particular caste in this order may be disputed, and that such order attaches a relative degree of 'purity' to each caste, or, is itself founded on the varying degrees of purity possessed by each caste.[32]

The issue of 'purity' naturally introduces a religious element into the caste structure, the Brahmanas being regarded as the purest; and Louis Dumont has forcefully argued in his *Homo Hierarchicus* that the 'Hindu' ideology of purity and pollution provides the real determining and organizing factor behind the caste system.[33] It follows that Hinduism, in fact, has created the caste system.

While much of what Dumont says has been widely disputed,[34] his ascription of a causative role to the 'ideology' of Hinduism (or, rather, Brahmanism) in the genesis, evolution, expansion and configuration of the caste system is often explicitly or implicitly taken for granted.[35] It would certainly be foolish to deny the connection and interaction between the two. The question is whether the evolution of the caste system could not have been a largely autonomous or separate process, which began to germinate appropriate justifications and theoretical rules within Brahmanical codes only *ex post facto*.

The argument here advanced is that the alternative hypothesis deserves to be given a hearing. While it would be wrong to disregard the *varṇa* order or underplay its importance,[36] the fact is that the *varṇa* order as it is described in the main Vedic corpus lacks the two essential elements of the caste system, namely, occupational fixity and endogamy, which have belonged mainly to the realm of *jāti*, the real unit of the caste system. The term *jāti* itself has not been traced in the Vedic corpus.[37] In its earliest occurrence in Sanskrit (fifth or fourth century BC) it seems still to be just a synonym of *varṇa*.[38]

As has been often remarked, *Rigveda*, IX.112, describes diverse occupations for livelihood with no suggestion of hereditary constraint. Rather: 'Striving for wealth, with varied plans, we follow our desires like cattle.'[39]

The *Vājasaneyi-saṁhitā*, XXX, provides a detailed list of occupations of men and women, and yet without any suggestion of hereditary fixity.[40]

How far the spirit was from endogamy is revealed by the assertion in the *Atharvaveda*, V, 17.8–9, that if a woman had had ten former husbands, and yet a Brahmana now claimed her for a wife, she would be his, not of a Vaishya or a Rājanya [K<u>sh</u>atriya].[41] This would be consonant, in a far-fetched interpretation, with a dogma of hypergamy; but, then, we have the rather casual way in which the *Vājasaneyi-saṁhitā*, XXIII.30–31, looks at the seduction of an Ārya's wife by a Shūdra, put at par with that of a Shūdra's wife by an Ārya. On the question of purity and pollution, something at least can be extracted out of the Vedic corpus. The *Shatapatha Brāhmaṇa* bars a consecrated person at a sacrifice from directly speaking to a Shūdra (III, 1.19.10) and enjoins a holy teacher to avoid contact with Shūdras and leavings of food, or even look at Shūdra and a woman (XIV.1.13).[42] But, all in all, the amount of evidence about the need for keeping such excessive distance from the lowly is rather small.

When we actually come to the *Rigveda's* own single statement about the *varṇas* in the *Puru<u>sh</u>a-sūkta*, where the Brāhmaṇa, Rājanya, Vaishya and Shūdra are shown as springing from the various parts of the body of the sacrificed Puru<u>sh</u>a, it is clear that it is a simple declaration of social hierarchy, the classes of priests, warriors, the masses, and the menials being placed in a descending order.[43] Such a description could have been given of the society of any ancient or medieval civilization, and by itself hardly implies the existence of the caste system, though once the caste system was incorporated within the Brahmanical code, this began to be cited as a narration of its original creation.[44]

Such silence about castes and their endogamous customs and fixed occupations in the Vedic corpus needs to be explained, since we have ample evidence from Buddhist literature going back to the fifth century BC, some of it possibly preceding in time most of the Upanishads, that the caste system, in the form we know it, had by then been well established in society at large, at least in Eastern India. It was essentially based on the *jāti* as a unit, and the status of a low or high *jāti* was fixed by occupations – the *jātis* of the Chaṇḍālas, basket-makers, hunters, charioteers and sweepers were held to be 'low' *jātis*; the Khattiya (Kshatriya) and Brahmana were the high ones. Endogamy prevailed – the Buddha is quoted as saying that the concept of *jāti* (*jātivāda*) was of no importance in matters of salvation; it was only of importance for marriage.[45] The Buddha's own clan, the Sakyas, were so conscious of their unmixed descent, that their ancestors, reduced to a set of brothers and sisters, married each other. The Buddha, after telling this story, emphasized that the Khattiyas were so firm in their belief in endogamy that while the Brahmanas would recognize as a Brahmana the offspring of the union of a Khattiya youth and a Brahmana maiden, the Khattiyas would reject the offspring as absolutely illegitimate.[46] The last statement is interesting as suggesting a greater espousal of endogamy on the part of the Kshatriyas than the Brahmanas.

One can fairly conclude from this evidence that the caste system arose not out of an overbearing and hugely infecting priestly ideology of purity, but out of internal social processes in which economic and political changes played a major role. From at least *c.* 700 BC the diffusion of iron, the increase in commerce (so well reflected in the importance assigned to merchants in early Buddhist lore), the rise of towns and strong states based on rising fiscal resources,[47] created space for a more and more specialized division of labour, the trend to protect one's occupation from outsiders by claiming hereditary monopoly for one's caste (*jāti*) and for the imposition of a hierarchical order by use of the power of the state. It is surely quite plausible that customs of occupational fixity, endogamy and the repression of large groups as lowly *jātis* arose in society first, and entered the Brahmanical codes, the *Dharmasūtras* and *smritis*, only later. The *sūtras* where the term *jāti* begins to occur, though much less frequently than the term *varṇa*, are all generally believed to have been compiled after the Buddha's time;[48] and the *Manusmriti* is generally assigned to the first century BC. Much of this literature is, then, subsequent to the important account of the Indian caste system, left by Megasthenes, the Macedonian envoy to the Mauryan court (*c.* 300 BC), surviving in the works of Diodorus (II, 40–41), Strabo (XV.1.39–41, 46–49) and Arrian (*Indica*, XI–XIII).[49] The influence of the *varṇa* order is present here but essentially the description suits the *jāti* organization, with occupational fixity and endogamy being emphasized. The *Arthashāstra* has also much interesting material on the caste system, with its intermediate and menial castes, and its varied use of the term *jāti*, but the times to which the text's various parts can be assigned is uncertain, and much of the work may contain material long posterior to Mauryan times.[50]

In view of the above, it seems particularly doubtful if the evolution and spread of the caste system can be attributed primarily to Brahmanical inspiration. Since the Buddha lived and preached in Eastern India (Eastern Uttar Pradesh and Bihar), the caste system that is described in early Buddhist literature must have been prevalent in that region. It is not certain that it had then also taken root in other parts of India. It is singular that classical accounts based on Greek narratives of Alexander's campaign in the Indus basin (327–325 BC) are absolutely silent about the castes, at best mentioning the Brahmanas only as philosophers and conspiratorial advisors of local kings.[51] It was Megasthenes who travelled up to Pataliputra who provides us with the first Greek account of a recognizable caste society. An inference can, then, fairly be drawn that caste institutions took time to spread, radiating from Eastern India. If so the kingdom of Magadha and, then, the Mauryan Empire may have played as important a part in its spread as any priesthood or monastic order.

Here we must consider the role of Buddhism (and Jainism). We have seen that the early Buddhist literature has much information to give about caste. The Buddha's sermons about morality in worldly life adopt a curiously neutral attitude towards caste – neither endorsement nor rejection.[52] Ashoka (reigned *c.* 270–234 BC), who drew on this legacy for his *dhaṁma* formularies, inscribed on rock and pillar, not once mentions either *varṇa* or *jāti*, and, except for his references to Brahmanas, mostly paired with *samanas* or Buddhist, Jaina and Ājīvika monks, bypasses the issue of caste altogether. And yet both Buddhism and Jainism, by their theories of life-cycles based on *karma*, and the doctrine of *ahiṁsa* (non-killing), provided an ideological underpinning for the caste system that was, perhaps, far more potent than the mythical *Purus̲h̲a* sacrifice of Vedic tradition.

It is possible that the *Brihadāraṇyaka Upanis̲h̲ad* (VI, 2.13–15) and the *Chāndogya Upanis̲h̲ad* (V, 3–10), the earliest texts of their genre to contain the doctrine of transmigration of souls, were composed during or after the times of Mahāvīra and the Buddha. But even if they were not, and are earlier in time, it is curious how the doctrine is said to have been discovered. A *rājanya* (Ks̲h̲atriya) asked Shvetaketu Aruneya some questions which he could not answer. His father Gautama then went to the King, who, after showing some perplexity, told him of secrets known till then 'to the Ks̲h̲atra class alone'; and the centrepiece of this teaching was the description of the transmigration of souls. At the end of it all came the following:

> Those whose conduct has been good [in earlier life], will quickly attain some good birth, the birth of a Brāhmaṇa or Ks̲h̲atriya, or a Vaishya. But those whose conduct has been evil, will quickly attain an evil birth, the birth of a dog or a hog or a Chaṇḍāla.[53]

One is, then, responsible for one's own low birth in the caste order, owing to one's deeds (*karma*) in the past life. The fact that this doctrine had not come out of the Vedic lore was itself so well known that the doctrine had to be acknowledged as an import into Brahmanical thought from the lore of the Ks̲h̲atriyas. It will not escape notice that both Mahāvīra and the Buddha were Ks̲h̲atriyas, and so probably drew directly on beliefs already in circulation among non-Brahmanical thinkers, and so not at second-hand, from what the Upanis̲h̲ads contained in respect of the theory of life-cycles. Moreover, whereas the theory remained only a peripheral element in Upanis̲h̲adic thought, it occupied a central part in the teachings of Jainism and Buddhism. The spread of these religions naturally greatly contributed to a strengthening of the popular belief in the legitimacy of the caste order as a product of past *karma*. This justification for the *varṇa* system duly appears, but still weakly, in the *Manusmriti* (e.g., XI. 24–26).[54]

The other element, that of *ahiṁsa*, arising out of the protest against Vedic animal-sacrifices and extending to avoidance of killing of living beings, was shared in different degrees by both Buddhism and Jainism. Implicit in this position was the disapproval of the occupations of hunting-and-gathering communities. Not only is non-killing of living beings given the pride of place in Ashoka's *dhaṁma* formularies, but it is claimed in his Aramaic inscriptions of Lamghan that he threw out of the prosperous populace those who lived by hunting and fishing.[55] Their occupations could thus be used as a reason for treating the forest folk and other gathering communities as outcastes. Once the *ahiṁsa* doctrine was accepted by Brahmanism as well, this attitude could easily find its reflection in *Manusmriti*, not only in its listing of the outcaste *jātis* as those engaged in hunting and gathering (X.32, 34, 36–37, 48–49), but also in its condemnation of peasants who use ploughs that kill earthly creatures (X, 84). This last sentiment is echoed in late Buddhist tradition – the scholarly pilgrim Yi-Jing (I-tsing) (*d.* 713) reported that monks were forbidden by the Buddha from ploughing and watering fields, since this destroyed 'lives'.[56] In time this could become one further argument for treating all peasants as Shūdras.[57]

The fact that the caste system obtained much of its classic shape and universality in India during the time that Buddhism spread over the country, and Prakrit, not Sanskrit, was the major language of inscriptions (third century BC to third century AD) represents a synchronism which might not be entirely accidental. It is not the intention here to assert that Buddhism alone generated the entire process of caste-transformation of the various regional societies within India. Complex political, economic and cultural forces were probably at play, which we cannot perhaps as distinctly identify as we would like to. But the point made here is that it was no simple process of Brahmanization. Buddhism and Jainism also contained ideological baggage with which the caste system could be explained, justified and lived with.

## IV
## Islam in India

The developments within Brahmanism subsequent to the formation of the caste system have been treated in three essays in our volume, by Professor K.M. Shrimali, who discusses the interaction of religious ideologies in post-Mauryan India (Chapter 2), by Professor Suvira Jaiswal, who treats of the social dimensions of the spreading cult of Lord Rāma in late ancient and medieval India (Chapter 3), and by Dr Nupur Chaudhuri and Professor Rajat K. Ray who jointly study the role of Tantricism in providing escape routes from a rigorously ordered society (Chapter 4). The period they cover broadly ends with the time around 1200 AD when Islam became a rival religion to a significant degree.

We have thought it best to reprint for our volume as Chapter 6 an essay by Professor M. Athar Ali, in which exploring the Islamic background to Indian history he touches on certain fundamental features of Islam's past, including secular developments. We shall here confine ourselves mainly to the history of Islam as a religion.

Islam, whose prophet, Muḥammad, died in Arabia in 632, is a strongly monotheistic religion, the absolute unity and power of God being strongly emphasized, along with a hostility to any kind of image-worship. In much of its lore about earlier prophets (the prophets of the Old Testament and Christ) it shares much with the Judaic and Christian traditions, as also in the belief in Satan and the Day of Judgement. It strongly stresses the individual human being's obligation to obey God, for which God would judge, reward and punish on the Day of Resurrection. From 622 to 632 Prophet Muḥammad was in control of an expanding community (*umma*) at Medina, a town north of Mecca, and this necessitated legislation of the code by which members of the community had to live. Some of its fundamentals were provided by Revelations (subsequently collected in the Qur'an), supplemented by the Prophet's own statements and practice (*sunna*), reports of which constituted *ḥadīṣ*. Muslim law (*sharī'a*) mainly grew on the basis of the Qur'ān, and the *ḥadīṣ* and the use of analogy and elaboration by jurists. There was undoubtedly a strong element of continuity of local Arab custom, some Jewish ritual (circumcision, ban on pork, kosher/*ḥalāl* meat, etc.), a notable stress on contract-fixed obligations, and some elements of reform, as in allowing a daughter to have a share in inheritance, though only to the extent of half the son's share. Islamic law allowed slavery, as well as concubinage, put women in a generally inferior position, and its detailed rules allowed for considerable differences of status by the side of a limited degree of male equality.[58]

After the Prophet's death, despite some internal conflicts, his successors (*khalīfas*, 'Caliphs') succeeded in not only subduing the Arabian peninsula, but also in conquering most of West Asia, Iran and Egypt. When the non-dynastic Caliphate (632–660) was replaced by the Umayyid dynasty (660–750), a fresh wave of expansion began that saw Arab armies occupy North Africa, Spain and Central Asia. In 712–714, much of the Indus basin (Sind and Southern Punjab) was annexed to the Arab Empire. It is possible that Arab (and some Iranian) Muslim traders had already settled in some of India's ports, but it was the conquest of Sind which established strong Muslim communities in a fairly large region within India.

By the time of the conquest of Sind the Arab rulers had worked out arrangements of coexistence with the conquered non-Muslim peoples elsewhere. The remarkable chronicle, *Chachnāma*, furnishes detailed evidence, which other Arabic sources corroborate, that the Hindus in Sind were placed at par with 'people of the book' (Jews and Christians), a large degree of tolerance being extended to them and to their places of worship, so long as they paid the land tax (*kharāj*) and the poll tax (*jizya*). The grants earlier made to Brahmanas out of the state revenues were continued.[59] So far did the new regime step into the older regime's shoes that the heavy disabilities imposed under the previous regime on the outcaste communities like the Jatts, a pastoral people of the Sind plains, were confirmed by the Arabic conqueror Muḥammad bin Qāsim.[60] On the other hand, a Brahmanical text, *Devālasmriti*, from Sind ascribed to the ninth or tenth century, prescribes rituals for cleansing men and women, tainted by contact with the *mlechchhas*, or Muslims, of the kind that Alberuni mentions in *c.* 1035.[61]

Islam began to have its internal convulsions not long after the Prophet's death. The great schism over the question of the privileges of the descendants of the Prophet, especially through the line of his cousin and son-in-law 'Alī, in time involved both theological and political issues. The establishment of the Fāṭimid Caliphate in North Africa and Egypt led to strong Shi'ite activity in Sind; and in or about 950 the rulers of Multan in southern Punjab shifted their allegiance to the Fāṭimid caliph, whereafter they came to be known as Qarāmiṭa (Carmathians), the Ismā'ilī branch of the Shi'ites. The community was virtually massacred by Maḥmūd of Ghazni upon his seizure of Multan in 1010. However, Shi'ite, as well as Ismā'ilī, communities survived in India into later times.

Another important development in Islam was that of *Ṣūfism*, or Islamic mysticism. In an obvious reaction to the growing theological prescriptions of ways of earning merit (*ṣawāb*) with God for reward in afterlife, there arose in eighth-century Irāq reputedly with the woman saint Rābi'a of Basra (*d.* 801) as its first declarant, an emphasis of love (*'ashq* or *'ishq*) of God, as the only valid reason for obeying Him. The logical corollary to an absorption in this love, was an implicit rejection of Paradise as the goal of ethical endeavour, and its replacement by an aspiration for *fanā* (annihilation), the elimination of self through the attainment of an absolute union with God. There has been much debate over whether any Indian (Buddhist or Brahmanical) ideas contributed to the genesis of Ṣūfism. The possibility of concepts like *nirvāna* or *bhakti* being transmitted from Sind to the Arab world cannot be ruled out, although the positive evidence for this still remains tenuous.[62]

By the eleventh century, Ṣūfism had become a recognized component of Islam. An early comprehensive text on different aspects of it was composed by 'Alī Hujwīrī (*d. c.* 1071), who wrote *Kashfu'l Maḥjūb* ('The Unveiling of the Veiled') in Persian at Lahore in Ghaznavid Punjab. The writing of this work does not only mark the maturity of Ṣūfism as a systematic body of beliefs and practices, but is also a firm announcement of the system's arrival in India.[63]

After the Ghorian conquests in the late twelfth century and the establishment of the Delhi Sultanate (1206), Muslim communities began to increase rapidly outside the Punjab and Sind, the older regions of Muslim settlement. A similar process took place in the Deccan north of the Tungabhadra river in the fourteenth century, the faith, so to speak, following the flag. Conversions on a large scale seem to have occurred especially in Eastern Bengal, probably between the thirteenth and fifteenth centuries.

By 1200, orthodox Islamic theology with the *ulamā* or *dānishmands* (scholars) as its spokesmen, had largely made their peace with mysticism, whose votaries were the ṣūfis or *darvīshes.* The ṣūfis ordinarily respected the domain of theology, just as the '*ulamā* tolerated the ṣūfis' practice of total subservience to the *pīr* or preceptor, though *samā'*, or the public recitation of love poetry addressed to God, still caused disputation.

Within Ṣūfism, the increasing authority assigned to the *murshid* or *pīr* over his disciples or devotees led to the formation of various *silsilahs* ('chains') or orders among ṣūfis. These arose as individual *pīrs* appointed *khalīfas*, successors or agents, often assigning them particular territories in which to operate. These could in turn accept *be'at* or allegiance from disciples, and, usually after the deaths of their own *pīrs*, appoint their own *khalīfas*. The *khānqāh* or hospice was the centre of Sufic activity. Here the *pīr* imparted instruction, held conversations and *samā'* assemblies, his chosen assistants inscribed slips for amulets, and a free kitchen (*langar*) was organized. The money for all this came from professedly unsolicited gifts (*futūḥ*). Many ṣūfīs expressed scorn for assured or regular gifts and land grants, but others were not so particular. Contemporary accounts show little concern on the part of ṣūfīs with conversions to Islam; nor, for that matter, do they appear noticeably as apostles of religious tolerance.[64]

In the thirteenth- and fourteenth-centuries, the two most influential orders among the ṣūfīs were the Suhrawardī, centred at Multan, and the Chishtī at Delhi and other places. The most famous Chishtī *shaikh* or saint, Niẓāmu'ddīn, offered a classical exposition of Ṣūfism of the pre-pantheistic phase in his conversations (1307–1322) recorded in the *Fawā'id u'l Fawād*.[65]

Ṣūfism began to turn pantheistic only when the ideas of Ibn al-'Arabī (*d.* 1240) began to arrive, first, through the Persian poetry of Jalālu'ddīn Rūmī (1207–1273) and 'Abdu'r Raḥmān Jāmī (1414–1492), and, then, diffused within India through the endeavours of Ashraf Jahāngīr Simnānī (*d.* 1436).[66] It is remarkable that this wave of qualified pantheism should have begun to dominate Indian Islamic thought about the same time that the pantheism of Shankarāchārya's school of Vedānta was attaining increasing influence within Brahmanical thought. Shankarāchārya's thought necessarily took time to spread, and significantly enough, it was not noticed at Akbar's court where no Hindu parallel to Ṣūfic pantheism was still known. That recognition seems to have been first registered by Jahāngīr early in the seventeenth century.[67] (This matter is also taken up in my essay on Kabīr in this volume.)

An important aspect of Islam in India was its very early recognition of a long-term coexistence with Hinduism, despite all the violence that occurred in military campaigns, conquests and depradations. The conqueror Mu'izzuddīn of Ghor (*d.* 1206) had stamped the image of the goddess Lakshmī on some of his gold coins – a device 'without a parallel in Muhammadan history'.[68] Under the Delhi Sultans, though Muslims dominated the upper levels of the nobility, the rural potentates remained mostly Hindu, and, in the fourteenth century, Hindus began to be appointed as the Sultans' governors and commanders as well. In the 1350s the historian Baranī noted with some bitterness how 'the Kings of Islam' showed respect to 'Hindus, Mongols, polytheists and infidels', by making them sit on the *masnad* (cushions) and by honouring them in other ways, and how the Hindus upon paying taxes (*jiziya-o-kharāj*) were allowed to have their temples and celebrations, employ Muslim servants, and flaunt their titles ('*rāi, rānā, ṭhākur, sāh, mahtā, paṇḍit*, etc.'), right in the capital seats of Muslim rulers.[69] This attitude was reciprocated. Muslims were employed as officers and soldiers in the Vijayanagara Empire, and when Rānā Kumbha in the fifteenth century built his famous Victory Tower at Chittor, he took care to have the sculptured Hindu pantheon of deities surmounted by the name 'Allāh' carved many times in excellent Arabic calligraphy.[70]

The question has often been raised as to how far Islam influenced developments of certain beliefs in Hinduism. The presence of Islam did not help to create a monotheistic trend in Hinduism; such a trend had long existed. Alberuni noted its strong presence in the Bhagavad Gīta;[71] and Amīr Khusrau in 1318 said emphatically that Hindus believed in only one God, without any associates whatever, contrasting them with the Christians who associated the Holy Spirit and the Son with Him.[72] But proximity to Islam did probably help to move monotheism to a more central position within Hinduism, and to dilute to that extent the influence of the Sāṁkhya belief in the duality of existence. Less certain is the extent to which the theoretical religious equality within the Muslim community generated criticism of the caste system raised within Indian society. The doubt arises because social hierarchy was in practice and in law a quite strongly established institution among the Muslims; and, indeed, one searches in vain for any explicit Muslim condemnation of the caste system in this period, whereas Islamic theologians both outside and inside India accepted hierarchy as a normal and, indeed, desirable state of social organization.

There was, however, a plane on which the influence of Islam could be felt – the very concept of religion. To Arabs and Iranians, India was Hind and the Indians were 'Hindus'. But as Muslim communities arose in India, the name 'Hindu' came, quite naturally, to apply to Indians who were not Muslims; and all the numerous religious beliefs current in India were put in one docket by the Muslims as the beliefs of 'Hindus'. A consciousness began correspondingly to take shape among the Hindus (as from the fifteenth century they began to call themselves)[73] of a common framework of belief. Starting from the existing internally conflicting body of beliefs, there was now a tendency increasingly to subject them to selection, syntheses and shifts of emphasis. The transformation of the massive Brahmanical tradition into Hinduism was thus largely on its own terms, however exotic in part the original impetus and the new name.

In the late fifteenth and early sixteenth centuries, both Islam and Hinduism encountered the popular monotheistic movement, associated with Kabīr's name (on which an essay is included in this volume as Chapter 7). Even an impeccably orthodox theologian such as 'Abdu'l Ḥaqq of Delhi (1551–1642) was compelled to recognize that besides Muslims and infidels, there were 'monotheists' (*muwaḥḥids*) on whom no judgement could be passed.[74] 'Abdu'l Ḥaqq himself says this with reference to Kabīr (early sixteenth century), the Muslim weaver of Banaras (Varanasi), who, in his verses, disowned both Islam and Hinduism and dedicated himself to God and to an ethical life unencumbered by identification with any sect. Kabīr undoubtedly was, and still is, a living influence among large numbers of ordinary Hindus and Muslims; and he probably also prepared the ground in the popular mind for the grand project of universal tolerance undertaken by the emperor Akbar (1556–1605).

Islam in India was now also influenced by millenary movements. The most notable of these was the Mahdawī sect established by Sayyid Muḥammad of Jaunpur (1443–1505), who claimed to be the Mahdī. He preached strict adherence to the prescribed mode of life and worship and criticized the worldliness of the scholars. He established *dā'iras*, or centres for his followers, who had to live in egalitarian conditions, relying on *futūḥ*, or gifts from the laity. Such puritanism led to considerable respect for the Mahdawīs in Gujarat and other parts of Northern India. The sect suffered from temporary bouts of persecution, but seems to have declined mainly from internal inertia after the enthusiasm of the first two or three generations had died down.[75]

A movement of a similar nature was that of Bāyazīd Raushan (*d.* 1572–1573), who was born at Jalandhar in Punjab and belonged to a family settled in Waziristan among Pashtoon tribes. He received a divine call and began to claim that he was the Mahdī and was receiving God's messages (*ilhām*). Anyone who did not admit his claims was thus defying God and must be treated as an unbeliever. It was not surprising that he and his successors came into conflict both with

Pashtoons of a more conventional Islamic bent and with the Mughal authorities.[76] Bāyazīd wrote a text, the *Khairu'l bayān*, in Arabic, Persian, Hindi and Pashto. It is the last version which has survived and it is hailed as the first prose text in the Pashto language. Ultimately the sect was decimated by war and its numbers dwindled when Bāyazīd's last successor, 'Abdu'l Qādir, surrendered to the Mughals during the early years of Shāh Jahān's reign (1628–58).[77]

What can only be described as spectacular developments occurred at Akbar's court, from the 1570s onwards. These are what Professor Shireen Moosvi in her essay (Chapter 9) in this volume endeavours to analyse from the point of view of Akbar's personal character and experience. The ideas of Ibn al-'Arabī had already become fairly well established among Indian ṣūfis by this time. The notion of *ṣulḥ-i kul* (Absolute Peace) and *insān al-kāmil* (the Perfect Man) gained particular prominence in Akbar's circle. The first held that all differences should be tolerated because the unity of God's existence embraces all illusory differences; and the second, that a Perfect Human Being was necessary to guide humanity to God in every age. Both principles provided the rationalization behind Akbar's policy of tolerance and his own claims to high spiritual status. To this was added the influence of Shihābu'ddīn Suhrawardī's Illuminationist (*ishrāqī*) philosophy, which, as interpreted by Abū'l Faẓl (1551–1602), Akbar's brilliant minister and ideologue, would clothe a just sovereign with divine illumination.[78] In Chapter 8 of this volume Professor Osamu Kondo discusses the text and significance of the scholars' *maḥzar* of 1579. But Akbar was probably not satisfied with the *maḥzar* (declaration) of 1579 making him, as a 'just king', the interpreter of Muslim law – he may have come to think of the position as too limited or sectarian. During the last 25 years of his rule, he freely expressed his scepticism both of the notion of prophethood and of human incarnations of God, and asserted the supremacy of reason (*'aql*). He extended his critique to social matters, condemning alike the Hindu practice of widow-burning (*satī*) and the smaller share in inheritance given to daughters in Muslim law.[79]

Akbar's views ceased to hold sway after his death, though the policy of religious tolerance he established continued to be respected and even invoked by his successors, with some departures from it only during the reign of Aurangzeb (1659–1707). Prince Dārā Shukoh (1615–1659) was notable not only for carrying forward Akbar's project of translations of Sanskrit texts (he himself rendered the Upanishads into Persian in 1657), but also for arguing that the path to gnosis (*ma'rifat*) is identical in both Sufi Islam and Vedantic Hinduism.[80]

It was not fortuitous perhaps that Dārā Shukoh was attached to the mystic order of the Qādirīs, which had been deeply influenced by the ideas of Ibn al-'Arabī. Its major figure was Miyān Mīr (1531?–1636) of Lahore. Of an ascetic bent, he spurned worldly affairs and advocated tolerance.[81] The popular Ṣūfī poet of Punjab, Bulhe Shāh (1680–1757?) was a Qādiri, and he often mirrors Kabīr in his verses.[82]

A contrary trend in Sufism was represented by Shaikh Ahmad Sirhindī (1564–1624). Attaching himself to the Naqshbandī order, he insisted on rigorous obedience to the *Sharī'a* and was bitterly intolerant of both Hindus and Shi'ites. He rejected Ibn al-'Arabī's theory of the unity of existence (*waḥdat al-wujūd*) as merely based on a passing stage of mystic experience. Yet he went outside the traditional realm of the *Sharī'a* by asserting that Islam needed a *mujaddid* (reviver or renovator) with special powers after every millennium and, later, that God would ordain for Islam a *qayyūm* (maintainer). It was natural that he should claim both these positions for himself. As was to be expected, this provoked considerable opposition, not only from the more traditional, but also from moderate theologians, like the Qādiri scholar 'Abdu'l Ḥaqq of Delhi, already mentioned in connection with Kabīr.[83]

Shaikh Ahmad Sirhindī's hostility to the Shi'ites had an especially Indian context, since under the tolerance extended by the Mughal regime and the patronage of Iranian émigrés, some of whom held high office, Shi'ism became an established part of Indian Islam. Nūrullāh Sushtarī (1542–1610) a Shi'ite theologian and martyr, served as the *qāẓī* (judge) of Lahore under Akbar. In 1602 he completed his best-known work, the *Majālisu'l mūminīn*, a collection of biographies of eminent Shi'ites; and in 1605, the *Iḥqāqu'l ḥaqq*, a refutation of Sunni critiques of Shi'ite beliefs.[84] Sunni–Shi'ite debates became a common feature in Muslim intellectual life in the 'free-for-all' atmosphere of Mughal India. The debates had, perhaps, a positive side as well. S.A. Nadeem Rezavi in his contribution to our volume (Chapter 10) assesses the influence of the Iranian scholar Mullā Ṣadrā (*d.* 1640) and his circle on the intellectual environment in India.

Aurangzeb was the most theologically inclined of the Mughal emperors. His interest in the *Sharī'a* led him to organize, under state auspices, the compilation of a comprehensive collection in Arabic of the expositions of the four Sunni legal schools on every imaginable facet of civil and personal law. This bore the title *Fatāwā'-i 'Ālamgīrī* and in its field it remained the most extensive and standard compilation in India.

The eighteenth century saw the very ambitious project of Shāh Walīullāh (1703–1762) of Delhi, which aimed to reconcile the *Sharī'a* with the Sufi path (*ṭarīqa*). Shāh Walīullāh sought to end the controversy over Ibn al-'Arabī's theory of the 'unity of existence' by declaring it as equally valid alongside the contrary theory of the 'unity of what one sees' (*waḥdat al-shuhūd*). He wrote numerous spiritual and legal tracts. Among the latter, his best-known work is the *Hujjatullāh al-bāligha*.[85] His son, Shāh Abdu'l 'Azīz (1746–1824) was a prolific writer who continued his father's mission, polemicizing against the Shi'ites and insisting on rigorous adherence to the *Sharī'a*.[86]

## V
## Religion in its Modern Phase

From the preceding short and rather pedestrian survey of the history of Islam in India, it would be obvious that though Islam is widely held by many of its own followers as well as others, as fairly inflexible in both its articles of faith and rules of conduct, it has been subject to considerable change over time. This was manifest to bolder thinkers like Abū'l-Fazl who, during the reign of Akbar, asserted: 'If the Great Imām [Abū Ḥanīfa] had lived in our time, he would have written a different [book of] religious law.'[87] With the coming of colonial times the altering circumstances and the wind of new ideas from the West caused religions in India to change even more considerably in both form and substance.

The two external streams, namely, Christian missionary activity and the influx of modern values, especially emanating from the French Revolution, need to be distinguished. The missionary propaganda against Hinduism and Islam, while it caused great bitterness, tended to induce both Hindus and Muslims to stress those elements of their religions, by which they could turn back the missionary barbs. Thus Ram Mohan Roy (1772–1833) began his career as a writer by publishing his *Tuḥfatu'l Muwaḥḥidīn* in Persian in 1801–02, arguing that 'belief in one Almighty God is the principle of every religion', that is, including Hinduism.[88] Thereafter he explored the Upanishads to reinforce his thesis that Hinduism is supremely monotheistic, and image-worship is an alien and unacceptable intrusion into the original creed.[89] The same impulse is seen in his rejection of *satī*, not only because this was a practice forbidden in 'every race of man', but also because this was not allowed in the Shāstras, especially Manu.[90] It would, however, be wrong to attribute Ram Mohan Roy's opposition to 'sati' merely because of the desire to protect Hinduism from the assaults of Christianity. There was a humanitarian attitude towards women and their miseries that now breaks forth.[91] Here we cannot ignore the influence of the new humanitarian values from the 'bourgeois–democratic' spring that the French Revolution represented, and which Established Christianity so universally denounced. The equal rights accorded in the French civil codes (1790, 1792) to women obviously inspired Ram Mohan Roy to assert that women had been granted considerable rights of inheritance in ancient Hindu texts, which had been denied to them by 'modern' jurists.[92] When he wrote to John Digby in 1828 inveighing against the prevalence among the Hindus of 'the distinction of castes, introducing innumerable divisions and subdivisions among them' that 'entirely deprived them of patriotic feeling',[93] he was even anticipating movements towards social equality which occupy such a noticeable place within the modern history of Hinduism. Other aspects of Ram Mohan Roy's work such as concern for scientific education and advocacy of liberty, though lying outside the area of religion, have behind them the same impulse from the same modern ideological impetus, which Marx in 1853 had held to be the unintended regenerative consequence of colonial rule.[94]

Ram Mohan Roy's reconstruction of Hinduism was the first important one in a series. Such constructions had liberal as well as conservative representatives: Keshav Chandra Sen (1838–1884) of the New Brahmo Samaj, for example, on one side, and Dayanand Saraswati (1842–1883) of the Arya Samaj, on the other. In some of these efforts, noticeably within the Arya Samaj movement, there was a tendency to perceive Hinduism in the same light as the Semitic religions, with a scripture-based faith and a single consistent body of law and ritual.[95] In this volume we include an important contribution by Professor D.N. Jha (Chapter 12) showing how unhistorical such reconstructions of Hinduism appear once they are put next to actual evidence.

A similar situation arose with respect to Islam faced with the challenge of modern ideas. Since Islam shared many features with Christianity, the trend of modern apologetics was to show that modern values in many matters already existed within early Islam. Of this trend a leading light was Ameer Ali (1849–1928) who published his *Spirit of Islam* in 1891.[96] This was, however, not a satisfactory way out for Syed Ahmad Khan (1817–1898). While defending Islam against what he held to be unfair attacks from European biographers of the Prophet like William Muir, he went beyond most Muslim thinkers in rejecting earlier extra-Qur'ānic literature if its prescriptions were not consonant with science and reason. He insisted on so interpreting the Qur'ān that there was left no inconsistency between the 'Word of God' – namely the Qur'ān – and the 'Work of God', which is discovered for us by science, and is consistent with reason.[97] This would naturally mean that the Qur'ān has to be continuously re-interpreted to keep pace with the growth in rational knowledge. It is probable that this is the extreme limit to which any interpreter can go in reconciling Islam with modern values, though, it is true, that Syed Ahmad Khan himself remained fairly conservative as far as social issues were concerned.

Unluckily, we were not able to get a contribution on the ideological trends in modern Islam for our volume. However, there is a study of Sikhism and the position of women by Professor Kamlesh Mohan, which treats of problems that arise over social issues, when certain texts and their traditional interpretations obtain scriptural status (Chapter 11). In Islam, this is particularly the case with the controversy over Muslim 'Personal Law'.[98]

With regard to the role of religion and resistance to colonial rule, there can be no doubt that before the rise of the modern Indian national movement, religion played a certain role in arousing defiance of British rule under adverse conditions. Rajat K. Ray has argued in his detailed and insightful study of 'the mentality of the Mutiny' that the recourse to religion in 1857 was inevitable in view of the lack of development yet of the idea of the nation. 'In an age', he writes, 'when the mentality of the people was steeped in profound religious convictions, it may be historically misleading to try and isolate the patriotic feelings that have come to stand on their own in the course of later developments.'[99]

What the events of 1857 show also, however, is that under the momentum of resistance the most deeply ingrained perceptions of religion can also change. The Revolt of 1857 was no exception.

I offer below two striking instances. Under the Rebel regime at Delhi (May–September 1857) the weekly *Dehli Urdu Akhbār*, edited by a Shi'ite scholar Muhammad Bāqir makes 'the native country' (*watan*) central to its concerns and shapes the cause of religion accordingly. In its issue of 14 July it contains an appeal to countrymen (*ahl-i watan*) calling upon both Muslims and Hindus to refer to their sacred books and beliefs, put their trust in God and unite to fight the English.[100] On 19 July the appeal is made to 'fellow countrymen' to consider each other to be organs of the same body.[101] Patriotism is here explicitly breaking the bonds of religious separation. Or take the case of the famous Rani of Jhansi. Dressed like a Pathan, she tells a Maharashtrian pilgrim that she had given up the common widow's *dharma* (*rāñdmuñdesa dharma*) to defend the pride of Hindu *dharma* (*hindudharmāchā abhimān*).[102] The transformation here of the concept of *dharma* from one of obedience to custom into a total disregard of it for the higher purpose of overthrowing British rule is remarkable.

The invocation of religion by Bal Gangadhar Tilak or in the Khilafat agitation was naturally important in early nationalist mobilizations. On the other hand, those who followed the path of social reform tended to turn to economic grievances which were felt by people across religious boundaries. In Chapter 13 Professor V. Ramakrishna studies how this process took place in Andhra in the late nineteenth century.

The growth of nationalism in India was unfortunately accompanied by a parallel growth of communalism, and ended in the Partition of India on religious grounds. The fact that India's nationalist leaders yet insisted on creating in India a secular republic makes theirs an unforgettable act of steadfastness to principle, hallowed by Gandhiji's martyrdom. Communalism has, however, persisted and, indeed, grown stronger over the decades, so much as to have become, in all but name, part of the official doctrine of India under the NDA Government around the turn of the millennium. Professor Nirmalangshu Mukherji in a perceptive article (Chapter 15) examines the roots of communalism in our culture and polity. This is an aspect of contemporary history which, important as it is for our people, this volume has not been able to treat in any further detail.

**Notes and References**

1 Karl Marx, 'Contribution to the Critique of Hegel's Philosophy of Right' (1844), in K. Marx and F. Engels, *On Religion*, Moscow, 1957, p. 42.

2 Ibid., p. 41.

3 Cf. Marx: 'The religious world is but the reflex of the real world' (*Capital*, I, Moore–Aveling translation, edited by Frederick Engels, London, 1887, p. 51; Dona Tarr's edition, London, 1938, has the same pagination).

4 Ludwig Feuerbach, *The Essence of Christianity*, English translation, 1854, pp. 31–32, quoted by T.A. Jackson, *Dialectics*, Indian reprint, Benares, 1945, p. 107.

5 *Capital*, I, p. 51.

6 This he did in his *The Protestant Ethic and the Spirit of Capitalism*, published in German in 1904–05, and then in 1920–21. For a summary of his arguments, see Anthony Giddeon, *Capitalism and Modern Social Theory*, Indian edition, New Delhi, 1992.

7 See, especially, R.H. Tawney, *Religion and the Rise of Capitalism* (originally published in 1926), Harmondsworth, 1980, which is a parallel account of the relationship between Reformation and capitalism; his comments on Weber, are on pp. vii–xii and 311–13.

8 US President George W. Bush's use of the evocative word 'crusade' for the United States' use of force was by no means a slip of the tongue – whether his or his speech-writer's.

9 K. Marx and F. Engels, *On Religion*, p. 42.

10 Bridget Allchin, 'Middle Palaeolithic Culture', in A.H. Dani and V.M. Masson, eds, *History of Civilizations of Central Asia*, Vol. I, UNESCO, Paris, 1992, p. 84.

11 J.M. Kenoyer, J.D. Clark, J.N. Pal and G.R. Sharma, 'An Upper Palaeolithic Shrine in India', *Antiquity*, Vol. LVII, No. 219, 1983, pp. 88–94. With such a time difference to bridge, the authors need not perhaps have attempted analogies with contemporary local beliefs and rituals.

12 G.R. Sharma, *From Hunting and Food Gathering to Domestication of Plants and Animals . . . (Excavations at Chopani Mando, Mahadaha and Mahagara)*, Allahabad, 1980, especially pp. 86–98.

13 On the Bhimbetka paintings, see Yashodhar Mathpal, *Prehistoric Rock Paintings of Bhimbetka, Central India*, New Delhi, 1984.

14 Editor's afterword in *History of Humanity*, Vol. I (*Prehistory and the Beginnings of Civilization*), edited by S.J. De Laet, UNESCO, Paris/London, 1994, p. 646.

15 For an example illustrating 'the dangers of taking living traditions directly back into history', see D.D. Kosambi, *Myth and Reality*, Bombay, 1962, pp. 117–18. Among all Indian historians Kosambi has been the foremost in calling for ethnological fieldwork for providing us with insights on prehistoric and early historic social conditions.

16 Among really primitive communities, not touched for long by relations with agricultural populations, the number of languages spoken tends to be

astonishingly large. In Papua, with a population of two million, over 700 languages are spoken, belonging to over 60 language families!

[17] First postulated by V. Gordon Childe, the broad features of it that he sketched in his *Man Makes Himself*, London, 1936, Chapter 5, have been remarkably confirmed by subsequent discoveries and application of improved scientific techniques for dating and biological analysis (see, e.g., David R. Harris, ed., *The Origins and Spread of Agriculture and Pastoralism in Eurasia*, London, 1996).

[18] See Pascal Sellier, 'Mehrgarh: Funerary Rites and the Archaeology of Death', in Michael Jansen *et al.*, *Forgotten Cities of the Indus*, Mainz, 1987, pp. 75–86.

[19] Catherine Jarridge, 'The Terracotta Figurines from Mehrgarh', in ibid., pp. 87–93.

[20] After noting that female figurines, generally interpreted as 'images of the "Mother Goddess"' are found at Neolithic sites 'in Egypt, Syria, Iran, all around the Mediterranean and in south-eastern Europe', Gordon Childe infers 'that the earth from whose bosom the grain sprouts has been imagined as a woman who may be influenced like a woman by entreaties (prayers) and bribes (sacrifices), as well as 'controlled' by imitative rites and incantations' (*What Happened in History*, Harmondsworth, 1942, p. 37).

[21] Damodar Dharmanand Kosambi, *An Introduction to the Study of Indian History*, Bombay, 1956, pp. 59–62. It is likely that Kosambi was influenced not a little by Mortimer Wheeler's judgement that 'whatever their source of authority – and a dominant religious element may fairly be assumed – the lords of Harappa [the other major Indus city besides Mohenjodaro] administered their city in a fashion not remote from that of the priest-kings or governors of Sumer and Akkad [in Iraq]' ('Harappa 1946: the Defences and Cemetery R 37', *Ancient India*, Bulletin of the Archaeological Survey of India, No. 3, January, 1947, p. 76).

[22] Kosambi, op. cit., p. 59.

[23] Ibid., pp. 59–60.

[24] The 'citadel' at Mohenjodaro and the 'citadels' found in other Indus towns have been usually seen as palace and defence complexes, with provision for ceremonial and religious or ritualistic functions. See, especially, Shereen Ratnagar, *Enquiries into the Political Organization of Harappan Society*, Pune, 1991, pp. 106–22.

[25] Stuart Piggott, *Prehistoric India, to 1000 BC*, Harmondsworth, 1950, p. 171.

[26] D.D. Kosambi, *Myth and Reality*, pp. 78–79.

[27] Iravatham Mahadevan, 'The Cult Object on Unicorn Seals: A Sacred Filter?', in K.N. Dikshit, ed., *Archaeological Perspective of India since Independence*, New Delhi, 1985, pp. 165–86.

[28] John Marshall, *Mohenjo-daro and the Indus Civilization*, London, 1931, Vol. I, pp. 52–56. See also Asko Parpola, *Deciphering the Indus Script*, Cambridge, 1994, pp. 184–90.

[29] Gregory L. Possehl, *The Indus Civilization, A Contemporary Perspective*, New Delhi, 2002, p. 152.

[30] These data are derived from the detailed lists in Iravatham Mahadevan, *The Indus Script*, New Delhi, 1977, pp. 793–98. Our count does not entirely follow Mahadevan's own classification.

[31] G. Possehl, *The Indus Civilization*, pp. 146–47.

[32] See J.H. Hutton, *Caste in India*, fourth edition, Bombay, 1969, pp. 71 *et passim.*

[33] Louis Dumont, *Homo Hierarchicus: The Caste System and Its Implications*, revised complete English edition, New Delhi, 1998.

[34] See Suvira Jaiswal's critique of Dumont in her 'Varna Ideology and Social Change', *Social Scientist*, Vol. 19, Nos 3–4, 1991, and my own in 'Caste in Indian History', in *Essays in Indian History: Towards a Marxist Perception*, New Delhi, 1995, pp. 160–64. Dumont himself discusses his critics (mainly from the field of sociology) in his preface to the revised 'Complete English Edition', pp. xi–xliii.

[35] For a discussion of various views on the evolution of the caste system, see Suvira Jaiswal's introduction to her *Caste: Origin, Functions and Dimensions of Change*, New Delhi, 1998, pp. 1–31.

[36] See Dumont's remarks, *Homo Hierarchicus*, pp. 72–75.

[37] See A.A. Macdonell and A.B. Keith, *Vedic Index of Names and Subjects*, London, 1912, I, pp. 281–82.

[38] In Nirukta, XII. 13, with reference to 'a woman of Shūdra *jāti*' (quoted by S. Jaiswal, *Caste*, p. 13).

[39] I follow Ralph T.H. Griffith's translation, edited by J.L. Shastri, Delhi, 1973.

[40] See R.T.H. Griffth's translation, *The Texts of the White Yajurveda*, third edition, Banaras, 1957, pp. 413–19.

[41] I have followed R.T.H. Griffith's translation, *The Hymns of the Atharvaveda*, third edition, edited by M.L. Abhimanyu, 2 volumes, Varanasi, 1962.

[42] See, for the textual references given within brackets, Julius Eggerton's translation, *The Śatapatha-Brāhmaṇa*, 5 volumes, Indian reprint, Delhi, 1963.

[43] It should be recalled that Vaishya in the *Rigveda* seems to have the sense of a common man, derived from *vish*, people. It is also noteworthy that the term *varṇa* is not actually used in this passage. The passage is repeated in *Atharvaveda*, XIX. 6, and *Vājasaneyi*, XXXI.11.

[44] As in *Manusmriti*, I.31 (G. Buhler's translation, Oxford, 1886, pp. 13–14).

[45] For these statements from early texts of the *Tipiṭaka*, viz., *Vinaya Piṭaka*, and *Dīgha Nikāya*, see Narendra Wagle, *Society at the Time of the Buddha*, Bombay, 1966, pp. 122–23.

[46] Wagle, op. cit., pp. 102–03, quoting *Dīgha Nikāya*.

[47] See Krishna Mohan Shrimali, *The Age of Iron and the Religious Revolution, c. 700–350 BC*, New Delhi, 2007, for a comprehensive survey of the period.

[48] K.M. Shrimali, op. cit., p. 65.

49 R.C. Majumdar, ed., *Classical Accounts of India*, Calcutta, 1960, pp. 224–26 (Arrian), 236–37 (Diodorus) and 263–68 (Strabo).

50 See Thomas R. Trautman, *Kauṭilya and the Arthaśāstra*, Leiden, 1971, and S.C. Mishra, *Evolution of Kauṭilya's Arthaśāstra*, Delhi, 1997.

51 For a summary of the information the Greek sources provide us with about the society and religion of North-Western India at the time of Alexander's conquest, see Irfan Habib and Vivekanand Jha, *Mauryan India*, New Delhi, 2004, pp. 1–4.

52 A notable text is that of the Buddha's counsels to *Sīgāla* in *Sīgālaka Sutta* in *Dīgha Nikāya*, often cited as a source on which Ashoka could have drawn upon in formulating his *dhaṁma* injunctions.

53 *Chāndogya Upaniṣhad*: The provocation for Gautama's approach to the King and the latter's reference to the Kṣhatriyas' secret knowledge occurs in V. 3, and the quoted passage in V.10.7. The translation used is that of F. Max Muller, *The Upaniṣhads*, I(1), reprint, New Delhi, 1990, pp. 76–82.

54 I have used G. Buhler's translation, *The Laws of Manu*, Oxford, 1886.

55 B.N. Mukherjee, *Studies in the Aramaic Edicts of Asoka*, Calcutta, 1984, pp. 9–22, especially pp. 12, 14.

56 *A Record of the Buddhist Religion as Practised in India and the Malay Archipelago*, translated by J. Takakusu, Oxford, 1896, p. 62.

57 Cf. R.S. Sharma, *Śūdras in Ancient India*, Delhi, 1958, especially pp. 232–34. Part of the argument advanced by me in the preceding paragraphs on the role of Buddhism was set out in my *Essays in Indian History: Towards a Marxist Perception*, New Delhi, 1995, pp. 168–69.

58 On the social aspects of Islam, one can easily commend Reuben Levy, *The Social Structure of Islam*, Cambridge, 1957, and Maxime Rodinson, *Islam and Capitalism*, London, 1974.

59 *Chachnāma*, edited by U.M. Daudpota, Delhi, 1939, pp. 206–14.

60 Ibid., pp. 214–16.

61 For the *Devālasmriti*, see Derryl N. Maclean, *Religion and Society in Arab Sind*, Leiden, 1989, pp. 78–82. Alberuni's remarks occur in *Alberuni's India*, translated by E.C. Sachau, London, 1990, II, pp. 162–63.

62 There is no doubt that R.C. Zaehner in his *Hindu and Muslim Mysticism*, London, 1960, greatly overstates the case for the Hindu sources of Sufism.

63 This work has been translated by one of the great authorities on Sufism, R.A. Nicholson, London, 1936.

64 See the pioneering writings of Mohammad Habib on early sufis, reprinted in his *Politics and Society during the Early Medieval Period*, edited by K.A. Nizami, Vol. I, New Delhi, 1974. There are two important works on early Indian Sufism: Saiyid Athar Abbas Rizvi, *A History of Sufism in India*, Vol. I [*up to 1600*], New Delhi, 1997, and Riazul Islam, *Sufism in South Asia: Impact on Fourteenth-Century Muslim Society*, Karachi, 2002.

65 The best edition is that of M. Latif Malik, Lahore, 1966.

66 Cf. S. Athar Abbas Rizvi, *Muslim Revivalist Movements in Northern India in the Sixteenth and Seventeenth Centuries*, Lucknow, 1965, pp. 52–53.

[67] Jahāngīr, *Tuzuk-i Jahāngīrī*, edited by Saiyid Ahmad, Ghazipur/Aligarh, 1863–64, p. 176.

[68] C.J. Brown, *The Coins of India*, Calcutta, 1922, p. 70.

[69] Baranī, *Fatāwā-i Jahāndārī*, India Office (London) MS, I.O. 1149, ff.118b–120b.

[70] H.B.W. Garrick in A. Cunningham, *Archaeological Survey Reports*, XXII (1883–84), pp. 116–17.

[71] E.C. Sachau, translation of *Alberuni's India*, I, pp. 27–32 especially pp. 29–30.

[72] Amīr Khusrau, *Nuh Sipihr*, edited by M. Wahid Mirza, London, 1950, pp. 164–65.

[73] In a Kannada inscription at Penukonda of 1354 the Vijayanagara ruler Bukka I is styled *Hiṁdu-rāya Suratrāṇa*, 'Sultan over Hindu rāyas', (*Epigraphia Indica*, VI, p. 327 and note), this particular title occurring in subsequent inscriptions as well until the sixteenth century. A Jaina inscription at Sādri, of 1438–1439, says of Rānā Kumbha of Mewar that he had obtained by his military successes the title of *Hiṁdu Suratrāṇa*, 'Hindu Sultan' (*Epigraphia Indica*, XIX–XXII, D.R. Bhandarkar's List of Inscriptions. No. 784 on pp. 109–10). In both these styles the use of Hindu still has an exotic air about it.

[74] 'Abdu'l Ḥaqq, *Akhbāru'l Akhyār*, Deoband, 1332/1913–14, p. 306.

[75] S.A. Abbas Rizvi, *Muslim Revivalist Movements*, pp. 68–134.

[76] S.A. Abbas Rizvi, 'Rawshaniyya Movement', *Abu Nahrain*, Leiden, Vol. 6, 1967.

[77] Anonymous (Kaikhusrau Isfandyār), *Dabistān-i Mazāhib*, (*c.* 1653), edited by Rahīm Rizā Zada, 1362/1983, I, pp. 279–86.

[78] Cf. Irfan Habib, 'A Political Theory for the Mughal Empire: A Study of the Ideas of Abu'l–Fazl', Proceedings Indian History Congress, 59th (Patiala) session, Aligarh, 1999, pp. 329–40.

[79] See the selection from Abū'l-Faẓl's record of Akbar's sayings in Shireen Moosvi, *Episodes in the Life of Akbar: Contemporary Records and Reminiscences*, New Delhi, pp. 126–29.

[80] This he did in his tract *Majma'u'l Baḥrain*, edited and translated by M. Mahfuz-ul Haq, Calcutta, 1929.

[81] Rizvi, *History of Sufism*, II, pp. 55–150, especially pp. 103–08.

[82] S.R. Sharda, *Sufi Thought: Its Development in Panjab and Impact on Panjabi Literature*, New Delhi, 1974, pp. 148–71.

[83] Rizvi, *Muslim Revivalist Movements*, pp. 202–313; J. Friedmann, *Shaykh Ahmad Sirhindi, an Outline of his Thought and a Study of his Image in the Eyes of Posterity*; and Rizvi, *History of Sufism*, II, pp. 196–249.

[84] Rizvi, *Muslim Revivalist Movements*, pp. 313–23.

[85] S.A. Abbas Rizvi, *Shah Wali Allah and his Times*, Canberra, 1980.

[86] Idem, *Shāh 'Abd al-Azīz*, Canberra, 1982.

[87] As reported by 'Abdu'l Qādir Badāūnī, *Muntakhabu't Tawārīkh*, edited by Ali, Ahmad and Lees, Calcutta, 1864–69, III, p. 79.

[88] See translation of this work in Jogendra Chunder Ghose, ed., *The English*

*Works of Raja Rammohan Roy*, Calcutta, 1906, pp. 941–58 (p. 957 carries the quoted words).

89 For example, 'A Defence of Hindu Theism' (1817), ibid., pp. 87–100, and 'The Monotheistical System of the Veds' (1817), ibid., pp. 101–26.

90 'Burning Widows Alive' (1818), ibid., pp. 321–63.

91 'Observe what pain, what slighting, what contempt, and what afflictions their virtue enables them to support!' (Ibid., p. 361, and pp. 361–63 for the whole passage.)

92 'Modern Encroachments on the Ancient Rights of Females according to the Hindu Law of Inheritance' (1822), ibid., pp. 373–84.

93 Ibid., p. 929.

94 'Future Results of British Rule in India', *New York Daily Tribune*, 8 August 1853; reprinted in *Karl Marx on India*, edited by Iqbal Husain, New Delhi, 2006, pp. 46–51.

95 See Romila Thapar's important essay, 'Imagined Religious Communities? Ancient History and the Modern Search for a Hindu Identity', reprinted in her *History and Beyond*, New Delhi, 2000, pp. 60–80.

96 On Ameer Ali see Wilfred Cantwell Smith, *Modern Islam in India: A Social Analysis*, London, 1946, pp. 49–55.

97 Syed Ahmad Khan's letter of 17 August 1892 to Sayyid Mahdi Ali Khan, printed in *Makātibāt al-Khullān*, edited by M. Usman Maqbūl, Aligarh, 1915, pp. 3–7, shows that he continued to hold uncompromisingly to these views till his very late days.

98 It is a curious lacuna in the Indian Constitution that whereas under the Directive Principles of State Policy, we have Article 44 prescribing the aim of a 'uniform civil code', there is no hint as to what it should contain besides being 'uniform'! There is not even a recommendatory provision that women should have equal rights with men in all civil matters, especially inheritance, control of property, etc.

99 Rajat Kanta Ray, *The Felt Community*, New Delhi, 2003, p. 375.

100 This passage is seriously mistranslated in William Dalrymple, *The Last Mughal*, New Delhi, 2006, pp. 268–69, where he makes it appear that the appeal is addressed only to Hindus, made under the belief that they were not supporting the Rebellion sufficiently.

101 I have used a rotograph copy of the file of this weekly journal in the library of the Department of History, Aligarh Muslim University.

102 Vishnubhat Godse's narrative, quoted in Rajat K. Ray, *Felt Community*, pp. 371–72.

# 1 In Search of the Roots of Religion or *Dharma*

## Linguistic and Social Routes

*D.P. Chattopadhyaya*

Objective studies in the concepts, institutions and practices of religion have shown with fair clarity their deep social roots. Their proclaimed spiritual underpinnings and divine sanctions may be disputed, but their social origins have often been quite convincingly traced. Here I would be mainly concerned with the social roots of religion and the methods followed are linguistic, anthropological and economic.

I propose to discuss, first, a few key terms of religious discourse from a comparative philological point of view. Incidentally, it will be seen that because of the social embeddedness of language, philological discussions always have sociological implications. Secondly, in Section II, I shall try to bring my anthropological or sociological discussion closer to the history of religions in India. Thirdly, in Section III, I try to illustrate my view with selective references to Chinese, Hellenic and Islamic philosophers of religion. Since this is a very large area, I cannot naturally, within the scope of my paper cover any of these important areas in a comprehensive way. With this in my mind I provide a select bibliography at the end of the paper in which one who is interested can see for himself the factual sources of my view and for his own further studies. Fourthly, in Section IV, I shall go into the relationships between mythology, sociology and history. In this Section, I propose to refer to the interface of the scientific and the Marxist views on religion. In this connection, I try to show how Marx was influenced by contemporary evolutionist and anthropological findings. Finally, in Section V, I discuss the professed unifying role of religion and its historically evident divisive workings in practice. I round off the paper by offering my own reflections in the light of the materials available to me. With all its limitations, I maintain, religion as an institution, has still a very important historical role to play. But it seems to me that for pressing socio-economic reasons the secularizing forces of society are still not able to overcome the forces of fundamentalism and, in quite a number of cases, those of terrorism. Notwithstanding these limiting tendencies, I am inclined to conclude that religion, in its transformed ethical and spiritual forms, definitely has its own future.

## I

### Comparative Philological Approach

Different authorities on religion, not surprisingly, have chosen different methods for understanding and explaining what religion is and what its associated views and observances mean. Philosophers and theologians speak of some unspeakable and supernatural reality as the source of religion. Sociologists and anthropologists, who often sail in the same boat, try to interpret religious beliefs and activities by relating them to humans' natural and social praxis. Their findings and conclusions, understandably, are basically empirical and historical, shunning metaphysical presuppositions and theological postulations.

Personally speaking, I find the linguistic routes to religion and religion-related concepts such as god, temple, sacrifice, worship, priest, holy or sacred, heaven, hell, angel, devil, pagan, magic, witch, fairy, ghost, etc., very insightful. Linguistic and etymological analysis provides us a clearer map of what religion is, what it means and practically entails. The relations between linguistic items and their social origin, association and reference exhibit the natural roots of 'the supernatural'.

'Religion' stands for belief in a supernatural being or power and the yearning of humans to be in satisfying and peace-giving relation to that being. Religion has two main aspects, cognitive and practical. One of the most widespread linguistic sources of 'religion' is belief or faith. In some cases, however, religion is kindred to worship or service of god.

There is no distinctive Sanskrit word for religion. It is generally covered by *dharma*, that is, what is established, law, usage and right conduct. The term is derived of *dhr-*, 'hold' or 'support'. Another Sanskrit word close to religion or *dharma* is *marga*, 'way'. It stands for the right way of life and this expression emphasizes the desirable code of conduct. The underlying concept has found wide support with the Buddhists. There is no distinctive early Greek word for religion. The word *theogonia* stands for genealogy of the gods, that is, mythology. Other related words mean: (i) piety toward gods or parents, and (ii) feelings of awe, reverence and worship. Another Greek word *thredkeia* denotes religious worship; in plural it denotes religious rites.

The modern English word religion and its widespread European cognates are, etymologically speaking, traceable to Latin, *religio*. On this issue there is dispute – whether *legere*, 'collect' and 'select' or *ligare*, 'bind', should follow after *re-* (repeated mental collections, selections, considerations). Some comparative philologists like Emile Benveniste are of the view that originally the Indo–Europeans did not think of any omnipresent reality underpinning religion as an institution. In those languages one finds no term to designate it. In Ionic Greek, in Herodotus, the term *threskeie* means observances of cult prescriptions. The term is not found in Attic Greek. It appears only at a late date, first century BC, meaning religion as a complex of beliefs and practices. Benveniste argues that religion must be related to *relegere*, 'to collect again, to take up again for a new choice, to return to a previous synthesis in order to recompose it.' According to him *religio*, 'religious scruple', was originally a psychological or *subjective* attitude, an act of reflection bound up with some fear of a religious kind. He thinks that it is due to the Christian influence and interpretation that the word *relegere* came to mean 'to tie' or 'to bind'. Under the new interpretation, '*religio*' becomes 'obligation', an *objective* tie or bond between the believer or the worshipper and the god. The Old English word *geleafa*, Old High German *gilouba*, Lithunian *tikyba* and Lettic *ticet* stand for 'belief' or 'faith' with or without an object. That is, it may be subjective or it may be objective. However, an element of objectwardness or a sense of transitivity is certainly present.

Another concept central to many, though not all, religions is god. There are several cognates of these words in Indo–Iranian, Italic, Celtic and Baltic languages. Most of these words are related to 'sky', 'day', 'sky-god' etc. Indo–European words *deiwo*, *dyew*, *diw* are clearly naturalistic. But many pro-religious interpreters endow these natural terms with a spiritual sense. The personified Greek words, *zeus*, *dios*, Latin *iuppiter* and Sanskrit word *dyaus* all denote the common notion of brightness and shining. These words represent an extension of a simple term *dei*, seen in Sanskrit *dideti*, 'shines'.

The naturalist association of the etymological roots of Greek, Roman and Sanskrit equivalents to such words as temple, sacrifice, prayer, worship, priest, heaven, hell, angel, devil, idol, superstition, magic, witch and ghost can be easily shown. For example, Greek words like *naos* and *ieron* denote dwelling place and holy place or shrine, respectively. The Latin word *templun* from which most of the equivalent Romance, Celtic and Germanic words are derived originally denoted the space in the Heavens marked out by the augur, a consecrated place or sanctuary. The Sanskrit words for temple have been *mandira, devalaya, caitya, vihara,* etc. Some of the roots of classical languages of these words are associated with light, burning, place for living and so on.

The Old Greek word for sacrifice or offering was *thydia.* In Latin the roots are *sacrificium,* making a sacrifice, *victima* or *hostia,* animal sacrifice. The Sanskrit word for sacrifice had been *yajna* (worship), *medha* (juice, sap), *hotra* (liquid offering). Different cognates of these words in their original forms denoted offerings of different types of meat, feast and festival.

Old Greek words, *euchomai, araomai,* Latin words, *preari, orare,* and Sanskrit words *yac, prarthaya,* are admittedly different in shades of their meaning, but they denote acts of speaking, saying, taking vow, pleading, asking for, longing for, etc. All these words are expressive of human needs and cravings, to ask some supposed supernatural power to grant, sanction or respond to the same.

Verbs for 'worship' are in most cases related with the verbs 'to pray' or 'to honour'. When these acts of praying and honouring are addressed to god and in an intensified form, the acts are designated as worship. The Greek word for worship is *debomai,* which stands for feeling awed. Sometimes it means fear leading to a sense of shrinking or withdrawing from the source of fear. The Sanskrit word *tyaj* has a somewhat similar sense of leaving, abandoning or shunning.

The Latin word *venerari,* derived from *Venus,* is indicative of love or charm. Here the sense is not of shunning or being afraid of; on the contrary, it means getting drawn towards. The other Latin word *adorari,* originally meant 'speaking to' and then 'praying'.

The Old English *witan,* and the Old High German *wizzan,* have the senses of 'seeing', 'knowing' and 'heeding'. The object of worship, by implication, is supposed to be a force or power to reckon with because of its holy character.

It is instructive to note that the Indo–European synonyms of the words like 'priest' and 'preacher' are closely related to the meanings of the words 'praying' and 'worshipping'. The origin of many of these words are pre-Christian and socially functional. It is clearly evident that in the pre-Christian societies such as in Vedic India, Babylonian and Judaic West Asia, and Chinese East Asia, the roles of priest and/or preacher were duly recognized.

Understandably, many of these words are derived from words for 'holy', 'god', 'sacrifice' or 'invoke'. Sanskrit work *ṛtvij* is derived from *ṛtu*, 'right time' and 'appropriate hour'. The priest is a person who pours an oblation and makes an offering. The Sanskrit word used in this context is *havate*; the Greek word for it is *cheo*; the Avestan word is *zavaiti*; and the Slovak word is *zovetu*. All these cognate words carry the senses of calling upon, invoking and worshipping with hymns and sacrifice.

Such words as related to Christianity, viz., clergyman, minister, parson and nun are relatively new. In the Greek language the word 'monk', traceable to *monos*, denotes someone who is a solitary hermit. In Greek it also meant 'old man', 'good man'. As its cognate in the Latin language one may take *monachus*. Similar words are found in Baltic languages, for example, *vienuolis* (Lithuanian) derived from Vienas.

Similar words are found in ancient India. During the pre-Buddhist times we hear of the single and wandering 'hermits', 'ascetics', 'sages' and *tantriks* living sometimes in human localities and sometimes in forest areas. It is in the later period of Buddhism that we find that the monk is being named *bhikku* (Pali); its Sanskrit equivalent is *bhikṣu*, beggar, religious mendicant, etc. The word *bhikkuni* is feminine and means nun. It is only during the Buddhist period that monks or sages started living together, forming the *sangha* (religious order).

'Priest' and 'preaching' are closely related words. Priest is a knowledgeable man, and he preaches what he knows particularly about the supernatural truths and social propriety. He is credited with some extraordinary power of knowing and the authority of proclaiming or announcing such knowledge to others. The Greek work *kerngma* and the Latin word *sermo* are the etymological roots of many European words of equivalent or related meaning. In many ancient societies preachers and priests were allotted the duties of telling the people about their duties and obligations. They had the power to summon people and excommunicate or exclude the wrong-doer from a social community for maintaining its intended right character.

It is also interesting to follow the etymological roots of such words as 'heaven' and 'hell'. In nearly all the Indo–European words for 'heaven', as the abode of gods, goddesses and the blessed spirits, are such as originally denoted the 'sky'. Among the Indo–European words for the abode of gods, we find such words as *yamasya bhavana, svarga, devaloka*; and contrary to popular belief, Yama is not necessarily to be taken as the king of the nether world. *Yama* literally means 'controller', 'regulator', 'driver', 'charioteer', who can check the wrong propensity in humans. *Yama* is regarded as the first of men and born from Vivasvat, the Sun, and his wife Saranyu. The solar association of *yama* is notable. The other Sanskrit word for heaven is *svarga*; here also one notices that *svar* (in Sanskrit) stands for 'sun', 'sky' and 'heaven'. In the compound form, *svarga* stands for the heavenly abode where the blessed ones can go (*gam*, 'go'). The other word for heaven is *devaloka*; here also *deva* is related to *diva* ('day') which gives us light.

The adjectival form of *naraka* is *naraka* and from it is obtained the word *naraka-loka*, the 'hellish world' (*Atharvaveda* 12.4.36). The Greek cognates of the world would be *enerteros*, pertaining to the nether or lower world. The Umbrian cognate is *nertru* and the Latin one is *sinistro.* Its impression is clear from the Vedic literature where it is said to be *adharad gṛha*, the house below or *adhama-tamas*, lowest darkness. A similar pejorative connotation is attached to Avestan words like those for the 'worst world', 'house of the worst spirits', etc.

It is to be noted here that the concepts of heaven and hell are being indicated by what is naturally good, like light, and naturally bad, like darkness. The other paired concepts like 'best world' and 'worst world', or 'upper world' and 'lower world', are also, by implication, natural.

The other words of negative connotation like 'devil' and 'demon' are, on analysis, found to be extensions of social approval and disapproval, blame and condemnation. Most of the European words for 'devil' are derived from a Greek word, *diabolos* or *diaballo* (original meaning 'slanderous' or 'slanderer'). Later on, the 'slanderer' became the 'devil'. The Latin word for devil is *diabolus.* The English word 'diabolic' is traceable to its Latin root, *diabolus.* Also, the Latin word *draco* denotes 'dragon', a fearful and reprehensible reptile. The Sanskrit words for devil and demon are numerous, viz., *pisaca, betala, apadevata* ('bad god'), *asura, raksasa, danava* and *nisacara.* Here also one may note that what is bad, wrong or evil, is likened to darkness, absence of light, and lack of divinity. The linguistic analyses of roots of these words unmistakably reveal their naturalistic connotations. It also makes it plain that natural phenomena and forces may be ingeniously used by humans for the purposes of social and moral approval or disapproval.

The linguistic root of the words for 'angel' may also help to make this point clear. In Sanskrit the word *aditya*, derived from *aditi*, the personified infinity, is taken in the angelic sense. Aditya is one of the seven deities of heaven. In Avestan the word for angel (*yazata*) literally means 'to be worshipped'. Angel is among a large group of holy beings subordinate to *ahura mazda*. In Greek language the angel is a messenger, *eggelos*. The highest and holiest among the angels is archangel.

Words like 'pagan', 'heathen' and other cognates stand for an exclusivist mind in the pejorative sense. The Greek word *ethen*, meaning people or nation, was used by Jewish writers with reference to non-Jewish nations. From the Jewish point of view, the non-Jewish nations were 'heathen'. The Latin *gentes*, in Gothic *piudos*, and Old English *peoda* were used in this sense. In other languages like Lithuanian (*pagonis, pagonas*), Old Prussian (*poganans*), and in Slovak (*poganu*) the words are used in an exclusivist and critical sense. In India, in Sanskrit and Sanskrit-based languages, the sense of pagan is conveyed by such words as *asadharmasevi*, *vigrahasevi* and *pratimapujaka*. It may be noted in this connection that the sense underlying the word *pratima* is that it is like (or *pratima*) the original deity, but *not* the original itself. In support of the worship of *pratimas* or images the concerned worshippers maintained that visual representation of deities facilitated their attention and concentration during the time of worship and prayer. Most of the places of worship of major religious groups – the Hindus' temple, Muslims' mosque, Christians' church, Buddhists' *stupa/vihara* and Jews' synagogue – have their distinct architectural designs. Indirectly that suggests the importance of visual representations. The distinctiveness of the languages of prayer is also indicative, in a way, of the necessary peculiar character of different modes of worship.

Most of the cognates of 'idol' in European languages are derived from the Greek word *eidos*, which means 'form' or 'shape'. The Greek word *idon* and the Latin word *videre* convey a sense of visibility. To prevent the impression that the visible forms of God are true, Jewish and Christian writers have often used the expression 'image of false God'. Hence, the worshippers of 'false God' have been critically referred to as 'idolaters'. But in some European languages, like Old

English and Gothic, we find similar expressions which mean 'holy images'.

Whether image worship is a 'good' act of religion or a 'bad' act of superstition is highly controversial and depends upon how words like 'religion' and 'superstition' are understood, i.e., whether in a value-loaded or value-neutral sense. Sociologically speaking, what is regarded now as 'superstition' was once, and still is among many groups, an integral part of their religious belief and practice. The line of demarcation between 'religion' and 'superstition' depends upon time and place.

The Greek word for 'superstition' denotes 'fear of supernatural power' either in a good sense or in a bad sense, but the latter seems to be the prevailing sense. The Latin word *superstitio* is apparently derived from *superstare* 'stand over', due to wonder, astonishment or awe.

In several Slavic languages the word is used in the sense of 'belief in absurdity', 'belief in phantom or ghost', 'bogey' and 'in vain'. In Sanskrit the sense of superstition is conveyed by such expressions as *atibhaktih* (excessive devotion), *sakunapisacadivisvasah* (belief in sinister beings) and *anythamargah* (different and bad paths). The words are clearly negative and critical in their implications. Those who depart from their own faith and path and follow other faiths and the wrong path are referred to as superstitious people.

Words like magic, witchcraft and sorcery are traceable to various linguistic roots. Many European words of this group are traceable to the Greek derivatives of the designation for the Persian priests, the Magi (Old Persian, *magus*). Magic has two connotations, one is positive, meaning wisdom (of a wise person), and another negative, meaning the ability to perform acts of deception and harm, or 'black magic'. Sometimes it has been used in the sense of charming or skilful acts. Magic is traceable both to Greek *magike* and Latin *magice.* The magician is credited with superhuman mastery over natural forces and objects and control of events. Often he is referred to as a practitioner of sorcery, witchcraft and enchantment with the help of wicked spirits.

In Sanskrit *maya*, *mayavidya*, *abhicarvidya*, *jalkarma*, *vasakriya*, etc., are used to convey the sense of magic. The practitioner of magic is credited to have the twin powers of suppressing the truth and also of projecting falsity. The word has been used both in ordinary and in metaphysical discourse.

Both in Sanskrit and in Avestan, *yatu* has been used to denote 'magic'. In Sanskrit magic has been taken as a sort of *kṛtya*, 'deed and act' with special reference to spreading an evil spell and practising witchcraft. It appears that the word *kṛtya* possesses Slavic (*caro*) and Russian (*carodejstvo*) cognates.

'Spirit', 'soul', 'ghost', 'spectre' and 'phantom' are often used in interchangeable ways and with reference to supernatural beings. In Sanskrit, the words used, in this connection, generally speaking, are *pitaras* (plural), *preta-bhuta. Preta* is used for 'the dead' (*pra-ita,* 'gone forth, departed'). It also denotes the spirit of the dead or ghost. *Bhuta* is a being. It is derived from *bhu* which means 'becoming' or 'being'. *Bhuta* is supposed to be a supernatural being and its existence is shadowy in character. The Greek word *dekia* also denotes 'shade', 'shadow', 'ghost' and 'phantom'. The Latin word for such beings is *manes* (plural), *larva* and *phantasma.* In Old English we find the word *gast,* meaning 'soul' and 'spirit'. In Middle English, the word is changed into *gost,* and in New English, as we know, it has become *ghost.* In Dutch the word *geest* is used in both senses of 'ghost' and 'spectre'. It is also used in the sense of Sanskrit *atma,* and *antaratma* ('disembodied spirit'). In Sanskrit, words like *nisacarah* (those who move in night), *narakah* and *smasanavasi* (those who live in the burning place), one perceives a sense of evil.

Most of the words briefly discussed above denote some supernatural or abnormal beings that are easily graspable. To account for their existence, the traditional writers speak of the paranormal (*alaukia*) cognitive capacities of human beings. But at the *laukika* (ordinary) level one finds it difficult to know them. Therefore, the discourse about them is generally found to be confined to the areas of belief or socially inherited faith.

## II

## From the Philological to the Historico-Anthropological Approach

It will be wrong to suppose that what is recognized now as religious beliefs, institutions and practices are exhaustively, or in a near exhaustive way, understandable by tracing the ancestry of the major religions of the world like Hinduism, Judaism, Buddhism, Christianity and Islam. From studies in the prehistory and anthropology of different forms of the surviving religions and other religions, not necessarily major, it becomes clear that the human reflection on its environmental phenomena, day and night, life, disease and death, etc., give rise to certain beliefs which cannot be completely reduced to natural events and processes. The contents of these beliefs, empirically determinate or not, had and still have their validity of a kind, and on that ground, these, as found in different languages and social practices, deserve objective analysis and understanding.

Simply because certain views and values are not *ours* and followed or practised by *others* must not be ignored, still less debunked. The distinction between 'we' and 'they', 'our' and 'their', has always exercised influence on minds. With the passage of time and development of human culture, facilitated by increasing interaction, humans have, however, certainly been overcoming the distance between 'the world of self' and 'the worlds of others'. Rightly understood, social space, unlike political territory, knows no boundary. It is clear from recorded history and historical linguistics that the territorial boundaries of different states, and cultural traits and limits of different human aggregates and their physical–geographical areas, have been undergoing intermittent changes.

For example, if someone however knowledgeable, tries to tell us where, culturally speaking, Asia ends and Europe begins, or tries to indicate the bounds of South Asia, one is destined to be unsuccessful. At best, we can have only a working idea on the narrow basis of our contemporary facts and figures, history and geography. The same point would seem to stand true for any attempted *cultural* definition between and within different continents, and even within a subcontinent like South Asia. We may recall that within many countries (like India, China and Russia) there are different cultures and languages. On the other hand, it may be shown that many languages are shared by many different countries and peoples. English and Spanish, for example, are in use in many countries. Within India itself there are many languages, religions and subcultures. The political identity of a country need not be confused with its cultural identity. Principled recognition of different religious communities, linguistic groups and ethnic groups does not amount to denial or dilution of the civilizational unity of the concerned human aggregates.

It may be profitably recalled here that in the Indian context and from the history of the country, we come across different religions, both those that are of indigenous origin, and those which came from without but have been internalized with the passage of time. Again a distinction between 'indigenous' and 'foreign' cannot be easily and sharply demarcated. The myths of 'pure race', 'pure religion' and 'pure culture' need to be discarded. Social entities and institutions, on careful analysis, are always found to be composite, complex or intermingled.

The most ancient forms of indigenous religions and languages of India are not Vedic. Several pre-Vedic, non-Vedic and even anti-Vedic cultures developed in South Asia. Many tribal groups and their religions and tongues in the main hilly tracts of the country, North-East India and the Andaman and Nicobar Islands, attest this simple point. The distinction and mutual interaction between the *agamic* and *nigomic* traditions are well recognized. Also recognized is the long process of their mutual accommodation, assimilation and dissimilation.

Generalizing this, one may rightly affirm, on the basis of the studied historical facts, that where different ethnic and religious groups share the same cultural space over a long period of time, they are obliged to learn the ways of mutual accommodation. It is a part of the civilizational process. One may say – it is a civilizational imperative. In this connection reference has been frequently made to how the pre-Vedic peoples (e.g., Dravidians, Lokayatas, Carvakas, Tantrikas and Kapalikas), the post-Vedic groups (e.g., Buddhists and Jainas), the followers of the early Saṁkhya and the early Vaisesikas (atomists), shared the same cultural space. It is interesting to recall that, at least theoretically speaking, Buddhists and Jainas did not share many religious tenets and philosophical views (like those of the Absolute (*Brahman*), immortal and substantive self, and causality) of the Vedic practitioners. It is also true that their mutual relations had not always been free of conflict. But that is not very surprising in human affairs. Even within and between the groups professing Vedic views, there were often bitter internecine fights. But both conflict and conflict-resolution mark the relations between different groups inhabiting the same territory. This complex process of acculturation has been taking place in all countries both at the political and the social levels. To assert this historically and anthropologically well-attested general truth is not intended in the least to rationalize the views and values favouring conflict. This is an integral part of the least interpreted *descriptive* history of India and that of many other long-lasting civilizations. The analogy of the relations between the Vedic people with non-Vedic and anti-Vedic ones, with suitable qualifications, may be extended to the peoples professing other religions like Confucianism, Christianity and Islam.

In India between 700 BC and 400 BC we find a number of emergent major religious and philosophical sects. If the Jaina Tirthankars (teachers) prior to Mahavira are taken into account, then the ancestry of Jainism goes back beyond, or, at least, to around 600 BC. Lokayata, Ajivika and other sects were also active at that time. It is well known that Mahavira and the Buddha were contemporaries. If the Jataka stories, like the lineage of Tirthankaras, are kept in view, then the ancestry of Buddhism and Jainism can be antedated by at least two hundred years. Some ancient historians interpret the pre-Buddhist and pre-Mahavira eras as preparatory to the differentiation or dissimilation of Buddhism and Jainism from the Vedic mainstream. Makkhali Gosala of the Ajivika sect was a contemporary of the Buddha and Mahavira. So was Kanada, the original *sutrakar* of the system of Vaisesika (logical atomism). Of course, many authorities trace some elements of logical atomism even in the oral versions of Indian epics. Between 400 BC and AD 900, a fairly longish span of time, the Buddhists, due to internal dissension and dialectic, developed into many sects, viz., Mahasanghikas and Sthaviras (Theravadins) (*c.* 400 BC), Pudgalavadins (*c.* 300 BC), Vaibhashikas (*c.* 200 BC), Sautrantikas (*c.* 200 BC), Mahayanists (*c.* 100 BC), Madhaymikas (*c.* 100 BC), Yogacaras (*c.* AD 300), and Vajrayana (*c.* AD 300). Between AD 800 and 1000 both Jainism and Vaishnavism gained much in popularity and acceptance, which would explain their spread to different parts of India.

The period between AD 400 to 900 may be characterized as the Buddhist–Hindu watershed. During this period some very influential Vedic and Buddhist thinkers appeared on the scene and interacted, both critically and constructively, between themselves. In this connection some names deserve special mention. In the tradition both individual authorities and their schools commanded much respect and remembrance. It may be added here that the elements of the Samkhya and Vaisesika systems are traceable in many works over a very long time before their being codified, e.g., those of Ishvarakrishna (*c.* AD 400), one of the earliest authorities on the Samkhya, Vasubandhu, a distinguished Buddhist logician, and Vatsyayana, a famous commentator on *Nyayasutra.* After Vasubandhu we find several very distinguished Buddhist logicians like Dharmakirti (*c.* AD 650), Shantarakshita, Kamalashila and Dharmottara. During the same period, Bhartrihari, the famous Kashmiri grammarian, and Uddyotakara, the Nyaya logician, Gaudapada, the Advaitin, Kumarila and Prabhakara, both

Mimamsakas of different persuasions, developed their doctrines and arguments. It appears that Dharmakirti, Kumarila and Prabhakara flourished between *c.* 600 and 700. Both Shankara and Mandana Mishra, two famous Advaitins, and Shantarakshita and Kamalshila, famous Buddhist logicians, seem to have flourished between 700 and 800.

Close scrutiny shows that the Advaitins, Naiyayikas and Buddhists closely interacted and influenced one another. Jayanta Bhatta, the Naiyayika from Kashmir, criticized the Buddhists' logic and metaphysics. Within Brahmanism, as the result of its long interaction with and assimilation of some elements of Buddhism, some strong pro-Vedic writers are found to refer critically to the Advaitins as crypto-Buddhist. For the purpose of assimilation through interaction, it has been said, some Brahmanic rulers exercised an element of coercion, not amounting to literal liquidation, against the followers of Buddhism in India. It may be recalled here that both Fa-hien (AD 399–414) and Hsuan-Tsang (AD 629–645), the famous Chinese scholars and monks, widely travelled throughout India. Both of them found at the places they visited many Buddhist towns and monasteries in a dilapidated state, suggesting that Buddhism *qua* Buddhism started declining from the fifth century onward. Later on, the pace of its decline increased. Many pro-Brahmanic writers tried to interpret it as the sign of assimilation of Buddhism within the Brahmanic fold. However, the critics defending the contrary interpretation maintain that Buddhists were persecuted and forced to give up their faith and return to the Hindu fold. The name of Shashanka, the King of Gauda, is often referred to in this context.

To understand the development, rise and fall, of India's religious and philosophical schools, one is required to bear in mind its political history, which is marked by a series of cycles between expansion of dominant states and their fragmentation into many small warring kingdoms. Except during the Maurya and Gupta periods, no state could establish itself as a relatively stable hegemonic entity. It seems that the Gangetic fertile plains were settled well before 600 BC, but the evolution of human settlements into forms of states took time. This had much to do with the beginning of the use of iron.

Around 500 BC there were several important states on the banks of the Yamuna and the Ganges. The notable among them were Kuru, Matsya, Surasena, Kausambi, Vatsa, Panchala, Kosala, Kasi,

Magadha and Anga. States like the Mallas, Kapilavastu, Videha, Vaisali, Chedi, and Avanti should also be mentioned in this context. With the states, came cities, like those of Mathura, Kausambi, Benaras, Pataliputra and Ujjain. Under the Mauryan empire (322–185 BC), these settlements (*janapada*) and states (*rajyas*) were brought together. Only a small southern part of the peninsula lay beyond this empire. But by the second century BC this vast empire disintegrated and there appeared different political entities, viz., the Shunga empire in the east, the Kushan empire in the north, the western satraps in Gujarat, and the Andhra kingdom in the south. These political entities formed an unsteady balance of power. Again, in the Gupta empire around AD 400, which was confined mainly to northern India we cannot discern, strictly speaking, a large, stable and strong political hegemony. But, culturally speaking, the Gupta period proved to be rich and of lasting value.

Within this political space emerged different religions. The decline of the Vedic cults, followed mainly by the emergence of different tribes or congeries of tribes, witnessed the twin controls of hereditary kingship and very influential priests attached to different regional kings. The Upanishadic period was in full bloom at this time. By 300 BC the Vedic insights were distilled into philosophical and religious aphorisms. The ideas started gaining logical, epistemological and systematic forms.

The Vedic ideology came under question with the rise of Jainism and Buddhism. India did not have a state religion familiar in the Chinese, Christian and Islamic orbits. State patronage meant not much more than permission to build monasteries and religious monuments, donating property, support for the monks and exempting these properties from taxation. Religious donations, in most cases, came from private persons like merchants and relatives of the royal families. Buddhist patronage was more institutionally organized than Hindu patronage which was extended to the followers of Hinduism. Under the Mauryan empire, Buddhism began to spread outside its Magadhan homeland due to the royal initiative in sending missions to different parts of the country and even beyond the country. During the Gupta empire, Hinduism flourished. But both Buddhism and Hinduism coexisted in the Gangetic plains. Buddhism and Hinduism in India have a common characteristic – neither allowed itself to become a state religion; admittedly Buddhism had a symbiotic relationship with strong states and Hinduism with weak ones.

The early spread of Jainism was parallel to that of Buddhism originating from Magadha. The shrines of Jainas reached Tamilnadu in the south and Mathura in the upper Ganges in the post-Maurya period. The Jainas had close ties with Guptas during the early period of the imperial build-up. Later on, the Jainas received patronage from some of the regional kings and coastal merchants. Buddhism flourished in the Gangetic heartland and in the north. With the passage of time different sects appeared within Jainism. While a group of them followed strict ascetic practices, many others took up urban professions like trade and commerce. The base of Jainism was narrower than that of the Hindus or Buddhists. Jainism was weakened and it was gradually displaced from the south after the middle of the twelfth century as new Shaivite and Vaishnavite movements made the Hindu caste system flexible, allowing Hindus to enter into the area of commercial activities, where they became powerful under the Mughals. Jainism was never as large a religion as Buddhism. But it survived longer because of its relatively stricter code of conduct and way of life. Unlike Buddhism, it did not allow itself to be influenced by the liberal gestures and flexible overtures of Hinduism. While the Buddhists agreed to share, perhaps unwillingly, and/or unwittingly, the same social and intellectual space, the Jainas preferred to remain cautious and watchful bystanders.

## III
## Brief Historical Excursion into Chinese, Hellenic and Islamic Philosophers and Religions

In shaping the course of Chinese philosophical ideas and religious practices the forces of opposition played a very important role. Confucius and his followers appeared on the scene around 500 BC. The old agricultural primitivists were still active and influential. Confucians were explicitly challenged by the Mohists. The moral activism of the Mohists and Confucian schools were contradicted by Yang Chu, defending a kind of self-centricity. Mencius, affirming the native goodness of human nature, criticized the Yang Chu movement. This view was attacked by Hsun Tzu who affirmed the natural evil tendency of the human mind, requiring social control and regulation. All these views developed approximately between 500 and 350 BC. By the time Mencius appeared on the scene (*c.* 300 BC) all these different, conflicting and affine views took the form of a network. The main parallel areas of the network can be designated as idealism versus naturalism, sophistry versus transcendentalism, changing names versus namelessness of the *Tao Te Ching.*

The major philosophers who dominated the philosophical scene of China between 350 and 250 BC are Kao Tzu, Mencius, Hui Shih, Chuang Tzu, Sung King, Kung-Sun Lung, Tsou Yen and Hsun-Tzu. Most of these philosophers were aligned to one or the other state structures. From Agricultural Primitivists and Mohists to Confucians and Tao Te Ching all had their different political leanings, articulate or inarticulate, and political affiliations, direct or indirect. Warring states like Ch'in, Chao, Ch'u, Ch'i and Wei had their philosophical and political theoreticians. It is even said that the innovation in ancient Chinese thought emerged from war between states and conflict and opposition between ideas. A dialectic of development is discernible in Chinese history of ideas and politics from a very early period. The emergence of the Han dynasty (200 BC–AD 200), giving rise to a highly centralized polity, strengthened Confucianism enormously. But its hegemony did not go unchallenged indefinitely. Confucian claims for ideological and administrative monopoly were challenged by other scholars. This opposition forced a sort of synthetic reformulation of Confucianism. But for the forces of opposition to Confucian hegemony, the creativity of the time cannot be explained.

The opposition gradually crystallized and centred around Taoism. The Taoist ideas, particularly those of Mo Tsu, Han Fei Tzu and Kung-sun Lung, were brought together into a syncretic unity, strengthening the appeal of the school. The dissension between the thinkers synchronized with the political dissidence within the state, leading ultimately to the fragmentation of the autocratic state itself into three Kingdoms. The internal weakness and dissension invited alien ethnic incursion. Before the rule of the Han dynasty came to an end, a very strong bureaucracy developed within it and the situation became very complex, with the effective rise of both Taoist and Buddhist sects. This was the period when monasteries became influential centres for intellectual production. Religious factionalism was brought to an end when China became politically reunified through military struggles under the Sui (581–618 BC) and the Tang (618–600 BC).

It is to be noted from the Chinese, Indian and Hellenic histories of ideas and politics that *opposition*, rather than *unity*, fosters the spirit of creativity. Unity gives and lends stability and solidity to the ongoing intellectual life. But in the absence of a dissenting space in a solidly united regime, the spirit of questioning and the search for new satisfactory answers, linking then to the past and a desired future, tend to atrophy. This hypothesis can be buttressed by piecing together the intellectual history of the Hellenic world, spanning West Asia, the Aegean Islands, Greece and southern Italy in the pre-Roman era. The notable intellectual centres were Miletus, Ephesus, Samos, Cnidus, Smyrna, Colophon and Clazomenae (located on the eastern side of the Hellenic world), Athens, Eritrea, Megara (on the mainland of Greece), and Elea, Locri, Croton, Metapontum, Acragas and Syracuse (all in southern Italy).

The early Hellenic philosopher, Thales (624–546 BC), Anaximander (600–546 BC), a disciple of Thales, and Anaximenes (*c.* 570–500 BC), a follower of Anaximander, were all born in Miletus. Each of them was a naturalist and cosmologist. Thales held that the ultimate 'element' of the world is water. According to Anaximander, the ultimate stuff of the world is a formless mass, *apeiron*, meaning the infinite. This concept of infinity reminds one of the Indian concept of *aditi.* Both Thales and Anaximander travelled widely in the Mediterranean world and were distinguished geometricians, having learnt geometry apparently from Egypt. Anaximenes, like his two predecessors, was also a cosmologist and interested in the study of heavenly phenomena. According to him, air was the fundamental element of the universe. Heraclitus (*c.* 540–475 BC), who believed that fire is the ultimate reality and the forces of opposition account for universal creativity, was born at Ephesus near Miletus. Xenophanes (*c.* 570–480 BC) believed that earth is the fundamental element of the universe. He did not believe in transmigration of souls or in the primitive Hellenic gods. Both Heraclitus and Xenophanes settled in Elea. Pythagoras settled in Croton. After the Persian conquest of West Asia many of the West Asian thinkers moved westward and settled in southern Italy and Sicily. Anaxagoras (*c.* 500–428 BC) is believed to have lived in Clazomenae, not far off from Miletus. He moved to Athens for his intellectual activities. He spoke of an infinite number of 'seeds' (apparently something like the atoms of Leucippus) as the ultimate stuff of the heavens and the earth. His relations with the leading Athenians like Euripides and Pericles were not good enough for him to be allowed to teach his rationalist philosophy in the city and he had to retire to Lampsacus on the Hellespont. Besides Pythagoras, several other

Hellenic philosophers like Parmenides (*c.* 540 BC–fl.) and Zeno (*c.* 450 fl.) moved to southern Italy to live in exile. Both Parmenides and Zeno, a prominent exponent of the Eleatic school, were defenders of permanentism and critics of Heraclitean fluxism. It is to be remembered here that many famous philosophers of the time like Democritus (*c.* 470 BC–fl.) and Empedocles (*c.* 490–*c.* 430 BC), a great synthesizer, lived far away from mainland Greece. Democritus lived in Abdera, Thrace, and developed the notion of indivisible, indestructible, unchangeable and eternal atoms. Besides atoms, he believed only in the void. All other things, according to him, are due to the void and atoms. The atomism of Democritus proved very influential. It was taken up by Epicurus (341–270 BC), who was also born in Samos, outside Greece. It is interesting to recall that some of the Greek philosophers took active interest, in the political affairs of the places they lived in. A citizen of Acragas, Sicily, Empedocles took active part in overthrowing the tyrant ruler of the city–state. All these seminal thinkers are often clubbed together and identified by Eurocentric historians as Greek, overlooking the distinction between 'Greek' and 'Hellenic'.

The intellectual space in which the Hellenic philosophers moved was exceptionally extensive. Early poets like Hesiod and Alcman tried to show an order in the genealogy of deities. They also criticized many absurd myths and tried to interpret them in a rational manner. Lovers of political freedom and free thinking, many Hellenic philosophers, left their homeland and went into exile to retain the integrity of their thought. The geopolitical upheavals due to the Persian wars and subsequent Athenian imperialism sent many thinkers of the time to places outside the centres of partisan politics. The naturalistic cosmologists, the atomists and the Pythagoreans (who developed the theory that numbers are at the base of all that is real) imparted a clearly rational essence to Hellenic thought.

The views attributed to Socrates in the different Dialogues of Plato are in effect a reorganization and reinterpretation of the pre-Socratic philosophical ideas in the light of the political state of affairs during Plato's own time at Athens. The death of Socrates is symbolic, both philosophically and politically. He preferred to die rather than to reconcile himself with the unethical political and juridical practices of his time. Plato's portrayal of Socrates should be understood as a defence of rationality, free thinking and morality.

In order to objectively understand the origin and development of Islamic thought in Arabia and the adjoining countries within a relatively short span of time, we will be well advised to remember one particular characteristic of the cultural history of Arabia. Both in India and China, when foreign ideas were imported/imposed, the local traditional base retained its own voice in defining the manner and extent of acceptance and assimilation of the non-indigenous religious and philosophical ideas. This may be illustrated by referring to the ways of interpreting and accepting Christian views in the Jewish and other non-Christian areas. Somewhat similarly, in Islam, the generations after the death of Muhammad interpreted prudentially and realistically the revelations he communicated (recorded in the Quran) and his own statements (in the form of *hadith* compiled by Muhammad's companions), keeping in view their own time and place. The extent to which, in the different religions, the later interpretations followed the original scriptural text or departed from it, depended on the way the original 'scriptures' survived. While the Buddha's views, though not allowed to be written down during his lifetime, commanded their authority continuously for a pretty long time before different schools like the Theravada and the Mahayana schools of interpretations started appearing on the scene, the Vedic world-view, on the other hand, was relatively decentralized right from the beginning and easily lent itself to diverse interpretations. In the case of Christianity and Islam the attendant organizational conditions were relatively well-defined, ensuring the continuity of the original holy canons. In this context, the question of the relation of the so-called reason and the so-called faith turned out to be very important. Both in the Sanskrit-based and the Latin-based languages the meaning of 'faith' is close to credibility and reverence, and the sense of blindness, ordinarily attached to the word, is not present. From 'reason' it differs only in the degree of directness or remoteness from the original and supposedly self-certified truths.

When religion is backed by coercive political power the range of permissible interpretation turns out to be rather limited. In self-protection the prudent thinker is obliged to state that the results of reasoning and those of faith are, at heart, harmonious. If the proclaimed harmony could not be persuasively established, faith was accorded superiority. Unless courageous thinkers are provided with dependable institutional protection, their interpretation of canons or scriptures, understandably, is likely to be defensive. A long line of metaphysical constructions in defence of scriptural legacy may be easily interpreted differently in terms of alternative logico–epistemological terms. In such cases, even those who, left to themselves, are conservative and dogmatic can present their case with philosophical sophistication, making it acceptable to the lay people in general and the believers in particular. One finds this sort of situation in Islam with al-Ghazzali and Ibn Taymiyah, and in Christendom the conservative condemnations of radically new interpretations which gave rise to the sophisticated positions of Scotus and Ockham.

The devious path from doctrinal orthodoxy to argumentative epistemology tends to become inevitable mainly when religion is state-enforced. The task of philosophers within the folds of Christianity and Islam proved very difficult. When God is believed to be a person, possessing human attributes like knowledge, power, goodness and will and this belief is sanctioned by the state, the philosophical space left for the thinker to express views at variance with God's knowledge becomes limited. Besides God, Islam introduced other supernatural powers and persons, viz., the Prophet himself and various angels, pronouncing their aims and objectives in the world and for the human race. In the context of Christianity, the philosophical space left for the freethinker was even more limited. Besides the all-knowing and all-powerful God, Christ was declared to be both a human being and a son of God, but of a virgin mother, endowed with miraculous powers like surviving or coming back to life after crucifixion. The doctrines of human sin and redemption, the Day of Judgement and the resurrection of human body to eternal life in heaven or hell obviously compounded the difficulties of the philosophers' task to fulfil it in a coherent and credible manner.

Unlike the eastern religions, their western counterparts took immense pains to prove the existence of God. The ostensible justification for it was to convince the 'unbelievers' and convert them to 'true beliefs'. The question of converting 'others' by *proving* God's existence did not hold good only when the targeted convert was a Jew, Christian, or Muslim, because they were all believers in God's existence and did not need anyone else to provide proof for it.

Islam began as a theocracy and after the swift Arabian military conquest of the Middle East, including Syria, Egypt, Iraq and Persia which were annexed between 634 to 654, Islamic fighters got divided over the lines of charismatic succession to the rulership. The Sunnites broadly accepted political status quo and followed the victorious lineage, and the Shi'ites remained loyal to the line of the Prophet's descendants. In spite of the initial wave of conquest, bringing the Arab tribes together, an uneasy stalemate was soon created. After the three civil wars, the Abbasid Caliphate, which assumed a centralized power, started losing it after 830. The de facto political powers went to the regional administrators and the de facto religious authority was assumed by the ulama or religious scholars. Their authority remained anchored to daily rituals, holy texts and practical laws. In the course of time, there emerged four factions, viz., (a) the practitioners of rational theology; *Kalam* (Mu'tazilites), (b) scriptural literalists, (c) Sufi mystics, and (d) the secular translators and practitioners of Hellenistic science and philosophy, the *falsafa.* All of them, except the rational theologists, came to occupy a semi-recognized position within the world of Islam.

## IV
## Mythology and Sociology of Religions

Religion may be, and in fact, has been, studied from different points of view. The standpoints of mythology and sociology are intimately connected with religion, but not in a uniform way. The importance and reality of religion is recognized even by those thinkers who themselves are not religious in the received sense.

In every language we come across many religious terms and myths. To the ear of the ordinary English-speaking persons of the modern times the term 'mythology' is likely to sound pejorative. To many professional and hard-headed scientists, religion may seem to be an outdated institution. Strictly speaking, there is no view or institution which is not criticized at all. And the same term may be used in more than one sense.

Many of the social beliefs of the ancient and medieval past appear to be mythical to many of us. Before a particular myth, whether it is about religion or about an area of science itself, is assessed critically, we should try to situate it in its appropriate historical and social contexts. Many gods and goddesses, who appear to be mythical, may convey a credible sense once the social setting is gathered philologically or historically, preferably from different points of view. Many beliefs and practices of a society or a religion appear unintelligible and bizarre, if not irrational, to people professing another religion or belonging to another society. This can be viewed either as a matter of historical distance or of social unfamiliarity. Many discarded scientific hypotheses of the ancient, medieval, and, in some cases, of the recent past, are derisively referred to as absurd or mythical. But the authors of those hypotheses may yet be deeply respected and seriously discussed in the history of science, and viewed as the builders of the modern tradition of science. There is no absolute distinction between 'tradition' and 'modernity', or between 'mythology' and 'sociology', or between 'logic' and 'myth-logic'. If we always insist on telescoping our own views into the minds of the peoples of the vanished past, we would be guilty of being 'scientistic', and not being 'scientific'. A good scientist always recognizes a problem as a problem even if he cannot solve it. He keeps on trying to *understand* it, studying and tackling it.

A somewhat comparable attitude should be taken by a rational historian or social scientist or philosopher. Problems of *other* peoples of *other* times should, at least in principle, be recognized by us. That explains why a Christian, if he is truly objective and rationalist, can write a reliable history of Hinduism or Confucianism or Islam. One's religious identity need not be necessarily taken as one's essential character, completely influencing or colouring one's judgement. In the democratic world of mutually intelligible and fruitful communication, views and values of the other need to be duly and respectfully recognized. Unless this condition of mutual intelligibility is satisfied, the self cannot expect its own views and values to be recognized and respected by the others. Unless we accept this ground rule of theoretical enquiry, every kind of our practice – social, scientific and religious – is destined to be unnecessarily and fruitlessly polemical. Acceptance or rejection of views and values is not the most important condition for academic or even for any other practical discourse. What is most important for correctly understanding one's views or values are the arguments and facts adduced in support of the same.

In the nineteenth century, particularly from the 1840s, many European scholars started paying serious attention to religion from mythological, anthropological and linguistic standpoints. The great German philosopher, Immanuel Kant, a self-professed Newtonian and materialist in his early life, did not believe in the existence of God. Hegel, who was a Christian believer, wrote at length on religion, the history and philosophy of religion. It is clear that Hegel himself studied in detail the available literature on religions of India, China and West Asia. His reference to the forms of religion of the Asian countries was highly critical and expressive of what he described as changeless and 'substantive' phases of human thought. His attitude was highly coloured by his Eurocentricity and his own accepted form of Christianity. Interestingly enough, he himself wrote a monograph on the *Gita* expressing his appreciation of the poetic content of the work.

Some of Hegel's left-wing followers like Feuerbach and the Bruno brothers deeply influenced the ideas of Marx and Engels, and, through them, of Lenin. Hegel himself was an Absolutist. To him, somewhat like Shankara, and his Advaitin followers, God is not the highest reality. To them the Absolute (Brahman) is the highest reality. People who worship Nature as their God, said Hegel, can never be free. Only when they conceive God as Absolute Spirit, standing above Nature, can they become free. Both Kant and Hegel initially welcomed the French Revolution. But later on, partly due to the Prussian state's pressure and partly due to the Reign of Terror, their references to the Revolution became very cautious. For a long time Kant totally stopped expressing his views on the Revolution and on God. But both he and Hegel believed that religion should be understood as it is expressed, minimally speaking, in the sphere of legislation, earthly rule and secular life. These cues were taken up later by Feuerbach and Marx.

Another scientifically minded philosopher who studied religion seriously is Auguste Comte, who, in his *Positive Philosophy*, speaks of his law of the Three Stages. The Three Stages of the development are Religion, Philosophy and Science, in that order. The traditional forms of religion and metaphysical philosophy did not find favour with Comte and his followers. He speaks of a 'new religion' for the people of the scientific age. According to him, humanity itself is an object of reverence and worship. He thought that scientific development would one day displace the traditional forms of religion and the metaphysical types of philosophy. It is true that as a fallout of the Enlightenment in the eighteenth century and the French Encyclopedists' influence, religion as an institution had partially lost its age-old influence on most urban minds. But this neither means that all people turned out to be anti-religious nor that some highly gifted scientists have totally rejected the concept of religion.

Religion in its modern forms is more akin to morality and law, rather than to some supernatural or metaphysical beliefs. But this kind of generalization is not very enlightening. The varieties of religious forms and experience demand that these should be studied objectively and, if possible, respectfully. Therefore it is not surprising to find that many anthropologists, sociologists and others engaged in scholarly pursuits have been studying specific forms of religions both from a descriptive and axiological, i.e., ethical and normative, standpoints. Many famous scientists from Max Planck (1858–1947) and Albert Einstein (1879–1955), to A.S. Eddington (1882–1944), Max Born (1882–1970) and Erwin Schrödinger (1887–1961) have defended some forms of religion, cognitive or emotive.

While many atheistic and agnostic scholars stress the inevitable demise of religion, social scientists in this context introduce and interpret the modern process of secularization very cautiously. To them secularization does not imply the decline and fall of religion, but its new historical transformation. They point out that religion should not be identified with institutional structures. The primary function of religion is to bestow meaning and value upon human existence, both individual and social.

Max Mueller (1823–1900), the famous Indologist, who studied Vedic and several other Asian religions, highlights in his writings the significance of solar mythology among the so-called Aryans. He explains the birth of the god and of the related myths as a 'disease of language'. What had originally been only a name, *nomen*, became the divinity, *numen*, later on. His thesis proved influential and its variations are found in such writers as Wilhelm Mannhardt (1831–1880), E.B. Tylor (1832–1917) and Andrew Lang (1844–1912). Mannhardt, expounding Max Mueller's view of religion as naturalistic mythology, speaks of the 'lower mythology' still surviving in the beliefs and rituals of peasants and tribals. According to Tylor, the primitive man believes that everything is endowed with a soul. He has no doubt that animism is the first stage of religion. From animism, he maintains, evolves polytheism which, finally, through abstract thinking, gives way to monotheism. Andrew Lang rejects the views propounded by both Mueller and Tylor. He rejects the idea that religious myths are a 'disease of language'. He argues, admittedly on the basis of some reliable anthropological findings, that belief in 'high Gods' was present even among the very primitive peoples like New Zealand's Maoris and the Andamanese Jarwas.

Animism and shamanism are similar in several respects. The followers of these creeds find no dualism between naturalism and spiritualism. They believe that 'natural things' have in them 'spiritual beings' and vice versa. In this matter they differ from professional philosophers and scientists who are often very eloquent on a dualism between the two. The etymological root of 'shaman' is doubtful: it may be Ural–Altaic or Persian or Tibetan (*sraman*). But shaman, a priest, magician or medicine man, is credited with the power to control the spirits, communicate with them and cure the diseases caused by them. Shamanism, in some form or other, is found in different parts of the world, but its practice in north-east Asia seems to be the strongest.

There are thinkers who defend pro-animistic theories and maintain that the origin of religion is to be sought in the experience of awe and wonder aroused by the encounter with a personal power like God, or an impersonal power like *mana*, a Melanesian word. Another very influential pro-animistic writer was James George Frazer (1854–1941) who expounded his views in his famous book, *The Golden Bough* (12 volumes, 1890). According to Frazer, magic precedes religion. Frazer's anthropological work, though it became a classic, is basically indifferent to stratification or the importance of historical process.

Theories of religion may indeed be profitably studied, broadly speaking, under two heads – historical and anthropological. The debate between them assumed complexity when Darwinian evolutionism, displacing creationism, began to command recognition. While the historical approach was defended, though in different ways, by neo-Hegelians and, in particular, Marx, the anthropological approach found its ablest defenders in Tylor and Frazer. Another school, which made its existence felt in the field of religion, was the psychological school led by Freud. His book *Totem and Taboo* opened a new horizon in the study of religion.

Marx's views on religion deserve special mention for various reasons, both positive and negative. Marx, himself a philosopher and historian by training, understood, though critically, Hegel very well. Besides, he was an admirer of Darwin's evolutionism. Further, the strongest feature of his work was his ability to see religious beliefs in their socio-historical context. Admittedly, Marx took his cues from Feuerbach's criticism of Hegel in which Feuerbach reduced both theology and speculative philosophy to anthropology. The concept of 'false consciousness', underlying Hegel's 'speculative philosophy', deeply influenced Marx. But, whereas Feuerbach seeks the roots of religious ideas in the *individual* psyche, Marx seeks it in the socio-economic conditions distorting the *true* origin of *false* religious ideas. Unlike

Feuerbach, Marx insists on understanding man in his enworlded condition. To him, 'man is the world of man, the state and society'. It is this state and this society which produces religion. In his view, this religion is 'a reversed world-consciousness because they [the state and society] are a reversed world'. In this reversed world man feels inwardly alienated. Religion is certainly distressing but Marx affirms that religious distress is the expression of real distress and, at the same time, it is a protest against the latter. Religion is said to be 'the heart of a heartless world', the 'spirit of a spiritless situation'. Then follows the famous sentence, 'it is the opium of the people' which is often quoted out of context, giving a highly misleading impression. Certainly Marx is a critic of religion, but he does not fail to see it in the context of man's social situation. To him, religious happiness is to be likened to a sort of drug-induced peace. He wants to show that unless the real causes of human unhappiness and alienation are objectively and truly ascertained and confronted, man cannot be made really free and happy. One may or may not accept this view of Marx. I, for one, do not accept it, but I do appreciate the hidden element of truth within it. Marx's critique of religion must not be caricatured to suggest that Marx himself did not know what he was saying.

During the lifetime of Marx (1818–1883) and immediately after him, various anthropologists and sociologists produced serious studies of religion, including Lewis Henry Morgan (1818–1881), Edward Burnett Tylor (1832–1917), Lucien Levy-Bruhl (1857–1939), Emile Durkheim (1858–1917) and Marcel Mauss (1872–1950). Of all these scholars Morgan's findings and conclusions influenced Marx and Marxism most. Morgan had no left-wing philosophical and political commitments. His two main works, *Systems of Consanguinity and Affinity of the Human Family* (1871) and *Ancient Society* (1877) were based on his own ethnological studies of the American Indian tribes. His main findings may be grouped under four heads: (i) human growth through invention and discovery, (ii) growth related to the idea of governance, (iii) the importance of the family and its growth, and (iv) the growth of the idea of property. He discusses both the idealistic and the materialistic theories of evolution. Morgan emphasized the importance of ecology and, particularly, of technology, in shaping human growth or evolution. In fact, both Marx and Engels were deeply influenced by Morgan's thought. This is borne out by Engels's monograph, *The Origin of the Family, Private Property and the State* (1884), which appeared soon after Marx died. Marx himself had thought of writing a book taking a cue from Morgan. Morgan had met Darwin, Huxley, McLennan, Lubbock and Henry Maine. In his studies of the primitivity of the matriarchal form of society he established contact with some Indians through correspondence and enquired about the Nair society of Kerala. Apparently, he was not well aware of the matriarchy in north-east India and the polyandry of the Indo–Tibetan border areas in and around Himachal.

Tylor was also an evolutionary ethnologist. He was influenced by the writings of Charles Lyell, J.S. Mill, Darwin, Huxley and Tyndal. Tylor's *Primitive Culture* was a rationalistic attack on the stronghold of religious orthodoxy. He questioned the divine inspiration of religious beliefs. The influence of Quaker humanitarianism was a major force in his thought. His first major work, *Researches into the Early History of Mankind*, clearly shows the influence of historicism. However, his most scholarly work was devoted to the development of the idea of animism, i.e., the belief in spiritual beings. He influenced, through his writings, many distinguished anthropologists and sociologists like Andrew Lang, James Frazer, L.H. Morgan, Emile Durkheim and Franz Boas. He thought of developing a 'Science of Culture', but mainly, perhaps because of his intellectually restless nature, he could not develop a coherent, systematic theory of religion.

Lucien Lévy-Bruhl had a highly original mind. He interacted, often critically, with his French contemporaries like Durkheim and Mauss. His famous book, *Ethics and Moral Science* (1903), shows some influence of Comte on him. His main objective was to develop a comprehensive theory of the primitive mind. He did not share the pro-positivist rationalism of his many contemporaries. According to him, primitive minds, all over the world, think in some kind of mystical and intuitive, not logical, manner. His numerous books on the nature of the primitive mind, like *How Natives Think* (1910), *Primitive Mentality* (1922) and *Primitives and the Supernatural* (1931) argue that the primitives do not think in logical ways. Their cast of mind and ways of thinking are *pre-logical.* Notwithstanding his disavowal of it, the influence of positivism on his thought is unmistakable. It must be noted that he admitted that all primitive peoples do not think in the same mystical and pre-logical ways; and he recognized psychological pluralism in his anthropological writings. Marcel Mauss, Emile Durkheim and Evans-Pritchard criticized Lévy-Bruhl, highlighting particularly the point that his views objectively amount to the assertion that primitives cannot be logical, and that the distinction between the primitive and the modern is not a matter of degree but of kind. The serious implications of this criticism were not unintelligible to Lévy-Bruhl, and he slightly revised his position in his later works. Even if it is admitted that A.R. Radcliffe-Brown (1881–1955) and Bronislaw Malinowski (1884–1942) distorted and misrepresented Lévy-Bruhl's refined Durkheimianism, the point remains that Lévy-Bruhl's revised position retained all the basic elements of his earlier theoretical position. At the same time it must be added that most of the Euro–American anthropologists and sociologists had a broad pro-positivist orientation, given which, it was difficult for them to view 'modern logical man' and 'pre-logical primitive man' at par and as equally capable of thinking and acting similarly in all sphere of life – scientific, political or religious. Oversimplifying the position, from an Archimedean standpoint one can maintain that in the intellectual world, as in the socio-economic world, the East–West divide still lingers. Among the exceptions to this position one can name only a few like Lévi-Strauss (1908–fl.) and Jean-Paul Sartre (1905–80), as is evident from their works like Lévi-Strauss's *Structural Anthropology* (2 volumes) and *Savage Mind* and Sartre's *Critique of Dialectical Reason* (2 volumes).

Every generalization in any branch of science – social or natural or even mathematical – on close analysis, turns out to be untenable or, domain-relative, i.e., restrictive. Though we often speak and hear words like 'Euro-centric', 'Asia-centric', 'Africa-centric' or 'America-centric', these are only approximative adjectives. Their value is purely heuristic.

While it is ordinarily believed that historians are basically concerned with *particular* events, this particularity has no clear definition. Events are related to and coincide with other events. Metahistorians and philosophers of history speak of 'general patterns', 'existential trends', 'rhythms' or 'laws' of history. A somewhat similar claim is made by anthropologists, particularly those who do fieldwork. But theoreticians among the anthropologists themselves speak of some general or even universal stages in the history or evolution of religions. For example, they speak of 'pre-animism', 'animism', 'polytheism' and 'monotheism'. There are several other generalized taxonomies.

But interestingly enough, there are some theoretically disposed anthropologists who speak of general structures among *all* primitive societies. In this connection, the famous anthropologist whose name readily comes to mind is Lévi-Strauss. In his many works he claims that all primitive societies exhibit some striking structural similarities, especially binary characteristics. His area of field study was South America. Some other anthropologists, e.g., Mayberry Lewis, having done fieldwork in the same area have contested his conclusions.

The most extensive criticism, if not refutation, of Lévi-Strauss's views has come from his own colleague, Jean-Paul Sartre. Both Lévi-Strauss and Sartre were philosophers by training and Marxist in their ideological inclination. Sartre affirms the primacy of history in the field of the social sciences and criticized Straussian structuralism. In response Lévi-Strauss argues that his version of structuralism is not tainted by any universalism because he takes historical particularism or peculiarities very seriously. What is more, he thinks that his structuralism is *doubly* historical and that Sartrean history is *unilayered.* Anthropology may be described as 'silted' or 'layered or structured history', and that it recognizes the particularity of every culture. Needless to say, the method of dialectics, as understood by Sartre, is primarily historical. It is an endless process, but neither cyclical nor repetitive – a process of 'totalization, de-totalization, re-totalization'. It is a variation of the Hegelian–Marxian thesis of the tri-rhythms of 'thesis–antithesis–synthesis'. Both formulations of the tri-rhythmic historical are said to be creative. Another formulation of the view, described in terms of 'construction', 'deconstruction' and 'reconstruction', is basically differentiative, and not creative.

In the limited context of religion, the question which looms large in one's mind is: why does not religion, as a key cultural concept, have any *universally* acceptable connotation or set of connotations? Another intriguing question is: why does religion, as a widely acknowledged institution, not exhibit any universal, theoretical, practical and structural characteristics? Why is it that within religion, humans are endlessly segmented, rather than being united?

## V

## Religion or *Dharma* at Work as Unifying and/or Divisive Force

In the end I would like to raise some questions. Close and objective studies of the history of all religions, particularly of the major ones, exhibit some common characteristics.

First, true to the spirit of the root words like *dharma* and 'religion', viz., *dhr* and *relegere/relegare*, all religions in the different stages of their career, have worked alternatively both as a unifying force and as a divisive force. No religion could work indefinitely and exclusively either as (a) a unifying and binding force, or as (b) a divisive and disintegrative force. To what is this general characteristic due? It seems to me that there are elements of bipolarity – both individual and social – and an inherent dialectical tension in every religion.

Secondly, religion, for many people is partly but intensely a personal matter. It has been said that religion is what one does with one's solitude. At the same time, every individual, as a user of language and embedded in a network of interpersonal relations, is unfailingly social. Every society, necessarily situated in a territory and propelled by human power, is subject to some political authority, internal or external. Internality or externality, in most cases, is a matter of degree. One can be relatively free even within a prison. One may be condemned to be unfree in a mass society, even if that society, is not externally restricted or coerced by any other person or agency.

Thirdly, the individual/social bipolarity is dispositional. But the interactions between these two poles of human existence are dialectical. Every religion has its ethnic ancestry and a historically circumscribed situation. Even those religions which are not recognized as major do not suddenly become socially visible. It is interesting to note that practically every major religion – Hinduism, Buddhism, Confucianism, Christianity and Islam – has a traceable ancestry. For example, Christ himself by birth was a Jew and started his life within a Jewish community. Islam itself acknowledges a continuity with Judaism and Christianity. Both Buddhism and Jainism had their Vedic or post-Vedic ancestry. Vedic Hinduism had pre-Vedic, non-Vedic and even anti-Vedic elements in it. This shows the *purity* claim of a religion is unhistorical and, therefore, unfounded. 'Pure religion' like 'pure race' is a myth. It is invariably socio-historically embedded, and so, subject to change.

Fourthly, the exclusive and the resulting intolerant character of many religions, on analysis, is found to have no justification. For example, words like 'pagan', *mlechchha*, *barbar*, 'heathen' and *kafir*, though often used in a derogatory sense, are not to be taken literally. In many contexts, the words refer to an external faith or religion. In the past, many religious groups used to view the world of religion in a simplistic manner, either as 'A' or as 'not-A', 'A' standing for one's own religion or *self*, and 'not-A' for the *other*, i.e., all other religions. It was assumed that there was nothing in between, no social space for that which was neither 'A' nor 'not-A', a notion which is untenable, both historically and socially. This way of categorizing religions and religion-related phenomena is still in vogue among many religious groups. Obviously, this anthropological fact, historically attested, will not be liked by 'modern' people affiliated to the major religions. As I observed before, the distinction often drawn between 'traditional' and 'modern', or between 'logical' and 'pre-logical', is highly suspect. As we know, there are many logics – two-valued logic, three-valued logic and many-valued logic. It must be added here that the idea of alternative logics is not peculiar to our time. It was there in the past in many cultures. The simplistic classification of religions, either as *self*-centric or as *other*-centric, has almost always been taken in a pejorative and value-loaded, rather than descriptive, sense. The application of this type of reasoning to religious faith and practices is bound to encourage intolerance, if not hostility, towards *other* peoples professing different faiths.

Fifthly, animism, shamanism, polytheism and the various unidentified religious cults are generally berated by modern, rational or scientific-minded persons and communities. But if the principle of 'A' and 'not-A' type of classifications is deemed dubious, the defenders of the so-called berated religions can rightly criticize the widely accepted 'major religions'. If religion is primarily a matter of value, faith or reverence, then the question of number of followers is immaterial. We must be prepared to accept the democratic principle in studying religions and we must show a spirit of toleration and accommodation to others' views and values, including their religious beliefs. If we reject this principle, our own commitment to views and values and profession of our own religious faith would turn out to be self-defeating. If not out of the ethical nobility of our nature, then for the sake of strict logical reason and in the larger self-interest, we should learn to live with others who differ from us.

This attitude does not entail tolerating the intolerable. And yet, if we become narrower in our outlook and refuse to see the world beyond ourselves, then, many, otherwise tolerable, if not admirable, views and values will appear intolerable to us.

Sixthly, given the extreme views for and against religion, we may take one of the several attitudes towards the issue: (i) We may reject all religions and claim indifference to all types of known religions. (ii) We may turn agnostic. (iii) We may remain silent on the debate between the believers and non-believers. (iv) We may assume science to be religion. (v) We may accept an ideology as religion. It must be mentioned here that there are historical evidences of well-known thinkers presenting science as religion or describing ideology as religion. Here, one may recall Comte's 'scientific humanism' as a kind of religion, and Russel's reference to 'communism as religion'. It should be remembered here that in these cases, words like 'religion', 'science' and 'ideology' are used in highly uncommon senses.

Seventhly, there are many religions, like Buddhism and Jainism, which are purely ethical and are not based on this or that conception of God. There are many well-known forms of religions which are basically ethical and not religious in the received sense. But even in those cases, one may point out that an element of supernaturalism or self-transcendentalism has been tacitly recognized.

Eighthly, there is an idea of religion which is basically humanistic. I know the word 'humanism' has been used in very many ways. But there is one sense of humanism which is based on the developing or evolutionary potentiality of the human body, mind, and the body–mind-based capacities – cognitive, active and emotive. Even if the idea of a superman is discarded and taken to be utopian, it is difficult to deny the self-transcendentalism or open-endedness of the human nature. This belief in the boundless development of human nature gives us a sense of optimism and hope.

Ninthly, whether naturalism and humanism are compatible, mutually supportive or antagonistic cannot be decided in a blanket manner within the context of any particular religious or scientific tradition. Within every major religion and scientific tradition there are several different views on naturalism and humanism. In recent literature on the subject, broadly speaking, there are two predominant views. First, some people hold that the human mind is essentially consciousness, and its sociality and creativity are not subject to or determined by the laws of physical nature. This view has an old dualistic lineage both in the East and the West. The exponents of the second view think that in man nature attains self-reflectivity. Nature and nurture or culture, according to this view, are terms and stages in a continuum. Many defenders of the second view maintain that old metaphysicians and modern scientists find that both human biology and human psychology have in them an endless potential for self-transcendence. Man's knowledge of nature is not a mere power of exploiting it for production and consumption. It is a kind of power which promotes human capacity and creativity, which facilitate man's understanding of nature, of the past, as well as the future of mankind. Among the defenders of the second view there are some who offer a theory that within the nature of man there lies the promise of evolving a supernature, facilitating the creative emergence of the superman. This romantic and utopian view finds acceptance at times even among cautious scientists like Julian Huxley. They interpret it as the existence and operation of the endless potentiality of the development of the human mind. Whether the highly developed state of mind should be called 'supermind' or 'omega point' is a matter of terminology. But in the meaning of this term lies hidden the suggestion that at this 'super' level, which itself is seen to be a dynamic level, the distinction between direct or intuitive knowledge and indirect, testable, ratiocinative knowledge gets gradually blurred.

Finally, it is to be considered that in the received sense of religion, there is a distinct element of otherworldliness, or a recognition of supernaturalism. Religion may be with God or without God. The concept of God itself is not free from ambiguity. In many religions in place of God some other concepts or realities, endowed with extraordinary powers, have been postulated. For example, in Buddhism and Taoism there is no explicit concept of God, but they accommodate a supernatural reality like Tao itself, or the Buddha with a cosmic body (*Dharma Kaya*). All these references to supernatural entities are to be understood as something more than a mere yearning for self-transcendence. Often the will of man to be higher or more than what he is makes him spiritual.

Spiritualism is not necessarily other-worldly or antithetical to naturalism. It is not surprising that in many godless value-systems the word 'spiritual' figures prominently. It is a clear indication of that human will for self-transcendence, self-transformation and self-development by which the self can be intimately united with its so-called 'other'. Both self and its 'other' are endlessly transformable and enlargeable according to laws which cannot be derived from the known laws of physical nature. The ideal of universalism itself is rooted in earthly humanism, in its boundless inspiration and aspiration.

**A Select Bibliography**

Al-Ghazali, 1951, *The Faith and Practice of al-Ghazali*, translated by Montgomery Watt, London: W.M. Watt, Allen & Unwin.

Antilla, R., 1972, *An Introduction to Historical and Comparative Linguistics*, New York: Macmillan.

Barbour, I., 1990, *Origin of an Age of Science: The Gifford Lectures 1989–1991*, New York: Harper Collins.

Basham, A.L., 1980, *The Origins and the Development of Classical Hinduism*, New York: Oxford University Press.

Beekes, R.S.P., 1995, *Comparative Indo-European Linguistics*, Amsterdam and Philadelphia: John Benjamins.

Benveniste, E., 1973, *Indo-European Language and Society*, Florida: Coral Gables.

Bongard-Levin, G.M., 1980, *The Origin of Aryans*, Delhi: Arnold.

Buck, Carl Darling, 1988, *A Dictionary of Selected Synonyms in the Principal Indo-European Languages: A Contribution to the History of Ideas*, Chicago and London: University of Chicago Press.

Bukharin, Nikolai, [1925] 1969, *Historical Materialism: A System of Sociology*, Ann Arbor: University of Michigan Press.

Ch'en, Kenneth, 1964, *Buddhism in China*, Princeton: Princeton University Press.

Chadwick, Owen, 1960–70, *The Pelican History of the Church*, 6 vols, Harmondsworth: Penguin.

Chakravarti, Uma, 1987, *The Social Dimensions of Early Buddhism*, Delhi: Oxford University Press.

Chan, Wing-Tsit, 1963, *A Source Book in Chinese Philosophy*, Princeton: Princeton University Press.

Chattopadhyaya, D.P., [1976] 1988, *Karl Marx and Sri Aurobindo: Integral Sociology and Dialectical Sociology*, Delhi: Macmillan and Motilal Banarsidass.

———,1990, *Anthropology and Historiography of Science*, Athens: Ohio University Press.

———, 1996, *Interdisciplinary Studies in Science, Technology, Philosophy and Culture*, Project of History of Indian Science, Delhi: Munshiram Manoharlal.

———, 1997, *Sociology, Ideology and Utopia: Socio-Political Philosophy of East and West*, New York: Brill.

———, 2001, *Societies, Cultures and Ideologies: Analysis and Interpretation*, Bombay: Bhartiya Vidya Bhavan.

Davidson, Herbert H., 1987, *Proofs for Eternity, Creation and the Existence of God in Medieval Islamic and Jewish Philosophy*, New York: Oxford University Press.

Grant, Michael, 1985, *Atlas of Ancient History 1700 BC to AD 565*, New York: Dorset Press.

Hermann, A., 1966, A. *An Historical Atlas of China*, Chicago: Aldin.

Hodgson, Marshall G.S., 1974, *The Venture of Islam*, 3 vols, Chicago: University of Chicago Press.

Kalupahana, David J., 1992, *A History of Buddhist Philosophy*, Honolulu: University of Hawaii Press.

Kant, Immanuel, 1960, *Religion Within the Limits of Reason Alone*, New York: Harper & Row.

Kirk, G.S., J.E. Raven and M. Schofield, 1983, *The Pre-Socrates Philosophers*, Cambridge: Cambridge University Press.

Kolokowski, Leszek, 1978, *Main Currents in Marxism*, 3 vols, New York: Oxford University Press.

Kosambi, D.D., 1975, *An Introduction to the Study of Indian History*, Bombay: Popular Prakashan.

———, 1977, *The Culture and Civilization of Ancient India in Historical Outline*, New Delhi: Vikas Publishing House.

Levin, S., 1971, *The Indo-European and Semitic Languages*, Albany: State University of New York Press.

Lévi-Strauss, Claude, 1972, *The Savage Mind*, London: Weidenfield Nicolson.

Mallory, J.P., 1989, *In Search of the Indo-Europeans: Language, Archaeology and Myth*, London: Thames & Hudson.

Mallory, J.P. and D.Q. Adams, eds, 1997, *Encyclopedia of Indo-European Culture*, London and Chicago: Fitzroy Dearborn Publishers.

Marx, Karl, 1975, *Critique of Hegel's Philosophy of Right*, in *Collected Works of Marx and Engels*, Vol. 3, London: Lawrence & Wishart.

Morrison, Karl F., 1969, *Tradition and Authority & the Western Church, AD 330–1140*, Princeton: Princeton University Press.

Murty, K. Satchidananda, 2002, *Life, Thought and Culture in India (From* c. *AD 300 To* c. *AD 1000)*, New Delhi: Centre for Studies in Civilizations and Munshiram Manoharlal Publishers.

Nakamura, Hajime, 1964, *Ways of Thinking of Eastern Peoples: India, China, Tibet, Japan*, Delhi: Motilal Banarsidass.

Palmer, I.R., 1980, *The Greek Language*, London: Duckworth.

Pande, G.C., ed., 2001, *Life, Thought and Culture in India (From* c. *BC 600 To* c. *AD 300)*, New Delhi: Centre for Studies in Civilizations and Munshiram Manoharlal Publishers.

———, 1999, *The Dawn of Indian Civilization (upto* c. *600 BC)*, New Delhi: Centre for Studies in Civilizations and Munshiram Manoharlal Publishers.

Renfrew, C., 1987, *Archaeology and Language: The Puzzle of Indo-European Origins*, London: Jonathan Cape.

Sartre, Jean-Paul, *Critique of Dialectical Reason*, 2 vols, London: Verso.

Sharma, Ram Sharan, 1991, *Aspects of Political Ideas and Institutions in Ancient India*, Delhi: Motilal Banarsidass.

Walter, Burkert, *Greek Religion*, Oxford: Oxford University Press.

Weber, Max, 1951, *The Religion of China*, Glencoe: The Free Press.

———, 1952, *Ancient Judaism*, Glencoe: The Free Press.

———, 1958, *The Religion of India*, Glencoe: The Free Press.

Yu-lan, Fung, 1952–53, *A History of Chinese Philosophy*, 2 vols, Princeton: Princeton University Press.

Zaehner, R.E., 1960, *Hindu and Muslim Mysticism*, New York: Schocken Books.

# 2 Religions in Complex Societies

## The Myth of the 'Dark Age'

*K.M. Shrimali*

In the first quarter of the twentieth century, when Indian nationalism was entering a new phase with the arrival of Mahatma Gandhi, a few historians sought to reinforce faith in the British imperial order by propounding the principle of a specific type of universal sovereignty. Vincent A. Smith is the characteristic administrator–historian of these decades. One of his works, viz., *Early History of India* was first published at the beginning of the century and continued to exercise quite a dominating influence for many decades. The following observations in the 1924 edition of this work deserve special attention:

> So much, however, is clear, that Vāsudeva was the last Kushān king who continued to hold extensive territories in India. After his death there is no indication of the existence of a paramount power in Northern India. . . . Probably numerous Rājas asserted their independence and formed a number of short-lived states . . . but historical material for the third century is so completely lacking that it is impossible to say what or how many those states were.
>
> . . .
>
> The period between the extinction of the Kushān and Andhra dynasties, about AD 220 or 230, and the rise of the imperial Gupta dynasty, nearly a century later, is one of the darkest in the whole range of Indian history.[1]

While, on the one hand, we are confronted with such a historical sense from Smith as reflected in the above paragraphs, on the other, we also get the manifestations of notions of history cherished by Kashi Prasad Jayaswal, who has the distinction of being characterized as a great 'nationalist' historian in Indian historiography. It is perhaps not a mere coincidence that the first edition (1924) of *Hindu Polity: A*

*Constitutional History of India in Hindu Times*, often considered Jayaswal's greatest work, was published in the same year when the edition of Vincent Smith's work that we have quoted was published. Yet another work of Jayaswal provides us with glimpses of extraordinary similarities between the historical sense of this 'nationalist' historian and that of Smith. In the 'Foreword' to his *History of India* (*AD 150–350*) dealing with the two early centuries of the Christian era and first published in 1933, Jayaswal wrote:

> The period 180 AD to 320 AD is called the DARK PERIOD. I undertake the work with the prayer: '*Lead me from darkness to light*'.

The notion of 'Dark Age' in the paradigm concerning the five post-Mauryan centuries (*c.* 200 BC to *c.* AD 300) available in such writings of the early twentieth century had the following two important components: (i) an absence of a universal, all-pervasive political authority or an extensive empire, disintegration of political forces, the rise of small and fragmented autonomous states, and India being reduced to a mere geographical expression; and (ii) distortion and disfiguring of Indian culture in general and its religions in particular by such 'foreign' disruptive forces as those of Yavanas, Shakas and Kushāṇas.

The context of such a portrayal of an important phase of Indian history was provided by the fact that in almost the same period (early twentieth century) the centuries of Gupta rule (*c.* AD 320–550) were being designated as a 'Golden Age'. Again, the so-called 'nationalist' historians were instrumental in creating such an image, which was sought to be located in and rationalized through concepts of political unification and the revival of an 'empire'. The Gupta kings, beginning with the first important king of the dynasty, i.e., Samudra Gupta, and coming down to the times of Kumāra Gupta I, are supposed to have created and nourished such a political authority. This period of the 'Golden Age' is also held to have facilitated the glorious 'Hindu Renaissance'. In order to underline the 'foreign' character of the Yavana, Shaka and Kushāṇa rulers of the pre-Gupta centuries, one such 'nationalist' historian has gone to the extent of characterizing the Gupta coinage as not only 'the earliest indigenous coinage of India', but also as 'thoroughly national in their art, motif and execution'.[2] It is true that historians of many other countries of the world have also invoked the concepts of 'Golden Age' and 'Dark Age' in writing their histories, and such notions have also been reviewed periodically. In the context of the writing of early Indian history, too, the historical rationality of the nomenclature of the 'Golden Age' for the Gupta period has been widely discussed and its myth exposed. D.D. Kosambi has even gone to the extent of saying: 'The golden age, if any, lies in the future, not in the past.'[3]

Comparatively speaking, unlike the discussion of a 'Golden Age', any comprehensive analysis of the historical rationale and relevance of the concept of 'Dark Age' for the post-Mauryan centuries has not yet been attempted. Partially though, our knowledge about the social and economic developments of these centuries has certainly increased considerably in the last few decades.[4] In the present context, the following questions may be considered:

(i) Should the political developments be treated as the sole axis for interpreting and reconstructing historical processes?

(ii) Should the Indian cultural heritage be compartmentalized and put in straightjacketed caskets such as 'indigenous' and 'foreign'? Could such compartmentalization form the basis for characterizing any period of Indian history in a specific garb?

(iii) What is more important for understanding historical processes: to establish points of disjuncture and crises or to identify elements of continuity and change?

Within the parameters of the objectives of Vincent A. Smith's notions of history, the rationale of accepting political developments as the sole axis could perhaps be his concern for establishing the validity of absolute British sovereignty in India and his keenness to defend his negative orientation towards the so-called disruptive forces. But what could be the compulsions of Kashi Prasad Jayaswal in reiterating Smithian notions of history? For a proper and scientific understanding of historical processes, the knowledge of the elements of fragmentation and/or agents of disruption is not particularly important. Even during the so-called political fragmentation, people's lives keep changing in positive terms. In this context, it needs to be underlined that instead of labelling the new political forces represented by the Yavanas, Shakas and Ku<u>sh</u>āṇas as 'foreigners' and rejecting them *en masse*, these forces should be seen as effective agents of significant socio-economic and cultural transformations and exchanges. It is possible that points of disjuncture may become useful reference points in certain contexts, but, relatively speaking, it is hard to accept them as major determinants in comprehending historical processes. If we try to identify elements of continuity and change in cultural processes in any given period of history, our potentialities to highlight multifaceted patterns within the concerned historical period are likely to increase considerably. Such an understanding of history would be more appropriate and judicious. That would also enable us to demystify and de-mythify such characterizations as the 'Golden Age' and the 'Dark Age', and the need for undertaking such an exercise is indeed paramount. Our objective in this essay is to reflect on the rationale and relevance of characterizing the post-Mauryan centuries as a 'Dark Age', which forms the cornerstone of reconstruction of these centuries by Vincent A. Smith and Kashi Prasad Jayaswal. The focus here would be on the constantly changing forms of Indian religions during these centuries.

In the present context, it would be appropriate to begin our proposed analysis by recalling Jayaswal's paradigm. The period of the Gupta rule was characterized as 'Golden Age' in the writings of some contemporaries of Jayaswal. However, Jayaswal's own remarks on Samudra Gupta, the first important king of that dynasty, reads as follows:

> Samudra Gupta, like Alexander, killed the free spirit of his country. He destroyed the Mālavas and the Yaudheyas, who were the nursery of freedom; and many of their class. Once those free communities were wiped out, the recruiting ground for future heroes and patriots and statesmen disappeared. . . . The social system of the republican communities was based on equality. They knew no caste. They consisted of one caste only. The orthodox system, on the other hand, was based on inequality and caste where mass patriotism could not be mobilized as it could easily be done amongst the Mālavas, the Yaudheyas, the Mādrakas, the Pushyamitras, the Ābhīras and the Lichchhavis. They were the exercise-ground for state-making, for patriotism, for individual ambitions, capabilities and leadership. But under Samudra Gupta and his descendants they all merged into an organized, officialised, orthodox caste system and an orthodox political system which recognized and fostered monarchy and imperialism. The seed-pod for the rise of a Krishṇa, the prophet of rightful war and the prophet of the cult of duty, the seed-pod to produce a Buddha,

the prophet of a universal religion and universal equality, was consumed for ever. . . . And the Hindu sank. . . . The Hindus did not remember the name of Samudra Gupta with any gratitude, and when Alberūnī came to India he was told that the Guptas were a wicked people. . . . They were tyrants to Hindu constitutional freedom. . . .

In yet another context, Jayaswal's sentiments about the Gupta dynasty are thus expressed:

> The history of the Imperial Hindu revival is not to be dated in the fourth century with Samudra Gupta, not even with the Vākāṭakas nearly a century earlier, but with the Bhāraśivas[5] half a century earlier still. . . . The rājavaṁśa (dynasty) of the Bhāra Śivas had performed Ten Horse-sacrifices on the Ganges which they had acquired by valour. . . . The Bhāra Śivas adopted Śiva as the presiding deity of the empire.

Invoking the evidence of the *Matsya Purāṇa* (257.13–14), Jayaswal draws our attention to descriptions of Apsarases, Gaja-Lakshmī and *Garuḍa-dhvaja-vāhinī* Vaishṇavī (Vaishṇavī carrying the banner with the *garuḍa* emblem). He also focuses on such monumental remains of the Buddhists and the Jainas as are found at Mathura, Nagarjunakonda, and Bodh Gaya. Further, arguing that the Kushāṇa emperors wilfully destroyed architectural remains of 'orthodox Hindu buildings' on a massive scale, Jayaswal almost caricatures these emperors as villains. In contrast, one century of Bhārashiva rule was a period of the germination of 'Hindu imperialism', of the foundation of a 'new tradition – the tradition of Hindu freedom and sovereignty', and the period which took the Āryāvarta and India out of the 'Dark Age' and enlightened them.[6]

Taking recourse to prognostication and a few verses of the Vanaparva of the *Mahābhārata* (chapters 188 and 190), Jayaswal designates the period of the Kushāṇas as 'Buddhist India' and draws inferences about the terrible state of the 'Hindu nation'. The *Mahābhārata* verses read as follows:

> The whole world will be Mlechchhanized; all rites and sacrifices will cease. The Brāhmaṇas, Kshatriyas, and Vaiśyas will disappear; at this time all men will become one caste . . . men will no

more gratify the Celestials with *śrāddha* or manes with libations. Prohibiting the worship of the Celestials, they will worship bones. In the settlement of the Brāhmaṇas, in the Āśramas of the Great Ṛishis, in places sacred to gods, in sacred spots and in temples which had been dedicated to the Nāgas – the land will be marked with tombs (*Eḍūkas* = Buddhist stūpas) containing bones. They will have no temples dedicated to the Celestials.

*Eḍūkān pūjayishyanti, varjayishyanti devatāḥ* ।
*Shūdrāḥ paricharishyanti [prabhavishyanti] na dvijānyugasaṃkshaye* ॥
*Āshrameshu maharshīṇāṃ brāhmaṇāvasatheshu cha* ।
*devasthāneshu chaityeshu Nāgānāṁālayeshu cha* ॥
*eḍūka-chihnā prithivī na devagriha-bhūshitāḥ* ।
*bhavishyanti yuge kshīṇe tadyugāntasya lakshaṇaṃ* ॥

Jayaswal comments, 'The description seems to be a description by an eye-witness.'[7] With such an assumption and ascribing these descriptions of the *Mahābhārata's* Vanaparva to *c.* AD 150–200, Jayaswal compares them with the descriptions of the Shaka rule in the *Garga Saṃhitā* and several Purāṇas. His own assessment of the Shaka rule is:

> The Śakan rule aimed at denationalizing the Hindus and at the basic destruction of their national system. The social revolution which the Śakas strove for with a calculated policy, was a scheme to depress the high and the aristocrat, the custodians of national culture and the trustee of national liberty – the Brahmin and the Kshatriya. . . . They (the Śakas) aimed at sapping character from the common people by systematic terrorization and proselytisation. . . . They must have carried away as well great wealth from the country to Bactria. Their infamous greed was notorious. . . . Hindu life, in short, was suspended. . . . It became, therefore, imperatively necessary for the Hindus to undertake to deliver their country from such a political and social scourge.[8]

The Bhārashivas are supposed to have taken upon themselves the responsibility of freeing the nation from this national calamity, and they also raised the yogic/ascetic and destructive Tāṇḍava form of Mahādeva Shiva as the symbol of 'National Cult and Faith'. Jayaswal emphatically writes:

The presiding God to whom political service was this time dedicated, was the God of Destruction. . . . The air is surcharged with the belief that the Destroyer Himself has founded the Bhāraśiva state, that He is the guarantor of the king and people of the Bhāraśiva kingdom. . . . Like Śiva's domestic polity, they [the Bhāraśivas] have a *gaṇa* of Hindu states around them. They are the true Śiva-made Nandi, the lord of the *Gaṇas.*

Since the Kus̲h̲āṇa emperors were killers of cows and bulls,[9] the Bhārashivas decided to make the Bull their sacred symbol, depicting it on their coins, and it was only thereafter that the sacredness of the Bull came to be recognized universally throughout the length and breadth of their empire, 'punctuating the difference of their age from the last political period when the bull was freely slaughtered for the kitchen of the Kushans. . . .' In total contrast to the rule of the Guptas, that of the Bhārashiva kings of the Nāga dynasty was responsible for raising a confederacy of states where considerable freedom and autonomy was reposed in the confederating units. The Bhārashivas were truly political Shaivas. Jayaswal concludes, 'The foundations of modern Hinduism were laid by the Nāga Emperors and that edifice was reared by the Vākāṭakas and elaborated by the Guptas.'[10]

Dharmanand Kosambi (father of the renowned historian D.D. Kosambi), who was a great scholar of Pali, Sanskrit and many other languages, has given us an alternative paradigm. Significantly, he has invoked the same sources, which have formed the bases of Jayaswal's exposition of 'Dark Age'. In 1948, Kosambi came out with his *Bhāratīya Sanskriti aur Ahiṃsā*, which is a Hindi translation of his Marathi work, *Hindū Sanskriti Āṇi Ahiṃsā*. Like Jayaswal, he also extensively discussed the verses of the Vanaparva of the *Mahābhārata*. Kosambi is of the view that the relevant 190th chapter (in effect, merely a repetition of chapter 188) was written *after* the arrival of the Muslims in India. European (especially British) historians, invariably interpreted the reference to *eḍūka-chihnāḥ* in the relevant verses of this chapter as Buddhist *stūpas* and *chaityas*, and Jayaswal, too, relied upon this reconstruction. In refutation of this, Kosambi has drawn our attention to a description *bhittiḥ strīkuḍyameḍūkaṁ yadantarnyastakīkasaṃ* occurring in the *Amarakos̲h̲a*. For him, the central argument rests on the word *bhitti (bhīta)*, i.e., a wall, and one cannot comprehend the real meaning of *eḍūka* by divesting it of this element. Western scholars, argues Kosambi, accepted the ordinary meaning of the word *kīkasa*, viz., bone, and, therefore, described *eḍūka* as a Buddhist *stūpa*. In contrast, Kosambi himself recalls Maheshvarabhaṭṭa's commentary on *Amarakoṣha* for expounding *kīkasa: Kīkasaṃ kaṭhinadravyasyopalakṣhaṇaṃ*, the commentator remarks. Kosambi understood this as *'yahān ukta shabda upalakṣhaṇa se kaṭhina dravyavāchaka hai'*, which in simple terms means the *bhīta* (wall) in which are inserted wood or bamboo or stone pillars at some intervals in order to strengthen it; and such a wall should be called an *eḍūka*. In other words, an *eḍūka* for Kosambi was either an *īdgāh* or a wall of a *masjid* (mosque).[11]

The post-Ashokan religious scenario also received Dharmanand Kosambi's attention. References to the Shakas, Kuṣhāṇas, and the Yavanas are quite frequent in this context. In the same context, there has been an extensive discussion on the process of the transformation of a violent Mahādeva into a non-violent Maheshvara. The Grihyasūtras, especially the *Āshvalāyana Grihyasūtra*, give an elaborate description of the Shūlagava sacrifice, which was marked by the offering and thereafter the killing of a high-shouldered bull to placate Mahādeva. The shift from such association with bull-killing to non-violence added to the god's popularity. Kosambi simultaneously underlines that Mahādeva's popularity kept on increasing along with the growth of the Shaka empire. The Shaka kṣhatrapas considered Him as the creator of the world. The southern contemporaries of the Shakas, viz., the Shālivāhana (Sātavahana) kings, too, accepted Maheshvara's grace, who was relatively a non-violent deity. Probably under the influence of Buddhism, the violent Mahādeva was transformed in this fashion. Commenting on this transformation, Kosambi says:

> The great pashupati Mahādeva, who needed to be placated with a sacrifice of a big bull, later became a protector of cows and bulls – bull became his mount and Nandi, the great Bull, was being installed in front of temples dedicated to Him. The coins of Vima Kadphises have depictions of Maheshvara in an anthropomorphic form along with the Nandi. The chronology of the reign of Vima has not yet been settled, nonetheless there is no harm in accepting his period as falling in the first century AD. The transformation of Mahādeva into *gorakshaka* (protector of the bovine) Maheshvara probably took place at least two or three centuries before that.[12]

Since the influence of Buddhism on the populace was considerable, the brāhmaṇas aspiring to receive royal patronage, had no alternative but to become priests of Maheshvara.[13] This provokes Kosambi to suggest that the *Shvetāshvatara Upanishad*, which is marked by characteristic Shaiva theism, was probably composed by a *pandit* named Shvetāshvatara in order to placate some Shaka king, just as some brāhmaṇas wanted to placate emperor Akbar through the *Allopanishad*. The *Mahābhārata* has a narrative of a sacrifice performed by Daksha, during which he insulted Maheshvara, who, in turn, finally destroyed that sacrifice. Its rationale may be seen in references to those anti-sacrifice forces and their nourishers, who are mentioned in texts of the post-150 BC, i.e., from the Shuṅga period onwards.

While, on the one hand, the senior Kosambi provided us a unique insight into the religious developments of the concerned centuries without invoking the notion of a 'Dark Age', his son (Damodar Dharmanand Kosambi) does characterize the socio-religious scenario of the post-Shuṅga period in terms of a 'Dark Age'. However, his exposition and rationale thereof are qualitatively different from those of Jayaswal.[14] Assuming that 'the revolution, inevitably in primitive times, had to take on a religious aspect', D.D. Kosambi opines that notwithstanding the brāhmaṇa rulers of the Kāṇva dynasty (who were successors of the Shuṅgas), this period formed the 'dark ages of the Brāhmaṇas'. Though a few brāhmaṇas gained wealth as ministers, yet it was a 'disastrous period for most of them by reason of the decay of fire-sacrifices.'[15] The brāhmaṇas responded to this situation in two ways. First, as the main force of resistance to the invaders because they had private property, family and magical formulae to achieve success in wars – 'the commonest Sanskrit word for minister, *mantrin*, means the possessor of a magic formula, which implies a Brāhmaṇa.' Second, and this is perhaps more significant, 'the main Brahmanical readjustment was the doctrine of non-killing engrafted upon the older ritual.' This is probably a reiteration of the senior Kosambi's proposition concerning the transformation of Mahādeva into Maheshvara.

The exposition of D.D. Kosambi, however, also incorporates a new mode of production arising out of ecological changes. According to him, this new mode involved a transition from cow to water buffalo in the marshy lower Ganga basin:

The cow does not thrive in wet lands, though it could have done

> well enough in the Indus valley. The cow is not hardy enough to hold out against wild beasts in the forest. The swampy lower territory of the Gangetic basin could only have been opened out for a new type of agriculture, wet-rice cultivation, by a new animal, the less edible water buffalo.

Kosambi further argues that 'buffalo is not a Vedic animal at all, and must have been a terrifying beast in earlier times for Yama, the god of death, comes riding on it to claim the souls of human beings at their final moments.' However, by the time of Pāṇinī, *mahishmat*, i.e., 'rich in buffaloes' became a term of respect. By the opening centuries of the Christian Era, breeding of buffaloes became a profitable proposition, and if the *Pañchatantra* allusion (V.8) is taken note of, then it becomes clear that its ranking was certainly above the cow, but below that of the horse. Significantly, however, from the ritualistic point of view, the buffalo had still not acquired any distinctive place in the brahmanical world-view. A recent study of the Dharmasūtras of Āpastamba, Gautama, Baudhāyana and Vasishṭha puts the period of these texts between the fourth century BC and the first century AD,[16] which evidently coincides with our period of study. A comparative assessment of the allusions to cow and buffalo in these Dharmasūtras throws up the following picture.

| *Dharmasūtra* | *Number of allusions to the cow* | *Number of allusions to the buffalo* |
|---|---|---|
| Āpastamba | 51 | 1 |
| Gautama | 43 | 3 |
| Baudhāyana | 49 | 2 |
| Vasishṭha | 50 | 2 |
| *Total* | *203* | *8* |

An illuminating example and a vivid description of the dynamism, variety and richness of the religious scenario of the period under study is available in the Pali *Chūlaniddesa*. Generally, this text is placed between the third century BC and the first century AD.[17] In a rather long passage, it refers to five *shramaṇa* (non-brahmanical) groups, viz., the Ājīvikas, Nigaṇṭhas, Jaṭilas, Paribbājakas and the Avaruddhakas. Thereafter follows a long list of as many as 22 sects, which must have been active in the middle Ganga valley. Those who kept *vratas* for, or worshipped, the elephant were called the *hatthivatikas* and they may have given rise to the sect involving worship of Gaṇesha, the elephant-headed deity. Those who kept *vratas* for, or worshipped, the horse were designated *assavatikas.* In a similar way, we read about the *govatikas* (worshippers of the cow), *kukkuravatikas* (worshippers of dogs), *kākavatikas* (crow worshippers), *Vāsudevavatikas, Baladevavatikas, Puṇṇabhaddavatikas, Maṇibhaddavatikas, Aggivatikas* (fire worshippers), *Nāgavatikas, supaṇṇa (garuḍa)vatikas, yakkha (yaksha)vatikas, asuravatika, gandhabba (gandharva)vatikas, Mahārājabbavatikas* (worshippers of Mahārājas), *chandavatikas* (moon worshippers), *suriyavatikas* (sun worshippers), *Indavatikas* (worshippers of Indra), *Brahmavatikas* (worshippers of Brahmā), *devavatikas* and *disāvatikas* (worshippers of directions). Other allusions to these multifarious sects are found scattered not only in rich and varied literature, but their existence is also corroborated otherwise. To illustrate, a headless image of Maṇibhadra was found at Pawaya (ancient Padmavati) village near Gwalior (Madhya Pradesh). An inscription on its base clearly indicates that Maṇibhadra was also called Bhāgavat. It is generally understood that his worshippers were called Bhāgavatas. Similarly, epigraphic notices testify the presence of the worshippers of Vāsudeva, Baladeva (Saṃkarshaṇa), Nāgas, Pūrṇabhadra, Yakshas, Gandharvas, etc. We are also made familiar with the belief of the ordinary people that four Mahārājas resided in the four cardinal directions and several *yakshas* and *devagaṇas* came under them. The allusion to the Mahārājabbavatikas in the *Chūlaniddesa* ought to be understood as a reflection of such practices. It may not be out of place to recall that the *Āṭānāṭiya* and *Mahāsamaya suttas* of the Pali *Dīghanikāya*, which are considered to be important testimonies of varied belief systems of the populace, describe in detail the four Mahārājas. These are: Dhritarāshṭra, the guardian of the East and lord of the Gandharvas; Virupāksha, the guardian of the West and lord of the Nāgas; Kubera, the guardian of the North and lord of the Yakshas; and finally, Mahārāja Virūḍha (Vīrūḷhaka), the guardian of the South and the lord of the Kumbhaṇḍas. Under the influence of the Buddhists, gods and goddesses fond of violence either got transformed into non-violent divinities or became followers of the Buddha; but under no circumstance were they completely destroyed.

A different type of cultural explanation of 'Dark Age/Ages' can be seen in the writings of Julian Haynes Steward. His works have been the cornerstone of the neo-evolutionary school in American social anthropology and also provided impetus for development of the processual school of American archaeology, especially in the 1960s and the 1970s. Some leading Indian archaeologists, too, have followed him. Steward had, in his writings, expounded a challenging theory of cultural change. In the decade of the 1940s, when D.D. Kosambi in India had been advocating his famous 'Combined Methods in Indology', involving integration of archaeological evidence, anthropology, linguistics and other disciplines, Steward also laid out the contours of what he called a 'Trial Formulation of the Development of Early Civilization', which centred round the interrelationship of 'cultural causality and law'. This was certainly an epoch-making hypothesis in the western world and its basic premise was similar to the method of Kosambi. Outlining his 'Trial Formulation', Steward says:

> In the irrigation areas, environment, production and social patterns had similar functional and developmental relationships.[18] . . . The eras are not 'stages' which in a world evolutionary scheme would apply equally to desert, arctic, grassland, and woodland areas. In these other kinds of areas, the functional inter-relationship of subsistence patterns, population, settlements, social structure, cooperative work, warfare, and religion had distinctive forms and requires special formulations.

Keeping such a notion of history in view, Steward constructed an ordered series of economic stages which are meant to be linked to levels of socio-political developments. These stages, which have served as working models for archaeologists, are:

(i) Hunting and gathering
(ii) Incipient agriculture
(iii) Formative (peasant community to state)
(iv) Emergent regional polity
(v) Initial Empire
(vi) DARK AGES
(vii) Cyclical conquest
(viii) Iron Age

The above classification mixes technological and social features. Everything from the 'Formative' stage downwards can be characterized as progressive development of irrigated agriculture, the freeing of labour, and its reintegration into an expanding division of labour. Characteristically, *'crises', which are seen as synonyms of 'dark ages' in this formulation,* occur as a result of over-exploitation of the environment, overpopulation and subsequent economic collapse and political fragmentation. They appear to alternate with periods of expanding empire until the onset of the 'Iron Age', or rather the incorporation of iron technology into the basic process of production.[19]

In the last 35 years, there has been considerable discussion of the 'Kali Age Crisis' to explicate the nuances of historical reconstruction of the post-Mauryan centuries.[20] These discussions have often centred around such descriptions as are essentially found in the Epics and the Purāṇas. R.C. Hazra, the great savant of Puranic studies, has dated the *yugadharma* descriptions of the *Vāyu* and the *Brahmāṇḍa Purāṇas* to between AD 200 and 275, and similar descriptions in the *Vishṇu Purāṇa* have been located between AD 275 and 325.[21]

The 'Kali Age Crisis' has been seen as a serious social crisis, when the primary producers [vaishyas, shudras and *varṇasaṃkaras* (mixed castes)] had either stopped engaging themselves in the work of production, or the vaishya peasants as principal taxpayers refused to pay taxes. Brāhmaṇa–kshatriya *versus* vaishya conflicts, on the one hand, as well as conflicts between brāhmaṇas and shudras, on the other, had taken the form of social crises. In all fairness, it may be underlined that historians undertaking historical reconstruction on the basis of *yugadharma* descriptions have not invoked the notion of the 'Dark Age'. Nonetheless, we suggest that the formulation of 'Kali Age Crisis' may be substituted by 'Dynamics of the Kali Age'. This would be a more positive way of looking at processes of historical changes. We do not aim here to undertake any comprehensive discussion of internal and mutual relations of social classes. And yet, we think that the scenario of the social fabric of five centuries of the 'Dark Age' that supposedly engulfed post-Mauryan India was marked by tendencies of tolerance, assimilation and adjustments. These tendencies not only gave new directions to different societies and communities, but were also responsible for giving them new identities. In a way, these centuries were extremely creative and constructive, for, in course of time, these tendencies prevented Indian societies becoming stagnant.

Non-brahmanical thinkers and philosophers had already dented brahmanical social philosophy and establishment. For example, even without completely condemning the caste system, the Buddha had raised serious questions against its basic roots. Who is a brāhmaṇa?

The answer to this question is provided by the Buddha in the *Dhammapada*:

> *Yassa kāyena vāchāya manasā n'atthi dukkatam*
> *saṁvuttaṁ tīhi ṭhānehi tam ahaṁ brūmi brāhmaṇam*
> [Him I call a Brāhmin who does not hurt by body, speech, or mind, who is controlled in these three things.]
>
> *na jaṭāhi na gottena na jachchā hoti brāhmano*
> *yamhi sachchaṁ cha dhammo cha, so sukhi, so cha brāhmaṇo*
> [Not by matted hair, not by lineage, not by caste does one become a Brāhmin. He is a Brāhmin in whom there are truth and righteousness. He is blessed.]
>
> *na chāhaṁ brāhmaṇaṁ brūmi yonijam mattisambhavam*
> *bhovādi nāma so hoti, sa che hoti sakiṁchano*
> *akiṁchanam anādānam tam ahaṁ brūmi brahmaṇam*
> [I do not call him a Brāhmin because of his origin or of his mother. If he be with goods he is called *bhovadi*. Him I call a Brāhmin who is free from goods and free from attachment.][22]

One of the most conspicuous examples of the kind of social dynamics of the post-Mauryan centuries mentioned above is certainly the *Manusmriti*. Almost all historians consider it to be a text of that period, while some historians even accept it as a product of the ideology of the Ganga valley. Notwithstanding the fact that in the contemporary politics of India, the slogan of 'Manuvāda' seems to have become a compulsion for some political parties, the *Manusmriti* deserves to be taken as a mirror of the social dynamics of its times. In enumerating more than 60 *varṇasaṃkaras* (mixed castes), Manu has provided us a very useful framework of the dialectics of the rise and fall of castes taking place within overall social changes. On the other hand, some non-brahmanical works, too, present almost similar traits of social fabric. An important example of such texts would be the *Aṅgavijjā*, a Jaina work of the Kus̲h̲āṇa times, i.e., the first three centuries AD.[23] Despite being essentially a work of prognostication, the *Aṅgavijjā* is indeed a reflection of newer bases of social changes. It seems that the fourfold brahmanical social order had lost its *raison d'être.* Allusions to several combinations of dual *varṇas* are amazing. Some of these are: bambha–khatta, khatta–bambha, bambha–vessa, vessa–bambha, sudda–khatta, sudda–bambha, vessa–sudda, etc.[24] This is, by no means an exhaustive list of such dual *varṇas*. Explicit glimpses of the paradigm of the *utkarsha* (rise) and *apakarsha* (fall) of *jātis* (castes) as a result of sexual intercourse between women and men of higher/lower *varṇas* are to be seen in the *Aṅgavijjā*. On the one hand, this text provides us with a twofold social classification in the form of *ajja* (*ārya*) and *milakkhu*,[25] but, on the other hand, we also notice that the suddas are classified under *ajja*.

The descriptions of society in the *Aṅgavijjā* also indicate yet another developmental process. Social classes were sought to be identified not on the basis of birth, but on that of wealth and property. The twofold classification, in the form of *ajja* (free and propertied nobility) and *pessa* (*dāsas*, *bhritakas*, hired labourers who were bound by different types of servitude), typifies such identity formation. Yet another description of almost a similar type is concerned with *gotras*. Instead of identifying *gotras* with reference to eponymous *rishis*, allusions to *dijātigotta* (relating to the twice-born castes or only the brāhmaṇa caste) and the *gahapatikagotta* (concerning rich householders) tend to stress interrelationship between material power and wealth as sources of social empowerment. We also get to read at several places that people belonging to the lower *varṇas* started adopting professions and occupations that were supposedly meant for people of higher *varṇas*. Such indicators of social dynamics are specially noticeable in the Buddhist and Pali *Jātakas*. The *Dasha-brāhmaṇa Jātaka*, for example, refers to brāhmaṇas collecting taxes and working as hunters, traders, armed escorts, servants, wagon-drivers, and even as menials of kings. Similarly, the *Kusha Jātaka* is a narrative of a prince (kshatriya) working successively as a potter, basket maker, reed worker, garland maker and cook. On the whole, it appears that from the point of view of the social (including religious) scenario, the post-Mauryan centuries acted as if a stone had been thrown in a stagnant pool of water causing several ripples. Some of the credit for this must certainly be attributed to the 'foreign' rulers (Yavanas, Shakas, Kushāṇas, Parthians, etc.) as well. As evidence of the blurring of the dividing lines between the 'indigenous' and the 'foreign', one may invoke the epigraphic allusions to matrimonial relations between the Shakas and the so-called unique brāhmaṇas, viz., the Sātavāhanas. Samudra Gupta, the famous Gupta emperor immortalized in the panegyric inscribed on the Allahabad stone pillar inscription, adopted different types of policies vis-à-vis varied political forces of the day. With reference to the 'foreign' powers we read: '*daivaputra-s͟hāhi-s͟hāhānus͟hāhi-Shaka-Muruṇḍaiḥ . . . kanyopāyanadāna*', which has also been interpreted in terms of establishment of matrimonial relations with them.

Accepting that varied religions were inseparable constituents of society, the kind of the religious scenario of the post-Mauryan centuries that unfolds before us, compels us to reject the notion of the 'Dark Age' for those 500 years. The tendencies of tolerance, adaptability and assimilation mentioned above could be seen influencing all religions, both brahmanical and non-brahmanical. Jayaswal had, in his exposition of the 'Dark Age', accepted Mahādeva Shiva as the symbol of 'National Cult and Faith'. Though we do not accept such an interpretation, yet it would be difficult to deny that this 'Great God' underwent significant transformation during the centuries under discussion. One may even go a step further and ask – why only Shiva? The fact of the matter is that during these centuries of the 'Dark Age', there is hardly any religion or religious sect, which does not betray phenomenal traits of unique consciousness about its dynamism and changing character.

Not only historians of Indian religions, but of Indian art as well accept the fact that numerous popular sects/faiths and forms of worship were prevalent during the post-Mauryan centuries. These included several *yaks͟has* and *yaks͟hīs* that adorned Buddhist and Jaina *stūpas* and other monumental remains. Both anthropomorphic images of such popular gods and goddesses, as well as epigraphic allusions to them are available. The passage of the *Chūlaniddesa*/mentioning as many as 22 sects has already been referred to. While talking about *yaks͟has*, it is not possible to forget Kubera, the king of *yaks͟has (yaks͟harāja)*. He too underwent a major transformation during the first three centuries AD. Reflections on this transformation show that it was not only indicative of the dynamism of the religious situation, but was also instrumental in contributing significantly to the development of Kubera's iconography.

The divinity of Kubera was not conceived in the period of our study. There are plenty of references to him in pre-Mauryan texts. Often he is known through his ugly form – one-eyed, pot-bellied and deformed body *(ku-tanu)* which are his distinguishing physical traits. The mythological allusions portray him as the chief of evil beings who were supposed to live in the abode of shadow and darkness. Some mythological allusions even make him a thief. On the one hand, he was the god of wealth and prosperity, but on the other, his '*naravāhana*'[26] form is perhaps indicative of his fierce character. It is not improbable that Kubera's popularity amongst the people of lower social orders may have been the reason for most of the negative portrayals of this deity. Anyway, more significant is the fact that during the rule of the Kushāṇas (first three centuries AD)[27] Kubera was not only being accepted by the Buddhists, but was attaining growing acceptability amongst the class of traders. Very interesting changes in the iconography of Kubera took place along with this expanding social base of the *yaksharāja*. Mythological notices reveal that while Kubera–Vaishravaṇa was the king of the *yakshas*, the general of their army was Pāñchika. Mahāyāna Buddhism essentially rose and spread during the first three centuries AD. The followers of this sect preferred to style Kubera himself as Pāñchika and started worshipping him along with his wife Hārīti. A sculptural depiction of this new couple (Pāñchika–Hārīti) was discovered during the 1949–50 excavations at Kaushāmbi (near Allahabad). The sculpture was placed between 250 and 325 AD.[28] Numerous such delineations of Kubera–Pāñchika are known to us from Takal (near Peshawar) to Mathura, and these can be conveniently assigned to the first three centuries AD. Sometimes, the donors of such images have also been described as Scythian chiefs.[29] The Buddhists not only accepted Pāñchika, but also gave birth to Jambhāla, who was simply a counterpart of Kubera with almost similar iconographic features – special accent being placed on his pot-bellied character. In some sculptural depictions of Kubera in these centuries also portray him with a purse (of wealth) in one hand,[30] which could perhaps be seen as an indicator of his popularity amongst traders and merchants. Incidentally, it is fairly well understood that from the point of view of large-scale urbanization and intensive, as well as extensive, trading activities taking place all over the Indian subcontinent, the first three centuries AD were very significant. Amongst the features of the transformation of Kubera during this period one may emphasize his royalization as an important component. He was no longer riding upon men (*'naravāhana'*). Instead, we now see him seated on a throne with lions as its decorative elements. It is generally accepted that Ashvaghosha was a contemporary of Kanishka, the Kushāṇa emperor. Kubera has been called *rājarāja* in his *Buddhacharita*. B.N.S. Yadava has drawn our attention to a passage (III.53.11) from the *Vishṇudharmottara Purāṇa* (ascribed to the early medieval centuries):

the connotation of '*nara*' in '*naravāhana*' in the allusion in this text is '*rājya*', i.e.,'state'.[31] Thus, Kubera has been conceived as the presiding deity of the state.

It has been indisputably established that some very significant changes were taking place in the domain of land rights in precisely the same first three centuries AD.[32] The oldest inscriptions referring to land grants belong to these centuries. These records underlining radical changes in the norms of land ownership, land revenue and land administration are not only indispensable for any understanding of the accompanying economic developments, but are also of value for enabling us to comprehend changing dynamics of the religious scene as well. Hitherto the historians of religions of early India have often argued that the rise of theism within Vaishnavism and Shaivism was the result of challenges posed by the growing popularity of Mahāyāna Buddhism, where considerable emphasis was placed on the worship of the Bodhisattva, i.e., anthropomorphic form of the transcendent Buddha. For us, this argument is something like the proverbial choice between the precedence of chicken and the egg. It is almost impossible to decide as to which sect initiated a particular step as a response or in reaction to developments within another religious sect. We are willing to accept that the roots of theism can be located even in the pre-Mauryan centuries. However, it seems to us an undeniable fact that the kind of simultaneous presence of theism noticeable in numerous religious sects of the post-Mauryan centuries, is not only reflective of its horizontal spread, but is also a useful parameter for determining the development of its particular form in the period. The *raison d'être* of this characteristic theism perhaps lies in a twofold development. First, the developments related with the genesis of land rights mentioned above compelled religious sects and orders to realize that in conducting their daily activities, they could not be oblivious of shifts in the distribution of wealth and power within society. Incidentally, it can also be said that in due course these religious sects became agents of legitimizing such land system as became in time the basis of Indian feudalism. The second development influencing the rise of theism may be seen in the conscious policies adopted by the so-called foreign rulers, whereby they immersed themselves completely in the soil of India. It is not improbable that there may have been some political compulsions, too, in the adoption of such policies.

In taking stock of the first course of development, theological developments within Mahāyāna Buddhism may first be investigated. It needs to be recognized at the outset that during the first three centuries AD, it was essentially the Mahāyāna form of Buddhism that was taken to the vast geographical region stretching from Afghanistan (brought to wide notice by the recent destruction of the Bamiyan sculptures by the Taliban) to Xinjiang (western China). The carriers of this movement were the Buddhist monks and their followers, who apparently accompanied traders and merchants traversing the Great Silk Road. In this context, it is important to stress that from the point of view of theological changes, the emergence of the images of the Buddha in human form was obviously an outwardly visible trait. But this cannot be taken as its sole trait. The theologians of Mahāyāna developed concepts of the *dāna-mahimā* (glories of gift making), *bhūmi* (land) and *kshetra* (domain) in a very calculated and conscious manner. In contrast to the *arhat* of the Hīnayāna sect, whose sole objective was merely the *nibbāna* (salvation) of the self, the Bodhisattva of the Mahāyāna was an Avalokiteshvara, who worked for the happiness and salvation of the entire suffering humanity. The underlining assumption of the concept of the Bodhisattva is that He becomes the Buddha in a specific period and at a specific place. The theologians ascribed a regional base to that world and designated it as the '*Buddha kshetra*'.[33] In this march towards Buddhahood, the Bodhisattva had to pass through ten or twelve stages in order to reach the highest stage of *bodhi*. It is perhaps not mere coincidence that the Mahāyāna theologians called these various stages '*bhūmi*' and even composed a separate and a specialized text, viz., the *Dashabhūmikasutra*.[34] Yet another important facet of the doctrinal developments within Buddhist sects during the time of the Kushāṇas was the association of the common people with the Buddhist community. This resulted in the Buddhist *saṃgha* taking considerable interest in the daily activities of ordinary people. As a consequence, the necessity of a strong economic base became an imperative for the horizontal spread of the *saṃgha*. This was perhaps the reason for the Mahāyāna theologians incorporating the philosophy of *dāna-mahimā* within their formulations. The Theravāda, on the other hand, laid emphasis on *paññā (prajñā* or wisdom), *sīla* and *samādhi*, as against the Mahāyāna's primacy to *dāna* (charity). In the list of six *pāramitās* (stages of spiritual perfection), the Mahayanists gave the first place to *dāna*, which was followed by *sīla* (morality or virtue), *kshānti* (patience or tolerance), *vīrya* (vigour or energy), *dhyāna* (meditation) and *prajñā* (wisdom or understanding). In the vast corpus of the Avadāna literature produced by the Mahayanists, one gets to read numerous stories about *puṇya* (merit) accruing on account of gifts of even small things.[35]

The incorporation of *dāna-mahimā* is also noticeable in the material remains of the Jainas, Shaivas and the Vaishṇavas of the post-Mauryan times. The monumental remains, inscriptions and sculptures lying scattered almost all over the Indian subcontinent bear witness to ordinary people emerging as a conspicuous category of donors on a very large scale. For example, out of more than 600 donative inscriptions from Sanchi, only three refer to donors coming from royal families; monks and nuns account for as many as 200 donations; and the ordinary people outnumber all of them. Amongst 300 donors of the last category were *gahapatis, ghāriṇī* (housewife), *seṭṭhi, vāṇija, sotika* (weaver), *lekhaka, rājuka* (surveyor), *kamika (shilpi* or artisan), *vaḍhika* (mason), etc. The material remains from Mathura also tell the same story. The Jaina *āyāgapaṭas* from Mathura are remarkable for the preponderance, indeed almost a monopoly, of women patrons, which should be taken as a characteristic feature of the place and the period (mainly the early centuries AD). Significantly, a donor of a first century AD Jaina *āyāgapaṭas* was a *gaṇikā* (courtesan) named Loṇāshobhikā. The Nanaghat cave inscription of Nāgamnikā (Nāyanikā?) ascribed to the Sātavāhana times (first century BC) and recording several types of donations, begins with an invocation of Dhaṃma (Prajāpati), Īda (Indra), Saṃkaṃsana (Saṃkarshaṇa), Vāsudeva, Chanda, Sūrā (Sūrya), the four Lokapālas, Yama, Varūna, Kubera and Vāsavā.[36]

The conscious state policies of the 'foreign' rulers were identified as the second course of development influencing the rise of theism in the post-Mauryan centuries. According to Jayaswal's notion of history, during the 'Buddhist India' of the Kushāṇa times, the 'Hindu nation' had gone to ruin before the Bhārashivas laid foundations of the 'imperial Hindu revival'. After all, what did the Kushāṇas and other 'foreign' rulers do which inflamed the religious feelings of Kashi Prasad Jayaswal and other strong-headed 'nationalists' of his class? Was it their fault that more than one ruler of the Kushāṇa line had Vāsudeva as their first name? Was it also their fault that all Kushāṇa kings (right from Vima Kadhphises onwards) delineated gods and goddesses of different religious communities in their long series of gold and copper coins? Apart from the depictions of Greek and Iranian (Zoroastrian) deities, several divinities of varied religions of the Indian subcontinent, too, found distinctive places in this numismatic repertoire. Any statistical analysis would reveal that the depictions of the Buddha and his symbols were almost negligible, whereas varied forms of Shiva were clear favourites of the Kus͟hāṇa emperors. Nor were Laks͟hmī and 'Durgā' riding on a lion absent in these delineations.

In the long lines of Shaka kings, the western Ks͟hatrapas ruling over western India (largely Malwa and Gujarat) deserve a distinctive place in Indian history. Both the Vikrama and Shaka *samvats* (we have no definite information about the originators of either of these systems of reckoning) received the recognition of the state of independent India in 1947. About 30 chiefs of the western Ks͟hatrapa line ruled for nearly 400 years – very few dynasties in the long history of the Indian subcontinent could really be credited with such an achievement. Is it possible that any political power could have had an uninterrupted rule for such a long period through villainous acts of undermining and crushing the feelings and sentiments of a large section of the populace? A glance at the personal names of these chiefs can be very instructive – many of them called themselves by Sanskritized names, Rudradāman, Rudrasiṃha, Prithvīs͟heṇa, Yashodāman, Vijayasena, Rudrasena, Vishvasena, etc. The issue here is not the 'Indianization' of 'foreign' rulers. What, after all, formed the basis for declaring them as 'foreigners' in the first instance? Most of the aforesaid 30 Shaka chiefs were born on Indian soil. These Shaka chiefs were the first to issue silver coins *with dates* in India. Is it not ironic that the coinage of the Gupta kings, whose silver coins were simply imitations of the Shaka silver coinage, has not only been given the credit of issuing 'the earliest indigenous coinage of India', but their coins have also been called 'thoroughly national', whereas the pioneering Shaka chiefs have remained 'foreigners'?[37]

The historians of Indian architecture have always believed that the credit for initiating the practice of structural temples in India should go to the Gupta kings, and that the temple at Gop in Gujarat was the earliest temple of that period in that region. For the time being at least, we would not like to undertake any detailed discussion of the view of Ananda K. Coomaraswamy, the renowned art historian. As early as 1930, he had, with the help of plans and line drawings of archaeological remains and literary allusions, documented the existence of single- and multi-storeyed *Bodhigharas* (Buddhist shrines) in different parts of India between the second century BC and the third century AD (it is not a mere coincidence that this period exactly corresponds to the 'Dark Agė' under discussion). Extending this line of argument further, U.P. Shah has invoked some Jaina Āgama texts, such as the *Aupapātika Sutta* and *Rāyapaseṇiya Sutta*, and established the presence of *yakṣha-chaityas* and *yakṣhāyatanas*, i.e., structural temples for the worship of *yakṣhas*.[38] Further, revisiting the Gop temple in Kathiawad (Gujarat), its stylistic similarities with the architecture of Kashmir have also been established. It is well known that one of the most distinguishing features of the Gop temple is its *shikhara* (tower) decorated with *chaitya*-shaped windows. It is equally well known that it would be impossible to link the Guptas with Kashmir. Coomaraswamy, too, has refrained from calling it a Gupta structure and identified it as an 'early mediaeval' structure after assigning it to the sixth century.[39] It may also be added that useful light has been thrown on the period of the Gop temple by the excavations conducted at Devnimori (about 160 kilometres north-east of Ahmedabad) on the banks of the Meshvo river in the Sabarkantha district of north Gujarat (ancient Ānarta). During the excavations of the 1960s at this site, remains of an exquisite and rich *mahāstūpa* (surrounded by a number of votive *stūpas*) made of bricks and decorated with terracotta plaques, two brick-built *vihāras* and an apsidal temple were identified. A tower-like structure of the *mahāstūpa* has also been referred to in this context. This structure is indicated by two receding *meḍhīs* (86 and 70 feet square) followed by an *aṇḍa* – a circular structure with an approximately 54-feet diameter. Amongst numerous remains of Buddhistic affiliations was found a relic casket in the *mahāstūpa*. The casket bears an inscription bearing a date of 127 of the era of 'Kathika' rulers. On the basis of this inscription, the date of the structural remains at Devnimori has been put around AD 375.[40] R.N. Mehta, the excavator of Devnimori, had also conducted a special survey of the Gop temple. On the basis of the information received from him, U.P. Shah has opined that from the point of view of the evolution of the *shikhara*, it would be reasonable to accept that such a type had already been developed and popularized by the Kṣhatrapas and the Kuṣhāṇas in western and northern India. Shah further added, 'one may even consider the possibility of the Gop shrine belonging to the kṣhatrapa art traditions of the fourth century . . . [it] was renovated and/or enlarged at a later date.'[41]

In the context of the conscious policies of the 'foreign' rulers of the post-Mauryan times, the Indo–Greeks come readily to mind. The narrative of King Milinda (the Indo–Greek king Menander), the hero of the Buddhist text *Milindapañho*, converting to Buddhism has become too old to require any detailed discussion. Similarly, it was almost a century ago that scholars came to know about the *garuḍa* pillar inscription at Besnagar (ancient Vidisha, near Bhopal, Madhya Pradesh) proclaiming the adoption of Bhāgavatism by Heliodorus (roughly of the same time as Menander, i.e., second century BC), the devotee of Vāsudeva. As is well known, this inscription is an important landmark in the religious history of India. It would perhaps be more relevant to discuss relatively recent discoveries unearthed by a team of French archaeologists at Ai Khanoum in Afghanistan.

The Délégation Archaeologique Française en Afghanistan excavated the site of Ai Khanoum between 1965 and 1978. These diggings yielded the remains of a vast Graeco–Bactrian city. It was probably founded around 280 BC and after a busy and prosperous existence for about 150 years, it was finally destroyed by nomad invaders around 145 BC. The excavations have yielded over one thousand coins. Of these numerous numismatic treasures found at Ai Khanoum, six drachms of Agathocles (180–170 BC) found in a hoard excavated in 1970, are of considerable historical significance, especially from the standpoint of the history of Vaishnavism. Weighing between 2.328 and 3.305 grams, these show two male figures between two vertical lines of legend in two languages and two scripts. The figures – one on the obverse and the other on the reverse – are identical in posture and dress but distinctive enough because of the attributes that they carry in their hands. On the obverse, we get the name of Agathocles in the Greek script, whereas the reverse has the king's name in Brahmi script as *Agathuklayesa*. Some other coins of Agathocles also show the use of Kharoshṭhi script, which was quite common in north-west India, as is clear from its use in the Shahbazgarhi and Mansehra versions of the rock edicts of Ashoka.

The uniqueness of these six drachms of Agathocles lies in the fact that they are probably the earliest anthropomorphic representations of two popular deities of the Vaishnavite pantheon, viz., Vāsudeva Krishṇa and his elder brother Saṃkarshaṇa Balarāma. These identifications are possible because of the specific attributes of the two figures. The god on the obverse, who carries a miniature *hala* (plough) and a *musala* (pestle) in his left and right hands respectively, is Saṃkarshaṇa Balarāma. The god on the reverse holds a large six-spoked *chakra* (wheel/ discus), which is the most distinguishing attribute of Vāsudeva Krishṇa. The object in the right hand is perhaps a *shaṅkha* (conch), which, together with the *chakra*, normally characterize Vāsudeva Krishṇa/Vishṇu. Both deities are adorned with a loincloth and a shawl and are notable for their frontal position on a horizontal line with their legs slightly apart. On the left flank, a large scabbard sticks out at a slant, the shawl hides the hilt of the sword it contains. An umbrella (or a tufted helmet?) surmounts the head of both deities.[42] The warlike aspect given to the divine brothers by the crested helmet (?) and the scabbard is somewhat unusual and may have something to do with the long Greek influence in the region. But equally significantly, the dress and the standing posture of both figures remind us of the famous headless stone sculpture of the Kushāṇa emperor Kanishka found at Māt (near Mathura). The garment and the long pointed shoes in Agathocles' coins show similarities with the details given by Nearchus (*c.* 325 BC), Alexander's admiral. Describing similarly dressed Indians in the Punjab, he speaks of 'a linen *chiton* down to mid-calf, with a piece of cloth wrapped round their shoulders'. Nearchus was also struck by rich Indians' taste for fancy shoes. He tells us: 'they wear richly ornate white leather shoes, with soles dyed in different colours and thick so as to appear taller' (Arrian, *Indika*, XVI).

Agathocles was the first Indo–Greek king to have issued coins in two languages (Greek and Prakrit) as well as in two scripts. This was a bold decision on the emperor's part. Apparently, in doing so, he consciously decided not only to proclaim himself king to the people of the region in their own language and in the two dialects they used, but also found space on his coins for images of their gods (the choice of Vāsudeva Krishṇa and Balarāma was a manifestation of his sensitivity to local traditions) and did not hesitate to entrust the engraving of these issues to a local mint. Even if it is granted that political overtones may have prompted this resolve, the fact that Agathocles, the 'foreign' king, demonstrated publicly his personal predilection for Indian civilization in his royal function by introducing Indian deities into the official pantheon of the state is reflective of cultural transactions between people of the Oxus valley and those who lived east of the Indus.

Between 1975 and 1978, the Department of Ancient Indian History, Culture and Archaeology of the Sagar University conducted excavations at Malhar (in the Bilaspur district of the present state of Chhattisgarh) in the region of ancient Koshala. These diggings were undertaken under the direction of K.D. Bajpai. An inscribed four-armed stone sculpture of Vishṇu was found at the site and the excavators have dated the image to second century BC.[43] The four arms of the deity carry *shaṅkha* (conch), *chakra* (wheel/discus), *gadā* (mace) and *asi* (sword). The whole delineation of the image is rather interesting. The figure is standing erect with two legs outstretched, and with both hands almost folded and held very close to the chest. This Vishṇu image carries a huge sword – an idea of the size of the sword can be had from the fact that its hilt is not in the hands but put upside down, touching the level of the feet; and the sharp point of the sword reaches the level of almost the headgear. In other words, the sword is almost life-size. The shape of the cap as well as the entire delineation of the image reminds us of those Scythian (Shaka) soldiers, whose representations in reliefs and sculptures from north India are very common during the first three centuries AD. Notwithstanding the uncertainties of the date of this Vishṇu image from Malhar, the discovery of the image makes at least one point very clear – the alleged villainous character and iconoclastic zeal of the Shaka–Kushāṇas and the tears shed by Jayaswal on the alleged destruction of the 'Hindu' religion have neither any justification nor any rationale.

Jayaswal's paradigm has also been refuted by the excavations at the mound of Sonkh near Mathura conducted between 1966 and 1974 by Herbert Härtel. These excavations have been particularly revealing from the point of view of structural remains and antiquities of different religious persuasions that can be definitely ascribed to the Kushāṇa period. Of very great significance in this context has been the discovery of an apsidal temple designated No. 2 by the excavators and identified as the shrine of 'a personified Nāgarāja', and the entire complex treated as an important centre of Nāga cult.[44] The large beam in the characteristic Mathura red sandstone depicting the Nāgarāja and Nāginī amongst numerous attendants is an exquisite piece and a priceless find. These excavations also yielded two landmark bronze images. One of these has been identified as 'standing figure of Skanda'. Of the other one, described as a 'standing divine couple', it is stated: 'while the female can be made out as a cat-shaped Mother goddess, the male figure is, for want of specific attributes, difficult to identify. Nevertheless, his appearance by the side of an animal-headed Mother goddess in this relief connects him fairly convincingly with great probability with Skanda.'[45] From the 'Early Kshatrapa' to the 'Kushāṇa levels' at Sonkh, i.e., between levels 24 and 16, several terracotta plaques and stone sculptures depicting Durgā as Mahishāsuramardinī (killer of the buffalo–demon Mahisha) have been reported. Many of them are four- and six-armed and betray several unique iconographic features. These are amongst the 'earliest depictions of the goddess.'[46]

If we rely on the historical reconstructions of the post-Mauryan times by Kashi Prasad Jayaswal and historians of his persuasion, then we would get the impression that nothing beyond the Buddhistic world existed in the religious domain of those five centuries. The reality, however, is shown by our evidence to be qualitatively, as well as quantitatively, different. Recent studies on the development of Vaishnavism and Shaivism make it crystal clear that processes involved in the making of the pantheons centring around Shiva and Vishṇu had begun long before the emergence of the Puranic Vishṇu and Shiva in the Gupta and post-Gupta times. Further, such studies also reveal the creative and constructive contributions of the post-Mauryan and pre-Gupta centuries in these processes. Interaction amongst different streams represented by the followers of Nārāyaṇa, Saṃkarshaṇa-Balarāma, Vāsudeva Krishṇa, Gopāla-Krishṇa, Shrī-Lakshmī, etc. was a major factor responsible for transforming the almost negligible Vishṇu of the *Riksaṃhitā* into a great god. Similarly, the transformation of Mahādeva into Maheshvara, as sketched above, did not represent the climax of the growth of Shaivism. The Shaiva pantheon was created around the family of Shiva, comprising of Umā/Pārvatī as wife, sons such as Gaṇapati (Gaṇesha) and Kārttikeya, the Nāga goddess Manasā becoming Shiva's daughter, and Gaṇgā as Umā's sister.[47]

Looking at the state of the Jaina religion, it is more than obvious that the post-Mauryan centuries were a period of significant fruition for its followers and that the Kushāṇa period, in particular, had a major role to play in it. Jaina monuments, *stūpas, āyāgapaṭas,* colossal stone images of *Jinas* and *tīrthaṅkaras* with huge umbrellas, and ascribable to these centuries, have been found in different parts of India. Mathura, which was a major centre of Kushāṇa power and also renowned for its characteristic art style, was a citadel of the followers of the religion. Archaeological remains unearthed at Kankali Tila bear eloquent testimony to the Jaina presence.[48] Sixteen out of a total of eighteen bronze images found at Chausa (Buxar district, Bihar) are those of *tīrthaṅkaras.* Some of these images are ascribed to the Kuṣhāṇa period and some even to pre-Kuṣhāṇa centuries. Some of them have been identified as 'pre-Gupta' or creations of the 'Kuṣhāṇa–Gupta transition' period. It has also been argued that though these have been found at Chausa in Bihar, they may actually have been the products of Mathura sculptors. In sum, the Chausa hoard of bronzes is essentially of post-Mauryan origins, and if we exclude the bronzes found at different centres of the Harappan civilization, then perhaps, these, along with the two images from Sonkh mentioned above, would be the oldest Indian bronzes.[49]

Commenting on the Jaina art of the 'early phase' (second century BC to third century AD), Pratapaditya Pal has drawn our attention to a 50 cm mottled red sandstone image of 'Harinegameshin with Boys', presently in the Russek Collection (Maennedorf, Switzerland), with the following description:

> Except for the goat's head, the figure is essentially human. As is characteristic of both mortals and immortals in the Kushan art of Mathura, he wears a dhoti held around the waist with a sash. A shawl comes down the left arm and goes around the right leg, and he is adorned with a necklace and heavy bangles. The right hand exhibits the gesture of reassurance and the left clutches the hand of a small boy. At least two more boys may originally have been near his feet. The two perched on his shoulders seem to be playing with his hair. The realistically rendered goat's head identifies the figure as Harinegameshin. An ancient folk deity, he was venerated for safe childbirth. . . . He was a constant companion of Skanda-Kumara, the divine general in Hindu mythology. Originally he may have been widely worshipped at Mathura, where a number of images have been found, though none as impressive as this example. He became associated with Jain mythology early on, which makes it possible that this image was part of a Jain shrine and was the focus of a cult. Each temple complex most likely had a separate shrine devoted to Harinegameshin, much as each Hindu temple today has a shrine to Ganesa.[50]

Such was the level of religious eclecticism in the post-Mauryan centuries.

In conclusion, it may be recalled that following the notions of history adopted by Vincent A. Smith and Kashi Prasad Jayaswal, the post-Mauryan centuries were identified as a 'Dark Age'. Such a view has been a positive hindrance in comprehending the actual historical processes at work. Unfortunately, it seems that historians of Jayaswal's persuasion have now been reborn. During the last two decades, in the domain of history, there has been a renewed attempt to exalt Jayaswal's views, and to impose on the medieval period of Indian history, what had been imposed by Jayaswal upon the post-Mauryan centuries. If the Shakas and Kushāṇas and numerous other 'foreign' rulers were villains in Jayaswal's paradigm of history, the 'Muslims' of the medieval period have been delineated in similar vein in the writings of the 'cultural nationalists'. For them, the 'Islamic' millennium (from the seventh to the seventeenth centuries) was as much a 'Dark Age' as were the post-Mauryan centuries for Jayaswal. For us, the construct of a 'Dark Age' of this sort can be no more than a myth. The perceptive observation made by Damodar Dharmanand Kosambi, though made in the context of the 'Golden Age', can be reproduced with a slight change for comprehending a 'Dark Age' – it can be looked for neither in India's past nor, hopefully, in its future.

The scheme of transliteration adopted here departs from the conventional one in the following particulars: the *'c'* of that system is represented by us as *'ch'* (as in 'chat'); *'ch'* is replaced by *'chh'*; *'ṛ'* is read as *'ri'* (as commonly pronounced); *'ś'* is represented by *'sh'*, and *'ṣ' by 'sh'*. The diacritics in quotations have been retained in their original form. We have also refrained from Sanskritizing the words of Pali and Prakrit.

I am grateful to Dr Pradeep Kant Choudhary, Reader in History, Deshbandhu College, University of Delhi, for making useful suggestions and comments on the first draft of this paper.

**Notes and References**

1 Vincent A. Smith, *Early History of India*, 1924, pp. 290, 292. Lest it be misunderstood that the conception of the 'Dark Age' is confined only to a period of about 100 or 150 years following the decline of the Kushāṇas, we would like to stress that there are numerous works that put the entire post-Mauryan to the pre-Gupta period (*c.* 200 BC to *c.* AD 300) within the broad paradigm of destructive 'foreign' rule. These writings, even when conceding some positive contributions of the Yavanas, Shakas, Kushāṇas, Parthians, etc., often harp on the overall political fragmentation and are unable to conceal their uneasiness at the presence of the so-called foreign elements. In a leading multi-volume history of India, which has been a major work of the post-Independence decades, serving for textbooks in several Indian

universities for more than the last fifty years, we get a clear example of such portrayal. K.M. Munshi, who planned and executed this series (R.C. Majumdar *et al.*, eds, *The History and Culture of Indian People*, Bombay: Bharatiya Vidya Bhavan, 1950 onwards), while covering the period between 150 BC and AD 320, wrote in the 'Foreword' to its second volume (*The Age of Imperial Unity*, 1951, pp. xviii–xxiv): 'In North-West India where the "contemptible and fierce" foreigners held sway, cultural purity was more than diluted and in consequence, there was absence of a collective consciousness dominated by Aryan values .... Under the influence of the foreigners, the spiritual disenfranchisement of women began .... As people with lax morals came into the social framework on account of the expanding frontiers of Dharma, the marital ties assumed great sanctity. . . .'

2 A.S. Altekar, *The Coinage of the Gupta Empire and its Imitations* (being Vol. IV of the Corpus of Indian Coins Series), Numismatic Society of India, BHU, Varanasi, 1957, p. 12.

3 D.D. Kosambi, *The Culture and Civilization of Ancient India in Historical Outline*, London: Routledge and Kegan Paul, 1965, pp. 26–28.

4 In this connection it would be pertinent to recall R.S. Sharma's writings providing insights on economic history of Mathura (cf. *Perspectives in Social and Economic History of Early India*, New Delhi: Munshiram Manoharlal Publishers, 1983, pp. 170–83) and urbanization (cf. *Urban Decay in India, c. 300–c. 1000*, New Delhi: Munshiram Manoharlal Publishers, 1987, especially Appendix 2, pp. 191–97) as well as Suvira Jaiswal's contributions on various stages of the evolution of the caste system (*Caste: Origin, Function and Dimensions of Change*, Delhi: Manohar, 1998). One may also recall in the same context Kameshwar Prasad's *Cities, Crafts and Commerce under the Kuṣāṇas*, Delhi: Agam Kala Prakashan, 1984.

5 The dynasty was called Bhārashiva because its kings carried the weight or load of the Shivaliṅga on their shoulders or heads.

6 For the aforesaid citations of K.P. Jayaswal, see his *History of India, 150 AD to 350 AD*, reprint of the first edition (1933), Delhi: Low Price Publications, 1990, pp. 4–6, 44–46, 208–10.

7 Why did such a witness resort to prognostication? Jayaswal does not provide any answer to this question.

8 Cf. Jayaswal, op. cit., p. 48.

9 It seems that Jayaswal forgot that numerous coins of the Kuṣhāṇas show Shiva in various postures. Of these depictions, the motif of 'Shiva with Bull' was apparently very popular.

10 K.P. Jayaswal, op. cit., pp. 48–52 and 61.

11 Dharmanand Kosambi, *Bhāratīya Sanskriti aur Ahiṃsā*, translated from Marathi by Vishwanath Damodar Sholapurkar, Bombay: Hemachandra-Modi Pustakmala Trust, second reprint, 1957, pp. 145–48. Quotes from this work have been translated into English here.

12 Ibid., pp. 125–26. According to Kosambi, 'Mahādeva became Maheshvara in the time of Pāṇinī.' A recent assessment about the date of Pāṇinī puts it

around 'early to mid-fourth century BC.' (Cf. George Cardona, *Pāṇinī: A Survey of Research,* Mouton: The Hague/Delhi: Motilal Banarsidass, 1976, p. 268).

13 Dharmanand Kosambi, op. cit., pp. 120–28.

14 *D.D. Kosambi: Combined Methods in Indology and Other Writings,* compiled, edited and introduced by Brajadulal Chattopadhyaya, New Delhi: Oxford University Press, 2002, pp. 204–07. This volume is a collection of scattered articles and the relevant article is 'Early Stages of the Caste System in Northern India', first published in 1946.

15 Ibid., p. 206. Coming from the pen of D.D. Kosambi, this concept looks somewhat bizarre because he has been a strong critic of such concepts as the 'Golden Age' for understanding historical processes. We would also like to share our reservations about Kosambi's contention that the cow as a productive force could have done well enough in lands which were not wet, such as the Indus valley. Looking at the vast repertoire of animals depicted in antiquities of the Indus (Harappan) civilization, especially the seals, the complete absence of the cow is conspicuous.

16 *Dharmasūtras: The Law Codes of Āpastamba, Gautama, Baudhāyana and Vasishtha,* Annotated Text and Translation by Patrick Olivelle, New Delhi: Motilal Banarsidass, 2000, *passim.*

17 Cf. K.R. Norman, *Pāli Literature* (being Vol. VII. 2 under Jan Gonda, ed., A *History of Indian Literature*), Wiesbaden: Otto Harrassowitz, 1983, pp. 84–87 and R.C. Majumdar *et al.*, eds, *The History and Culture of Indian People,* Vol. II: *The Age of Imperial Unity,* Bombay: Bharatiya Vidya Bhavan, 1951, chapter on Vaishṇavism by D.C. Sircar, p. 437.

18 This can be compared with the transition from cow to water buffalo propounded by D.D. Kosambi, for, it also seeks to rationalize differences in modes of production on the bases of ecological variations.

19 Cf. 'Cultural Causality and Law: A Trial Formulation of the Development of Early Civilization', first published in 1949. It is also included in Julian Haynes Steward's *Theory of Cultural Change,* University of Illinois Press, 1955.

20 R.S. Sharma, 'The Kali Age: A Period of Social Crisis', in S.N. Mukherjee, ed., *India: History and Thought* (Essays in Honour of Professor A.L. Basham), Calcutta, 1982; and B.N.S. Yadava, 'The Accounts of the Kali Age and Social Transition from Antiquity to the Middle Ages', *The Indian Historical Review,* Vol. V, Nos 1–2, July 1978–January 1979, pp. 31–63. Both these contributions have been reprinted in D.N. Jha, ed., *The Feudal Order: State, Society and Ideology in Early Medieval India,* New Delhi: Manohar, 2002, pp. 61–77 and 79–120 respectively.

21 The lists of prohibited practices and methods of the Kali Age, viz., the *Kalivarjyas,* were not compiled before the eleventh century. These *Kalivarjyas* were comprehensively codified in the seventeenth century by Dāmodara in his *Kalivarjyanirṇaya.*

22 *Dhammapada,* Brāhmaṇavaggo, verses 391, 393 and 396. Cf. *The Dhammapada* with introductory essays, Pali text, English translation and

notes by S. Radhakrishnan, London: Oxford University Press, 1966, pp. 179–81.

[23] *Aṅgavijjā*, Prakrit Texts Series, 1957, Introduction by Vasudeva Sharan Agrawala. It seems that some refinement of the text took place in the Gupta period. Nonetheless, scholars are inclined to ascribe the text to the Kushāṇa period on the basis of allusions to such numismatic terms as the *dīnāramāshaka*, as well as to such Greek and Iranian deities as Apalā (Pallas), Aṇāditā (Anāhitā), Airāṇi (Irene) and Sailimāliṇī (moon-goddess Selene).

[24] Allusions to brahma–kshatra, brahma–kshatriya, brahma–vaishya, etc. are found in inscriptions of the early medieval centuries. Such characterizations have particularly been found in respect of the 'Rajput' dynasties such as the Guhilas and the Paramāras of Malwa and Rajasthan in the same centuries. The issue has been comprehensively discussed in Vishwambhar Sharan Pathak, *Ancient Historians of India: A Study in Historical Biographies*, Bombay: Asia Publishing House, 1966, pp. 164–66.

[25] This usage occurs in the sense of a *mlechchha* and according to P.V. Kane (*History of Dharmashāstra*, Poona: Bhandarkar Oriental Institute, 1968, Vol. II, Part 1, p. 383), generally, Indian literature is familiar with the use of *mlechchha* both in the sense of indigenous tribes and of foreigners. In this classification of the *Aṅgavijjā*, suddas (shudras) are called *mlechchhas.* It needs to be recalled that Patañjali's *Mahābhāshya*, which is generally ascribed to the second century BC, both Yavanas and Shakas are called shudras, whereas Kauṭilya's *Arthashāstra* differentiates between shudras and *mlechchhas.*

[26] This refers to the deity whose mounts were *naras* (human beings). This appellation of Kubera also occurs in the *Rāmāyaṇa* and the *Mahābhārata.* E. Washburn Hopkins (*Epic Mythology,* first published in 1915, reprinted, Delhi/Varanasi: Indological Book House, 1968, pp. 142–45) thinks that '*nara*' could mean both 'spirits' and humans. A sculptural delineation from Bharhut shows a deity on a pillar with folded hands as a dwarf supports the deity on his hands and feet. A label inscription below the sculpture reads *kupiro yakkho*, i.e., 'yaksha Kupira (Kubera)'. In this context it would not be out of place to recall the remains of a circular *stūpa* found at Sanghol (village in tahsil Samrala, district Ludhiana, Punjab) in 1985. Numerous railing pillars around the *stūpa* show sculptural depictions of such *yakshīs* as could be seen standing upon crouching, prostrate and 'servilely [sic] bent' dwarfs. For descriptions of such delineations, see S.P. Gupta, ed., *Kushāṇa Sculptures from Sanghol (First-Second Century AD)*, second edition, New Delhi: National Museum, 2003, specially plates 1, 7, 8, 16-A, 19-B, 20, 23 and 24 and their descriptions on pp. 124–33.

[27] It is not imperative to give the credit for developmental changes in any aspect of people's lives to contemporary rulers. Allusions to specific regnal years or dates in any era found in inscriptions and/or other sources should simply be understood as referring to the period to which a sculpture, inscription, monument or any other artefact may belong. As long as

we do not get any specific evidence of direct patronage extended by any specific ruler of a specific dynasty, we should exercise utmost caution in attributing the concerned process to the work of any specific king/dynasty.

[28] G.R. Sharma, *Excavations at Kaushāmbi (1949–50), Memoirs of the Archaeological Survey of India*, No. 74, New Delhi, 1969, pp. 21, 76 and plate XLIX.A.

[29] John M. Rosenfield, *The Dynastic Arts of the Kushāns*, Berkeley: University of California Press; reprint, New Delhi: Munshiram Manoharlal Publishers, 1993, p. 245, plates 47 and 62.

[30] Even today one can see such a delineation of the *yakṣharāja* at the entrance gateway of the main building of the Reserve Bank of India, Parliament Street, New Delhi.

[31] B.N.S. Yadava, 'Some Aspects of the Changing Order in India During the Shaka-Kushāṇa Age'. This was presented at the International Conference of the History, Archaeology and Culture of Central Asia in the Kushāṇa Period, held at Dushanbe (Tajikistan) in 1968 and was published in the Proceedings of the Conference entitled *Central Asia in the Kushāṇa Period*, Vol. II, pp. 123–38. It has also been included in a volume entitled *Kushāṇa Studies* published by the Department of Ancient History, Culture and Archaeology, University of Allahabad, 1968 (reprinted 1998), pp. 75–97.

[32] R.S. Sharma, 'A Survey of Land System in India: 200 BC–AD 650', *Journal of the Bihar Research Society*, Vol. 44, 1958, pp. 225–34; *idem, Perspectives in Social and Economic History of Early India*, New Delhi: Munshiram Manoharlal Publishers, 1983, pp. 136–45; and two contributions of B.N.S. Yadava mentioned above in notes 20 and 31. In addition to these sources, see also B.N. Mukherjee, 'Revenue, Trade and Society in the Kuṣāna Empire', *The Indian Historical Review*, Vol. VII, Nos 1-2, July 1980–January 1981, pp. 24–53.

[33] For a discussion of the material background of these theological developments within the Mahāyāna order and their relationship with Indian feudalism, see A.K. Warder, 'Feudalism and Mahāyāna Buddhism', in R.S. Sharma and Vivekanand Jha, eds, *Indian Society: Historical Probings: In Memory of D.D. Kosambi*, second edition, New Delhi: People's Publishing House, 1977, pp. 156–74.

[34] For a few other theological changes within Mahāyāna Buddhism and the contributions of the Kushāṇas in bringing about those changes, see the contributions of L. Mäll ('Some Problems Related to the Rise of Mahāyāna') and A. Zelinsky ('The Kushāṇas and Mahāyāna') in Proceedings of the International Conference held at Dushanbe (see note 31 for publication details). These contributions were originally presented in Russian and their summaries in English have been included in Volume II of the Proceedings at pp. 222 and 235–36 respectively.

[35] For references related to glories of *dāna*, see G.P. Malalasekera, ed., *Encyclopaedia of Buddhism*, volume II, *q.v.* 'Avadāna'; John S. Strong, 'The Transforming Gift: An Analysis in Devotional Acts of Offering in Buddhist Avadāna Literature', *History of Religions*, Vol. 18, 1979, pp. 221–37.

[36] For the text of the Nanaghat cave inscription, see Dines Chandra Sircar, *Select Inscriptions bearing on Indian History and Civilization, Vol. I (from the sixth century BC to the sixth century AD)*, second edition, University of Calcutta, 1965, p. 193, specially notes 3 and 4. For a discussion of the social base and patterns of patronage noticeable in the arts and the monumental remains of the post-Mauryan centuries, see contributions of Romila Thapar, Vidya Dehejia and Janice D. Willis, in Barbara Stoler Miller, ed., *The Powers of Art: Patronage in Indian Culture*, New Delhi: Oxford University Press, 1992, pp. 19–53.

[37] For a discussion of the monetary policy and coinage of the Kshatrapas, see Amiteshwar Jha and Dilip Rajgor, *Studies in the Coinage of the Western Kshatrapas*, Nashik: Indian Institute of Research in Numismatic Studies, 1974.

[38] U.P. Shah, *Studies in Jaina Art*, 1955, pp. 39–84. This work is based on three lectures delivered by him under the auspices of the Jaina Cultural Research Society, Varanasi in 1954. See also U.P. Shah, 'Beginnings of the Superstructure of Indian Temples', presented at a symposium organized by the American Institute of Indian Studies (now in Gurgaon, Haryana) at Varanasi in (1967) and later published by that Institute in Pramod Chandra, ed., *Studies in Indian Temple Architecture*, Delhi, 1975, pp. 80–89.

[39] Ananda K. Coomaraswamy, *History of Indian and Indonesian Art*, 1927, reprinted, New York: Dover Publications, 1965/New Delhi: Munshiram Manoharlal Publishers, 1972, p. 82.

[40] R.N. Mehta and S.N. Chowdhury, *Excavations at Devnimori*, M.S. University, Baroda, 1966; Michael W. Meister, M.A. Dhaky and Krishna Deva, eds, *Encyclopaedia of Indian Temple Architecture*, American Institute of Indian Studies/New Delhi: Oxford University Press, 1988, Vol. II, Part 1 (Text), pp. 16–17.

[41] U.P. Shah, 'Beginnings of the Superstructure of Indian Temples' (for publication details, *supra* note 38), pp. 84–85.

[42] For a fuller description of these coins of Agathocles found at Ai Khanoum, and an analysis of their significance in the history of Bhāgavata religion and Indian art, see *Graeco-Bactrian and Indian Coins from Afghanistan*, edited and compiled by Olivier Guillaume (translated from the French by Osmund Bopearachchi and published as Vol. V under the series 'French Studies in South Asian Culture and Society'), New Delhi: Oxford University Press, 1991, pp. 80–116 and plates IV and VI.

[43] K.D. Bajpai and S.K. Pandey, *Malhar* (1975–78), Department of Ancient Indian History, Culture and Archaeology, University of Sagar, 1978, specially plate 10. Michael W. Meister, M.A. Dhaky and Krishna Deva, eds, op. cit., p. 3, endorse the originally suggested date of the sculpture.

[44] Cf. Herbert Härtel, *Excavations at Sonkh: 2500 Years of a Town in Mathura District*, with contributions by Hans-Jürgen Paech and Rolf Weber, Dietrich Reimer Verlag, Berlin, 1993, pp. 413–27 and relevant plates thereafter.

[45] Ibid., pp. 281–82. In an earlier publication on the excavations at Sonkh, Härtel described the 'standing figure of Skanda' as 'the oldest Hindustic

[sic] bronze so far found in India' (cf. Herbert Härtel, *Some Results of the Excavations at Sonkh: A Preliminary Report*, p. 90. This publication of 1976 was reprinted and circulated at the time of the exhibition on Sonkh excavations held at the National Museum, New Delhi in October/November, 1977). On the identification of the 'standing divine couple' in the final Report, Härtel thinks along the same lines as P.K. Agrawala (*Early Indian Bronzes*, Varanasi, 1977, p. 64) who comes, through the interpretation of the feline figure, to the following conclusion: 'From the iconographic evidence provided by some contemporary stone plaques from Mathura itself and by certain texts we have no doubt this goddess is Charchikā-Ṣaṣṭhī, a mother goddess presiding over childbirth and assimilated with Devasenā-Ṣaāṣṭhī, the spouse of Skanda.' We wonder if this 'divine couple' could also be a joint depiction of the goat-headed Harinegameshin and Skanda-Kumāra.

46 Cf. Herbert Härtel, *Excavations at Sonkh: 2500 Years of a Town in Mathura District*, pp. 101, 105, 112f, 120, 122f and 245 and relevant plates.

47 For a discussion of the processes involved in the creation of Shiva-centred and Vishṇu-centred pantheons during the post-Mauryan centuries, see Sukumari Bhattacharji, *The Indian Theogony: A Comparative Study of Indian Mythology From the Vedas to the Purāṇas*, Cambridge: Cambridge University Press, 1970, *passim*; and Suvira Jaiswal, *The Origin and Development of Vaishṇāvism*, second edition, New Delhi: Munshiram Manoharlal Publishers, 1981, *passim.*

48 Incidentally, Kankali Tila had also yielded exquisite antiquities of faiths other than that of the Jainas. For example, 'the earliest Indian image of Sarasvatī' has come from this mound. Now housed in the State Museum, Lucknow, the headless image is dated to the (Shaka) year 54 or AD 132). It has a long dedicatory inscription on its two-tiered pedestal. Gova, who was a smith, donated this image at the inspiration of his teacher Āryadeva. For further details of this image, see Pratapaditya Pal, ed., *The Peaceful Liberators: Jain Art from India*, Los Angeles County Museum of Art, California/London: Thames and Hudson, 1994, p. 26 (figure 12) and p. 171 (Catalogue No. 55).

49 For the monumental and art remains of the Jainas in the post-Mauryan centuries, see A. Ghosh, ed., *Jaina Art and Culture*, New Delhi: Bharatiya Jnanapith, 1974, Vol. I, chapters 6–9; U.P. Shah and Ernest Bender, 'Mathura and Jainism', in Doris Meth Srinivasan, ed., *Mathura: The Cultural Heritage*, New Delhi: Manohar/American Institute of Indian Studies, 1989, pp. 209–13; Smita Sahgal, 'Spread of Jainism in North India between *circa* 200 BC and *circa* AD 300', in Narendra Nath Bhattacharyya, ed., *Jainism and Prakrit in Ancient and Medieval India: Essays for Professor Jagdish Chandra Jain*, New Delhi: Manohar, 1994, pp. 205–32. For details of bronzes from Chausa, see Pratapaditya Pal, op. cit., pp. 24–25; Nihar Ranjan Ray, Karl Khandalavala and Sadashiv Gorakshkar, *Eastern Indian Bronzes*, New Delhi: Lalit Kala Akademi, 1986, pp. 17–19, 93–95, 103–06 and plates 1–17. A bronze image of Pārshvanātha (its place of origin is unknown) in the

*kāyotsarga mudrā*, now in the Prince of Wales Museum in Mumbai, has been ascribed to 100 BC or perhaps even earlier and compared with some *Jina* images from Chausa. From a stylistic point of view, this image of Pārshvanātha has also been compared with the famous bronze 'dancing girl' found at Mohenjodaro.

[50] Pratapaditya Pal, op. cit., p. 26, 170 (Catalogue No. 54).

# 3 Social Dimensions of the Cult of Rāma

*Suvira Jaiswal*

There is general consensus among scholars that the cult of Rāma, the hero of the epic *Rāmāyaṇa*, originated later than that of Vāsudeva-Kṛṣṇa. It is also generally conceded that although Rāma was recognized as an incarnation of Viṣṇu by the time the *Bālakāṇḍa* of the *Rāmāyaṇa* acquired its present form and the *Rāmopākhāyāna* of the *Mahābhārata* was composed, Rāma became an object of personal devotion much later.[1] R.G. Bhandarkar, one of the early pioneers in the field, was of the view that the cult of Rāma came into existence as late as around the eleventh century AD.[2] However, claims have been made of the existence of Rāma temples in the Gupta period. On the other hand, the rise of the Rāma cult has also been interpreted as a defensive response of the Hindus to the conquest and rule of northern and central India by Muslim invaders.[3] In order to analyse the social content and context of the cult of Rāma-*bhakti*, it is necessary naturally to have an accurate mapping of its chronological and spatial setting.

The popularity of the Rāma story led to the carving of the episodes from the Rāmāyaṇa on the panels of Vaiṣṇava as well as Śaiva temples; and a number of such panels from the fifth–sixth centuries onwards are found at various places, such as Bhitargaon near Kanpur (U.P., fifth century AD), Deogarh (Jhansi district, *c.* sixth century), Paunar (near Wardha, sixth century), rock-cut caves of Uṇḍavalli Vijayawada (seventh century), Calukyan temples at Paṭṭadakal (seventh century) and the Rāṣṭrakūṭa temple of Kailāśanātha at Ellora (eighth century). However, these cannot be taken as indicative of his cultic worship, which is sought to be established on the basis of a couple of epigraphic sources, and these need to be examined carefully.

The Rithpur copper plate inscription of the Vākāṭaka Queen Prabhāvatī Guptā, daughter of Candragupta II, records an order issued by the queen from the 'foot of Rāmagirisvamin' (*rāmagirisvāminaḥ padamulat*).[4] As Kālidāsa too in the *Meghadūta* pays homage to the hills of Rāmagiri (identified with modern Ramtek near Nagpur), which according to him are marked by the footprints of Raghupati,[5] it has been argued[6] that this provides clear evidence of the cult of Rāma existing in the fifth century AD. However, it is more plausible to infer from these references that some natural crevice or spot on the hill was supposed to have been marked by the footprints of Rāma during his southern wanderings and worshipped as such. The cultic worship seems to have been confined to the sacred footprint and localized in nature; it does not indicate the growth of a general cult of Rāma Dāśarathi.[7] It is important to note that for Kālidāsa, Rāma is only a partial incarnation of Viṣṇu embodying a quarter portion of the great god. He is the first among equals, with each of his three brothers being the embodiment of one or the other quarter portions (*aṃsa*) of Viṣṇu.[8]

The other epigraph is the Bhitari stone inscription of Skandagupta. It speaks of the installation of an image of god Śārngin,[9] the bearer of the bow Śārṅga, by the Gupta king; and on this basis it has been argued that since among the incarnations of Viṣṇu only Rāma Dāśarathi is described as the wielder of *dhanuṣa*, it unmistakably proves the existence of a Rāma temple and installation of his image in the Gupta period for the purpose of worship. However, the *Rāmāyaṇa* of Vālmīki nowhere speaks of the bow of Rāma as Śārṇga *dhanuṣa*. The *Rāmāyaṇa* story reflects a culture in which bows and arrows are the most important weapons, and not only Rāma, but almost all human-heroes are expert archers. All his brothers are shown wielding bows and arrows and Daśaratha is said to have killed the son of a blind ascetic couple by discharging an arrow at the sound created by the filling of water in a jar, which he mistook for the roar of an elephant. Indeed, there is no doubt that Viṣṇu was the original Śārṅgin, the wielder of the Sārṅga bow, just as Śiva was Pinākin, the wielder of the Pināka bow. The *Rāmāyaṇa* of Vālmīki narrates[10] that god Viśvakarmā made two powerful bows – one for Viṣṇu and the other for Śiva. In a fight between the two gods Viṣṇu's bow proved to be superior and Śiva was defeated. Paraśurāma gave the same bow of Viṣṇu to Rāma Dāśarathi for testing the strength of the latter, who himself, finally gave it away to god Varuṇa. At another place[11] in the same epic, sage Agastya bestows upon Rāma the bow of Viṣṇu fashioned by Viśvakarmā. Although in these passages the bow of Viṣṇu is described simply as the

'Vaiṣṇava bow', in the *Dhanurveda* Śārṅga is specifically associated with Viṣṇu.[12] The *Raghuvaṃśa* of Kālidāsa provides clear evidence of the fact that originally Śārṅgin was a designation of Viṣṇu, and not of Rāma, for, in a verse[13] which compares Rāma's joyful welcome of Śatrughna on his killing the demon Lavaṇa with Indra's delighted reception of god Viṣṇu on his killing of Kālanemi, the poet mentions Rāma simply as *agraja*, the elder brother of Śatrughna, but uses the term 'Śārṅgin' to refer to Viṣṇu. Again, at another place,[14] the poet speaks of the serpent Śeṣa as becoming the bed of Śārṅgin, which description fits Viṣṇu and not Rāma. Obviously in Ramology Rāma acquired this epithet through his identification with Viṣṇu, but in the Gupta times it seems to have served as just another name of Viṣṇu.

The earliest expression of exclusivist devotion to Rāma is found in a hymn of Namma Āḷvār (ninth century) wherein he asserts that he has taken refuge in the Daśaratha alone and none other.[15] Although the cowherd god Vāsudeva-Kṛṣṇa was the favourite deity of the Āḷvār hymnologists, they have also sung in praise of Rāma and a number of hymns extolling the achievements of Rāma composed by Poygai, Pudam, Pey, and other Āḷvārs are collected in the *Nālāyiradivyaprabandham* ('The Four Thousand Sacred Hymns') comprising the final redaction of their songs.[16] The Rāvaṇāntaka (killer of Rāvaṇa) form of Rāma is celebrated by Tirumaṅgai Āḷvār, who also speaks of Rāma, Sītā and Lakṣmaṇa as forming an inseparable group.[17] The burning of Laṅkā and related incidents figure prominently in the poems of Namma Āḷvār; and later Śrīvaiṣṇava tradition regards him as the incarnation of the wooden sandals of Rāma.[18] However, the sentiment of Rāmabhakti is most pronounced in the poems of Kulaśekhara Āḷvār, who perhaps lived in the first half of the ninth century and ruled over parts of Kerala. In his *Perumāḷ Tirumoḷi* he narrates the entire story of Rāma in eleven decades using every situation to express a deeply personalized and loving relationship with the deity. In the final stanza, the poet claims that the worshippers of Rāma obtain final union with Him through love.[19]

It is generally conceded that the emotional, ecstatic form of *bhakti* originated with the Tamil Āḷvārs. This is the implication of the *Bhāgavata Purāṇa – Māhātmya* – which, allegorizing the sacred geography of the *bhakti* movement, speaks of the birth of *Bhakti* (personified as a female) in the Draviḍa country.[20] The tradition is reiterated in a later Hindi saying.[21] It has been convincingly argued[22] that the Āḷvārs had inherited the heroic–erotic ambience of the *aham* tradition of Śaṅgam classics and had a positive anthropocentric concept of the deity, which was life-affirming and in tune with the Tamil cultural milieu. Friedhelm Hardy has suggested that the Āḷvārs were reacting against the suffocating life-negating ideological pressures of Jainism and Buddhism, which had become dominant in the period between the Śaṅgam age and the rise of the Āḷvārs. He repudiates the thesis that the Āḷvārs represented a 'mass movement' against caste oppression and argues that they spoke the language of the Tamil elite,[23] who rejected 'northern' influences represented by Jainism and Buddhism. He regards their movement as a product of 'Tamil renaissance', which ended the 'long historical night', using the words of Nilakanta Sastri.[24] Earlier Kamil Zvelebil also interpreted the *bhakti* movement of the Āḷvārs as an expression of a 'strong Tamil national feeling' against Jainism and Buddhism, which, in his view were perceived by the Tamils as 'alien', 'connected with foreign non-Tamil powers, chiefly the Cālukyas', and inimical to their 'national self-identification'.[25]

However, there is hardly any evidence to show that the Cālukyas posed a threat to Tamil powers in the period preceding the advent of the Āḷvārs and the Nāynārs for a reaction to set in. The rise of the Cālukyas of Bādāmi, the Pallavas of Kānci (of Sanskrit Charters) and the Pāṇḍyas of Madura took place about the same time in the sixth century. The denunciation of Jainism and Buddhism by the Śaiva and Vaiṣṇava *bhakti* poets cannot be explained as an assertion of Tamil nationalism and a subtext of the conflict among the Cālukya, Pallava and Pāṇḍya powers for the simple reason that although Jainism had a considerable presence in the Cālukyan kingdom, members of the Cālukyan royal family were generally devotees of Śiva and Viṣṇu and they built some of 'the most important temples of the time' at Bādāmi, Paṭṭadakal and elsewhere in honour of these gods.[26] Moreover, one cannot regard the period antedating the *bhakti* movement as the 'dark period', at least for Tamil literary and cultural activities. Most of the works grouped under the title 'The Eighteen Minor Works' (*Padinenkiḷkaṇakku*) and the Tamil classics *Śilappadikāram* and *Maṇimekalai*, as Nilakanta Sastri himself points out, were written during this period. Many of these authors seem to have been Jainas or Buddhists, but there is no break from the earlier Tamil literary traditions. The *Śilappadikāram*, written by a Jaina poet, celebrates both love and war 'in the tradition of classical Tamil poetry'[27] and ends with the deification of the heroine Kaṇṇaki and her union with the hero Kovalan in a divine chariot, which takes them to heaven.[28]

For a proper analysis of the nature of conflict and opposition to Jainism and Buddhism, spearheaded by the *bhakti* poet–saints, one has to examine the social base of these heterodox religions during the Kaḷabhra interregnum (*c.* AD 250–500) for which unfortunately the data are meagre. The Pāndyan Velvikuḍi grant speaks of the Kaḷabhras as a tribe of evil rulers, who uprooted many *adhirājas* and revoked *brahmadeya* grants.[29] The Tamil literary tradition speaks of their having kept the kings of the Cera, Coḷa and Pāṇḍya dynasties in confinement. A Kaḷabhra ruler, who is said to have occupied Madurai, was a Jaina and another named Accyuta Vikrānta, a patron of Buddhists.[30] Nilakanta Sastri interprets the overthrow of the Kaḷabhras and the rise of the *bhakti* movement in terms of a 'Hindu revival', characterized by an outspoken hatred of Buddhists and Jainas.[31] But according to R.S. Sharma,[32] the Kaḷabhras were tribal peasants who had risen in revolt against Tamil landed powers, and in his view, the anti-Brahmanical religions must have played a role in polarizing peasants against their oppressors. Their overthrow would thus mean the revival of the patronage of Brāhmaṇas and Brahmanical institutions. Friedhelm Hardy suggests that the collapse of the Gupta empire may have resulted in the immigration of a large group of Northern intellectuals and religious leaders to the South, accelerating Brāhmaṇa–Tamil interaction and providing an incentive to the *bhakti* movement.[33] Whatever be the social underpinning of the flowering of *bhakti* in the Draviḍa country, there is no doubt that the symbols of 'intellectual *bhakti*' as propounded in the *Bhagavadgītā* were given a new meaning and structure by the Āḷvārs, who endowed them with a humanist, emotional and ecstatic content bordering on the erotic. This anthropocentric concept of *bhakti* propagated by the Āḷvārs laid the foundations for the emergence of the cult of Rāma-*bhakti*.

One can discern gradual stages leading to the growth of a full-fledged Rāma cult in the Draviḍa country. The Āḷvārs sang in praise of local cult spots as haunts of their favourite deities, and this gave scope to the identification of various places as scenes of the events associated with the characters of the Rāma story and celebration of existing temples as those of Rāma. For example, Tirumaṇgai and Kulaśekhara Āḷvārs speak of the deity installed in the Govindarāja temple, situated within the Naṭarāja temple-complex at Chidambaram, as lord Rāma accompanied by his devotee Hanumān. They visualize the temple as Citrakūṭa. On the basis of these references it has been suggested[34] that although at present the Govindarāja temple enshrines an image of Nārāyaṇa in his *śayana* form, in the time of the Āḷvārs, it must have had an image of Rāma Daśarathi. But we may point out that the Śaiva saint Māṇikkavāśagar, who lived in the ninth century and was perhaps a contemporary of Kulaśekhara Āḷvār, has provided us with a vivid description of the iconography of the famous Naṭarāja and Govindarāja images at Chidambaram. In a verse of his well-known poem *Tirukkovaiyar*, he describes Nārāyaṇa as lying in front of Naṭarāja, 'absorbed in the contemplation of the foot lifted in his dance', and entreating Śiva to grant him the view of his other foot as well.[35] Apparently the Govindarāja temple, even in the time of the Āḷvārs, had an image of Nārāyaṇa-Viṣṇu in the lying posture, but they still claimed to see in it Rāma, attended by Hanumān and figuratively describe the location as Citrakūṭa.

Such devotional impulses may be seen operating in Central India as well. The Rājivalocana temple at Rajim, a village in the Raipur district of Chhattisgarh, has two inscriptions on the left wall of its *maṇḍapa*, one assigned to the middle of the seventh or early eighth century on paleographic grounds, and the other possessing a date, which corresponds to 3 January 1145. From these two records we learn that originally a king of the Nala dynasty (probably king Vilāsatuṅga)[36] built a temple of Viṣṇu in the eighth century. It was later rebuilt in the twelfth century by Jagapāla, also called Jagatsiṃha, a minister of the Kaḷacuri king Pṛthivīdeva of Ratnapura. The composer of the twelfth-century inscription speaks of the temple as 'manifesting the splendour of Rāma' (v. 22). We are told that Jagapāla was well versed in the duties of a kśaṭriya, worshipped the Brāhmaṇas, gods and Fire, listened to the recitation of the Purāṇas, Āgamas and Śāstras such as the Bhārata and read the *Rāmāyaṇa* (vv.20–21).[37] The temple is a famous place of pilgrimage for the devotees of Rāma who believe that an idol of Rāma is enshrined inside. But, as Cunningham reports,[38] 'the figure is actually one of the common four-armed representations of Viṣṇu himself with the usual symbols of the club, the discus, the shell and the lotus', confirming the hypothesis that with the growing popularity of the hero of the Rāmāyaṇa, certain Viṣṇu temples were transformed into cult centres of Rāma.[39]

A similar superimposition of the *Rāmāyaṇa* characters over

earlier Vaiṣṇava symbols seems to have taken place at Khajuraho. The so-called Lakṣmaṇa temple at Khajuraho, built in 954, was, in fact, dedicated to Viṣṇu in his Vaikuṇṭha form, and the principal image is a composite of the Viṣṇu Vārāha and Narasiṃha forms.[40] The eleventh-century Ramachandra temple at the place, also known as the Chaturbhuja temple, shows the four-handed male deity embracing the female deity and touching the left part of her breast. The female deity is in a Tribhaṅga pose,[41] and the depiction is close to Lakṣmī-Nārāyaṇa images popular in early medieval times.[42] Krishna Deva describes[43] the central image as that of Caturbhuja Viṣṇu in the Laltāsana pose. Obviously the substitution of 'Ramachandra' in place of Caturbhuja Viṣṇu in naming the temple is a later development.

Clear evidence of shrines erected in honour of Rāma comes from the Coḷa and Pāndya kingdoms, which had been the scenes of Āḷvār activities. Several inscriptions of the time of the Coḷa king Parāntaka I (907–955) indicate the existence of Rāma temples in his kingdom. The earliest of these is dated in the seventh year of his reign. It records the gift of land to the Lord of Ayodhyā (Tiruvāyottiperumāḷ, i.e., Rāma) of the Kodaṇḍarāma temple in Madurāntakam in the Chingleput district.[44] Another inscription dated in the fifteenth year of his reign records a gift of land to the god named Ayodhyā-perumāṇdigal of the village Uttaramerur Cāturvedimaṅgalam.[45] A third inscription dated in the thirty-fourth year of the same king from the shrine of Kāmākṣī Amman in the Kailāśanātha temple records a gift of ten Kaḷañjus of gold by the queen Seyyabuvana Sundara-Maniyr for the purpose of burning a perpetual lamp in the temple of Sri Rāghavadeva, who was pleased to take his stand at Tiruvāyodhi temple at Pulavelur in Eyirkottam.[46] A little later, an epigraph fixed on the north wall of the Vaikunṭha Perumāḷ temple at Uttaramallur (district Chingleput) records the setting up of an image of Rāma in the temple of Tiruvayottiyai (sacred Ayodhyā), situated in Uttaramerur, by Villavan Mahādevī, the queen of Pārthivendrādhipatiivarman (i.e., Āditya II, Karikāla – 955–69).[47] The Ammangudi record of Rājarāja I dated in his ninth year (992–93) speaks of the reconstruction of a shrine under the name Tiruvaiyotti (sacred Ayodhyā) for the god Rāmadeva-perumāḷ and consecration of his image.[48] Another temple of the same deity, described as Rāghavadeva, mentioned in an inscription dated in the thirteenth regnal year of Rājarāja I was situated in Ukkol in the Chingleput district.[49]

It seems that initially Rāma temples were built as subsidiary shrines within larger Vaiṣṇava temple complexes. Champakalakshmi writes that numerous references to Rāma or Rāghavacakravartigal are found in the inscriptions of Rājendra I in the Narasimha temple at Ennāyiram (South Arcot district).[50] Quite interesting is the record of Rājendra Coḷa's twenty-fifth regnal year (1037) from the Ādikeśava temple at Vaḍamadurai in the Chingleput district. It speaks of the celebration of the marriage of the goddess Nambirāṭṭiyar, i.e., Sītā, with the *cakravarti* king of Ayodhyā (*Tiruvayoddhicakravarti*, i.e., Rāma). An areca garden was gifted to the goddess as dowry on the occasion.[51] A Rāmasvāmin temple of roughly the same date is also reported to have existed at Śermadevi in the Tirunelveli district.[52]

The pieces of evidence cited above are substantial enough to cast doubt on all attempts to interpret the rise of the cult of Rāma-*bhakti* as a 'Hindu' reaction to the 'Muslim' invasion of India in the twelfth and thirteenth centuries.[53] Nevertheless, recurrent references to the deity as the *cakravarti* (universal monarch) or the lord of Ayodhyā emphasize his connection with kingship. Although the Coḷa kings were worshippers of Śiva and constructed a number of magnificent temples in honour of their favourite deity, several of them assumed titles referring to the Rāma incarnation of Viṣṇu. Āditya Coḷa (871–907), who claimed to have built several Śiva temples on the banks of Kaveri, assumed the title of Kodaṇḍarāma (the bow-wielding Rāma). His son Parāntaka I built a sepulchral temple on the remains of his father, at the site of his death at Toṇḍaināḍ near Kalahasti in the Chittor district of Andhra Pradesh, naming it Kodaṇḍarāmeśvara.[54] Parāntaka himself assumed the title of Saṇgrāma-Rāghava, 'Rāma in battle'. His eldest son Rājāditya, too, had the title of Kodaṇḍarāma like his grandfather. The correspondence between the god–king and earth–ruler is strongly suggested in the *Rāmāyaṇa* (*Irāmāvatāram*) of Kamban, who lays particular stress on the royal nature of this incarnation.[55] The imperial Coḷas claimed to have belonged to the solar lineage, the line in which Rāma Dāśarathi was born; and Kamban's patron, named Śaḍaiyan, a chieftain of Vennainallur, was apparently a feudatory of the Coḷas. So, Kamban made the ancestors of his patron bring the crown to Rāma at the time of his coronation, implying that the relationship between Rāma and the ancestors of his patron was fundamentally of the same nature as the relationship between the Imperial Coḷa ruler and Śaḍaiyan. Kamban's own date continues to be controversial, scholarly opinions varying from the ninth to the twelfth century.[56] In any case, he lived in the time of the Imperial Coḷas, and it is said that his description of Kosala presents an idealized account of the features of the Coḷa country.[57]

The device of using religious myths and symbols for the glorification of contemporary rulers is not exclusive to Ramology. The concepts of divine origin of kingship and divinity of the king are traceable in later Vedic literature.[58] The *Mahābhārata* and the Purāṇas repeatedly state that kings are partial incarnations of Viṣṇu.[59] The idea became so ingrained in traditional thinking that the *Caitanyacaritāmṛtam* of Kṛṣṇadāsa Kavirāja, a famous work of Bengal Vaiṣṇavism written in the early seventeenth century, depicts a Hindu officer of the Muslim Court addressing quite ṇaturally his master, 'an unconsecrated Yavana', as a part of Viṣṇu.[60] The notion was buttressed by the doctrine of incarnation. The Gupta kings are depicted on their coins with a nimbus round the head, a sign of divinity and several of their inscriptions and coin-legends describe them as veritable gods and incarnations of Viṣṇu. In the fifth–sixth centuries, the Cālukyas of Bādāmi assumed the title of Śrī Pṛthvī Vallabha, 'the beloved of Śrī and Pṛthvī', the two wives of Viṣṇu in Puranic mythology. Later, in the ninth century, the Gurjara Pratihāra king Mihira Bhoja claimed his identity with Viṣṇu's Boar incarnation, by assuming the title of *ādivarāha*. The character of the Rāma incarnation was even more suitable for such uses. Hence, the Śaiva kings of the Coḷa dynasty could easily appropriate it for their exaltation in the context of the growing popularity of the Rāma saga through the songs of the Āḷvārs and the *Rāmāyaṇa* of Kamban.

Kamban's *Rāmāyaṇa* shows that the poet was well versed both in the Sanskrit and in the Tamil traditions, the written as well as oral.[61] In the main, he follows the account of Vālmīki, but introduces a number of minor episodes which provide him room to develop themes of love and war in the spirit of the *aham* and *puram* conventions of the Tamil classics. Thus, he invents a meeting between Rāma and Sītā prior to their marriage or *svayaṃvara*, which allows him to give a beautiful poetic description of their premarital mutual attraction and pangs of separation (*viraha*) felt by the lovers at night.[62] Kamban's interpretation of the characters of Rāvaṇa, Kumbhakarṇa and Indrajit provides flashes of heroic valour; and his Rāma is the ideal king, a perfect *cānror* at the earthly level, and the Supreme Being, whose grace alone can rid one of the cycle of births and deaths, at the divine level. According to some scholars, Kamban was a Śaiva,[63] as his work begins with a homage to Śiva. But in his narrative Śiva figures only as one of the gods in the Trinity (*trimūrti* of Brahmā, Viṣṇu and Śiva) and the highest position is repeatedly assigned to god Tirumāḷ (i.e., Viṣṇu). Tirumāḷ is the origin of everything. Taking the *trimūrti* form it is he who creates, protects and destroys the universe. He alone is eternal, constituting the twenty-sixth principle, and it is expressly stated that one who seeks liberation has no other place of refuge than his divine feet.[64]

Kamban is supposed to have belonged to the Uvacca community, a caste of temple priests performing worship in the temples of Mariamman and similar deities. In the Dharmaśāstras, temple-priests are regarded as low-ranking Brāhmaṇas.[65] However, the *Kamba Rāmāyaṇa* reflects a typically Brahmanical world-view, referring to the law-code of Manu with deep reverence at a number of places.[66] Vasiṣṭha, instructing the future king Rāma, describes the Brāhmaṇas as superior to the Trinity of Brahmā, Viṣṇu and Śiva and the Five Buddhas. It is said that countless gods have suffered on account of having incurred the wrath of the Brāhmaṇas and an equal number of gods have attained greatness by receiving their compassion. Rāma too worships the Brāhmaṇas and does their bidding. Even Fate awaits the command of the Brāhmaṇas. So, one should always extol them in this birth, as well as in the next.[67] Kamban closes his epic with the Yuddhakāṇḍa, with the narration of Rāma and Sītā returning to Ayodhyā and their coronation, and makes a very brief mention of the Rāma rājya. We are told that Rāma ruled over his kingdom in accordance with the laws of Manu, protecting the world in such a manner that goddess Lakṣmī and the Earth were not hurt in the least.[68] The message of devotion to Rāma, the incarnation of Tirumāḷ, is closely linked with the authority of the Vedas, efficacy of Vedic sacrifices and veneration of Brāhmaṇas. It is not surprising that the *Kamba Rāmāyaṇa* should have become a target of attack by the protagonists of the Dravidian Movement in the early twentieth century.

The close connection of the cult of Rāma with Brahmanical social order and its social implications are often underplayed by stressing its so-called liberating potential, as it opened the path of *bhakti* to all, irrespective of caste and gender. But the entire range of religious literature on Rāma-*bhakti* in the *Saguṇa* stream has a very clear social message. God is universally accessible and grants salvation to all those who worship him with devotion, but He does not allow any transgression of the *varṇa dharma*, i.e., violation of caste rules and disrespect to Brāhmaṇas regardless of their qualifications. Concern about the religious needs of the Śudrā and depressed castes in Ramology figures in texts written after the thirteenth century, and is reflective of a changed social scenario. An analysis of the subtle variations in the telling of the Śambūka episode in the texts of different settings and periods is useful in revealing the contextual significance of these narrations.

The Uttarakāṇḍa of Vālmīki's *Rāmāyaṇa*, which narrates the killing of Śambūka is no doubt a later addition to the original epic, but the story was known in the early centuries of the Christian era, as it is mentioned by Kālidāsa. In the Uttarakāṇḍa of Vālmīki, we are told that when Rāma was ruling over Ayodhyā, a young son of an aged Brāhmaṇa died an untimely death. Rāma learnt from the sage Nārada that his death was caused by the act of some evil-minded Śudrā, practising ascetic rites (*tapaścaryā*) in violation of the *dharma* rules. This sent Rāma on his Puṣpaka Vimāna searching for the Śudrā. When he went towards the south, he found a Śudrā ascetic named Śambūka practising severe austerities on the Śaivala mountain with the object of attaining godhood and entering heaven in his physical form (*saśarīra*). Rāma promptly cut his head off with his sword, for which act the gods extolled him and granted him the boon of bringing back to life the dead son of the Brāhmaṇa.[69] A little later,[70] we are told that the child got back his life on account of Rāma having performed his *dharma*. The purpose of the anecdote is to depict Rāma as the ideal ruler, firmly devoted to the maintenance of the *varṇa-dharma*, which is an important duty of the king according to the Śānti Parva of the *Mahābhārata*, the *Manusmṛti* and other Brahmanical law books.[71] It provides a concrete example of what the *Bhagavadgītā* emphasizes repeatedly,[72] that the consequence of performing the *dharma* of some other *varṇa* is frightening, even if performed in a better fashion. No concern is shown here for the Śūdra. He deserved the extreme punishment for his presumptuous ambition and Rāma is praised as *śudrā-ghātin*, the śudrā - killer.

A minor change in the story may be noticed in the narration[73] of the incident in the *Raghuvaṃśa* of Kālidāsa. Rāma learns from an aerial speech of the goddess Sarasvati that the prevalence of some evil practice (*apacāra*) among his subjects has caused the death of the infant son of a Brāhmaṇa. Rāma finds Śambūka practising severe asceticism and beheads him for this transgression of the *varṇa dharma*. The act not only revives the child, but also sends the Śudrā ascetic to heaven, for we are told that 'the śudrā by the punishment inflicted upon him by the king himself, obtained the position of the virtuous, a position which he could not secure even by his severe austerity, being as it was in violation of the rules of caste.'[74] Interestingly, there is no hint of the doctrine of grace or compassion shown by the divine Rāma, and the possibility of a Śudrā obtaining heaven through *tapas* is clearly ruled out. The passage reiterates the view of Manu that those who are given punishment by the king himself are absolved of all sins and go to heaven.[75]

However, the Brahmanical version of the Śambūka incident was not acceptable to the Jaina narrators of the Rāma story and Vimalasūri in his *Paumacariyam*[76] makes Śambūka, the son of Candranakhā (Surpanakha of the Brahmanical lore), sister of Rāvaṇa. He is a Vidyādhara. He practises severe penance for twelve years to obtain a divine sword, but is killed by Lakṣmana. Vālmīki's version is broadly followed by Bhavabhūti in his *Uttara Rāmacarita*, written in the first half of the eighth century AD, but he dramatizes the event by making the murdered Śambūka reappear in the form of a heavenly person (*divya purusa*) singing praises of Rāma for having inflicted punishment on him. The Brāhmaṇa child is brought back to life and Rāma's action has bestowed glory on Śambūka, for 'even death arising from the contact of the good brings salvation.'[77] The Śudrā expresses his feeling of devotion to Rāma by stating that he is greatly indebted to his performance of penance, as this made Rāma search for him, a mere wretched Śudrā. Rāma grants him the attainment of Vairāja or heaven. Thus, while the socio-religious disabilities of the Śudrā are recognized unhesitatingly, Rāma is depicted as a compassionate god in human form. Despite carrying out his kingly duty of killing the offending Śudrā, his attitude towards him is humane. Basically, Bhavabhūti's version of the Śambūka story is the same as that of Kālidāsa, the treatment bearing the stamp of the former's poetic genius.

However, by the time the *Ānanda Rāmāyaṇa* was composed in the fifteenth century,[78] the intensity of the Brāhmaṇa–Śudrā antagonism was much reduced in the changed socio-economic environment, with the category of Śudrā subsuming a number of the so-called 'clean' (*satśudrā*) and 'unclean' (*asatśudrā*) castes. A story which was apparently invented to emphasize the exclusion of the Śudrā from what was conceived as the privilege of the upper *varṇas* is narrated in this text in such a way that its central message becomes incorporative. It tries to bring the Śudrā castes within the fold of Rāma worshippers without in any way mitigating their social disabilities. In Vālmīki's *Rāmāyaṇa* Nārada explains at length that in the Kṛta age only Brāhmaṇas could practise asceticism. In the Tretā age, even Kṣatriyas did so and acquired strength (*vīrya*) equal to that of the Brāhmaṇas. In the Dvāpara, the third epoch, the Vaiśyas could practise *tapa* but the Śudrās have never been allowed to do so in the purer three *yugas*, although, it is acknowledged that in the Kaliyuga, the Śudrās would violate the *dharma* by practising *tapa*. Hence, Rāma is exhorted to seek out the evil transgressor of *dharma* and punish him to ensure the well-being of his subjects. The *Ānanda Rāmāyaṇa*,[79] developing this story, asserts that the violation of the *varṇa dharma* by the Śudrā ascetic led to the death of not only the five-year-old son of the Brāhmaṇa couple of Ayodhyā, but also of six others. These were the husband of a Brāhmaṇa woman from Śṛṇgaverapura, a Kṣatriya, a Vaiśya, an oil presser, the daughter-in-law of a blacksmith and the daughter of a leather worker (*carmakāra*). The killing of Śambūka revived them all. And, before cutting off the head of the Śudrā, Rāma asks him to seek a boon. The Śudrā wants the liberation of not only his own self, but that of his entire community. Rāma tells him that the Śudrās may achieve salvation merely by reciting his name (*japa*) and chanting it collectively (*kīrtana*). But Śambūka points out that in the Kaliyuga Śudrās would be too ignorant and engrossed in agricultural work and other pursuits to earn a living to find time for *japa* or *kīrtana*. Rāma then tells him that in the Kali age the Śudrās would attain heaven simply by saying 'Rāma, Rāma' while greeting each other and Śambūka too would go to heaven, having been killed by the god himself. Thus, the hostile attitude towards the Śudrā reflected in the earlier version becomes so much more subdued in the *Ānanda Rāmāyaṇa*, where the whole tenor is inclusive rather than exclusive.

It may not be without significance that the offending Śudrā is situated in the South. Vālmīki locates him on the northern side of Śaivala mountain, beyond which lay the hermitage of the sage Agastya. Bhavabhūti places him in Janasthāna, also described as Daṇḍakāraṇya, the extensive forests between Narmada and Godavari, which were the habitats of aboriginal tribes. Henri Cousens[80] records a 'local legend' which identifies the Ramtek hill in the Vidarbha region as the place where Rāma had executed the Śudrā Śambūka. We have already noticed that the *Raghuvaṃśa* as well as the inscriptions of the Vākāṭaka queen Prabhāvatī-Gupta describe the Ramtek hill as marked by the footprints of Rāma. It is likely that the story of Śambūka reflects the antipathy of the custodians of Brahmanical culture towards the aboriginal population of the Deccan in the early centuries of the Christian era, when this area was coming increasingly under Brahmanical domination. An inscription of the second century AD speaks of the Sātavāhana king Gautamīputra Śātakarṇi as the 'unique Brāhmaṇa who zealously supported the brahmanical order by preventing the fusion of the four varṇas.'[81] In the third century AD, Vindhyaśakti, a Brāhmaṇa of Viṣṇuvṛddha gotra, carved out the Vākāṭaka principality in western Madhya Pradesh or Berar. The ascendance of Brahmanism in the Deccan does not seem to have been entirely peaceful. In the fifth century, a descendant of Vindhyaśakti, the Vākāṭaka king Pravarasena II, granted the village Carmāṇka near Illichpur in the Vidarbha region to one thousand Brāhmaṇas on the condition that they would not resort to arms, harm other villages or commit treason against the kingdom. If they acted otherwise or assented to such acts, the king would commit no theft in taking the land away.[82] R.S. Sharma[83] has drawn attention to a Pallava grant of about the same time made by *Yuvamahārāja Viṣṇugopa*, by which the prince gifted a village named Neḍḍuṇgarāja in the Maṇḍarāṣṭra region to a number of Brāhmaṇas as a 'Śaraṇikagrāma', that is, as a refugee settlement. Neḍḍuṇgarāja is identified with a place in the Nellur district of Andhra Pradesh. Apparently, these Brāhmaṇas must have faced more persecution at the hands of the aboriginal 'non-Brāhmaṇa' population of the area. The hostility of the Kaḷabhras towards Brāhmaṇas and Brahmanical institutions has been referred to above. We may also refer to an inscription of the Nandivarman Pallavamalla, who ruled in the sixth century. It records the grant of two villages named Kumāramaṇgala and Vennatturaikotta, free of all taxes, to 108 Brāhmaṇas after removing from these villages all those whose conduct was offensive to religion. The practice of dispossessing earlier settlers and giving villages to Brāhmaṇas as Vidyābhogaṃ was quite common under Pallava rule.[84] In such an environment the emphasis on the king's duty of protecting the *varṇa dharma* and honouring the Brāhmaṇas by the proponents of Rāma-*bhakti*, such as Kamban, could not have been incidental.

Medieval religious literature provides ample evidence of the growing popularity of the Rāma cult in Brahmanical circles. Śrīvaiṣṇava's hagiography depicts several Śrīvaiṣṇava ācāryas, the inheritors of the Āḷvār tradition as devout worshippers of Rāma. It is also believed that Rāmānuja (b. 1018) had received his initiation in the temple of Kodaṇḍarama at Tirupati.[85] The present Rāma temple at Tirupati known as Rāma Medal dates from not earlier than the thirteenth century and has copper idols of Rāma (known as Raghunātha), Sītā, Lakṣmana and Sugrīva in the sanctum sanctorum, traditionally supposed to have been installed by Rāmānuja himself.[86] It is difficult to ascertain the historicity of such beliefs, but Raṅganātha Muni, who is said to have been a pupil of Namma Āḷvār and is the first of the Śrīvaiṣṇava Ācāryas, is described as a great devotee of Rāma in the *Āḷvandār stotra* of his grandson Yāmunācārya (also known as Āḷvandār).[87]

The growing importance of the Rāma cult is also indicated by the composition of the sectarian Upaniṣads which attempt to connect it with the ancient Vedic tradition. The three sectarian Upaniṣads, the *Rāmapūrvatāpanīya*, *Rāmottaratāpanīya*, and *Rāmarahasya Upaniṣad* are of uncertain date, but may not be later than the twelfth century AD.[88] These advocate his worship in the Brahmanic mode with the use of *yantra* (a geometrical diagram drawn on stone, metal or any other material and identified with the body of the deity) and sectarian Rāma and Sītā *mantras*. Rāma represents the highest male principle (*parama puruṣa*) and Sītā the undivided primal matter (*mūla prakṛti*). These are also passages explaining Rāma *bhakti* in *advaitic* (non-dualistic) terms.[89] Rāvaṇa is said to have abducted Sītā to ensure his salvation.

A philosophical text of a different genre is the *Vasiṣṭha Rāmāyaṇa*, also known as *Yoga Vāsiṣṭha*, written in Kashmir and dated variously between the eighth and the twelfth centuries AD.[90] It presents in the character of Rāma, a model of spirituality, that of *jīvana mukta*, in opposition to the ideal of *sanyāsa* or renunciation, celebrated by Buddhism and the Vedānta philosopher Śaṇkarācārya. Buddhism was quite influential in Kashmir in early medieval times. To combat it the author of the *Yoga Vāsiṣṭha* preaches attainment of liberation without abandoning the householder's life and synthesizing 'knowledge' and 'action' (*jñāna-karma samuccaya*). *Karma* is interpreted not in the sense of rituals or devotional acts of worship, but as search for truth and religious experience. The devotional theme is carried forward in later texts such as the *Agastya Saṃhitā*[91] and the *Adhyātma Rāmāyaṇa*,[92] which are regarded as canonical by the Rāmānandī sect of Rāma worshippers.

Both the *Agastya Saṃhitā* and the *Adhyātma Rāmāyaṇa* in their present form do not seem to be earlier than the fifteenth century AD. The Marathi poet–saint Ekanātha who lived in the sixteenth century refers to the *Adhyātma Rāmāyaṇa* as a modern work,[93] hence it is generally assigned to the fifteenth century. The *Agastya Saṃhitā*, on the other hand, is dated by Hans Bakker[94] to the twelfth century on the ground that passages dealing with the *Rāmanavamīvrata* found in it are quoted in the *Caturvargacintāmaṇi* of Hamādri (thirteenth century) and the *Kālanirṇaya* of Mādhavāchārya (fourteenth century). It is also extensively quoted in the sixteenth-century treatises, such as the *Tithitatva*, *Nirṇayasindhu* and *Rāmārcanacandrikā*.[95] But it needs to be noted that the work mentions Rāmananda giving his date of birth as Kali era 4400, corresponding to AD 1299–1300, on which basis R.G. Bhandarkar[96] placed Rāmananda in the fifteenth century, a dating accepted by Hans Bakker too. Apparently, in its present form, the *Agastya Saṃhitā* cannot be earlier than the fourteenth century, when the cult of Rāma was gaining popularity. This work contains elaborate instructions for the worship of Rāma along with Sītā (*Rama Sītā Samanvitaṃ*). He is to be worshipped internally through *dhyāna* (meditation), *nyāsa* (placing of sacred letters in different parts of the body) etc., and externally by performing the 16 *upacāras* (services). It equates Rāma with the Vedantic transcendent *brahman* (*parabrahman*), who is the highest god[97] and the exclusive object of worship. While making the worship of Rāma open to all, regardless of caste and sex, it is strictly enjoined that one has to observe one's *varṇa dharma* scrupulously; women have to follow *pativrata dharma* and the Śudrās have to serve the twice-born. Religious teaching is to be given in accordance with one's caste rules (*tattajjātyānusārataḥ*).[98] The work seems to have been written for the use of *pujāris* or priests of Rāma temples.

The *Adhyātma Rāmāyaṇa*, on the other hand, narrates the story of Rāma beginning with Viṣṇu's assurance to gods, that he would incarnate himself as Rāma and kill the demon Rāvaṇa. It follows the framework of Vālmīki's Rāmāyaṇa, but, as Frank Whaling remarks, 'the humanity of Rāma in the *Adhyātma* Rāmāyaṇa is seen, as it were, from the godward side whereas Vālmīki views it from the manward side.'[99] Rāma is identical with Viṣṇu and is the highest god, worshipped by Śiva and other deities. He is the *Brahman* celebrated in the Vedas and is all enveloping, as well as unmanifest and without attributes. Almost every character in the story is aware of this fact and every incident provides the author an occasion to expatiate on Rāma-*bhakti*, which was open to all. However, this stress on *bhakti* is combined with veneration to the Brāhmaṇas, and the holding of Brahmanical rules of caste and order. Thus, lord Rāma explains to Lakṣmana that for attaining the knowledge of liberation, performance of one's duties in accordance with one's caste and status is a necessary precondition. Heedlessness in this regard had turned king Nṛga into a chamelion.[100] Rāma himself worshipped with great devotion the innumerable Brāhmaṇas who came to him for their protection, headed by the sage Cyavana.[101] Vaiṣṇava tradition regards this work as a part of the *Brahmāṇḍa Purāṇa*, but it seems to have been an independent treatise incorporating within it several other compositions, such as the *Rāmahṛdaya* and the *Rāmagītā*, the latter evidently inspired by the more famous *Bhagavadgītā*. The *Adhyātma Rāmāyaṇa* also borrowed the story of Vālmiki from the *Avanti-Khaṇḍa* of the *Skanda Purāṇa*, which describes the transformation of a Brāhmaṇa, who had become a robber and a virtual Śudrā due to his evil deeds, into the sage Vālmīki, the author of the *Rāmāyaṇa*, through the intervention of the seven sages.[102] In the *Skanda Purāṇa*, the sages instruct the Brāhmaṇa to practise meditation and severe asceticism and recite the sacred *mantras*, but the author of the *Adhyātma Rāmāyaṇa* uses this story to emphasize the merit of reciting the name of Rāma. We are told that sinful as the Brāhmaṇa was, the sages taught him to repeat with a concentrated mind the word *marā*, being the inverted syllables of the name of Rāma. The Brāhmaṇa did so for thousands of years and was enveloped by an anthill. The sages came again and asked him to come out of that *vālmīki*, i.e., the anthill. They praised him as a great sage born a second time and called him Vālmīki.[103]

There is a tradition that both the *Agastya Saṃhitā*, also known as *Agastya Sutīkṣṇa-Saṃvāda*, and the *Adhyātma Rāmāyaṇa* were brought to the North by Rāmānanda who came from South India.[104] However, internal evidence goes against this supposition.[105] More dependable is the account of the *Bhaktamāla*, which makes Rāmānanda a disciple of the Śrīvaiṣṇava teacher Rāghavānanda, who came to Vārānasī from the South and initiated Rāmānanda in devotion to

Rāma. However, Rāmānanda did not strictly adhere to the practices of the Śrī Vaiṣṇava sect founded by Śri Rāmānuja, and he is regarded as a radical reformer, who did not differentiate between his Brāhmaṇa and non-Brāhmaṇa followers. He made them dine together, breaking the taboos on commensality. An oft-quoted couplet in Hindi attributed to him, states: 'Do not enquire to which caste or community one belongs, whoever worships Hari (the Lord) he belongs to Hari.'[106] He also used the vernacular language to propagate his creed among the masses.

Nevertheless, there was a strong resistance to the use of vernacular languages for religious narratives among orthodox Brahmanical circles, and a *śloka* of uncertain authorship commonly cited in this connection asserts: 'whoever listens to the eighteen purāṇas and the story of Rāma in the vernacular language, would be condemned to Raurava hell.'[107] The suggestion[108] that the *Adhyātma Rāmāyaṇa* is a later attempt to Brahmanize the Rāmānandi community by providing it with a 'scripture' based on *advaita* philosophy, appears quite plausible. Even the *Ānanda Rāmāyaṇa* which, as we have seen, has a more inclusive approach towards the Śudrā castes and has provided rich material for religious discourses at popular *kīrtans* and *kathā* performances,[109] is written in Sanskrit. Tulsī (Tulasī) had to face stiff opposition from the orthodox Pundits of Vārāṇasī who denounced him for writing in the vernacular. But Tulsī was not the first to write a *Rāmāyaṇa* in Hindi (Awadhi dialect). Before him, some time in the fifteenth century, Viṣṇudāsa had rendered a translation of Vālmīki's *Rāmāyaṇa* in a Hindi dialect, titled *Bhāṣā Vālmīki Rāmāyaṇa.*[110] It was in verse and used the *Caupāyī* metre, later adopted so successfully by Tulsīdās. In fact, if we leave out the Tamil *Rāmāyaṇa* of Kamban, the period from the fourteenth to the sixteenth century saw the flowering of *Rāmāyaṇa* in almost all major regional languages. Some of these seem to have been inspired by the human drama inherent in the Rāma story,[111] but most were deeply imbued with the sentiment of *bhakti* as well, indicating the growing popularity of the Rāma cult among the common people. However, Tulsīdās's *Rāmacaritmānas* towers above all the rest in terms of its literary beauty, lyrical quality and popularity. It is remarked that it 'takes the place of the Bible and Shakespeare combined for the teeming millions of North India.'[112] What has been its social significance?

It is often said that Tulsīdās was not a social reformer, but a poet. He was certainly a saint, a devotee of Rāma par excellence. Nevertheless, he did not write only for self-satisfaction or liberation of his own soul; his societal concerns find clear expression in his writings. He begins the *Rāmacaritmānas* with a prayer to Śiva and Pārvatī that his poetic composition in the vernacular language should have the effect of turning all those who listen to it, or recite it, into devotees of Rāma, devoid of the sins of the Kali age, and so transformed into blessed beings.[113] Along with the message of Rāma-*bhakti* runs the message of unquestioning acceptance of the hierarchies of caste and patriarchal family structure. The *Rāmacaritmānas* conveys an explicit subtext of belief in the natural, inborn superiority of the *dvijas* (the twice-born) and innate and intrinsic inferiority of those who are born as Śudrās or women. Tulsīdās repeatedly gives vent to his anger against those who are *vipradrohī*, hostile to Brāhmaṇas. The fire provoked by the hostility to Brāhmaṇas is even more destructive than the weapon *Vajra* of Indra, the Trident of Śaṇkara, the Rod of Yama and the Discus of Hari.[114] A person who reviles a Brāhmaṇa is condemned to many hells and is finally born as a crow.[115] Rāma himself preaches in the Rāmāgītā section to all his subjects including Vasiṣṭha and other sages that there is nothing so meritorious in this world as worshipping the feet of the Brāhmaṇas with mind, action and speech, i.e., with complete dedication.[116] The *Uttarakāṇḍa* of Tulsi's *Rāmāyaṇa* is quite different from Vālmīki's *Uttarakāṇḍa*. It does not speak of the killing of Śambūka and the banishment of Sītā, but mentions the birth of Lava and Kuśa, briefly presenting a happy and blissful picture of Rāmā's kingdom and his family life. The story ends here but what follows gives a clear exposition of the poet's social outlook and purpose, a lengthy description of the Kali age, when religion and sacred texts disappear, and arrogant persons bring into existence numerous sects prompted by their own imagination and having no scriptural sanction.[117]

Hazari Prasad Dwivedi has convincingly established[118] that Tulsī is not only aware of Kabīr and his teachings, but has repudiated him strongly, using vitriolic language. In an obvious reference to Kabīr's oft-repeated assertion[119] that the Supreme God Rāma was not the son of Daśaratha and he never took birth in human or any other physical form, Tulsī remarks[120] that it is only the ignorant, blind, crooked, lascivious and deceitful hypocrites who say that the Supreme God Rāma is different from the son of Daśaratha. The attributeless (*nirguṇa*) Supreme God Rāma was born as the son of Daśaratha in the family of Raghu for the love of his devotees, for the well-being of the Brāhmaṇas, cows and gods, for the destruction of the wicked and the protection of the Vedic religion.[121] For Tulsī there is no difference between *nirguṇa* Rāma and *saguṇa* Rāma. It is one and the same Rāma, who is celebrated in the Vedas and pervades the entire universe.

In a seminal article[122] Irfan Habib has analysed the rise of popular monotheistic movements of the *nirguṇa* stream led by Namdev, Kabir, Raidas and other like-minded preachers in the backdrop of social and economic changes following the establishment of the Delhi Sultanate, which had generated, among other things, an increase in demand for craft-goods and the consequent expansion of the old and formation of new professional artisan groups. The development led to some social mobility as well as transitional instability among the lower castes engaged in these professions, providing a fertile ground for questioning the age-old barriers of caste and religion. Obviously the custodians of Brahmanism, too, could not have remained unaffected by social turmoil. Elsewhere, I have drawn attention to the fact that material changes in the early centuries of the Christian era had brought about a modification in the traditional concept of the *varṇa* duties typical of the Vaiśya and Śudrā *varṇas*, with 'vaiśya' becoming a synonym for trader and communities subsisting on peasant agriculture, as well as with other manual tasks being dubbed Śudrā.[123] The spread of this modified concept of the *varṇa* theory in the regions of the South and the East during this period led to an anomalous situation within the so-called Śudrā *varṇa*. It included powerful Kammas and Kapus of Andhra Pradesh, Veḷḷālas of Tamil Nadu and Kālitas of Assam at one end of the spectrum, and depressed Māḍigas, Paraiyas, etc., at the other, necessitating conceptualization of the fifth *varṇa* (*pañcama varṇa*), or an *avarṇa* (outcaste) category. The virtual absence of Kṣatriya and Vaiśya *varṇas* in the regions outside the Gangetic valley may be explained historically,[124] but in practice it meant that in these regions the high caste Śudrās enjoying pure status stood only next to the Brāhmaṇas.[125] At least in medieval times the term Śudrā did not carry the same pejorative meaning in the South as in the North, and many ruling families had no hesitation in proclaiming their Śudrā status,[126] as they came from communities which were ascribed the *satśūdra* (pure Śudrā) status by the Brahmanical lawmakers. P.V. Kane[127] lists as many as 31 books written in the period extending from the thirteenth to the seventeenth century, which deal with the religious rights and duties of the Śudrās. Viśveśvarabhaṭṭa, who was a Southern (*Dākṣinātya*) Brāhmaṇa and wrote his *Smṛti Kaumudī* at the behest of Madanapāla, the ruler of a petty kingdom near Delhi, begins his work by stating that the earlier lawgivers have generally dealt with the *dharma* of the three higher varṇas and have paid little attention to the *dharma* of the Śudrās. Therefore, he says, he has taken up the task of clearly expounding the *dharma* of the Śudrā castes.[128] In the sixteenth century, Śeṣa Kṛṣṇa wrote the *Śūdrācāra Śiromaṇi*[129] under the patronage of Pīlāji Rao, a king of the South (*dākṣinātya*).[130] The attempt of these *smārta* Brāhmaṇas to cater to the ritual needs of the Śudrā castes within the framework of *smṛti* rules was made in the background of both Southern as well as Northern developments, for, whereas some had their patrons in the South, others were located in the North near Dehli and as far as Mithilā. Vācaspatimiśra, the author of *Śūdrācāracintamaṇi*, dealing with the rules of conduct for the Śudrās, lived in Mithilā in the latter half of the fifteenth century and was the advisor of the Mahārājādhirāja Harinārāyaṇa.[131] The Brahmanical preachers of Rāma-*bhakti* almost went to the South to give the message of *bhakti* to Śudrā castes by making proper performance of the *varṇa dharma* its *sine qua non*. We have seen how the author of *Ānanda Rāmāyaṇa* introduces in the story of the Śudrā Śambūka the daughter-in-law of a blacksmith, the daughter of a *carmakāra*, an oil presser and other castes too, and preaches, through Rāma, that in the Kali age menial castes could attain liberation merely by saying 'Rāma, Rāma' while greeting each other. Kabīr's reaction to such preaching is remarkable. He says, 'The Pandit is preaching a false doctrine. If people could attain salvation merely by uttering Rāma, one would taste sugar merely by saying "sugar".'[132]

Kabīr is often placed in the line of Vaiṣṇava *bhaktas* apparently for two reasons. Legend makes him a disciple of Rāmānanda, and he speaks of God as 'Rāma', albeit his disclaimer is that his Rāma is without attributes and not the son of Daśaratha. The historicity of the story that he was trampled by Rāmānanda and received Rāma *mantra* from him on the steps of the bathing ghat in Vārāṇasī is doubtful.[133] It was apparently invented to give his followers greater legitimacy and respectability. Moreover, the fundamental principle of Vaiśṇavism is the doctrine of incarnation with the Vedic god Viṣṇu at its centre. But this is firmly rejected by Kabīr. In fact, he uses not only 'Rāma', but all the words current in his time to denote God in a monotheistic sense –

Allah, Khuda, Karim, Kṛṣṇa, Govinda, Nirañjana, Nātha and so on.

The earliest use of 'Rāma' for God in a monotheistic sense may perhaps be traced to the Tamil *Siddhas*. In the tenth century, Śivavākkiyār uses both 'Rāma' and 'Śiva' to refer to the eternal omnipresent God 'described almost exclusively in negative terms'. Revolting against Brahmanical orthodoxy he condemned image worship, repudiated the authority of the Vedas, and rejected the caste system and the theory of transmigration unequivocally.[134] The usage of 'Rāma' as a general word for God seems to have been facilitated by the fact that in contemporary Brahmanical literature like the *Kamba Rāmāyaṇa* and sectarian Upaniṣads, Rāma was no longer looked upon as a partial incarnation of Viṣṇu, but identical with Viṣṇu in his *parama-brahma* form, who is beyond activity, immanent as well as transcendent, and beyond the reach of human experience. The *Bhāgavata Purāṇa* tried to synthesize the emotional *bhakti* of Kṛṣṇa with the *advaita* of Śaṇkara and similar attempts were made by the Brahmanical preachers of Rāma-*bhakti* in the *Yoga Vāsiṣṭha, Adhyātma Rāmāyaṇa* and other texts. It was the growth in the religious significance of Rāma which led to the general use of his name for God.

However, Tulsī's ire against Kabīr is not merely over differences in the conceptualization of God. It stems from his divergent social perspective and location. Kabīr came from a depressed weaver caste and must have had personal experience of the demeaning, exploitative caste system and religious establishments, Hindu as well as Muslim. He is critical of both. Tulsī, on the other hand, was a pious Brāhmaṇa who had to suffer persecution at the hands of the orthodox Pundits of Vārāṇasī, jealous of his popularity and fame. His outburst against his persecutors shows that even in his pique his reference points were the caste system and the Brahmanical order:

> Some call me a cheat, some others an *avadhūta* (an ascetic who has renounced all worldly attachments and norms), some say I am a Rajput and some others call me a Jolaha (a low caste of Muslim weavers). My name is Tulsī and I am a slave of Rāma. Let any one say what he feels like. I am not asking anyone to give his daughter in marriage to my son! I am not ruining anybody's caste! I shall beg for my food and sleep in a mosque, but shall have nothing to do with such people. (*Kavitavali*, VII.106)

Paying respect to caste hierarchy and its rules, despite the irrelevance of caste status in the pursuit of liberation has been the essential feature of Vaiṣṇavism from its first exposition in the *Bhagavadgītā*. Tulsī thoroughly imbibed this upper-caste attitude. No doubt the main message of the *Rāmacaritmānas* is that of complete devotion and surrender to God, but along with this is conveyed a moral code of conduct which is Brahmanical and patriarchal; the *Rāmāyaṇa* story provides examples for every situation in life conforming to these norms. Celebration of the patriarchal joint family had a strong appeal to all classes in medieval times, whether they were peasants, artisans or belonged to the upper castes or nobility, as there was nothing in the material milieu of the age which would have encouraged subversion of the long established subordination of the female sex. Caste identities depended on it. The image of Rāma as an ideal family man (*gṛhastha*) was further buttressed by the *Rāmacaritmānas*, although it seems that even earlier Rāma was never worshipped singly and was always accompanied by at least Lakṣmana and Sītā.[135] The Mūlla *mantra* for worshipping Rāma as given in the *Agastya Saṃhitā* visualizes Rāma in company with Sītā,[136] and the *Adhyātma Rāmāyaṇa* advises the devotee to complete his worship of Rāma by giving offerings to his companions.[137] The *Vaikhānasāgama* enjoins that Rāma should be shown along with Sītā, Lakṣmana and Hanumāna.[138] Rāma temples of the early Vijayanagara phase had images of Rāma together with Lakṣmana and Sītā installed in the sanctum sanctorum (*garbhagṛha*).[139] The inscriptions of Vijayanagara rulers mention the installation of the image of Rāma along with his family (*saparivārakaṃ*).[140] But the term *parivāra* is used here in the sense of the 'circle' (*āvaraṇa*) of attendants and not in the sense of a patriarchal household. Rāma is envisioned as a divine king surrounded by his retinue consisting of his brothers and Sugrīva, Hanuman, Vibhīṣaṇa, Aṅgada and Jāmbavant. Such representations suggest a homology between the divine ruler and the earthly ruler. But the celebration of the *gṛhastha* (householder) Rāma in folk songs and popular narrations mentioned by Tulsī is at a different level.[141] Tulsī too wrote *Rāmalalā Nahachū* (ceremonial pairing of nails of Rāma) and *Jānakī maṇgala* (marriage of Jānakī) in the style of folk songs sung on such occasions. This aspect of the Rāma story added colour to the life of the common people and was an important factor contributing to the popularization of the Rāma cult, which, through the *Rāmacaritmānas*, spread social values essential for the stability of a caste society based on the subordination of the lower classes and of women. It is said that already in the life time of Tulsī this work had acquired a sacred character and its recitation was deemed holy. It encouraged the construction of Ṭhākurbāḍas[142] (literally, the house of god), which were shrines containing images of Rāma and his family, often including his favourite attendant and devotee Hanumān as well, attached to the residences of the rich and the well-to-do people. Perhaps the earliest of such temples of a 'gṛhastha Rāma' was established in Kanaka Haveli at Vārāṇasī in 1585.[143] But this aspect of the cult of Rāma needs further investigation.

**Notes and References**

1 Suvira Jaiswal, *Origin and Development of Vaiṣṇavism*, Delhi, 1981, pp. 9, 140.

2 R.G. Bhandarkar, *Vaiṣṇavism, Śaivism and Minor Religious Systems*, 1913, reprint 1965, p. 46f.

3 Hans Bakker, *Ayodhyā*, Part I, Groningen, 1986, p. 66; Sheldon Pollock, 'Rāmāyaṇa and Political Imagination in India', *The Journal of Asian Studies*, Vol. 53, No. 2, 1993, pp. 261–97. In his *The Wonder That Was India*, A.L. Basham wrote somewhat cryptically, 'It is perhaps significant that his [i.e., Rāma's] cult only became really popular after the Muslim invasion', Calcutta, 1971, p. 306.

4 D.C. Sircar, *Select Inscriptions bearing on Indian History and Civilization*, Vol. I, 1942, p. 415, line 1 of the inscription.

5 *Meghadūta*, vol. 12, edited by V.V. Mirashi; *Epigraphia Indica*, XXV, p. 12fn.

6 Ajay Mitra Shastri, *India as Seen in the Bṛhatsaṃhitā of Varāhamihira*, Delhi, 1969, pp. 131–32.

7 Many initial cult spots located on the hills were later associated with Śiva or incarnations of Viṣṇu, and brahmanic worship was superimposed on them. For such antecedents of spots connected with the worship of Narasiṃha and Hayagrīva incarnations of Viṣṇu, see Suvira Jaiswal, 'Evolution of the Narasiṃha Legend and its Possible Sources', *Proceedings of the Indian History Congress*, Chandigarh (34th session, 1973), pp. 140–51; *idem*, 'The Demon and the Deity: Conflict Syndrome in the Hayagriva Legend', *Studies in History*, I, I, n.s., 1985, pp. 1–13.

8 Raghuvaṃśa, X, 65–86. References are to the *Raghuvaṃśa of Kālidāsa*, edited and translated by Gopal Raghunath Nandargikar, Delhi, 1971.

9 J.F. Fleet, 1888, *Corpus Inscriptionum Indicarum*, III, No. 13, lines 17–19.

10 *Srimadvālmikiya Rāmāyaṇa*, Gita Press, I.75.

11 Ibid., III. 12. 32–36.

12 Vaman Shivaram Apte, *Sanskrit English Dictionary*, s.v. *Śārṅga*.

13 *Raghuvaṃśa*, XV.40.

14 Ibid., XII. 70.

15 *Tiruvāyamoḷi*, III.6.8, edited and translated by S. Satyamurthi Ayyangar, Bombay, 1981.

16 For references, see R. Champakalakshmi, *Vaisnava Iconography in the Tamil Country*, Delhi, 1981, p. 119, 154 notes, 165–67.

17 Ibid., p. 119.

18 Bhagwati Prasad Singh, *Rāma Kāvya Dhārā: Anusadhāna Aivam Anucintana*, Allahabad, 1976, p. 10. For a different and perhaps earlier hagiological tradition of the Āḷvārs regarding Rāma being a portion of Viṣṇu and his various attributes, see Champakalakshmi, op. cit., p. 240.

19 K.C. Varadachari, *Āḷvārs of South India*, Bombay, 1966, pp. 76–80.

20 *Bhāgavatu Purāṇa*, Samvat 2027, Gorakhpur, Gita Press (Bhāgavata Māhātmya, I. 48–50).

21 The couplet runs as follows:
*Bhaktī Drāviḍ ūpajī lāye Rāmanand.*
*Pargat kiyo Kabir ne sāt dvīpanau khaṇḍ.*

22 Kamil Zvelebil, *The Smile of Murugan: On Tamil Literature of South India*, Leiden, 1973, p. 198; A.K. Ramanujan and Norman Cutler, 'From Classicism to Bhakti', in *Essays on Gupta Culture*, edited by Bardewell L. Smith, Delhi, pp. 177–214; Friedhelm Hardy, *Viraha-Bhakti: The Early History of Kṛṣṇa-Devotion in South India*, Delhi, 1983, pp. 130, 227, 478.

23 For the elite background of the Āḷvārs, see Suvira Jaiswal, 'Change and Continuity in Brahmanical Religion with Particular Reference to Vaiṣṇava *Bhakti*', *Social Scientist*, Vol. 29, Nos 5–6, 2000, pp. 1–23.

24 K.A. Nilakanta Sastri, *A History of South India*, third edition, Madras, 1966, p. 144, quoted by Hardy, op. cit., p. 123.

25 K. Zvelebil, op. cit., pp. 196–97.

26 K.A. Nilakanta Sastri, *A History of South India*, third edition, Madras, 1966, p. 144; quoted by Hardy, op. cit., p. 123.

27 K. Zvelebil, op. cit., p. 176.

28 This reminds us of Bhavabhūti's turning of the tragic story of Rāma and Sītā into a happy ending in the *Uttara Rāmacaritam* by reuniting them, in the last scene.

29 K.A. Nilakanta Sastri, *The Coḷas*, Madras, 1975, pp. 101–02.

30 K.R. Venkata Raman, 'A Note on the Kalabhras', *Transactions of the Archaeological Society of South India*, 1956–57, pp. 94–100. According to Venkata Raman, the Kaḷabhra tribe came from the Karnataka region and one of the Kaḷabhra chiefs ruling in Tondaināḍu and designated as 'king of Kalaṇdai' was canonized as Kuṟṟuva Nāyanār, being one of the sixty-three Śaiva saints (p. 99).

31 Nilakanta Sastri, *History of South India*, Chapter XV.

32 R.S. Sharma, *Early Medieval Indian Society*, Hyderabad, 2001, pp. 221–22, 225.

33 Friedhelm Hardy, op. cit., pp. 123, 434f.

34 R. Nagaswamy, 'Sri Rāmāyaṇa in Tamilnadu in Art, Thought and Literature', in V. Raghavan (ed.), *The Rāmāyaṇa Tradition in Asia*, Delhi, 1980, pp. 414–45.

35 Nilakanta Sastri, *The Coḷas*, p. 643.

36 D.C. Sircar, in *The History and Culture of the Indian People*, Vol. III (*The*

*Classical Age*), R.C. Majumdar and A.D. Pusalker (eds), Bombay, 1970, p. 190.

[37] V.V. Mirashi, *Corpus Inscriptionum Indicarum*, Vol. IV, Part II, Ootacamund, 1955, pp. 450–57.

[38] A. Cunningham, *Archaeological Survey of India*, Report, Vol. XVII, p. 322; quoted in Hans Bakker, *Ayodhyā*, Groningen, 1986, p. 764, note 6.

[39] Hans Bakker also speaks of the evolution whereby Viṣṇu of the main sanctum was turned into Rāma, op. cit., p. 67.

[40] Devangana Desai, *Erotic Sculpture of India*, New Delhi, 1975, p. 49.

[41] R. Awasthi, *Khajuraho ki Deva Pratimāyen*, Agra, 1967, p. 111, plate 36.

[42] Kalpana Desai, *Iconography of Viṣṇu*, New Delhi, 1973, pp. 31–36.

[43] Krishna Deva, *Temples of Khajuraho*, Vol. I, New Delhi, ASI, 1990, p. 230f.

[44] Annual Report of the South Indian Epigraphy, Year 1896, No. 126, *South Indian Inscriptions* (henceforth *SII*), V, 991; quoted in R. Champakalakshmi, 1981, p. 122.

[45] *SII*, No. 297, quoted in P. Banerjee, *Rama in Indian Literature, Art and Thought*, Delhi, 1986, p. 215.

[46] *Annual Report of South Indian Epigraphy*, 1922–23, No. 46, quoted in P. Banerjee, op. cit.

[47] *Annual Report of South Indian Epigraphy*, Vol. 32; 1898, *SII*, III, No. 193; R. Champakalakshmi, op. cit. Incidentally, this also shows that Ayodhyā was conceived as a mythical city, the abode of Rāma, with hardly any connection with the geographical entity situated in the Faizabad district of U.P. Hence the temples of Rāma are described as Tiruvayoddhi, the sacred Ayodhyā. Also see note 50 below.

[48] *SII*, XIII, No. 203; P. Banerjee, op. cit.

[49] *SII*, III, No.2; R. Champakalakshmi, op. cit.

[50] Champakalakshmi, op. cit.

[51] *Annual Report of South Indian Epigraphy*, Year 1952–53, No. 262; Champakalakshmi, op. cit.

[52] Ibid.

[53] For one such attempt, see Sheldon Pollock in *Journal of Asian Studies*, 1993, (see note 3). Pollock hypothesizes that a temple-centred cult evolved around Rāma as a result of 'Hindu' reaction to the 'transformative encounter' with the Ghaznavids, Ghurids, Khaljis and 'perhaps even earlier with the Arabs', that is, with the Muslim conquerors. According to him, the Rāma narrative was a deliberate, 'representational instrument of choice' made by a communal consciousness, which deified the Hindu ruler and demonized the Muslim as the 'other'. B.D. Chattopadhyaya has countered these arguments in his *Representing the Other?: Sanskrit Sources and the Muslims*, Delhi, 1998, pp. 98–115. Pollock's essay reflects a trend in western scholarship which seeks to sidestep the role of colonial politics in the creation of homogenized and antagonistic Hindu and Muslim identities, and he tries to locate the roots of the Sangh Parivar's battle-cry for Hindutva in medieval Indian history.

[54] Nilakanta Sastri, *The Coḷas*, p. 115, 453.

55 Comparing the conception of Rāma rājya in the *Rāmāyaṇas* of Kamban and Tulsīdās, A.G. Menon and G.H. Schokker point out that while Kamban 'emphasizes the royal nature of the king/god, Tulsīdās stresses his divine aspect'. Menon and Schokker, 'The conception of Rāma Rājya in South and North Indian Literature', in A.W. Van Den Hock, D.H.A. Kola, M.S. Oorts (eds), *Ritual State and History in South Asia: Essays in Honour of J.C. Heesterman*, Leiden, 1992, p. 611.

56 K. Zvelebil, *The Smile of Murugan*, p. 208; Nagaswamy, op. cit., places him in the ninth century AD.

57 Nilakanta Sastri, *History of South India*, p. 377.

58 U.N. Ghoshal, *A History of Indian Political Ideas*, Madras, 1966, p. 25f.

59 For a detailed discussion, see S. Jaiswal, *Origin and Development of Vaiṣṇavism*, pp. 174–83.

60 U.N. Ghoshal, 'Hindu Theories of the Origin of Kingship and Mr. K.P. Jayaswal', *Indian Historical Quarterly*, Vol. I, 1925, p. 384.

61 K. Zvelebil, *The Smile of Murugan*, p. 210.

62 *Kamba Rāmāyaṇam*, I. 10, translated by H.V. Hande, Mumbai, Bharatiya Vidya Bhavan, 1996, pp. 41–50. The episode influenced later poets. For some other versions, see C. Bulcke, *Rāmakathā* (in Hindi), sixth revised edition, Allahabad, 1999, p. 286.

63 M.S. Purnalingam Pillai, *Tamil Literature*, Tinnevelly, 1929, p. 223, quoted by C. Bulcke, op. cit., p. 176. According to a story current in Kerala, Śiva was born as Kamban and wrote the *Kamba-Rāmāyaṇa*. Plays based on it are regularly enacted in the annual festivals celebrated in the Śiva temples of Kerala. K. Zvelebil, *The Smile of Murugan*, p. 209. However, according to another view, the Narasimha form of Viṣṇu was Kamban's family deity. H.V. Hande, op. cit., p. xxv.

64 Ibid., pp. 726–28.

65 Suvira Jaiswal, *Caste: Origin, Function and Dimensions of Change*, Delhi, 1998, pp. 56–57.

66 *Bālakāṇḍam*, Chapters 5 and 10, pp. 22, 57 and elsewhere.

67 *Ayodhyā Kāṇḍam*, Chapter 2; A.G. Menon and G.H. Schokker, op. cit., pp. 616–67.

68 *Yuddhakāṇḍam*, Chapter 39, translated by Hande, p. 752.

69 *Rāmāyaṇa* of Vālmīki, VII.73–76.

70 Ibid., VII.76.27.

71 R.S. Sharma, *Aspects of Political Ideas and Institutions in Ancient India*, third revised edition, Delhi, 1991, p. 233f.

72 *Bhagavadgītā*, III.35, XVIII.47. For the 'fixed' (*niyata*) nature of one's *karma*, see *Bhagavadgītā*, III.8.

73 *Raghuvaṃśa*, translated by G.R. Nandargikar, XV, 42–57.

74 Ibid., p. 478. Also see note 53 on the same page.

75 *Manusmṛti*, VIII, 318 (Pt. Gopala Sastri Nene, edited by fifth edition, Varanasi, 1997. A slightly changed version of this verse is found in the *Rāmāyaṇa* (IV.18.31). This is, however, considered to be an interpolation. See Bulcke, 1999, p. 493, note 1.

[76] *Paumacariyam*, edited by H. Jacob, Bhavnagar, 1914, Hindi translation by Shantilal M. Vora, Varanasi, 1962. References are to Parva 43.

[77] *Uttararāmacaritam*, Act II, edited by P.V. Kane and translated by C.N. Joshi, fourth revised edition, Delhi, 1962.

[78] C. Bulcke, *Rāmakathā*, p. 134.

[79] *Ānanda* Rāmāyaṇa, VII. 10.50–122, second edition, Mumbai, 1926.

[80] Henri Cousens, *List of Antiquarian Remains in the Central Provinces and Berar*, Calcutta, 1897, p. 7, quoted in Sheldon Pollock, op. cit., pp. 266–67.

[81] *Epigraphia Indica*, VIII, No. 2, p. 60f. R.S. Sharma thinks that the Sātavāhanas were 'improvised brāhmaṇas, which accounts for their zealous support of the brahmanical order' (*Aspects of Political Ideas and Institutions in Ancient India*, third revised edition, 1991, p. 288).

[82] J.F. Fleet, *Corpus Inscriptionum Indicarum*, Vol. III, London, 1888, reprint, Varanasi, 1963, No. 55.

[83] R.S. Sharma, *Early Medieval Indian Society: A Study in Feudalization*, Hyderabad, 2001, pp. 67–68.

[84] T.V. Mahalingam, *Inscriptions of the Pallavas*, Delhi, 1988, pp. 454–59.

[85] *Prapannāmṛta*, quoted by Bhagavati Prasad Singh, *Rāma Kāvya Dhārā Anusandhana aivaṃ Anuncintana*, Allahabad, 1976, p. 16.

[86] N. Ramesan, *The Tirumala Temple*, Tirupati, 1981, pp. 125–26.

[87] Bhagavati Prasad Singh, op. cit., p. 15.

[88] Bulcke, *Rāmakathā*, p. 119.

[89] Ibid.

[90] Ibid., pp. 131–32. Also see T.G. Manikar, *The Vasiṣtha Rāmāyaṇa: A Study*, New Delhi, 1977, p. 248. For the text, Rai Bahadur Lala Baij Nath's edition with a Hindi translation by Thakur Prasad, *Shri yogavaṣistha maharāmāyaṇa*, Bombay, 1903, 2 volumes.

[91] *Agastya Saṃhitā*, edited and translated into Hindi by Rāma Narayana Das, Lucknow, 1904.

[92] *The Adhyātma Rāmāyaṇa*, edited by Nagendranath Siddhantaratna, 2 volumes, Calcutta, 1935; English translation by Rai Bahadur Lala Baij Nath, Varanasi, 1979.

[93] R.G. Bhandarkar, op. cit., p. 48.

[94] Hans Bakker, op. cit., p. 68f.

[95] P.V. Kane, *History of Dharmaśāstra*, Vol. V, Part I, Poona, 1958, p. 88.

[96] R.G. Bhandarkar, op. cit., p. 67.

[97] Hans Bakker, op. cit., p. 71.

[98] *Agastya Saṃhitā*, 8.14–16, quoted ibid., p. 74.

[99] Frank Whaling, *The Rise of the Religious Significance of Rāma*, Delhi, 1980, p. 196.

[100] *Adhyātma Rāmāyaṇa*, VII. 5.2–7.

[101] Ibid., VII.6.2–5.

[102] *Skanda Purāṇa*, Avanti Khaṇḍa, Chapter 24; *Adhyātma Rāmāyaṇa*, II.6.65–88.

[103] Although little is known of Vālmiki's social origins, and Brahmanical texts

invariably give him a Brahmanical ancestry, some of these speak of him as having become a hunter, a robber, a great sinner and, at one place, even a *Brahmaghna*, the killer of a Brāhmaṇa. He was emancipated on practising severe ascetism for thousands of years and only then could he write the *Rāmāyaṇa*. Bulcke suggests that perhaps these myths disguise his low-caste origin. In the Bālakāṇḍa of Vālmīki's *Rāmāyaṇa*, Vālmīki having invented the *śloka* metre composes the *Rāmāyaṇa* in this verse form on the orders of the god Brahma and teaches it to his two Kuśālava disciples. Kuśālavas were bards, singers and actors of the lowly Śudrā status. Bulcke suggests that as the poem was originally sung and transmitted by them, they added the story of Kuśa and Lava being the sons of Rāma, giving their caste-name a new etymology. The low-caste association of Vālmīki led the Brahmanical composers to invent the myth of his having been a robber or hunter. Later, the rise of the Rāma-*bhakti* cult led to the introduction of the motif of the recitation of Rāma-name into this account, as given in the *Adhyātma Rāmāyaṇa*. Bulcke, *Rāmakathā*, pp. 25–35. However, in the *Bhaktamāla* of Nābhādāsa (*c.* AD 1600) Vālmīki is described as a Śvapaca (*Kavitta* 72, quoted in ibid., p. 33).

104 J.N. Farquhar, *Outline of the Religious Literature of India*, London, 1920, p. 323f; Hazari Prasad Dvivedi, *Kabīr*, eighth reprint, Delhi, 2000, p. 85.

105 For the *Adhyātma Rāmāyaṇa*, see Frank Whaling, op. cit., pp. 112–13.

106 H.P. Dvivedi, op. cit., pp. 84–85.

107 *Aṣṭādaśa Purāṇāni Rāmasya Caritāni ca, Bhāṣāyāṃ mānavaḥ śrutvā rauravam narakam vrajet.* Quoted by Bhabatosh Datta, 'The Rāmāyaṇa in Bengal', in V. Raghavan (ed.), *The* Rāmāyaṇa *Tradition in Asia*, 1980, p. 548.

108 Frank Whaling, op. cit., pp. 112–13.

109 V. Raghavan, 'The Rāmāyaṇa in Sanskrit Literature', p. 18, in Raghavan, ed., 1980.

110 C. Bulcke, *Rāmakathā*, p. 199.

111 Biswanarayan Shastri writes that the Assamese poet Mādhava Kandalī, who composed the *Rāmāyaṇa* in Assamese in the fourteenth century, claims that he had avoided interpolations and taken only the substance of Vālmīki. Unlike Tulsīdās and Kṛttivāsa he did not impose 'supreme divinity' on Rāma ('Rāmāyaṇa in Assamese Literature', in V. Raghavan, ed., 1980, pp. 584–86).

112 R.A. Dwivedi, *A Critical Survey of Hindi Literature*, Varanasi, 1966, pp. 53–54, quoted in Whaling, op. cit., p. 227.

113 *Rāmacaritmānas*, Bālakāṇḍa, p. 22, verses 5–6, and *doha* 15, edited with a commentary by Hanuman Prasad Poddar, Gorakhpur, 2001.

114 *Uttarakāṇḍa*, Bhuṣuṇḍi Samvāda, ibid., p. 998.

115 Ibid., p. 1018, verse 12.

116 Ibid., p. 936, verse 4.

117 Ibid., p. 983, *doha* 97k.

118 Hazari Prasad Dvivedi, op. cit., pp. 98–101.

119 Quoted in ibid., p. 98. See also ibid., p. 100, note 1.

120 *Bālakāṇḍa*, op. cit., p. 111.

121 *Sundara Kāṇḍa*, ibid., p. 733, verse 2. Also see *Bālakāṇḍa*, ibid., p. 57, and elsewhere.

122 Irfan Habib, 'Medieval Popular Monotheism and its Humanism: The Historical Setting', *Social Scientist*, Vol. 21, Nos 3–4, 1993, pp. 78–88.

123 S. Jaiswal, *Caste*, pp. 71–77.

124 Ibid., pp. 67–70.

125 M.N. Srinivas, in his article entitled 'The Dominant Caste in Rampura' (*The Dominant Caste and Other Essays*, Delhi, 1987), writes that in the multi-caste village of Rampura (near Mysore in Karnataka) the peasant caste of Okkaligas constitutes the dominant caste. Although they belong to the Śudrā *varṇa*, 'this does not mean much in Rampura, as there are no "genuine" Kshatriyas or Vaishyas.... While it is true that peasants are not ritually high, they command respect from everyone in the village including the priestly castes of Brahmins and Lingayats.' Extract included in Dipankar Gupta, ed., *Social Stratification*, Delhi, 1991, p. 309.

126 The Kākatīyas are described as belonging to the fourth *varṇa*. Pratāparudra Kākatīya was, however, a Sanskrit scholar and is supposed to have written a Sanskrit work entitled *Nītisāra*. One of the Kākatīya rulers laid claim to being a Kṣatriya and married a Brāhmaṇa girl (*South Indian Inscriptions*, Vol. X, No. 395), but such isolated claims remained inconsequential and did not give rise to a concrete category of the Kṣatriya groups in the South. For the failure of the emergence of Kṣatriya and Vaiśya *varṇas* in the South, see S. Jaiswal, 1998, pp. 61–70. Panegyrists of śudrā rulers and Śudrā communities in the South have often indulged in lavishing high praise upon this *varṇa*, claiming it to be even superior to the brāhmaṇa varṇa! Such hyperbole was possible only because empirically the so-called Śudrā castes were not insignificant in terms of economic and political power. See S. Jaiswal, *Caste*, p. 29, note 93 and p. 120, note 223.

127 P.V. Kane, *History of Dharmaśāstra*, Vol. I, pp. 640–41, 1930.

128 Ibid., pp. 383–86.

129 Edited by Gopinath Kaviraj, with an introduction by Narayana Sastri Khiste, 2 volumes, Varanasi, 1933 and 1936. According to Khiste, Śeṣa Kṛṣṇa also wrote *Kaṃsavadham* at the request of Giridhārī, son of Todarmalla, the celebrated finance minister of Akbar.

130 It is interesting to note that Kamalākara Bhaṭṭa, who wrote *Śudrā Kamalākara* in the seventeenth century, also belonged to a family of Dakṣiṇatya Brāhmaṇas. P.V. Kane, *History of Dharma*, Vol. I, 1930, p. 419.

131 Ibid., pp. 399–405.

132 '*Paṇḍit bād badante jhūṭhā. Rām kahyān duniyā gati pāve, khāṇḍ kahyān mukh mīṭhā.*' *Kabir Vāṇī*, No. 153, edited by H.P. Dvivedi, op. cit., p. 243.

133 Charlotte Vaudeville, *Kabir*, Vol. 1, Oxford, 1974, pp. 46ff; Irfan Habib, op. cit., p. 84.

134 K. Zvelebil, *The Smile of Murugan*, pp. 221–32.

135 G.S. Ghurye, *Gods and Men*, Bombay, 1962, p. 193, quoted in Frank Whaling, op. cit., p. 131.

136 *Agastya Saṃhitā*, 25.19, quoted in Bakker, op. cit., p. 6.

137 *Adhyātma Rāmāyaṇa*, IV.4.32–33, Lala Baijnath's translation, p. 99.

138 Quoted in Sheo Bahadur Singh, *Brahmanical Icons in Northern India*, New Delhi, 1977, pp. 83–84.

139 For example, the Penukonda temple of Anantapur district, Andhra Pradesh. See V. Kameshwar Rao, *Select Vijayanagar Temples of Rayalaseema*, quoted in P. Banerjee, op. cit., p. 212.

140 Mangalagiri pillar inscription of Kṛṣṇadevarāya, verses 31–32 and 47, quoted in P. Banerjee, op. cit., pp. 210–11.

141 *Rāmacaritmānas*, I.10 *khaṇd* mentions the recitation of the fame of Rāma and Sītā in the language of the rustics, which is sung and listened with great attention by the good and the wise (*sujana*); Gita Press, p. 15.

142 Ṭhākurbāḍī appears to be a literal translation of Sanskrit *devakula.*

143 Shukadeva Singh, 'Ramakathā: Aitihāsika Sāmājika Sandarbha', in Kunvarpal Singh, ed., *Abhinava Bharati Viśeṣāṅka*, 1991–92, p. 90.

# 4 Eros and History
## Sahajiya Secrets and the Tantric Culture of Love

*Nupur Chaudhuri and Rajat Kanta Ray*

The distinctiveness of a civilization derives in part from its culture of love. The erotic culture of a civilization, in turn, is rooted in its unique sex–gender system. Each sexual orthodoxy redefines, as a matter of course, its deviant mode.[1] No two gender systems are alike. Every gender system, indeed, seeks to channelize and control the force of libido, but it does so in its own particular manner.[2] Familial and social arrangements differ accordingly, as do the violations of these arrangements. The social formation is shaped thereby into many different formations. Al Biruni, the eleventh-century polymath, was aware of this. The fact that every society has its specific gender system, and its own erotic culture, finds mention in his account of the Hindus. By 'Hindus', he meant the Indians, and the category included in his eyes the 'Shamanyya', or the Buddhists.

Al Biruni's remarks deserve to be quoted in this context. No nation, said this keen investigator, can exist without a married life. The uproar of passions that might otherwise tear society apart dictates the necessity of this institution. 'Every nation has particular customs of marriage, especially those who claim to have a religion and law of divine origin.'[3] He then proceeds to describe the particular sex–gender system of the people governed by the Brahmanical codes, and notes with curiosity the prevalence of child marriage, the institution of life-long widowhood, the absence of divorce, and the then growing custom in India that every man must marry within his own caste. These things were not familiar to the Muslim world he knew.

As regards the specific erotic culture of the Hindus, he noted that homosexuality ('sodomy') was greatly abhorred at the time, immediately preceding the conversion of the Hindu ruler of Kabul to Islam. Marriage and sex, his account of the prevalent Garbhana ceremony implied, were oriented towards procreation. He dwelt on the fact that during the first four days of the wife's menstrual course, the husband was not allowed to cohabit with her, or even to come near her in the house, because during this time she was considered to be impure.[4] This account makes it clear that the Brahmanical codes, like the contemporary Islamic codes and the injunctions of the Christian church, sought to confine the erotic urge to heterosexual, genital and marital sex.[5] It is also evident that the Brahmanas laid special stress on procreative sex and on sex uncontaminated by menstrual impurities.

These Brahmanical values shaped the erotic culture of an entire subcontinent; and Islamic sexual norms, as they evolved in India, strengthened the same sexual orthodoxy. The use of sex for pleasure was admitted as a worthwhile goal, but only with the wife, and not during her period. Yunani physicians (*hakims*), Indian Muslims were told, forbid love in which 'the man is below and the woman above'.[6] Certainly, going to another man's wife (*aurat*) was considered to be shameful (*sharm*),[7] and it was laid down that the lawfully wedded wife of the Muslim household 'should cohabit only after her menstrual flow ceased and a bath had been taken'.[8]

Al Biruni was too observant a scholar not to notice some of the deviations from the prevalent sexual orthodoxy in India. He saw that Hindu kings had a habit of making courtesans an attraction for their cities, 'for no other than financial reasons'.[9] He also witnessed sexual preferences other than those of the men who followed the orthodox Hindu code. 'The catamites', he recorded, 'and the men who are incapable of enjoying the sex pleasure, the *Pushandilas*, who do the oral sex, swallowing the ejected semen, pity these (orthodox) men.'[10] Such actions were of course considered deviations from the norm. There were, however, other erotic deviations which had a religious sanction, and of which he was quite unaware, because of his limited scholarly access to the India of his times. He derived his information primarily from Brahmanical and Sanskritic sources, and not from the Buddhist and vernacular lore that was then flourishing in Eastern India and which was in the process of spreading to Tibet and inner Asia. Had he been able to tap these sources, he might have come across a secret, esoteric cult of love which reversed virtually all the prevalent Brahmanical norms.

The earliest contemporaneously recorded evidence of this esoteric, anti-Brahmanical cult is the collection of vernacular songs, known as the *Charyapadas*, which the pundit–cataloguer of the Bengal Library, Haraprasad Shastri, stumbled upon in the library of the Nepal Durbar in 1907.[11] They were written in a then unknown Indian vernacular language. Later on Prabodh Chandra Bagchi searched through the sacred Buddhist scriptures of Tibet and came across Tibetan translations of the songs discovered by Shastri. This was a source which helped in interpreting the concealed meaning of the songs, and the same source revealed that there had been many more *Charyapadas* (in all numbering about a hundred) than the ones discovered by Shastri. Subsequently, Rahul Sankrityayan discovered some more *Charyapadas* in a palm-leaf manuscript preserved in a Tibetan Buddhist monastery, but these were judged to be of a later date on linguistic grounds. Still more recently, Shashi Bhushan Dasgupta came across some *Charyapadas* which were judged to be older.[12] The secret literature thus discovered spanned Eastern India, Nepal and Tibet.

Debates among scholars[13] regarding the date of these songs established that they could not have been written earlier than the eighth century, nor later than the twelfth. However, the discovery of a contemporaneous manuscript of the *dohas* dated 1100–1101, which Prabodh Chandra Bagchi found in the Nepal Durbar library, indicated that the main body of the *Charyapadas* might have been composed in the tenth and eleventh centuries. Atisha Dipankara, who himself composed some *Charya* songs, available only in Tibetan translation, embarked on his journey to Tibet from the Vikramshila monastery around the year 1038. This was about twenty years after Al Biruni's exile to India by Sultan Mahmud of Ghazni. Even as the Turkish troopers from Ghazni spread devastation in upper India, lower down the Gangetic plains, the *Ċharya* composers continued to sing their esoteric songs among the peaceable rural folk.[14] Nor did the flow of pilgrims, both Indian and Tibetan, who carried the secret meanings of these songs in Sanskrit commentary and Tibetan translation across the Himalayas, stop immediately. When six generations later, the Khalji and Turkish troopers of Muhammad Ba<u>kh</u>tyār overran the great eastern plains, the songs and their secrets survived only in the cold upland desert across the high Himalayas.

As regards the identity of the vernacular in which the Buddhist *Siddhas* (adepts) composed their songs, it was thought at first, especially by European scholars of Shastri's generation, that the language was a form of Buddhist Prakrit, or Apabhramsa[15] (terms which were interchangeable at the time). Heraprasad Shastri demurred, and made the claim that this was an early form of Bengali, being its oldest surviving specimen. Suniti Kumar Chatterjee, in the first ever scientific study of the matter, concluded that the *Charyapadas* were written in a western dialect of the old Bengali language.[16] Rahul Sankrityayan rejected this, and put in a claim for Hindi. Scholars of Maithili, Oriya, Bengali and Assamese sought to appropriate the songs for their own respective languages. These languages were all derived from Magadhi Apabhramsa, the language that prevailed in Eastern India in late antiquity. The recent discovery of some clay tablets in lower West Bengal (*c.* 750–1200), the language of which is thought to be Bengali and akin to the language of the *Charyapadas*, has produced a renewal of the Bengali claim to the mysterious *Charya* songs, but the inscriptions on the earliest tablets contain no full sentences and the number of words, never more than six or seven,[17] are too few to arrive at a firm conclusion about the nature of the language.

The claims and counterclaims are, in a sense, historically misplaced. At the time in question, the differentiation of the modern Indian languages out of the parent stock of Prakrit or Apabhramsa dialects had not proceeded far enough to merit a serious consideration of the current disputes between the advocates of Hindi, Bengali and Oriya regarding the language of the *Charyapadas*. Contemporaries were not aware of such distinctions, and the modern vernacular languages did not assume firm shape until three centuries later. Al Biruni, in around 1030, perceived the language of Hind in terms of a simple distinction between the classical Sanskrit language used by the Brahmanas, 'and a neglected vernacular one, only in use among the common people'.[18] Three centuries later, the poet Amir Khusrau saw that this common language of the people had assumed differentiated regional contours, consisting now of Sindhi, Lahori, Kashmiri, the language of Dugar (Dogri), Dhur Samundar (Kannada), Tilang, Gujarat, Ma'bar (Tamil), Gaur, Bengal, Oudh and Delhi.[19] The Ladnun inscription (1316) made separate mention of Banga, Tilanga, Gurjara, Karnataka, Gauda and Pandyan, confirming the impression we gather from Amir Khusrau's text that the popular dialects of Gauda (North and West Bengal) and Banga (East Bengal) had still not consolidated into the common Bengali language of modern times.[20] The names 'Banga' and 'Bangali' are the only place and race names that occur in the *Charya* songs, a fact that Haraprasad Shastri took as proof for his claims. But, in fact, the names occur in a pejorative sense: 'No sooner did you take a wife from Banga than your knowledge vanished';[21] 'You, poor Bhusuku, have become a Bengali today, and have taken for wife a [low] Chandali.'[22]

Haraprasad Shastri found intelligible Sanskrit commentaries on the ambiguous vernacular songs in the palm-leaf manuscript itself. Tibetan translations subsequently discovered by Prabodh Chandra Bagchi made it clear that a *Siddha* ('the fulfilled one') named Munidatta had written these Sanskrit commentaries. Munidatta, who chose 50 *Charya* songs for comment soon after they had been composed, stated unambiguously that the songs were written in Prakrit.[23] What was more important, the commentator added, was that the songs were composed in 'the language of the twilight' (*sandhya bhasha*),[24] a sort of double language in which more than one secret sense could be concealed below the surface meaning.

For our purposes, the senses of the text (which was entitled *Ashcharya-charyachaya*)[25] may be classified into three logical groups: (i) the apparent sense grasped by the common folk who listened to the songs; (ii) the erotic sense which the more knowledgeable among them might understand and enjoy; and (iii) the esoteric Yogic sense which only the initiates could decode with the Guru's help. To illustrate these distinct senses, let us take the first line of a well-known and often-quoted song by Bhusukupada:[26]

*vaj nava padi pauna khale bahiu*

(i) The literal meaning is:
I set off on the 'Thunderbolt' boat
And sailed up the channel of the Padma.

(ii) The erotic meaning embedded in this is as follows:
My thunderlike organ pushed up
The vestibule of the lotuslike *mons Veneris.*

(iii) Munidatta's Sanskrit commentary[27] offers the following Yogic sense:
I entered into knowledge by means
of the true Guru's guidance.

The reference to the Padma, which was still the narrower channel (*khal*) of the immense Ganges, is reminiscent of the natural setting of the songs. The ecology is closely related to the social (or, in Brahmanical terms, 'anti-social') context of the *Charya* composers.

The villages and townships are precariously interspersed among marshes and forests in which wild beasts and hunters stalk one another and herds of deer.[28] The settlements are never far from bottomless rivers flowing deep and fast between slippery banks.[29] Individuals living on the margin between nature and society stand out sharply and vividly.

Among the highly individualistic portraits in the text, we may mention the hefty old oarswoman who ferries the passengers safely across the vast waters;[30] the aboriginal young huntress bold enough to spend the night with her lover in a cave up the deeply wooded hills;[31] the untouchable Dom woman who lives on the border of the town and sells wicker baskets for her living;[32] the polyandrous young woman of the toddy-tapper caste (*shundini*) who wears nothing but smooth tree bark as she moves about distilling liquor;[33] and the poor but philosophic milkman of the rickety cottage with no neighbour and no rice in his pot.[34]

Instead of putting on parade royalty, priesthood, warriors and celestial nymphs, the Sahajiya Buddhist *Siddhas*, who composed the *Charya* songs, brought into focus men and women in the lower walks of life, living on the margins of settled existence. This was unusual for the times, but by no means accidental. The fact is that the composers were closely acquainted with this section of society. The culture of love among the lowly and marginal individuals threatened the ordered society of the four orders (*varnas*), 36 castes (*jatis*) and the indefinite number of lineages (*kulas*) supposed to constitute every Brahmana-dominated settlement. The religious exercise (*sadhana*) of the *Siddhas* was a heterodox cult rooted in this defiant culture of love on the margins of society. The songs were composed by secretive Buddhists following the In-born Way (*Sahaja-yana*, a sect of Buddhists whose quest for liberation was based on locating and developing the in-born or *sahaja* powers of the body).

The kind of love (*pemha*)[35] and sex (*sanga*)[36] idealized by the *Siddhas* of the *Sahaja-yana* school was no less heterosexual and centred upon the genitals,[37] than what the Brahmanical legislators prescribe, but beyond that their paths diverge radically. The Brahmanical norms stress the maxim that a man takes a wife for producing a son,[38] and hold out the dire threat that the man who does not visit his wife for this purpose, when her menstrual cycle makes her ready for congress, becomes an animal in his next incarnation.[39] The Sahajiya Buddhist

*Siddhas*, on the contrary, seek release from the endless cycle of birth and rebirth, and they seek it in a love of the 'contrary' sort, in which there need be no 'issue'.[40] Once the need for a son is cancelled, the need for a married wife is sublated too.

What the Tantric practitioner of Yoga needed was a female partner, preferably outside marriage and outside his caste, who would help him in a difficult eroto-Yogic exercise (*sadhana*). The exercise involved *coitus reservatus* and its goal was the attainment of what is technically defined in the *Ashcharya-charyachaya* as *sahaja-ananda* (self-generated joy not caused by any external circumstance) or *maha-sukha* (the supreme bliss).[41]

For want of an equivalent from common experience, this is compared to the orgasm[42] produced by the exact fit (*sama-rata*) between the same-sized male and female organs. The common notion at the time was that this produced the highest bliss. Courtesans were supposed to earn merit (*dharma*) by conferring sexual favour on penniless men needing erotic treatment, wealth (*artha*) by consorting with rich men, and pleasure (*kama*) by uniting with men of the right genital size.[43] The Tibetan translation of the *Ashcharya-charyachaya*, being stripped of the multiple layers of meaning in the original Prakrit text, is unambiguous on the point:

> They have entered the war of the Thunderbolt and the Lotus,
> These soldiers of the Union of the same size.[44]

Gundaripada speaks of the sensation produced by the union of the Lotus and the Thunderbolt as a fire in the region around the navel, where the embedded nerve force, technically known as the *Chandali*, blazes forth.[45] Fulfilment in this exercise is not easy to attain and Yogic texts speak of a compliant female partner (*nari vashavartini*) as an essential requirement.[46] Gundaripada described in another song an extramarital affair in which the daughter-in-law escaped from the household to become the Yogini (female practitioner of Yoga) of a *Sadhaka* (practitioner of the exercise):

> Pressing down [on the penis] with your triangular zone [mons veneris], O Yogini, give me a tight embrace. By allowing the Thunderbolt to churn the Lotus, let us surmount the barrier of time. O Yogini, without you, it is impossible to survive even for a moment. Thrust out of your place, you can no longer be contained.

> Your sensation peaks and you enter your goal. Imprisòn your mother-in-law (alternatively, breath) using a strong padlock and disrupt the twin motions of the sun and the moon. Gundaripada proclaims that he has shown bravery through the practice of Kundura Yoga and the barrier of cloth has disappeared between man and woman.[47]

Gundaripada's Yogini was apparently a housewife who fled her home, leaving the mother-in-law locked up in the house. Later Sanskrit *Tantra* texts make it clear that there was no caste bar in this *sadhana.* Nine types of woman were named ideal as partner (*shakti*): a dance-woman (*Nati*), a Kapalik's daughter, a prostitute, a washer-woman, a barber's wife, a Brahmana woman, a Shudra woman, a milk-maid, and a flower woman. Indeed, any woman from a household specially experienced in the ways of men (*vishesa-vaidagdhya-yutah sarva eva kulanganah*)[48] would do – what was considered essential in *sadhana* was the worship of a woman who was not one's own, but 'one belonging to another man' (*parakiya*).[49] The woman who locked up her '*Sasu*' (mother-in-law, alternatively, breath) and escaped in order to become Gundaripada's Yogini was, accordingly, eminently fit to be a partner.

Yet another *Siddha* named Bhusukupada described his experience of sailing up the Padma and landing in Eastern Bengal (*Vangala*) to find an untouchable Chandal woman as his housekeeper (*gharani*).[50] He specially mentions that she brought him the supreme bliss, or *maha-sukha*, which men might experience through orgasm (or alternatively by an exercise in which the five senses are, in his own word, 'burned').[51] This, he said, was an experience in which the distinction between the living and the dead disappears (*jivante maile nahi vishesa*), a state strongly suggestive of the *fanà* (annihilation), with which the Sufi saints in Khurasan at the time were familiar. Indeed, it is sometimes speculated that forms of Tantric Buddhism prevalent in Central Asia prior to the expansion of Islam in that region might have been instrumental in passing on the 'secrets' to the incoming adepts of Sufism (*Tasawwuf*).[52]

Among the sharply etched female partners who find mention in the palm-leaf manuscript preserved in the Nepal Durbar, a Dom woman is celebrated in no less than three songs. Krishnapada, the unusually explicit composer, is mentioned in Tibetan sources as a native of Orissa. This is how Krishnapada introduces the great love of his life:

> O you Domni; You live outside the town,
> You, you reach out and touch the tonsured
> Brahman whenever you get a chance. Come Domni,
> let me unite with you. I am a shameless Kapalik, a naked Jogi . . .
> O my Domni, you sell looms and wicker baskets, for you I am willing to forsake this stage of a world. You are a Domni, I am a Kapalik, for you I have donned the necklace of bones.

Bringing her under control is a difficult exercise. Kanha resolves, at the end of the first song, to kill the Domni and take her life.[53] In the second song, he finds her alive and well, a shameless woman with her nose metaphorically cut off (*Dombi to agali nahi chhinali*).[54] The girl is capable of sending every man on the chase. Kanha, among them all, is asleep in his orgasmic state (*mahasukha lila*). In the third song, he proceeds to marry the Domni to the deafening accompaniment of drums. The ceremony over, he spends all night in the dense vapour of her erotic emanations. Unable to get a wink of sleep in course of the nocturnal and day-long motions of love, he finds that no man who has ever engaged with her is able to break out of the mad spell. Her infidelities are legion. He is trapped in a marriage without any issue.[55] It is a relationship in which she keeps scores of householders hovering outside, and a homeless Kapalik at home.[56] The 'marriage' itself is nothing but defiance hurled at a caste-bound society.

Despite the commentator Munidatta's hint that a particular Yoga was being mastered by Kanhapada, nowhere do these or any other songs in the *Ashcharya-charyachaya* explain what the eroto-Yogic exercises were exactly. Sanskrit works of a later date speak of *coitus reservatus*, and suggest procedures for recovery of any semen that might be spilt. Unite with her, advises a much clearer late Sanskrit text used by Bengali Hindu Tantriks, as soon as her menstrual flow starts (*rtau sati*); and during the union draw up spilt semen and her menstrual fluid through the shaft of your penis. To subjugate her, control breath and take her three, five, seven or nine times every day, and on each occasion give her strokes with your organ two, three or six times.[57] The exercises vary a great deal. A medieval Sanskrit text in use among the Yogis hints at similar exercises,[58] but the *Charyapadas* are more reticent in the matter. The Sanskrit Tantric texts current in medieval

Bengal seem to suggest that among the more conventional Brahmanical circles which embraced *Tantra* and made it more orthodox, there was no bar on the spilling of seminal fluid during intercourse,[59] as there certainly was among the heterodox sects of Bauls and Yogis.[60] The exact differences in the eroto-Yogic practices remain elusive. Significantly, however, the Bauls had no issue; the Tantriks did. It is likely that the eroto-Yogic exercise underwent transmutations during the passages through place, time and sect. However, these changes can no longer be traced with any certainty in the records. The picture we get in the *Ashcharya-charyachaya* is one of illicit, but strongly bonded pairs, who secretly pursued the *sadhana* as a single couple. In later times the Bauls of Bengal alone seem to have preserved this tradition intact, especially through the lineages (*silsilas*) of heterodox (*Beshara*) Muslim fakirs. These heterodox lineages might be traced back to Sahajiya Buddhist *Siddhas* who were compelled to conceal themselves among the incoming Sufis during the troubled period of the Turkish campaigns.[61] Shortly after the manuscript of the Nepal Durbar library had been transcribed, the Khalji raiders are said to have devastated the Buddhist monasteries in Eastern India. The Sahajiya Buddhist secrets, which had originated in the hot and densely wooded Gangetic plains, shifted to the cold highland desert of Tibet. Carefully preserved through translation in the Tibetan *Tengur*,[62] the *sadhana* had to adjust to a different set of conditions, especially a polyandrous society, an organized complex of Lamaist monasteries, and an art inspired by the religious conceptions of Yab and Yum. In the plains where Sahajiya Buddhism never recovered from the blow, the secrets were reworked into a Brahmanical framework which sanskritized and appropriated them in the Sanskrit *Tantras*.

What the postures and motions prescribed in the eroto-Yogic exercises of the *Sajaha-yana* in Tantric Buddhism might have been, is therefore, shrouded in profound obscurity. Evidence from later times and from other lands seems to suggest a reversal of the conventional sexual role. Conventionally, the female is a passive partner. But there is hard evidence of deviation from this assumption in late medieval Tantrism. Even earlier, at the time when scores of *Siddhas* were churning out *Charya* songs in a game of hide-and-seek with their puzzled audience, a more active role for women is unambiguously recorded by Al Biruni: 'They (i.e. the Hindus) perform coitus, both standing, like post and vine, the women moving up and down, as if occupied in ploughing, whereas the husband quietly relaxes.'[63] Al Biruni implied that this was the marital convention in the normal Indian household. In washing, he said, Indians begin with the feet, and then wash the face. They wash themselves before cohabiting with their wives. Then they perform the sex act standing like the support of the vine, while women move from the bottom upward in plough-like motions.

From the glimpses of Indian married life in the forbidding Dharmashastras, it seems that Al Biruni mistakenly generalized a more specific erotic experience in a certain quarter, which could be no other than the courtesan's mansion. Elsewhere he speaks of prostitution at temples, courts and towns, where this practice might have flourished, but not perhaps in the normal Hindu household. Kanhapada's Domni, a woman of the singing and dancing class (Dom), and a highly skilled dancer, hailed from a disreputable quarter. His songs hint at her active role in the married bed/Yogic exercise,[64] though we can no more than speculate upon what he meant.

What is more explicit is the visual evidence of frescoes in the Lamaist monasteries of Bhutan, Sikkim, Nepal, Ladakh and Tibet. In those representations of the Tantric eroto-Yogic exercise, the typical Yab–Yum posture[65] closely resembles the Indian 'marital' practice specified by Al Biruni. Later Sahajiya manuscripts in use among the Bauls of Bengal specify a ritual posture in which even the equality of the Yab–Yum standing posture is left behind, and the *shakti* sits upon the horizontal *sadhaka*.[66] Representations of Kali standing upon the corpse-like Shiva in the illuminated manuscripts of India and Nepal also spring to mind in this context.[67]

In this connection, we may note that Tantrism got the seal of approval from the Brahmana Pandits, as the Buddhist *Siddhas* disappeared from the Gangetic valley. The *Dabistan-i Mazahib*, a seventeenth-century Persian account of religious sects, confirms this. It describes the *shaktis*, whose scriptures taught the six circles (*shat shakra*), as a flourishing Hindu cult:

> In many places and among a great number of the Hindus, this worship exists: a great many follow the Agama, in which wine drinking is approved, and if, instead of a common cup, a man's skull (which they call kapala) be used, the beverage is much more agreeable. They hold the killing of all animals, even of a man, to be permitted and call it *bala*. At night they go to places which they call

> *smasana*, and where the dead bodies are burnt; there they intoxicate themselves, eat the flesh of the corpses burnt, and copulate before the eyes of others with women, which they call *Sakti puja*; and if the devoted woman be that of another, the good work is so much more valuable, and it is certain that they offer their wives to each other; the disciples bring their wives and daughters to their preceptor; they unite with their mothers, sisters, paternal and maternal aunts, which is against the custom of the Hindus, who do not take daughters of near relations. . . . This sect holds women in great esteem and calls them *Saktis* (powers); and to ill treat a *sakti*, that is, a woman, is held a crime.[68]

The medieval Sanskrit *Tantras* composed by Brahmanas confirm many of the lurid details, and there is an injunction that if other women are not available, one's own daughter, sister, aunt, mother, or mother's co-wife be worshipped as a *shakti*.[69]

The eroto-Yogic exercise, which we have traced from late antiquity into the high medieval period, might be divided into what Brahmanical Tantrism defined later on as the Right Hand and the Left Hand. The Right Hand confined themselves to *ekak sadhana*, while the Left Hand were involved in *yugal sadhana*. When a *sadhak* (performer of exercise) pursued the *sadhana* (exercise) himself, without the assistance of a *sadhan-sangini* (female partner-in-exercise), it was called *ekak sadhana*, or exercise on one's own. When, however, the *sadhak* pursued the exercise with the help of a female partner known as *shakti* (a woman embodying power), it became *yugal sadhana*, or 'exercise as a couple'. It should be noted in this context that in late antiquity, when the *Charya* songs were being composed, the Kanphata Yogis of Gorakhnath pursued *sadhana* singly,[70] while the Sahajiya Buddhist *Siddhas*[71] and their partners practised *sadhana* as couples.[72] Later on, Brahmanical Tantrism formalized the distinction as Right Hand and Left Hand. The *dakshinachari* or Right-Hand Tantrik pursued the *sadhana* without a sex partner (*shakti*). On the other hand, the *vamachari*, or Left-Hand Tantrik, had a female partner to assist him sexually.

In both types of *sadhana*, the exercise was centred upon the body and the eroto-Yogic objective was the same – Supreme Bliss (*maha-sukha*). For want of a sensible equivalent, this may be compared to a kind of super-orgasm, attained within the universe that is the body. The essence of the *Yoga* (Union) was to induce the serpent power, an energy located in the region between the rectum and the organ, to rise along the spinal column and penetrate to the top of the cranium. This was imagined as the union between the rising serpent and the topmost lotus (there were other lotuses penetrated by the serpent during its ascent). It happened within the body, with or without the aid of the female partner. Three exercises were commonly used for achieving this union within the Yogi's body. They were: (i) breath control (*pranayama*), (ii) sexual intercourse with a female partner (*shakti-sadhana*), with or without *coitus reservatus* (*ulta piriti*),[73] and (iii) ingestion of body fluids (*charichandra-bheda*), preferably, performed by exchange between the partners.

In the late medieval period, we find the Bauls of Bengal, both Muslim and Hindu, pursuing all three exercises together, and the Vamachari Hindu Tantriks doing only *pranayama* and *shakti-sadhana* to the exclusion of *charichandra-bheda*. The Sufis and the Nath Jogis, on the other hand, mostly confined themselves to breath-control exercises and had no resort to female partners or body fluids.

The surprising resemblances in the body-centric breath-control exercises of both *Tasawwuf* and *Yoga Tantra* might have a common origin, which could be the earlier and secret Buddhist exercises hinted at in the *Charya* songs. In fact, the Sufis of Iran and Central Asia were adepts in breath-control exercises, even before Islam came to India. In this connection it is interesting to note that Buddhism was prevalent in Central Asia before the region's conversion to Islam. From Al Biruni's account,[74] it would appear that the Shamaniyya were still remembered in his time. It has accordingly been speculated that the commonality of breath-control exercises in *Tasawwuf* and Tantrism might have had a common source in the Tantric Buddhism that had earlier been prevalent in Trans-Oxiana (Mawara-un Nahar). The expansion of Islam from Arabia to Ajam was accompanied and preceded by the spread of Buddhism to Tibet and Central Asia. An interaction between *Tasawwuf* and Tantrism (in its Buddhist version) before the coming of Islam to India cannot therefore be ruled out. In any case, the body-centric eroto-Yogic exercise was common to the Sahajiya Buddhist *Siddhas*, Sufis, Kanphata Yogis, Tantriks, Sahajiya Vaishnavas and Bauls (both Hindu and Muslim). Breath control by itself, or coupled with *shakti-sadhana*, was designed to achieve the super-orgasmic liberation produced by the union of the powers lying within the body at its opposite ends, namely the rectum and the cranium.

The Buddhist *Siddhas* of *Vajra-yana* (Thunder Path) and *Sahaja-yana* (Inborn Way) practised both breath control and a form of sexual intercourse, but the sources seem to indicate that the erotic exercise might not quite have been the same as the one we find in later Hindu Tantrism. The *Ashcharya-charyachaya* contains no explicit hint whether the *Siddhas* practised *coitus reservatus*, but one *Siddha*, Sarahapada, does exhort himself, 'Row upstream' (*sonte ujaa*),[75] in a well-known metaphor for semen retention during intercourse. If the *Siddhas* were secretive, there must have been a reason for it. In view of the practices prevailing among the *Darveshi* (Muslim) and Vaishnava (Hindu) Bauls and their direct lineal descendants, they are not unlikely to have practised 'reverse love' (*coitus reservatus*). What we do know is that the more orthodox Tantriks of the Brahmanical persuasion did not systematically practise *coitus reservatus* as the principal part of the exercise, for there are unambiguous references in the Sanskrit *Tantra* texts to the spilling of semen.[76] In any case, there was no bar against having offspring among the Tantriks (as there was among the Bauls).

The *Charya* composers are silent on, and probably unfamiliar with, a feature that emerges in later Brahmanical Tantrism. This is the circle (*chakra*). In the *Charya* songs we glimpse the joint *sadhana* of strongly bonded couples who are devoted to each other. The *Siddha* and his beloved invariably live in a house of their own. There is no collective mingling of several men and women in a hidden conclave on the cremation ground. It is quite otherwise with orthodox Hindu Tantrism as it evolved later on. Akshay Kumar Datta, who investigated Tantric practices in the nineteenth century, speaks of secret female circles.[77] These were big mixed circles which the Brahmana and Kayastha landlords patronized. Tantric circles were quite unlike the obscure and lowly Baul pairs whom Datta also investigated. The Baul couples probably preserved the Sahajiya *sadhana* of the Buddhist *Siddhas* in a more authentic form. Typically, the Baul lived with his female partner in a home of his own.[78]

The Tantric circle came alive at night, set in motion by riotous indulgences which were prohibited by day. These were the five M's, viz., *Madya* (liquor), *Mamsa* (meat), *Matsya* (fish), *Mudra* (snacks accompanying liquor), and *Maithuna* (sexual intercourse). Indulging in these by day would have invited censure. So, the *Tantras* advised that Vedic rituals should be practised by day, and Tantric rituals by night.[79]

They would have to resort to deceit and must feign to act as conventional members of society in order to preserve the secrecy of their practices.

This is how the circle is formed. A woman deemed to be the black goddess Kali in person is placed at the centre. Men and women in couples sit around her in a circle. In this circle, all castes mingle. Some of the female partners (*shaktis*) might belong to the lowest orders. The women should consider their male partners in the circle as their true husbands, and cease to regard their lawful husbands as spouses. However, this relationship obtains only within the circle and not outside of it. The consecrated women are urged to act like prostitutes in order to satisfy their male partners. The Tantric, as opposed to the Vedic, husband is deemed to be Lord Shiva in person. It would not be a sin to desert one's husband at the time of worship. But as soon as the circle dissolves, these relationships cease. The lawfully wedded husband becomes the master once again, and he takes over as the rightful partner in the discharge of obligations dictated by the Vedas.[80]

This is how the *Kularnava Tantra* describes the activities in the circle as the night wears on. The Yogis and Yoginis get into a drunken stupor. They indulge in whatever takes their fancy. The men begin to dance with the liquor vessels on their heads. The women clap their hands and join the men with staggering steps. The drunken woman takes another man to be her husband. As she goes over to him, the man receives her in a fit of wild rapture. Then comes the finale: 'Stupefied by wine, the Yoginis fall on the men and they happily fulfil one another's desires.'[81]

The cult around the eroto-Yogic exercise introduced by the *Siddhas* of Sahajiya Buddhism caught the popular imagination and became sufficiently powerful for orthodox Hinduism to try and absorb it by a ritual compromise based on the deceitful distinction between day and night. Vedic rituals were assigned to day, and Tantric rituals to night. For the woman of the Brahmanized cult, it was laid down specifically that she 'should not desert her lawfully wedded husband (*vivahita pati*) in the (daily Vedic) rites';[82] but she would incur no sin if she abandoned him for the Tantric husband (*agamokta pati*) during the worship at night. Orthodoxy was thereby redefined and reinforced. The eroto-Yogic exercise, now absorbed within the Brahmanical fold, and defined as *Kaula* (Tantric heterodoxy), was set off from its other, technically redefined as *Vaidik* (Vedic orthodoxy).

In popular Islam, as it spread to Bengal, a similar process was at work and this gave rise to the technical distinction between *Shariati* (orthodox path based on the Qur'an and Hadith) and *Marfati* (heterodox path shown by the *be-shar'a* dervishes). Within the *Vaidik–Shariati* complex, designed to uphold the world (*samsara/duniya*) and propagate the species, there continued to exist an eroto-Yogic outlet towards liberation from the world's bonds. Sahajiya Buddhism, wiped out by the onslaught of orthodox Hinduism and Islam, obtained an inverted victory by its penetration of the conventional religions.

Beyond the world of controlled domestic sex, there lay a secret, wild, turbulent, erotic universe, with no nationality, no racial identity and no social distinction. It subverted whatever civilization stood for at the time and bespoke of another culture of love. The women of that cult could enter into and exit from the secret world with equal ease, remaining a part of the structured world by day and becoming partners in wild orgiastic release by night. At night a person could be everything he or she could not be by day. Whatever the structured world denied to the individual who was straining at the bonds, she or he would obtain in a secret universe where procreation was not a duty and the propagation of the biological and social species not a consideration. Characterized by a highly individualistic, and almost unsocial pursuit of supreme bliss, the eroto-Yogic exercise created by night an equal society in which all social distinctions were temporarily forgotten.

To sum up the evidence, the first sign of this hidden world may be detected in secret *sadhana* of the *Sahaja-yana* sect of Buddhism, and its earliest surviving relic is the *Ashcharya-charyachaya* manuscript discovered by Haraprasad Shastri in the Nepal Durbar library. The cult was probably very different then from what it became later. At one time, this secret universe might have extended its sway from Bengal to Tibet and Central Asia. The hidden world shifted, contracted, expanded, evolved, metamorphosed. But it was unmistakably there, its trail in history deliberately obfuscated by 'the language of the twilight' (*sandhya-bhasha*).

The heterosexual, genital, marital, procreative, caste-bound, inter-menstrual, man-above-woman union prescribed by the orthodox code was meant to ensure the continuation of the lineage (*kula*), the reproduction of the world (*samsara*), and the upholding of caste and the ordered way of life (*varnashrama dharma*). The love (*pemha*) and sex (*sanga*) secretly taught by the Tantric gurus was no less uncompromising in its objective of the heterosexual uniting of the genitals to the exclusion of other sexual pleasures, but beyond that it differed radically in its extramarital, non-reproductive, anti-caste ideal, with a propensity towards intra-menstrual union in upstanding or woman-above-man posture. The visitor from abroad, Al Biruni, might have chanced upon the upstanding posture, but he did not uncover the secret behind it. What he was told was the conventional injunctions of the Brahmanas about the way men and women should relate to each other.

What he deduced unerringly from his exposure to a differently constructed world was that the gender system of one land might differ considerably from that of another. Furthermore, he deduced that the gender system might evolve over time within the same culture. He described this discovery in a striking manner:

> However, I must not reproach the Hindus only with their heathen practices, for the heathen Arabs too committed crimes and obscenities. They cohabited with menstruating and pregnant women; several men agreed to cohabit with the same woman in the same period of menstruation; they adopted the children of others, of their guests, of the lover of their daugher, not to mention that in some kinds of worship they whistled on their fingers and clapped with their hands, and that they ate unclean and dead animals. Islam has abolished all those things among the Arabs, as it has also abolished them in those parts of India the people of which have become Muhammadans. Thanks be unto God.[83]

Shorn of the ethical judgements, this contains an ancient insight into the relativity of eros and the passage of time. Even though 'the language of the twilight' conceals the passage of eros through time, there are fleeting glimpses that suggest important transformations in the culture of love. The secret cult we have come across was part of a protest against the predominant gender ideology, which emphasized intercourse with the wife alone, in the man-above-woman position, for the specific purpose of procreation, and during the period when she was 'clean'. The Sahajiya Buddhist *Siddhas* of late antiquity practised heterosexual intercourse, too, but there the similarity ended; their *sadhana* was built on intercourse with a female partner of low caste, who was not the wife, and in a non-conventional posture. This love moved 'upstream', to unite the powers at the opposite ends of the body. The propagation of the species was not the aim; nor was menstruation a bar. Initially, the *sadhana* was pursued by couples in their own homes. Brahmanical Tantrism, as it appropriated the *sadhana*, invented the circle, and thereby transformed the cult in the high medieval period. A protestant cult became orthodox, even as it became more and more riotous; and though the sanskritized Tantrism permitted progeny, the violation of convention persisted through this transformation of eros.

Love exists in all ages, but is never the same. The nature of eros cannot be grasped without its history, a history specific to place, time and station in life. That is the key to the splitting of love between high and low, Vedic and Tantric, day and night, open and secret. The secret component evolves, too, just as the open does; for they interact tensely, all the time.

**Notes and References**

1 On the deviant variety of India's culture of love, which is explored in this essay, see Mircea Eliade, *Yoga: Immortality and Freedom*, Princeton, 1971; Edward C. Dimock, *The Place of the Hidden Moon: Erotic Mysticism in the Vaishnava Saahajiya Cult in Bengal*, Chicago, 1966; Sanjukta Gupta, Teun Goudrian and Dirk Jan Hoens, *Hindu Tantrism*, Leiden, 1979; Jeanne Openshaw, *Seeking Bauls of Bengal*, Cambridge, 2002.

2 For this argument, see Rajat Kanta Ray, *Exploring Emotional History: Gender, Mentality and Literature in the Indian Awakening*, New Delhi, 2001.

3 Edward C. Sachau (ed.), *Alberuni's India: An account of the religion, philosophy, literature, geography, chronology, astronomy, customs, laws and astrology of India about AD 1030*, reprint, New Delhi, 1983, Vol. II, p. 154.

4 Ibid., p. 156.

5 See in this context Gulia Leslie, 'Some Traditional Indian Views on Menstruation and Female Sexuality', and Patricia Crawford, 'Sexual Knowledge in England 1500–1750', both in Roy Porter and Mikulas Teich (eds), *Sexual Knowledge, Sexual Science: The History of Attitudes to Sexuality*, Cambridge, 1994, pp. 77, 93.

6 '*Marad niche thake oupare aurat/hakimera mana kare e rup sohabat*', unknown Bengali author, *Sahi Elaje Lokmani Ba Lajjate Duniya* (n.d., n.p.), printed poetical work in *Dobhashi* or *Musalmani Bangla* (nineteenth century), p. 5.

7 Ibid., p. 6.

8 '*Hayejer muddat jabe gojaria jabe/Gosal karile tabe Sohabat karibe*', ibid., p. 5.

9 *Alberuni's India*, II, p. 157.

10 Edward Sachau, translating this sentence from Al Biruni's Arabic original, fastidiously switched over from English to Latin. We have retranslated the

Latin into English with the help of Father P. Bronckers, S.J., and Father Adrian Wavreil, S.J., of the Jesuit Society of Calcutta. Ibid., I, p. 181.

[11] Haraprasad Shastri published these *Charyapadas*, serially numbered 50 (but a part of number 23 and all of 24, 25 and 48 were missing), in 1916. He included in this certain other materials, including two collections of *dohas*. The whole was published as a book by the Bangiya Sahitya Parishad of Calcutta in 1916. We have used the following edition: Haraprasad Shastri (ed.), *Hajar Bachharer Purana Bangla Bhashay Bauddha Gan o Doha*, introduced by Bratindra Nath Mukherjee, Mahabodhi Society, Calcutta, 2000.

[12] See B.N. Mukherjee's introduction, ibid., pp. 1–50.

[13] For the development of the debate on the language and date of the vernacular manuscripts found in Nepal (including the *Charyapadas*), see C. Bendal, *Subhashita Samgraha*, Brussells, 1905; Haraprasad Shastri, *Hajar Bachharer Purana Bangala Bhashay Bauddha Gan o Doha*, Calcutta, 1916; Suniti Kumar Chatterjee, *The Origin and Development of the Bengali Language*, London, 1926; Muhammad Shahidullah, *Les Chantes Mystique de Kanha et de Sraha*, Paris, 1928; P.C. Bagchi, 'Materials for a Critical Edition of the Old Bengali Charyapadas' (a comparative study of the Text and Tibetan Translation), *Journal of the Department of Letters*, Calcutta University, Vol. XXX, 1938; Rahul Sankrityayana, *Hindi Kavyadhara* (in Hindi), Allahabad, 1945; Sukumar Sen, *Charyagiti-Padavali* (in Bengali), Calcutta, 1956; P.C. Bagchi and Shanti Bhikshu Shastri, *Charyagiti-kosha of the Buddhist Siddhas*, Shantiniketan, 1956; Rahul Sankrityayana, *Dohakosha* (in Hindi), Patna, 1957; Tarapada Mukherjee, *The Old Bengali Language and Text*, Calcutta, 1963; Aloka Chattopadhyay, *Atisa and Tibet*, Calcutta, 1967; Per Kvaerne, *An Anthology of Buddhist Tantrik Songs: A Study of the Charyagiftis*, Oslo, 1977; Shashi Bhushan Dasgupta, *Nava Charyapada* (in Bengali), edited by Asit Kumar Bandyopadhyay, Calcutta, 1989; B.N. Mukherjee, 'New Epigraphic and Paleographic Discoveries', in *Pratnagamiksha*, Vol. I, edited by G. Sen Gupta, Calcutta, 1992; Saiyad Ali Ahsan, *Charyagitika (Baudhda Gan o Doha)* (in Bengali), second edition, Dacca, 1997; Nirmal Das, *Charyagiti Parikrama* (in Bengali), Calcutta, 1997.

[14] A *Charyapada*, it should be stressed, is a song and not merely a poem. Song no. 2 of Shastri's collection specifically says: 'Kukkuripada sang this kind of *Charya*' (*aisana charya Kukkuripae gaira*), ibid., p. 46. Tibetan sources also mention that Atisha Depankara not only composed the songs, but sang them himself. See Bratindranath Mukherjee's introduction to Shastri, op. cit., p. 17.

[15] C. Bendal, *Subhashita Samgraha*, Brussells, 1905, discussed in ibid.

[16] Suniti Kumar Chatterjee, *The Origin and Development of the Bengali Language*, reprint, London, 1970, first published in 1926, p. 117.

[17] For an argument in favour of Bengali, see Bratindranath Mukherjee, *Banga, Bangala o Bharata*, Calcutta, 2000, pp. 53–62; also B.N. Mukherjee, 'New Epigraphic and Paleographic Discoveries', *Pratnagamiksha*, Vol. 1, 1992, pp. 135–54.

[18] *Alberuni's India*, Vol. I, p. 19.

[19] *Nuh Sipihr* of Amir Khusrau, in H.M. Elliott and John Dowson (eds), *The History of India as Told by its Own Historians*, reprint, Allahabad, 1964, Vol. III, p. 556; and *Ashiqa* of Amir Khusrau in Elliot and Dowson, Vol. III, p. 562.

[20] Rajat Kanta Ray, 'Bangali: Ke, Kabe ebam Kena', *Desh*, 11 November 2000, pp. 21–30.

[21] Song no. 39 by Sarahapada, in Shastri, op. cit., p. 103.

[22] Song No. 49 by Bhusukupada, in Shastri, op. cit., p. 116. Advocate of the notion that the *Charya* songs were composed in Bengali have an explanation for the pejorative use of the terms Bangal and Bangali. According to them, the language of the songs was the West Bengal dialect, and West Bengalis used to make fun of East Bengal (originally Bangal referred to East Bengal) and the East Bengalis (even nowadyas called Bangals in fun). This argument is misleading. As we have noted above, Gauda and Banga were separate countries at the time, and there was no common Bengali language. The vernacular languages had not yet taken distinct shape in 1000.

[23] '*Prakr (ta) – Bhasaya rachayitum*'. Shastri, op. cit., p. 42.

[24] Ibid., p. 46.

[25] The Sanskrit commentary states that the title of the text was *Ashcharya-charyachaya* (ibid., p. 41). Haraprasad Shastri named the collection *Charyacharya-vinishchaya*, but nowhere does this title occur in the MS.

[26] Song no.49, Shastri, op. cit., pp. 116–17.

[27] *Prajna-aravinda-kuhara-hrade sad-guru-charana-upayena praveshitam*, Munidatta, ibid., p. 117.

[28] See the following songs in Shastri, op. cit., nos 6, 23, 27, 28.

[29] Song no. 5. The thought of drowning in the depth of these rivers is constantly present in the mind of the composers, and there is the memory of sweeping currents suddenly overflowing the banks (Song no. 38). No one could afford to be forgetful of the crocodiles which infested the dreadful waters (Song no. 2).

[30] Song no. 14.

[31] Song no. 28.

[32] Song no. 10.

[33] Song no. 3. She keeps house for two lovers with separate households.

[34] Song no. 33.

[35] '*Pemha rati pohaili*', 'You spent a night of love', Shabarapada (Song no. 28).

[36] *A lo Dombi toye sama karibe ma sanga*, 'Come, Dombi, I will have sex with you', Kanhapada (Song no. 10).

[37] No other type of sexual pleasure than the uniting of the male and female organs is conceived. The frequent use of the metaphor of the Thunderbolt and the Lotus conveys this unmistakably.

[38] A Sanskrit proverb reads, 'One takes a wife for begetting a son. A son is necessary for food after one's death.' (*Putrarthe kriyate bharya/Putrah pinda-prayojanah*).

[39] 'He who does not visit his wife after her period, becomes an animal in his

next incarnation' (*Ritu-snatam-cha yo bharyam na adhigachchhati/ tyaktva kalevaram sa-api pashu-yonau cha jayate*).

[40] 'I married the Dom woman and put an end to (literally ate up) birth (*Dombi bihahia ahariu jama*), Krishnapada. '*Utpada-bhanga-adi dosa nashitah*', Munidatta. Song no. 19, Shastri, op. cit.

[41] Song no. 27, ibid.

[42] The ICS officer John Woodroffe, who is commonly recognized as having mastered the secrets with the help of a Tantric Guru, remarks: 'By the term Samarasya is meant the sense of enjoyment arising from the union (Samarasya) of male and female. This is the most intense form of physical delight representing on the worldly plane the Supreme Bliss arising from the union of Siva and Sakti on the "Spiritual plane".' *The Serpent Power*, Madras, 1989, first edition, 1918, pp. 238–29.

[43] Damodar Gupta, *Kuttanimatam*, Sanskrit text with Bengali translation by Tridib Nath Roy, Calcutta, 1953, p. 129.

[44] Alternatively, 'These soldiers of the Yoga of Equation', Shastri, op. cit., p. 53. This is the Tibetan translation of Song no. 48, of which the original, by Kukkuripada, is missing in the Nepal Durbar library MSS.

[45] Song no. 37, Shastri, op. cit., See also the Sanskrit commentary by Munidatta.

[46] *Hathayoga-Pradipika*, III, 26.

[47] Song no.4, Shastri, op. cit. This is the erotic sense. The Yogic sense, an obscure breath-control exercise, can be explicated only by a Guru.

[48] *Gupta-Sadhana-Tantra*, edited by Harichara Sadhak, Calcutta, 1886, pp. 2–3; Krishnananda Agambagish, *Vrihat Tantrasara*, (*c.* seventeenth-century Sanskrit text), edited by Rasikmohan Chattopadhyay, Calcutta, 1991, p. 104.

[49] '*Parakiya-narim dikshitam pujayet*', ibid., p. 704.

[50] Song no. 49, Shastri, op. cit.

[51] Arthur Avalon (pseudonym of Sir John Woodroffe) says that this is a *sadhana* for sublimating the sexual force, which ordinarily descends into gross seminal fluid, into a subtle force which is conserved and integrated with the deathless life force. 'With the extinction of sexual desire, mind is released of its most powerful bond', *Serpent Power*, p. 224.

[52] See, for instance, Muhammad Enamul Haq, *A History of Sufism in Bengal*, Dacca, 1975, but more especially his earlier Bengali work, *Bande Sufi Prabhab*, Calcutta, 1935. One might recall, in this context, that the great Buddha statues of Bamian survived the coming of Islam, though, unfortunately, not the regime of the Taliban.

[53] Song no.10, Shastri, op. cit. Alternatively, to storm her genitals and make her his slave in body and mind (*paran*). Or, differently, to conquer his own breath and make himself deathless. For yet another technical sense, see Munidatta's commentary, Shastri op. cit., p. 62.

[54] 'Dombi, there is no one more shameless [alternatively, woman with nose cut off] than you', Song no. 18, ibid.

[55] Song no. 19, ibid.

[56] Song no. 18, ibid.

[57] Unknown author, *Pavana-Vijaya Svarodaya* (nineteenth century?), edited

by Rasik Mohan Chattopadhyay, Calcutta, 1994, verses 238–41, p. 17.

58 *Hathayoga-Pradipika*, III, 26–27. The exercises for re-drawing the spilt semen up the penis is named *Vajroli Mudra.*

59 Krishnananda Agambagish, *Vrihat Tantrasara*, p. 702.

60 Among the latter, any spilt semen woud have to be pulled through the penis. Or it would be mixed with menstrual blood, and drunk. Upendranath Bhattacharya, *Banglar Baul o Baul Gan*, Calcutta, B.S. 1364, Vol. II, pp. 367–437, 476–81. The orthodox Tantriks might or might not do this, and would be permitted to spill semen for procreation.

61 Upendranath Bhattacharya, *Banglar Baul o Baul Gan*, Calcutta, B.S. 1364, Vol. I, pp. 127–29; Rajat Kanta Ray (ed.), *Mind, Body and Society: Life and Mentality in Colonial Bengal*, Calcutta, 1995, p. 16.

62 Haraprasad Shastri, op. cit., p. 6. Tibetan translations from Indian literature were divided into *Kengur*, which contained the Buddha's words, and *Tengur*, which contained all other matters.

63 We are grateful to Fathers Wavreil and Bronckers for translating the above sentence in *Alberuni's India* from Latin into English. Here again, in accordance with Edwardian conventions, Edward Sachau had resorted to Latin while translating Al Biruni's Arabic into English. *Alberuni's India*, Vol. I, p. 181.

64 Shastri, op. cit., Song nos 10, 18, 19.

65 For visual evidence of the Tibeto–Tantric standing posture, see the Tibetan Thanka named 'Vajrakila (r Dor rje phur bu) with his Sakti' (early seventeenth century, Indian Museum, Calcutta, Accession no. 645). This is discussed in Sipra Chakravarti, *Tibetan Paintings in the Indian Museum*, Calcutta, 2000, p. 14. In this picture, Vajrakila unites with his Shakti, standing on two legs set wide apart. Shakti stands on one foot, her other leg encircling his buttocks. This seems to be the type of sexual intercourse in the standing posture described by Al Biruni.

66 *Panchanan Daser Karcha*, quoted in Upendranath Bhattacharya, *Banglar Baul*, Vol. 1, pp. 422–23.

67 In one of the representations, the horizontal Shiva has an erect penis, and Kali is standing poised above the organ, preparatory to sitting down over it. See also 'Chhinnamasta', early nineteenth-century oil on canvas (Bengal) exhibited in CIMA Art Gallery, Calcutta, November 2000, and printed in *Art of Bengal, Past and Present 1850–2000*, CIMA, Calcutta, n.d., p. 42. This painting exhibits the woman-above-man posture, with the goddess Chhinnamasta standing over the copulating couple and cutting her own head off in the well-known Tantric stance. Here, however, the woman lies upon the horizontal man and does not sit upon him, as in the recommended Sahajiya posture.

68 David Shea and Anthony Troyer (translation), *The Dabistan or School of Manners*, Washington, 1901, pp. 251–52. For a much earlier obscure response to 'Tantric' practices prevailing among both Buddhist and Hindu sects, see Bhavabhuti (AD 700–736), *Malati Madhava* (Sanskrit play), IX, 32 and passim.

[69] Krishnananda Agambagish, *Vrihat Tantrasara*, p. 706. The question whether the close female relations should act as full partners in the eroto-Yogic *sadhana* is left unclear in the text, but is not specifically ruled out. It is possible that these females were worshipped by Right-Hand Tantriks who did not do *yugal sadhana* with an eroto-Yogic partner (as the Left-Hand Tantriks did).

[70] This is the unmistakable impression conveyed by the evidence of Ibn Battuta. *The Rehla of Ibn Battuta* (*India, Maldive Islands and Ceylon*), translated by Mahdi Husain, Baroda, 1953, pp. 164–66 and passim.

[71] *Siddha* means one who has attained fulfilment (*siddhi*) in the exercise (*sadhana*).

[72] The *Charyapadas* are clear on this point.

[73] Ali Raja alias Kanu Fakir, *Jnana Sagar*, edited by Abdul Karim, Calcutta, B.S. 1324, p. 36. This is an eighteenth-century *darbeshi* book by a Muslim dervish. The Muslim fakirs carried on the *sadhana* of the Buddhist *siddhas.*

[74] *Alberuni's India*, Vol. I, p. 21.

[75] Song no. 38, l. 9, in Shastri, *Hajar Bachharer Purana Bauddha o Doha.* 'That Thunderbolt of a knowing mind moves upward' (*Yo bodhi-chittavajrah sa urddham gachhati*), Munidatta's commentary, p. 103.

[76] 'Know sexual intercourse to be the ablution, and spilling of seed, the concluding rite' (*maithunam tarpanam biddhi, bijapato visarjanam*). *Vrihat Tantrasara*, p. 702.

[77] Akshay Kumar Datta, *Bharatvarshiya Upasak Sampraday*, Vol. II, second edition, Calcutta, B.S. 1314, p. 170.

[78] This is evident from the biographical sketches of Lalan Fakir and Raj Khyapa. See 'Mahatma Lalan Fakir', unsigned article in the *Hitakari* magazine, 31 October 1890, reprinted in Raicharan Das, *Maner Katha*, Calcutta, B.S. 1378, pp. 135–38; Jeanne Openshaw, 'Raj Krsna: Perspectives on the Worlds of a Little-known Bengali Guru', in Ray (ed.), *Mind, Body and Society*, pp. 108–51; Akshay Kumar Datta, *Bharatvarshiya Upasak Sampraday*, Vol. I, Calcutta, B.S. 1394, pp. 231–35.

[79] 'The Tantric act should be done at night, and the Vedic act by day' (*Ratrau kulakriya Kuriyat, diva kuryach-cha vaidikim*). *Niruttara Tantra*, quoted in Akshay Kumar Gupta, *Bharatvarshiya Upasak Sampraday*, Vol. II, p. 166.

[80] 'Except during the ritual, the woman should not touch another man even in spirit. During the ritual, O goddess, she should serve him like a prostitute' (*Puja kalam vina na-anyaṃ purusham manasa sprishet. Pujakale cha deveshi veshyeva paritoshayet*). *Uttara Tantra*, quoted in ibid., p. 171.

[81] *Madakulash-cha yoginyah patati purushaupari. Manoratha-sukham purnam kurvanti cha parasparam. Kularnava Tantra*, V, quoted in extenso in ibid., pp. 173–74.

[82] *Vivahitam patim na-eva tyajed-ukta-karmani. Niruttara Tantra*, ibid., p. 171.

[83] *Alberuni's India*, Vol. I, pp. 185–86.

# 5 Religion and Material Life in Ancient India

## D.D. Kosambi and Niharranjan Ray

*Barun De*

Historians do not generally study together two modern giants of the profession in twentieth-century India. D.D. Kosambi is by common consensus one of the first Marxist scholars who brought logical and rational methods to the study of prehistoric and ancient India, and of the survivals and accretions over time to myths and legends, discretely originating in the uncharted past, that are still with us today. Niharranjan Ray, on the other hand, was a historians' historian *par excellence*, who brought his knowledge of iconography in particular and art and aesthetics in general to bear on the analysis of regional cultures in different parts of India, particularly his native Bengal, but also in the Punjab and North India, where he spent some of his most creative years in the last decade of his life.

Kosambi was a rigorous analyst of base–superstructure relations reflected in varying class structures that were created by the forces and relations of production which themselves changed over broad historical periods. Ray, on the other hand, has been recognized, particularly after he passed away in 1981, as an integrationist who sought to encompass all elements of social production, including environmental determination, polity, forces and relations of consumption, distribution and production, and a variety of forms of aesthetic creativity, within his explanations of social change. A detailed reading of their texts shows that despite certain differences in style, mental approach, temperaments and sophistication, there were similarities in their approach to history.

One such similarity is to be found in their understanding of the multiple ways in which society, groups, and individuals influenced each other, with distinct qualitative changes over periods of time, that are themselves not determined by external religious impact – first Aryan/Hindu, then Central or West Asian/Muslim, and then Christian/British, corresponding to the familiar European historical division of ancient, medieval and modern. Both emphasized the endogenous and overlapping character of phases of Indian historical development. A second similarity was their use of what Kosambi, in a very felicitous title of one of his articles, called 'Combined Methods in Indology'.[1] B.D. Chattopadhyaya in his excellent compilation of Kosambi's articles on different aspects of ancient India, has given this title, adding the words 'and other Writings' to his volume. When he comes out with the work that we expect from him on Ray, he will surely find the same 'redefinition of the scope of history, which broke down the compartmentalization of earlier history in terms of his designing integrated methodology for harnessing diverse sources and in terms of his emphasis on asking questions which these diverse sources and the society they emanated from alone could generate', as well as the 'conception of the power of ideology, [which] followed from attempts to answer a query about wherein the history of India differs from other countries' in the writings of Niharranjan Ray, that he spotlights in Kosambi.[2]

The approach of using combined methods, not only those of history, but also of statistical inference, logical analysis of all relevant phenomena, field research in anthropology, and inference backwards to the antiquity of present primitive practices as referred to in texts of similar societies in similar locations, and of economics, political science and the sciences of behaviour, was the 'paradigm shift' of the mid-twentieth century that enthusiastic votaries of Kosambi have ascribed to him (vide Chattopadhyaya's reference to an article of Romila Thapar on 'The contribution of D.D. Kosambi to Indology').[3] A careful analysis on strict historiographical lines of the work of scholars like G.S. Ghurye and Iravati Karve on Hindu society, particularly in Maharashtra, of Ananda Coomaraswamy and Stella Kramrisch from abroad working on Indian artistic symbolism and creativity, and of lesser known scholars such as Bhupendranath Dutta on the study of the Indian land system and its impact on society, will show that the combination of methods leading to a holistic approach to the evolutionary phases of our subcontinental history came up by the 1930s and 1940s – about the time that the circumstances of the Second World War brought about significant changes in the pace of democratization and modernization in India.

The writings of Kosambi and Ray are both remarkable examples of the practical exemplification of that approach, in the study of ancient Indian history, particularly of the Gangetic plains and the Deccan in the case of the first, and of ancient Burmese and Bengali art and of the regional ancient history of Bengal in the case of the second. Both foreshadow[4] the approaches of British historians, writing in the 1950s and 1960s, such as E.H. Carr and Geoffrey Barraclough[5] whom present-day historians have credited with the innovation of using the present as the reference point to query the past. Kosambi and Ray were pioneers who brought a secular, contemporary vision to bear on the material conditions in Indian life.

One of the ways they did this was to search for the chronological development and stages in the progress of Indian ideology. Both emphasized the paucity of direct chronicle records, bearing irrefutable testimony of having been composed at the time of the events of which they spoke, or being completely reliable in being based on hearsay. Kosambi more than Ray tended to interlocute and deconstruct his sources to the point of seeing them as records about the age in which they were written, rather than about the age to which they refer. Ray, more business-like about preparing a social chronicle of Bengal that historians of its political dynasties had previously neglected, and to write this as the account of the rise and fall of pre-Muslim culture in the region in a fully secular way, selected only those sources that he found more reliable than others. But he eschewed detailed footnotes, relying more on the attention of lay students without a knowledge of the old scripts and languages, such as Pali, Prakrit, Tibetan, Greek as well as Sanskrit in which they were written, for whose instruction he wrote, and proceeded to give the least controversial and more straightforward version of historical events. Reading Kosambi one can almost hear him thinking combatively about his arguments with other interpretations on points of detail. Going through the sonorous cadences of Ray's prose, particularly in the Bengali that he wrote with élan, one is lulled into ignoring the nature of the sources taken from a variety of little traditions in backward tracts and monastic establishments, gathered and translated by different scholars, that he expects us to take for granted. The source materials, however, lie open for inspection in Kosambi's articles. In the case of Ray, built as they are on the very different methodologies of collation and edition, practised by scholars such as Mahamahopadhyaya Haraprasad Sastri, Prabodhchandra

Bagchi, or Dinesh Chandra Sarkar, they are embedded into the texture of Ray's own version, without a chance given to the reader by means of footnotes, which he stylistically disliked, to check and corroborate the argument.

Despite this difference in methods of presentation, both saw religion as dependent on particular conditions of production of knowledge, its patronage structure under different social circumstances (in Ray's case, dynasties as opposite to each other in their relations with the masses as the indigenous Palas and the Senas of external southern origin), its rewards or frustrations as social construction rather than as immanent and semi-eternal tradition or heritage, to be necessarily revered and preserved, as earlier scholars of the nineteenth and early twentieth centuries had done. They were closer to more explicit nationalists such as Swami Vivekananda, Rabindranath Tagore or Mahatma Gandhi than to more spiritualist thinkers such as Devendranath Tagore, Dayanand Saraswati or Aurobindo Ghosh. If religion could be deconstructed by scholarship, according to the material periodicity of its provenance, religion to them was also a force of ideology, which created different traditions. Out of these traditions came interpretations about origin myths, which were incorporated into religious history and its iconographic representation. Earlier scholars had taken the lineage of the traditions as being composite – whether Śakta, Śaivite, or Vaishnava, or Buddhist of different creeds, Jaina, or different forms of animism. Both Kosambi and Ray questioned this compositeness of tradition.

Historians are quite aware of the way in which the Krishna myth is accepted as a living force in Indian art and values. This is differentiated by Kosambi in order to analyse different forms of interpretation, religious practice and quietism or social activism and reform in reading the *Bhagavad Gita*. His famous article on the latter[6] should be supplemented by reading his article on 'The Historical Krishna', which, with striking pictures from eighteenth-century paintings and prehistoric cave drawings as well as early ancient coins, was first published in *The Times of India Annual* 1965 and is republished by Chattopadhyaya.[7] It would be useful to compare this social analysis of Indian religious tradition and its accretive force in later popular religious art with Ray's many writings on Buddhist and later Brahmanical symbolism, syncretism and symbiotic development in the art of the Mauryas and Sungas, and, then, later in the roughly late Gupta and Pala periods in Bengal.

Ray's method is not deconstructive like that of Kosambi. In his different books on Maurya and Sunga art, on Brahmanical and Buddhist cults in Burma as an outlier in ancient Indic culture, and in his magnum opus, *Bangalir Itihas: Adiparva* (Calcutta 1949, later translated into English by John W. Hood), Ray sees religion as being moulded by the relevant stage of social development. In his case, religion is free and individualist among primitive peoples, surviving in social backwaters away from settled-plains agriculture or over-sophisticated urbanism. It develops rituals of fertility, maternity, and social authority based on paternalist power in the culture of plains civilizations, such as developed after the widespread use of iron for cultivation, and warfare, that are to be found in the Mauryan and later imperial states, which created various feudal forms of the Indian variant. It tends to become overgrown when these cultures focus on nodes of commerce and artisan production in large towns, concentrated in trade routes or river navigability with the spread of luxury production. The spread of secret devotional jargon, mystic practices based on sexuality and human contact, a textual literature meant only for initiates – such as is to be found in the Nāthapanthi, Siddha and Yogic cults spread all the way from Eastern U.P., Nepal and Tibet to the eastern boundaries of Bengal, Tripura and Assam, or in the Tantrayana forms of debased Buddhism with an even further eastern spread into Southeast Asia – and of eroticism in attendant literary descriptions and practices that are to be found in the Sena period poetry till the times of the *Gitagovinda* and Dhoyi's *Pavanadutam*, showed, in Ray's opinion, signs of social decay, which were due to the enervating influence of excessive luxury.

Kosambi sees religion as the epiphenomenon of material life at a particular stage of development, on the one hand, and, on the other, in its secondary form, as the survival of outmoded ideas, tranquilizing social discontent in later stages. His model of social development is explicitly based on the classic lines from the preface by Karl Marx to his *Critique of Political Economy*:

> It is not the consciousness of men that determines their social being, but on the contrary their social existence that determines their consciousness. At a certain stage of their development the material productive forces of society come in conflict with the existing relations of production, or – what is but the legal expression for the same thing – with the property relations within which

> they had moved hitherto. From forms of development of the productive forces these relations turn into their fetters. Then begins an epoch of social revolution. With the change in the economic foundation the whole vast superstructure is more or less rapidly transformed. In considering such transformations, it is necessary always to distinguish between the material revolution in the economic condition of production, which can be determine with the precision of natural science, and the juridical, political, religious, esthetic or philosophic – in short, ideological forms in which men become conscious of this conflicts and fight it out.

So, Kosambi makes religions dependent on the development of the forces of material production, both in their rise and in their collapse.

Ray, on the other hand, has no such guiding model. Yet to him also, on the basis of the study of eastern Indian religious texts studied from a secular standpoint with a view to establishing a rounded view of society, and writing at a time only slightly a few years before Kosambi – the *History of the Bengalis: Ancient Period* was composed in the years of the Second World War and published just after Independence – religion changed along with social relations. A detailed study of the text of the *History of the Bengalis* shows that he is critical of placing religion in the secondary level (in the definition of religion as Kosambi sees it). He is unsparing in a critique of religion which loses its primordial vitality as spiritual force; it then becomes the obsolete formalization of social practices. This leads, in his opinion, to an age whose decadent traditional organization persists while its relations of production have changed. Thus the broad and ample fluidity of movement of the rustic characters depicted in the sculptures of the plaques of the Paharpur temple complex in central Bangladesh, he says, both in his English article on sculpture in the *History of Bengal*,[8] and in his *History of Bengalis*, is to him indicative of the stability, as well as vitality and creativity of the rural peace brought by the Pālas after a long period of anarchy (*matsyanvaya*) in rural Bengal. On the other hand, the excessive ornamentation and turgid eroticism of art and literature in Sena Bengal is indicative of the decay of the Hindu civilization. In the first, there is creative religious symbiosis between Buddhism and Brahmanism in their period of growth. In the second, there is subservience to the overweening formalism of the latter, just before Brahmanism itself became subservient to the creative religious puritanism and aggressive missionary activity of Islam, about to establish its sway over northern India. Ray arrives at this formulation without reference to any Marxian text. It is notable that his secular analysis of religion as a positive (spiritual) as well as a negative (formalistic and ritualistic) force within and over society was arrived at about a decade ahead of Kosambi's major writings on the subject which stuck close to the Marxian text, at least with regard to the analysis of religion.

It is this that represents the inner conflict within the modern tradition of Indian socio-economic historical analysis. Early modern historians of India, from the nineteenth to the early twentieth centuries saw religion as something above social life – neither tradition, immutable and not questioned by the conditions of the material change – or consciousness were within the realm of general social enquiry. In the 1920s and the 1930s, the influence of revolutionary ideology, Marxism included, but also social democracy to which Ray subscribed, challenged such a transcendental outlook. Not all modern historiography based itself, as Kosambi sought to do, on Marxian exegesis, as Ray said in the last years of his life to one of his most favourite students, the Marxist philosopher and historian of Indian materialist thought, Deviprasad Chattopadhyaya, in an interview.[9] He said:

> [Marxism] is a fine analytical tool and a sophisticated method of evaluation and interpretation. . . . I have been using it whenever and wherever I found it to my advantage to do so, but hardly altogether exclusively and with any claim to absolute certainty or to its infallibility as an argument, but certainly by providing a hypothesis, which might or might not help a step toward a rational generalization. . . .[10]

Ray was a forerunner of the present trend in modern Indian thought in which a plurality of variant paths of history, subject indeterminately to the possibilities of chance, form the structure of either development or regression, which are both historical trends. His last pages in *History of the Bengalis* deserve study for the note of doom they convey as early as 1949 in the aftermath of the 1947 Partition of Bengal for those who fall under the sway of traditionalist obscurantism and superstition. Only a few horsemen had been sufficient to frighten away the courtiers of Lakshmanasena from their pleasure house in Nadia and end the ancient history of Bengal. Perhaps the same supineness of culture led to the collapse of the Bengal Nawabs of the eighteenth century faced by the onrush of colonialism.

In his later writings after retirement, an analysis of which is offered by John W. Hood,[11] Ray has a complex series of observations on the bearing of these tendencies on the course of recent Indian history and the future of national authenticity and secular independence in an age of renewed attack from religious revivalist and neo-colonial forces. However, that is the subject for another paper. In this paper, I have sought to open the topic of how religion has to be studied in terms of the force of spiritual creativity and the flowering of individual mental consciousness, as a force for social welfare, on the one hand (examples being Gautama Buddha, Kabīr and Rammohun Roy), and, on the other, an instrument of obscurantism and traditionalist superstition seeking to enforce elitist authority on democratic creativity.

**Notes and References**

1 *Indo-Iranian Journal*, Vol. 6, 1963.

2 D.D. Kosambi, *Combined Methods in Ideology and Other Works*, edited by B.D. Chattopadhyaya, 'Introduction', pp. xxvii–xxviii.

3 Romila Thapar, *Interpreting Early India*, second edition, New Delhi, 1994.

4 E.H. Carr, *What is History?* Harmondsworth, 1959.

5 Geoffrey Barraclough, *An Introduction to Contemporary History*, Harmondsworth, 1967.

6 See D.D. Kosambi, *Myth and Reality*, Bombay, 1962.

7 D.D. Kosambi, *Combined Methods and Indology and Other Works*, No. 21.

8 'Stages of Indian History', *ISCUS: Journal of the Indo-Soviet Cultural Society*, I (1), January 1954, reprinted in *Combined Methods in Indology and Other Works*, No. 4, p. 57.

9 Niharranjan Ray, *History of Bengal*, edited by R.C. Majumdar, Vol. I, Dacca University, Dacca, 1943.

10 *History and Society: Essays in Honour of Professor Niharranjan Ray*, edited by D.P. Chattopadhyaya, Calcutta, 1978, pp. 12–13.

11 *Makers of Indian Literature: Niharranjan Ray*, New Delhi, 1997, Chapter IV.

# 6 The Islamic Background to Indian History

## An Interpretation of the Islamic Past

*M. Athar Ali*

The medieval period of Indian history, as conventionally fixed by historians, *c.* 1000 to 1750, received a deep imprint of Islam. Islam greatly influenced the political structure, the fiscal system and even much of the network of internal commerce and external trade, so it is crucial to understand the context of Islam in Indian history, or in other words, to understand Islamic history till the arrival of Islam in northern India, *c.* 1200.[1] A pioneering effort to do so was provided by Professor Mohammad Habib in his introduction to a reprint of Volume II of Elliot and Dowson's *History of India as Told by its Own Historians* (1952).[2] A year later Hamilton Gibb came out with his well-known essay, 'An interpretation of Islamic History', published in the *Journal of World History* (1953).[3] Nearly 35 years have passed since then, years during which much has been written on the theme, and many new insights obtained. The present essay proposes to offer a rather personal reappraisal of the first 600 years of Islamic history based, admittedly, on only a partial reading of the vast literature on the subject and with a confessed bias towards what seems more relevant from an Indian point of view, though not deliberately neglecting other possible angles of vision.

### I

In any narration of the events of the past, the emergence of Islam within a neglected, seemingly 'wild' desert, and its rapid transformation into one of the great historical cultures of the world, presents a subject of great drama and wonder. There have been greater and more rapid conquests. The Mongols in the thirteenth century, too, arose out of the steppes to create the sole world empire in premodern history, twice or thrice the size of the Islamic caliphate at its greatest extent; and they achieved it in far less time. But the Mongols created no international culture. Their own language was overwhelmed by the babel of tongues of their subjects; and instead of assimilating, like the Arabs, they were themselves assimilated by others. Clearly, then, without denigrating the claims of *Pax Mongolica* for historical analysis, one may still assert that an analysis of Islam is likely to tell us much more about what has happened in a large part of Asia and Africa during the last 1500 years.

How does one set about the task? There has recently been a spate of criticism of the 'Orientalists'. Amidst this protest, Edward W. Said's critique is perhaps the most comprehensive as well as reasonable.[4] In so far as 'Orientalism' is conceived as an attempt to study eastern cultures, especially Islam, in the way one studies zoology, or animals of lower orders, many of the criticisms are, perhaps, quite valid. From this valid objection, however, there has been a tendency to go on to assert that Islamic history can be understood only by those who believe in Islam, who can study it on its own terms, and still better, interpret it in *its terms*. This is a very attractive notion, and by ruling out all comparisons with other cultures or systems (for each of them must then be studied on its own terms), it sweeps away the possibility of any arrogantly Eurocentric interpretation of Islamic history. One may, perhaps, see the most learned practitioner of this kind of exposition in Muhammad Hamidullah, with his well-known biography of the Prophet.

Without totally denying the claims of this school to legitimacy, I would still argue that the basic premises here are not acceptable. A believer has a perfect right to expound the tenets of Islam 'on its own terms', in its terminology; but this would be theology – without any indignity necessarily attaching to that term. Can it be history? Islam as a historical phenomenon has always interacted with other elements that have indisputably originated and existed outside its fold. Will it be valid to see them on terms supposedly proper only to Islam? If not, how is the interaction to be interpreted? For if one is to understand the Islamic phenomenon in a historical perspective, the interaction is not peripheral but central to any analysis. The conclusion is inescapable that whether it is the history of feudal Christendom or of Lama–Buddhism or of Islam, one would need the same critical apparatus, the same freedom from assumptions or given premises, and the same sharp critical faculty.

This can be illustrated with the very first problem one faces: the emergence of Islam within the womb of what Muslims call the *Jahilliya*, the society and culture in which the Prophet was born. Is Jahilliya to be understood 'on its own terms' (hardly known to us now, at first hand) or on those of Islam, whose followers understandably exaggerated the allegedly evil customs of the Jahilliya? One must now rather examine the degree of exaggeration in the Islamic traditions about that period and reconstruct, by additional use of other sources, what was really happening in the Arabian peninsula before the rise of Islam. There is no proof that the pre-Islamic Arabian society was in a primitive, communal stage, as E.A. Belyaev has argued; nor, as he further asserts, that it was being converted into a slave-owning one.[5] One would rather say that the Bedouin society, based on tribe, was indeed pastoral; but it had long developed individual property, even if this was counted in terms of camels and date palms rather than money. Slavery was a convenient, but not essential, prop of this property system. Outside Yemen, agriculture was only of secondary importance; but this, along with date palm cultivation, would again emphasize individual right and economic and social differentiation. Thus, clearly, private property, which is the basis of Islamic civil law, already existed in Arabia. Islam helped at best to standardize and systematize its norms. As far as slavery is concerned, it is possible that slavery increased after Islamic conquests (with the train of captive slaves they generated); but it is unlikely that here too Islam either greatly modified or intensified slavery. It recognized slavery virtually just as it had found it.

Where then was there, in a sphere other than ideological, a true break with Jahilliya? Montgomery Watt's thesis of town–nomad conflict may be taken to develop a proposition of the triumph of urbanism over pastoral rusticism.[6] The essential difference between the town-dweller and the Bedouin is recognized in the Quran, where the nomad is spurned (*Sura* IX.98). There is no doubt that the initial success of Islam is related to the existence of commercial oases, notably Mecca, within the desert wastes of the peninsula. One can trace this situation, perhaps, to the discovery of the monsoons that occurred around the time of Christ. This discovery suddenly shifted the main ports to the mouth of the Red Sea. The Red Sea itself is unaffected by the monsoon winds, and so posed a tedious barrier to sailing ships within its waters. The trade between the Mediterranean and India had, therefore, to be carried overland through Hijaz, connecting the Levant and Egyptian ports with those of Yemen. Of this overland caravan trade, Mecca became the undeclared capital. It also became apparently, the entrepôt from where some of the luxuries of civilization were distributed among the nomadic tribes (or rather among their chiefs and 'wealthy' families). Mecca sealed its position by installing, in the Ka'ba, the images of gods (including the one called Allah) and goddesses to establish for itself a position of a pilgrimage centre for the tribes of the peninsula. The response of Mecca to Islam was governed, among other factors, by this alliance of commerce with religion. Could Islam offer a more attractive alternative in terms of persuading the tribes to respect the security of the Quraysh in the name of religious sanctity? As Shaban and Rodinson argue, the moment Islam would be shown to offer a far more effective claim on the nomad than Lat and Manat,[7] the older gods, the Ka'ba would assume an even greater sanctity upon its Islamic transformation. The Meccan reaction to Islam passed quickly from surrender to reconciliation, and, ultimately, to dominance.[8]

If these are reasonable notions, do we assume that Islam was simply a development of institutions, already present in Arab society and economy? This, indeed, is precisely Shaban's conclusion. Islam 'was definitely Arab, based on Arab traditions, and shaped in Arab forms'.[9] It seems to me that this represents an exaggeration that may dangerously mar our understanding of early Islamic history.

What is missing in Shaban's thesis is any recognition that the essential elements of the Islamic faith cannot be shown to have grown historically out of Arabian soil. If one does not care to contest the believer's faith in the message of Abraham, that message had admittedly long been forgotten in Mecca and it had left no living tradition. What was intruding into Arabia were the ideas of Judaism and Christianity radiating from the Roman Empire, and later Byzantium. The notorious missionary gibe that Islam is a rehash of Judaism and Christianity has undoubtedly inhibited free discussion of the matter. But Islam's link with both religions is explicitly recognized in the Quran, where God's message to Prophet Muhammad clearly reinforces, succeeds or supersedes that sent through Moses and Christ; the tradition of the Old Testament is appealed to in considerable detail. Its hearers did not deem these to be strange and incomprehensible narrations, for, already, all over Hijaz and Yemen, there were Jewish and Christian communities of tradesmen, peasants and even pastoralists, who often lived as at Madina, among pagan populations. The basis, introduced from outside, for challenging pagan beliefs already existed; without it, the reception given to Islam in pagan Arabia, after an initial hesitation, would have been inconceivable. The ideology of Islam was, then, by no means 'Arab', if it is intended to mean that its acceptance was the product of internal questionings spontaneously sprouting in nomad Arabia.

The core of what was new to pagan Arabia was *umma*, a concept which rapidly evolved from the sense of a federation of tribes or communities, pagan, Jewish and Muslim, with the Prophet as the arbitrator, into a community of Believers. There was no precedent of this in Arabia. The only precedents were external to the Arabs, in the Jewish community, for instance, but still more, the Christian realm, embracing all, irrespective of race and tribe, who believed in God. His Son and the Holy Ghost. If Allah was central to the faith of Islam, the *umma* was central to its organization; and the latter, at any rate, was in its evolved form a purely external phenomenon.

Here one might also note that 'Arabism' in the age of the Prophet would have been a total anachronism. The Arabs were conscious of no sense of superiority; and there were good grounds for their lack of such consciousness. They envied the wealth and prosperity of their neighbours. That Allah in His mercy had sent them the last of the Prophets was a matter of Divine Grace, not a thing expected or natural. Believers could be proud if those other than Arabs became Muslims; Islam was thus, quite self-consciously, not an Arab but a universal faith. Things were to change only later, when the Arabs subjugated other people in the name of Islam. Then alone could Islam become, in the eyes of its neo-aristocratic believers, the peculiar privilege of the conquering race.

Yet it was the externally introduced concept of *umma* that made the conquests possible; a unity to which tribal diversity became subordinate, and a unity that could, therefore, give cohesion and direction, if its leadership came into such able hands as those of Abu Bakr and Umar, the first two caliphs. The unity did not, however, imply equality or democracy. For one thing, the Quraysh, as the sacred tribe of the past and now the tribe of the Prophet, enjoyed a rising prominence. Within the tribes, the chiefs (*saiyyids*, *shaykhs*) had from the beginning retained their places upon joining the Islamic banner. There were thus all the elements present for a rapid evolution of an aristocracy within the *umma*, though such evolution could not but bring in the infusion of family and tribal feuds – the real 'Arab' heritage.

## II

On the actual process of conquests little need be said, since much has been written. It is difficult to know what the initial reactions of the conquered people were. The Byzantine Empire was undoubtedly ridden by sectarian quarrels, and the Sassanid Empire had been shaken by a revolt of the poor, led by Mazdak in the preceding century. But the factors behind the first successes of the Arabs lay probably more within their own new-found unity of purpose than in any support they would arouse among the ranks of their opponents. Yet once the initial military advantage had been attained, the Arab conquests were relatively swift, and the vast structures of the two empires, with their taxes and rents, lay in the hands of the conquerors, even before the Pious Caliphate came to an end (AD 661).

What took place may now be studied from two angles: what happened to the conquerors, and what happened to the conquered.

First, I venture to think that Wellhausen's analysis, though demanding modifications in detail, still stands in its essentials.[10] On a close scrutiny of the traditions incorporated in Ṭabarī, Wellhausen argued that with the ultimate rise to dominance of the aristocratic Qurayshite house of the Ummayyads, there developed three basic contradictions among the ruling classes of Islam: (a) between the tribal leaders of two great tribal federations, which evolved within the aristocracy of tribal leaders, namely the Muzarites and the Yemenites; (b) between the Arab tribal leaders settled in Iraq (the conquerors of Persia) and the Syrians (who hosted, so to speak, the Ummayyad Caliphate); and (c) between the Arabs, in general, and the non-Arab Muslims who tended to increase in numbers with 'unauthorized' conversions, that is with people becoming Muslims without actual acceptance as clients (*mawwālī*) by any Arab tribe. I do not think that Shaban in his *The Abbasid Revolution* has really brought down Wellhausen's major theses, though one would readily agree that Wellhausen's implied supposition of the continuation of pagan Arab rivalries in an Islamic form, probably goes too far.[11] The Abbasid Revolution was seen by Wellhausen as an alliance of the Iraqites with the *mawwālī*, with loyalty to the House of the Prophet (the 'Alīds) as an ideological cloak for their ambitions. One could, of course, agree that the natural result of such an alliance, when successful, was bound to be 'the assimilation of all Muslims', but whether this was a conscious immediate 'objective' of the 'Abbāsid Revolution, as Shaban supposes, may perhaps be doubted.

This brings us to the question: who were the *mawwālī*? We must now ask the second question, what was happening to the conquered? It may be seen from the actual records of the Arab conquests, for example of Sind (712–14), given in splendidly detailed narration in the *Chachnāma*, that the first converts to Islam, the 'clients' accepted by Arabs, belonged to the high and middle nobility rather than the masses who remained unconverted for a much longer time. Muhammad ibn Qasim, the conqueror of Sind and his successors, even continued the Brahmanical restrictions on the pastoral 'unclean' community of the Jatts.[12] The conquerors also continued the earlier taxes, so that a very heavy tax (*kharāj*) assimilated and incorporated the earlier burdens. It is doubtful if the Arab conquests meant any kind of liberation or even relief to the poor of the conquered lands.

The converted aristocracy, such as the *marzbāns* and *dihqāns* of the Sassanid regime, became inevitable adjuncts and middlemen to the Arab rulers. In course of time, they would be Arabicized in culture, and, perhaps, speech; they would never be tribalized. In essence, therefore, they came to represent a more coherent and homogeneous class than the tribally divided Arab rulers. As conversions percolated downwards. Hajjāj ibn Yusuf, the powerful Umayyid viceroy of Iraq, might inveigh against the rising *mawwālī*, but in vain. The future belonged to them.

### III

We may yet, with Wellhausen, suppose the Abbasid Revolution to have been the work of a coalition between the Iraqite Arabs and the *mawwālī*, the latter still probably a minority among the subject population, but indispensable to Iraqite rule.

The Abbasid caliphate was the period when the classical world of Islam really took shape. A subterranean Persian basis, influx of Hellenic and Hellenistic thought and sciences, Arabic as the vehicle of expression – such was the trinity of Abbasid high culture. It saw the emergence of the great juridical schools, the formulation of the orthodox (Ash'arite) theology, the beginnings of Sufism. This high culture, with Arabic as its main vehicle, was the obvious result of a tremendous amount of cross-cultural fertilization.

Alongside the development of this culture whose last great representatives in the eastern lands were Avicenna and Alberuni (early eleventh century), there seems to have occurred a process whereby Islam, from being the religion of an elite minority, became the faith of the masses. By the time of the Mongol conquests, the Muslims obviously formed the vast bulk of the population of Western and Central Asia. The Christians, Zoroastrians and Buddhists had been reduced to small minorities. It was probably this basic fact that saved Islam in Asia, when its splintered political fabric was all but destroyed by the Mongols in the thirteenth century.

The process of conversion, as it neared completion, created new problems for Islamic polity, now a state where the rulers and subjects were both Muslims, and where, therefore, the Muslims must bear the brunt of the taxation. For such a state neither the practices of the Prophet, more suitable for a semi-pastoral economy, nor the policies of Umar I, when the Muslims were the conquerors and all other people their subjects, could form a precedent. If Muslims were to pay *'ushr* or one-tenth of the produce, no state could subsist financially. Inevitably, law adjusted to circumstance. The notion of *kharāj* as a tax on all peasants, comprising the surplus, irrespective of the faith of the taxpayer, came to be upheld by the jurists of the Hanafite school.[13] In practice, this prevailed from the Atlantic to the Altai mountains. Conversely, the ruling class could no longer claim legitimacy on the basis of its Arab or Islamic origins. The Arab tribal claims on conquered lands in the form of *ziyā'*, which the early caliphs had had to admit, similarly disappeared as the *iqṭā* or transferable revenue charge became universal. The ruling classes came to be detached from earlier roots, and, but for exceptional cases like the Siljuq tribe under the Siljuqids, the nobility became a class totally dependent not on hereditary claims, but on the pleasure of the ruler. The classic new state was that of Ghaznin, whose ruler Mahmud (999–1030), the great conqueror, was supposed to be the first Sultan of Islam. Thus arose the characteristic state of medieval Islam, which seems to have formed the model of Marx's 'Asiatic Despotism'.[14]

In spite of these rather ominous features, the medieval states of the Islamic world (from the thirteenth century) had many positive features which may be readily admitted – patronage of commerce, a high level of urbanization, some degree of security. There were other features, which no longer appeal to the modern mind – oppression of the peasantry, growing orthodoxy and stagnation in science and learning. But these questions, though important, are outside the area of our present concern, which has only been to raise issues about the stages of evolution of the Islamic polities and societies of the early period, before the Ghorian conquests of *c.* 1200.

**Notes and References**

1 Here I am ignoring the Arab conquest of Sind, in the early eighth century, the Muslim communities in various parts of India in the subsequent period, and the Ghaznavide conquests of the eleventh century. Islam, as an important social and cultural factor in Indian history, begins its history mainly with the Ghorian conquests and the establishment of the Sultanate around the beginning of the thirteenth century.

2 Reprint, edited by M. Habib, S.A. Rashid and K.A. Nizami, Aligarh, 1952.

3 Reprinted in H.A.R. Gibb, *Studies on the Civilization of Islam*, edited by Stanford J. Shaw and William R. Polk, London, 1912, pp. 3–33.

4 Edward W. Said, *Orientalism*, New York, 1979.

5 E.A. Belyaev, *Arabs, Islam and the Arab Caliphate*, London, 1969, p. 115.

6 Watt's major works are *Muhammad at Mecca*, Oxford, 1953; and *Muhammad at Madina*, Oxford, 1956.

7 M.A. Shaban, *Islamic History*, AD *600–750: A New Interpretation*, Cambridge, 1971, pp. 13–14; Maxime Rodinson, *Mohammed*, Penguin, 1973, especially pp. 264–25.

8 Shaban, p. 15.

9 Ibid.

10 J. Wellhausen, *The Arab Kingdom and its Fall*, translated by Margaret Graham Weir, Calcutta, 1927. One of the important modifications was introduced by D.C. Dennet in respect of Wellhausen's theory of the history of *kharāj* and *jiziya* (Dennet, *Conversion and the Poll Tax in Early Islam*, Cambridge, Massachusetts, 1950).

11 M.A. Shaban, *The Abbasid Revolution*, Cambridge, 1970, especially p. xiv. Clearly Shaban is much harsher on Wellhausen than the evidence warrants.

12 *Chachnama*, edited by N.A. Baloch, Islamabad, 1983, pp. 163–64.

13 The most useful compilation for the jurists' opinions on taxation is Aghnides, *Theories of Mohammadan Finance*, Lahore, 1961.

14 See M. Athar Ali, 'Political Structures of the Islamic Orient in the Sixteenth and Seventeenth Centuries', in his *Mughal India: Studies in Polity, Ideas, Society and Culture*, New Delhi, 2006, pp. 94–105.

# 7 Kabīr
## The Historical Setting

*Irfan Habib*

Religion has been an undoubted component of human civilization in its various stages of evolution. The time is past – if ever there was one, except in the case of a very simplistic variant of Marxism – when one could dismiss religion as either too insignificant a factor in history or, alternatively, see its various forms as mere reflexes of social environments, which could themselves be narrowed to a few standard 'modes'. Contemporary events have retold us with renewed force that ideas, prejudices, superstitions, that is, the entire complex that constitutes the mental part of religion, does not arise automatically out of certain economic phenomena, or disappear with them, but has a life, a momentum of its own, which acts upon as well as responds to the whole social structure. For the present theme it is not of much relevance to defend Marx here, or to recall his many statements, indeed his whole theoretical work on capitalism, which often placed ideas at the centre of the universe of practice. What is unfortunate is that we have often tended to forget in our discussions of conveniently standardized stages of social evolution, the important truth that historical complexities go far beyond any possible straightforward unilinear schemes; and that the history of class struggles, carried on consciously or unconsciously, loses its richness and lessons for us when it is forced into the artificial mould of a blind and automatic process. Religion has played its role, not only in acting on behalf of the ruling classes and so justifying the suppression of popular revolts, but also, on the other side, in rallying the rebels, as in India in 1857 – a role that was inescapable when national or class consciousness was still undeveloped, as, say, in the case of peasant revolts during sixteenth-century Germany.[1]

It must at the same time be insisted that the study of history is subject to the same universal criteria of scientific enquiry as apply to all other aspects of history. It is unreasonable to demand that any religion must be analysed only on its own terms, that is, only after accepting certain premises which its followers declare to be indisputable truths.[2] No historian can regard any religion or any religious belief as *ipso facto* true or untrue, or as absolutely original or God-given, not bearing marks of precedent or external influences nor susceptible to change or evolution. For purposes of its historical significance, as against its theology, any religion or religious system has to be seen as it was understood by its followers (and different groups of them), as well as by outsiders, at each different point of time. How it is understood by the believers *now* is only a matter of interest for contemporary history, not for earlier epochs.

These general principles are as relevant to our understanding of the genesis of the ideas of Kabīr (fl. *c.* 1500) and the monotheistic movement of the late fifteenth and early sixteenth century, of which he was a unique representative. Primarily, the movement has to be seen in the realm of both social circumstances and inherited religious ideas.

It is customary in much non-academic writing to use the word 'Hinduism' to cover the varied systems of beliefs and social customs that prevailed in ancient India, as if there, then, existed a dominant religion in terms of common beliefs, which also defined the legally prescribed structure of society. It is obvious that such use of 'Hindu' and 'Hinduism' is linguistically anachronistic. The word 'Hindu' in Indian languages is a medieval loanword from Arabic and Persian, being derived from the ancient Persian (or Achaemenian) word 'Hindu' (=Sindhu) for the Indus or Sind, whence the Greek 'India'.[3] But the matter is not merely one of misapplied nomenclature. That there is not even an alternative Sanskrit or indigenous term to define a person who held beliefs ancestral to those held by Hindus today, e.g., an Indian, let us say, who was not a Buddhist or a Jaina, living in AD 600, shows that the concept of an integrated 'Hinduism' and of a 'Hindu', as the common votary of it, did not then exist. When Ashoka spoke of religious persons in India, he spoke of 'Samanas and Brahmans'.[4] Brahmanism, comprising the large pool of divergent ideas and rituals held by various schools of Brahmana priests and philosophers, was a basic fact of Indian religious situation, but only accounted for one part of it, as its coexistence with the faiths of Samanas, notably Buddhists and Jainas, implies. There was greater consonance, however, in the social sphere, notably the customs and practices of the caste system, which engulfed all, whether devotees and patrons of the Brahmanas, or of the Buddhists and Jainas.[5] The creation of 'Hinduism' out of the framework of social custom and ritual and of the various earlier schools of Brahmanical thought seems to occur practically with the diffusion of Islam in India, and some historians would argue that the process has continued into modern times.[6]

The view long prevailed among some modern writers that Islam brought a fresh wind of equality in this land of Homo Hierarchicus. This led even R.C. Majumdar to say that 'the democratic ideas of the Muslims, leading to a wonderful equality among the brothers-in-faith, offered a strong contrast to the caste system and untouchability of the Hindus.'[7] The fact, however, is that there is no sign of commitment to any element of social equality among the writings of Muslim theologians and scholars of the period. Minhāj Sirāj, himself a theologian of some eminence, speaks (1260) of the importance of the ruling class being confined to 'Turks of pure lineage and Taziks of select birth'.[8] Nearly a hundred years later, Ẓiyā Barani, acutely orthodox and exceptionally learned in Islamic theology and history, gave an uncompromising argument in favour of a rigid hierarchy of birth, which, alas, could not in practice be fully realized.[9] It is, therefore, characteristic that while Hindus were denounced as 'infidels', polytheists and image-worshippers, there is in the entire range of medieval Islamic literature no word of criticism of the caste system, the theory of pollution and the oppression of untouchables. In the late years of the sixteenth century, 'Abdu'l Qādir Badāūnī, in a work on ethics claims no superiority for the social ethics of Muslims over others, but concedes that Muslims had additional vices, including that of selling free people into slavery, though he claims that this evil had abated somewhat in his own time.[10] Indeed, the sanction for full-fledged slavery and even concubinage in Islamic law should strongly modify any attribution of equality to historical Islam.

There was a difference, however, between the social inequalities that the Islamic law and usage sanctioned, and those of the Indian caste system. Most notably, whereas upward or vertical mobility was restricted in both to varying degrees, the caste system also hindered horizontal or inter-craft and inter-professional mobility, a restriction absent in Islamic societies. This relative flexibility might have had some significance in making the economies of the caliphates and their successor polities more open to technological change, especially such as could be absorbed within the framework of manual crafts. Moreover, except for slavery, hierarchy in Islam tended to be based mainly on the possession of wealth and political power, birth playing its part largely on the basis of inheritance. The institutions of *kharāj* and *iqṭā'*, i.e. tax-rent and temporary assignments of revenue, led to greater dependence on the sovereign's will than was probably the case within the structure of 'Indian feudalism' of late ancient times, where the 'feudatories' (*rāṇakas*, etc.) were practically hereditary potentates.[11]

The establishment of the Delhi Sultanate was, therefore, accompanied by certain social and economic changes. In so far as the caste system pressed down the wages of the lower and menial castes serving as labourers and craftsmen, it increased the surplus out of which revenues came. It was, therefore, not to the interest of any ruling class, whatever its faith, to take up cudgels against caste restrictions. The Arab government in Sind, right from Muhammad ibn Qasim's time (713–14), characteristically enforced the disabilities and humiliations imposed on the pastoral Jatts of Sind, in line with those imposed by the previous Brahmana dynasty.[12] In spite of the view set forth by Professor Mohammad Habib that the Ghorian conquests were, in one respect, a 'liberation' of the low-caste craftsmen,[13] there is no specific evidence that any previous rules of caste were deliberately overthrown or abolished by the new regime. In fact, the fact that 'Alā'uddin Khalji (1296–1316) even withdrew tax-concessions from the village-menial, *balāhar*, on his small service-holding, shows not only that the menial castes were kept in their place, but that their members could not now claim from the fiscal authorities the customary exemption necessary for their subsistence.[14]

Such continuance of the constraints of the caste system was, however, accompanied by the simultaneous process of the expansion of communities of Muslims, among whom caste could not legally be the basis of hierarchy. Muslim populations grew by immigrations initially, not only from Central Asia and Iran, but also from Sind and southern Panjab where Muslim communities had flourished since the early eighth century.[15] (It was from southern Panjab that the rich and important Hindu community of Multānīs also came.)[16] Most immigrants from the Islamic regions had, of course, no caste backgrounds. Then, there were the large numbers of captives who had been made slaves: the augmentation of their ranks was a continuous process during the thirteenth and fourteenth centuries. Torn from their original castes and localities, the slaves were made to work as labourers, artisans and domestic servants. Converted to Islam simultaneously with enslavement, and often freed later on, they must have formed a significant group among Muslims[17] – their original enslavement being simultaneously a 'liberation' from caste. As Badāūnī notes towards the end of the sixteenth century, the slave trade (and, therefore, enslavement) was then in decline. It is possible to ascribe this decline and the relatively unimportant position of slavery in the Mughal Empire to the relative fall in profitability of using slave labour when free artisans became available in large numbers to pursue the imported crafts and skills.[18]

To the caste-free core of Muslim populations formed by immigrants and slaves were thus added infusions of free converts, quite possibly passing over in groups as their headmen took to the new religious allegiance. Unfortunately, the entire process is still obscure, and later traditions of large group or clan conversions (or fictitious collective migrations) can hardly be cited as reliable evidence in support of our supposition. If such group conversions occurred, caste customs and barriers would continue until, in course of time, the increasing influence of the Shari'a would begin to dilute the strength of earlier customs. It is possible to argue that living around 1500 Kabīr was a member of such a weaver community in transition.[19] A hint of this may be located in his indifferent use of 'Korī' and 'Julāhā' for himself, whereas the latter word derived from Persian is generally used for Muslim weavers alone.[20]

Such Neo-Muslim groups marked their conversion by slaughtering cows at the two 'Ids and revering Shaikhs, *shahīds* (martyrs) and *pīrs*, as Ravidās tells us of Kabīr's father.[21] But, next to such converts were still other professional groups not converted, and yet living and working closely with Muslims. Hindu masons in thirteenth–fifteenth centuries have left their epigraphic traces on the Qutb Minar and Jaunpur mosques.[22] This is certainly remarkable since in building construction there was such a fundamental alteration of technique, involved in the shift from trabeate to arcuate construction, and from stone to brick and rubble bonded with lime mortar.

It is difficult to say why some artisan groups converted to Islam, and others did not. It is, however, important to see that there was a pull, not so much from the deliberate blandishments of an alien egalitarian faith, as from the demand created for craft and urban labour by a new series of changes. When Kosambi (1956) spoke of 'Islamic raiders . . . breaking down hidebound custom in the adoption and transmission of new techniques',[23] he made an insightful suggestion which has been justified by subsequent detailed work. Besides the changes in construction techniques and the arrival of paper manufacture, we now know that devices like the spinning wheel, pedals in the loom, pin-drum gearing for the 'Persian' waterwheel, tinning, more efficient liquor distillation, etc., were also adopted and diffused in the wake of the Sultans' armies.[24]

Simultaneously, the urban demand for craft goods was probably enlarged by the flow of wealth into towns generated by a more efficient (possibly more oppressive) and successful system of revenue extraction from the countryside, well established by the end of 'Alāu'ddīn Khaljī's reign (1296–1316). There was correspondingly a marked expansion of trade, shown by the growth in the Sultanate gold and silver coin-minting. Finally, there was a sizeable urban expansion, so well attested by archaeological remains.[25]

It should be inferred that the technological infusion and the new demand created not only the ground for expansion of new professions, but also for a large number of entrants into old professions. This could initially, but only partly, be met by immigration and enslavement, then by conversion; ultimately, it required suitable adjustments within the established caste system. It could be argued that the very flexibility provided by a relatively large size of caste-free labour within the Muslim fold acted as a safety valve for the caste system, which could continue with its own rigidities in the domain where old occupations remained unaffected by the limited changes in craft technology. However, the enslavement, the conversions, and the new professions, could also introduce an element of instability in which old barriers of both caste and religion would be brought into question among groups affected by the new economic and social pressures.

It seems to me that here must be sought the explanation for one of the most dramatic aspects of the popular monotheistic movement, namely, its low-caste, artisan character. While Chaitanya, Mīrā Bāī, Tulsīdās and Sūrdās, who represented the *sagun bhakti* movement, belonged to either the priestly or the aristocratic class, the leaders of popular monotheism who are listed in a memorable hymn composed in the name of Dhannā Jāṭ by Guru Arjan (d. 1606), came from the opposite side of the social spectrum: Nāmdev, 'the petty calico printer' (*ādh-dām ko chhīparo*); Kabīr, 'the low-caste weaver' (*nīch kulā jolāhra*); Ravidas, 'the carrion remover' (*dhuvanta ḍhor*); and Sain, 'the barber and village-menial' (*nāi butkārīa*). Their access to God (Govind) encouraged Dhannā too, though 'a mere Jat' (*jāṭaro*), or peasant, to seek Him.[26] This list could of course be extended: Guru Nanak, the petty trader or accountant (*Khatrī*), whose successors would make such a strong appeal to the Jat peasantry and lower classes of the Panjab;[27] Dādū, a cotton-carder (*naddāf*); and Harīdās (d. 1645), a Jat slave.[28] They were not unconscious of their roots – Kabir himself not only triumphantly proclaimed his own profession of weaving, but could also see God Himself as a Weaver (Korī).[29] Ravidās owned that his family used to remove dead cattle in Banaras,[30] and explicitly claimed that 'caste and non-caste' (*baran abaran*) mattered not for God's love, it being open equally to all – 'Brahman, Bais, Sud (Shudra) and Khyatrī (Khatri), as well as Dom, Chandar (Chandal) and Malechh'.[31] Well might Tulsīdās (*c.* 1575–76) exclaim that the appearance of Shudras as religious preachers was the most certain sign of the degradation of *Kali-jug*, the Kali Age.[32] He must have been disturbed still more at what these monotheistic Shudras taught – a wholesale rejection of Hinduism and Islam, in bold preaching addressed directly to the poor, demanding an acceptance of God and rejection of all formal religion. The immense radicalism of such wholesale rejection was unprecedented in the history of India – unique, perhaps, till then in the world.

> The Hindu when dying, cries out 'Rām!', the Musalman 'O Khudā!'
> Says Kabīr, he (alone) is alive, who never accepts this duality.
>
> Kaba then becomes Kāsī, Rām becomes Rahīm
> Moṭh (coarse grain) becomes fine flour, and Kabīr sits down to enjoy it.[33]

Kabīr was recognized in the sixteenth century, not as a Muslim or Hindu, but eminently as a 'monotheist' (*muwaḥḥid*). This is the purport of a conversation which 'Abdu'l Ḥaqq reported as having taken place between his grandfather and father as early as 1522.[34] It is also the essence of Abū'l-Fazl's two celebrated notices of Kabir in 1595:

> Many truths emanating from his speech and reports of his actions circulate among the people. Out of the broadness of his path and the elevatedness of his vision, he held in affection both

> Muslims and Hindus. When he left this physical frame, the Brahmans came to cremate him, the Muslims to take him to the graveyard.

Elsewhere:

> He lived in the time of Sikandar Lodi. The door of spiritual truth became open to him somewhat, and he abandoned the obsolete customs of the age. He has left behind many Hindi verses containing the truths he preached.[35]

Another early summary of his teachings comes from Nābhājī's *Bhaktmāl* (*c.* 1600):

> Kabir refused to recognize caste rules (*varnāshram*) and the six [Brahmanical] schools. He held that without devotion (*bhakti*), religion (*dharm*) would be irreligion (*adharm*). Asceticism (*jog*), fasting and charity are useless without adoration (*bhajan*). By means of *ramainis, shabdis* and *sakhis*, he preached to both Hindus and Muslims (Turaks). He showed no partiality to any one, but spoke for the benefit of all. He spoke boldly and never tried to say what would please the world.[36]

This is how Kabir's preachings were seen by those who had access to his compilations within a century or so of his death. It is not necessary here to support these very accurate near-contemporary perceptions by quoting chapter and verse from Kabīr. These assessments, however, did not locate the source of Kabīr's thought in any single tradition, and Kabīr himself refrains from mentioning any teacher or precursor. Yet attempts to find precursors for Kabīr were soon not lacking. One precursor was supposed to be Nāmdev, the dyer or calico-printer from Maharashtra, whose verses find a place in the *Gurū Granth Sāhib*, and who, in the seventeenth century tradition, was seen as a monotheist very much in the mould of Kabīr.[37] This would then essentially place the origin of Kabīr and his school only within a like tradition of an earlier time. But all we know of Nāmdev comes from post-Kabīr times; and Kabīr himself has no mention of him. Such also is the case with Rāmānand through whom an effort has been made to trace Kabīr's movement indirectly to Rāmānuja (d. 1137).[38] But in the *Dabistān* (*c.* 1653), where the legend of a Brahmanical preceptor of Kabīr is first given credence, his name in the first version of the work is

Gang, and only in the second is the name of Rāmānand substituted for Gang. Clearly, the legend was in the process of formation as late as the mid-seventeenth century, being obviously an 'invention of tradition' at par with the still later one of a Brahmanical birth for the lowly weaver–saint.[39] At best Kabīr's frequent use of the name of Rām for God (also referred to as Hari, Gopal, Rahīm, Karīm, Khudā, etc.) apparently provided the justification for the supposed Vaishnavite affiliations. But any reference either to Rām's family, or to the Vaishnavite pantheon, is entirely absent in his verses. The author of the *Dabistān*, who places Kabīr among the Bairāgīs, and the latter among the Vaishnavites, himself insists that Kabīr was a monotheist (*muwaḥḥid*) and his Rām was really the Almighty God (*Īzid-i muta'āl*).[40] Kabīr's 'Rām' has as much affinity to the deity Rām, as the Muslims' Allah has to the god of that name in the idol house of the pagans of Mecca.

As against the Vaishnavite affiliations, the possibility of a Shaivite influence has also been urged, notably by Hazari Prasad Dwivedi, who has seen in Kabīr a continuation or reassertion of the Shaivite Nāth-Yogī tradition.[41] Here one must distinguish between Kabīr's use of terms and words, familiar to himself and his hearers, borrowed from the popular Yogic tradition, and his own ideas. In the latter realm, except for the rejection of Brahmanas, there is no perceptible Yogic or Tantric element in Kabīr. On the other hand, there is a scornful rejection of the claims set forth by the Yogīs. Any further discussion of this question is not necessary here, because of a fairly full treatment of it by Charlotte Vaudeville.[42] We can also dispense with the supposition of any impact of Shankara's Vedānta on Kabīr as well. This is because the total omission of any reference to Shankarāchārya's views in Abū'l Faẓl's description of Brahmanical philosophy in the *Ā'īn-i Akbarī* (*c.* 1595), based on extensive inquiries from erudite pundits, shows that Shankarāchārya had not yet acquired much eminence in North India. It was only in the *Dabistān* written in the middle of the seventeenth century that Shankarāchārya came to be recognized as the 'select among the later seers', with his stamp put fully on Vedānta, if not Hinduism.[43] There seems to be no recognizable reflection of Shankarāchārya's Vedānta in Kabīr's verses. Here *māyā*, for example, is used in its significance of worldly life,[44] and not as the Illusion of reality conceived by Shankarāchārya.

It is possible to argue nevertheless that concepts of monotheism and pantheism were already present in India's pre-Islamic tradition. Alberuni (*c.* 1035), the world's first 'orientalist', detected these elements in the *Bhagavadgīta*, though he shows no awareness, of course, of Shankarāchārya.[45] Of pantheism, Kabir seems hardly to display a trace; on the other hand, his monotheism is not just simply explicit, but is trenchantly and repeatedly proclaimed – God is one, God is everywhere, etc. It would seem, therefore, that what existed on the periphery of ancient Indian philosophy, became with Kabīr the centre of everything. One can, then, legitimately ask whether in this movement from the periphery to the centre, one can detect a strong influence of Islam.

The influence of Islam on Kabīr certainly needs to be discussed, but a certain amount of discrimination is called for. That there was only a limited amount of direct influence of Muslim theology and its vocabulary on him can be easily demonstrated linguistically. In the sphere of belief and ritual, Kabir rejected the Ka'ba and the mosque, just as he rejected images and the temple. It has been supposed, notably by Tara Chand, that he was influenced by Sufism.[46] We must remember that Sufism is a doctrine which rests man's obedience to God essentially, even solely, on the seeker's love of God as the Beloved. The rigour of preceptor (*pir*)–disciple (*murīd*) relationship is based entirely on the need to pursue the esoteric path prescribed for such supra-sexual love. The sufic doctrine of love and practice of preceptor and disciple had been fairly well developed by the thirteenth century, before Islam reached Kabīr's own region. And yet, in Kabīr's verses the theme of love as the cornerstone of the man–God relationship is rather weak (weaker still, perhaps, in the *Gurū Granth Sāhib* recension than in the Dādūpanthī one). While it is justifiable to see the sufic concept of communion or self-effacement (*fanā*) in some verses of Kabīr,[47] the 'pantheism' of Ibn al-'Arabī (d. 1240), which had had achieved some following in India by the late fourteenth century, and thereafter spread more widely among sufic circles,[48] is not recognizable. Almost predominant is God's position as the Judge, which is, perhaps, the most central element in ordinary non-sufic Islam. On this Kabīr uses imagery (God as Moneylender or Merchant or Account-taker) unacceptable or unfamiliar to orthodox Islam, and yet corresponding so well to the central Islamic notion of the relationship between man and God:

> Kabīr, the capital belongs to the *Sāh* (Usurer), and you waste it all.

There will be great difficulty for you at the time of the rendering of accounts.[49]

Or:

My Lord (*Sāīn*) is a Baniyā (Merchant). He conducts his commerce with ease (*sahaj*).
Without scales and balances, He weighs the entire universe.[50]

Or, again:

[Your] term of office (*amal*) is over,
Strict agents (*dūt*) have arrived to exact
what you have collected (*jama*).[51]

It is perhaps the most 'economical' inference that this sense of Divine Judgement on human thought and deed essentially comes from Islam, as seen by ordinary people, to whom the Quranic insistence on Reward and Punishment, set the major reason for obedience to decrees Divine. We have here again an illustration of Kabīr's characteristic distillation of a common belief to obtain first principles.

Yet Kabīr, goes beyond this. He preaches a monotheism which in its total surrender to God and rejection of all ritual, transcends the limits of orthodox Islam. The unity of God becomes for Kabīr the means of comprehension of the unity of man; and so, there comes an absolute rejection, explicit and vocal, not only of the concept and practice of purity and pollution of the caste system, but also of conventional mode of worship and all ritual. Not only Kabīr's verses, but also the anecdotes related of him became a perennial means of popular expression of revulsion against untouchability and religious differences.[52] The earliest anecdotes are found in the *Dabistān* (*c.* 1653). We are told how Kabir made fun of Brahmanas when they refused to drink Ganges water from his hands because he was 'weaver-born and therefore of a low class of people'. Another tells us of how he ridiculed image-worship; and yet another recalls his desperate poverty. Finally, the author gives the anecdote of how both Muslims and Hindus claimed his body, and how a recluse (*faqīr*) came to tell them that Kabīr was 'a gnostic ('*ārif*), and free (*fārigh*) of both these religions'. He ends by quoting for Kabīr the couplet of 'Urfi, the Persian poet at Akbar's court:

So live with the good and the bad, O 'Urfi,
that when you die
The Muslim bathes your body in holy water
and the Hindu cremates it![53]

The lowly penniless devotee of God thus became for the common man the apostle of humanity.

Tracing Kabīr to his various ideological contexts and sources is important. Equally important, however, is to see his action as essentially a negation of some gross inequities of our culture, and not a mere synthesis of its divergent elements. I have attempted in this modest contribution to examine the circumstances, material, social and ideological, amidst which the thought of Kabīr and other like-minded preachers took shape. But the radicalism of the response was their own achievement, not simply a 'determined' one. Their vision and boldness is a precious national heritage whose relevance is not bound by time.

**Notes and References**

1 See F. Engels' evaluation of the Protestant leader Thomas Munzer's ideas and beliefs in *The Peasant War in Germany*, English translation, Moscow, 1956, pp. 55–59, 70–78.

2 Cf. M. Athar Ali, 'The Islamic Background to Indian History: An Interpretation of the Islamic Past', in his *Mughal India: Polity, Ideas, Society and Culture*, New Delhi, 2006, pp. 4–5.

3 Irfan Habib, Introductory essay, in *India: Studies in the History of an Idea*, New Delhi, 2004, pp. 4–5.

4 Ashokan Rock Edicts III, IV, IX and XIII. In his Rock Edict XIII, Ashoka recognizes that among Yonas 'there are no groups of Brahmans and *samanas*'.

5 This is borne out by the description of the Indian caste system by the Chinese Buddhist scholar and pilgrim Xuan Zhuang (Hsuan Tsang) (602–64), in which there is no suggestion that the Buddhists did not subscribe to the system (*Si-yu-ki, Buddhist Records of the Western World*, translated by Samuel Beal, London, 1884, Vol. I, p. 82; Thomas Watters, *On Yuan Chwang's Travels in India, 629–645* AD, London, 1905, Vol. I, pp. 168–70).

6 Cf. Romila Thapar, 'Imagined Religious Communities?: Ancient History and the Modern Search for a Hindu Identity', in her *History and Beyond*, New Delhi, 2000, pp. 60–88, especially pp. 78–81; and D.N. Jha, *Looking for a Hindu Identity*, Presidential Address, Indian History Congress, 66th session, Santiniketan, January 2006.

7 *History and Culture of the Indian People*, edited by R.C. Majumdar, VI, Bharatiya Vidya Bhavan, p. 624.

8 Minhāj Sirāj, *Ṭabaqāt-i Nāṣirī*, edited by Abdu'l Hai Habibi, Kabul, 1343, II, p. 66.

9 See Irfan Habib, 'Barani's Theory of the History of the Delhi Sultanate', *Indian Historical Review*, VII (1–2), New Delhi, pp. 99–115, and idem, 'Ẓiyā Baranī's Vision of the State', *Medieval History Journal*, II(1), 1999, pp. 19–36.

10 'Abdu'l Qādir Badāūnī, *Nijātu'r Rashīd*, edited by S. Moinul Haq, Lahore, 1972, pp. 239–40.

11 The major study of 'Indian feudalism' is R.S. Sharma, *Indian Feudalism*, second edition, 1980; see especially pp. 127–212.

12 *Chachnāma*, edited by Umar bin Muhammad Daudpota, Hyderabad-Deccan, 1939, pp. 47–48, 214–15; al-Balāzurī, translated by Murgotten, *Foundations of the Islamic State*, II, New York, 1924, pp. 216–19, 223.

13 Mohammad Habib, Introduction to H.M. Elliot and J. Dowson, *History of India as Told by Its Own Historians*, Vol. II, reprint, Aligarh, 1952, pp. 54ff.

14 Ẓiyā Barani, *Tārīkh-i Fīrozshāhī*, edited by Sayyid Ahmad Khan and W.N. Lees, Calcutta, 1862, p. 287.

15 On such migrations see I.H. Siddiqui, 'Social Mobility in the Delhi Sultanate', *Medieval India: 1*, edited by Irfan Habib, Aligarh/New Delhi, 1992, pp. 23ff.

16 See Irfan Habib, 'Merchant Communities in Pre-Colonial India', *The Rise of Merchant Empires*, edited by James D. Tracy, Cambridge, 1990, pp. 381–82.

17 On slaves in the Delhi Sultanate, see T. Raychaudhuri and Irfan Habib, *Cambridge Economic History of India*, Vol. I, Cambridge, 1982, pp. 89–93, where detailed references are provided. See also Irfan Habib, 'Slavery in the Delhi Sultanate, 13th and 14th Centuries – Evidence from Sufic Literature', *Indian Historical Review*, XV (1–2), pp. 248–56.

18 Cf. Irfan Habib, 'Economic History of the Delhi Sultanate', *Indian Historical Review*, IV(2), p. 294.

19 Kabīr's date around 1500 is fixed by Abū'l Faẓl's statement (1595) that he lived during the reign of Sultan Sikandar Lodī (1489–1517) (*Ā'īn-i Akbarī*, edited by H. Blochmann, Bib. Ind., Calcutta, 1867–77, I, p. 433). In what may be the earliest recorded reference to Kabīr in Persian texts, 'Abdu'l Ḥaqq in 1590–91 reports a conversation about Kabīr between his father and grandfather that took place on 19 February 1522 ('Abdu'l Haqq, *Akhbāru'l Akhyār*, Deoband, 1332/1924, p. 306). Earlier dates going beyond 1450 seem to be as unhistorical as the myth of Kabīr's Brahmanical parentage.

It may be mentioned here that since Kabīr's verses in popular circulation continued to be added to, the safest course is to confine oneself to the two earliest collections of his verses, (i) *Shrī Gurū Granth Sāhib*, completed by Guru Arjan in 1604, and containing, among the verses of the Gurūs and various *bhagats*, a large number of verses of Kabīr under various *rāgs*. The authoritative Nagari edition, published by Shiromani Gurdwara Prabandhak Committee, Amritsar, 1951, has been used by me. (ii) The Dādūpanthī collection, made apparently early in the seventeenth century. These were conveniently collected in a manuscript whose text is published in *Kabīr Granthāvalī*, edited by Shyāmsundar Dās, Kashi, VS 2008/1951. They are apparently included also in *The Sarbangi of Rajjabdās*, edited by Shahabuddin Iraqi, Aligarh, 1985, but the absence of a proper list of contents or index makes the volume practically useless for purposes of reference. All manuscripts of Kabīr's *Bījak*, the standard text in use among the Kabīrpanthīs of Uttar Pradesh and Bihar are late and the restoration of the earliest core of it, which might go back to the seventeenth century is not apparently achievable with the materials we have. See Linda Hess and Sukhdev Singh's translation of *The Bījak of Kabīr*, Delhi, 1986.

[20] For example,

'The weaver (*julāha*) looks into his own hut and recognizes
God (Rām) there;
Says Kabīr: I have broken my loom (*kargah*), and the
weaver (*korī*) ties yarn with yarn [to make warp].'

(*Gurū Granth Sāhib*, Āsā Kabīr 36, Nāgari edition, p. 484)

See Hazariprasad Dwivedi, *Kabir*, Bombay, n.d., pp. 5–6 and note; and C. Vaudeville, *Kabir*, I, Oxford, 1974, pp. 83–85, 87–89. In U.P. in 1891 there were 9,19, 614 Koris (Hindu weavers) as against 7,80,231 Julahas (Muslims). (William Crooke, *Tribes and Castes of North Western Provinces*, London, 1897, III, p. 70, 73; IV, pp. 94, 96).

[21] *Gurū Granth Sāhib*, Rāg Malār, Ravidās: Nagari edition, p. 1923.

[22] Pushpa Prasad, *Sanskrit Inscriptions of Delhi Sultanate*, Delhi, 1990, pp. xxviii–xxx.

[23] D.D. Kosambi, *An Introduction to the Study of Indian History*, second edition, Bombay, 1975, p. 370.

[24] For a preliminary effort, see Irfan Habib, 'Technology and Society, 13th and 14th Centuries', Presidential Address, Medieval India Section, *Proceedings of the Indian History Congress*, Varanasi Session, pp. 139–61; and a subsequent paper, 'Medieval Technology: Exchanges between India and the Islamic World', *Aligarh Journal of Oriental Studies*, II(1–2), pp. 197–222.

[25] Cf. Irfan Habib, 'Economic History of the Delhi Sultanate', *Indian Historical Review*, IV(2), pp. 289-97. The archaeological evidence from the thirteenth century onwards has to be set side by side with that adduced by R.S. Sharma for urban decline till *c.*1000 in his *Urban Decay in India (c. 300–c. 1000)*, New Delhi, 1987.

[26] *Gurū Granth Sāhib*, Āsā Dhana; Nagari edition, pp. 487–88.

[27] For a seventeenth-century comment on this, see *Dabistān-i Mazāhib*, p. 186.

[28] Ibid., pp. 173–74.

[29] 'No one knows the secret of the Weaver (Korī)
He has set the warp of the whole world'
(*Gurū Granth Sāhib*, Āsā: Kabīr 36, Nagari edition, p. 484). See also the assertion: "I am a *julāha* of Kāsī" (*Kabīrgranthāvalī*, p. 128).

30 *Shri Gurū Granth Sāhib*, Malār: Ravidās, Nagari edition, p. 1293.

31 Ibid., Rāg Bilāwalu, Ravidās; Nagari edition, p. 858.

32 *Rāmcharitmānas*, Uttarkand, Gita press edition, Gorakhpur, V.S. 2046, pp. 520–22.

33 *Kabīr Granthāvalī*, edited by Shyamsundar Das, p. 42.

34 'Abdu'l Ḥaqq, *Akhbāru'l Akhyār (Takmila)*, Deoband, 1332/1913–14, p. 306.

35 Abū'l-Faẓl, *Ā'īn-i Akbarī*, edited by H. Blochmann, Bib. Ind., Calcutta, 1867–77, I, pp. 393, 433.

36 *Shri Bhaktmāl*, edited by Ganeshdas, first edition, Govardhan, n.d., p. 171.

37 *Dabistān-i Mazāhib*, litho., published by Ibrahim bin Nūr Muḥammad, Bombay, 1875, pp. 160–61.

38 For example, Tara Chand, *Influence of Islam on Indian Culture*, second edition, Allahabad, 1963, pp. 143–44.

39 This matter is discussed in Irfan Habib, 'A Fragmentary Exploration of an Indian Text on Religions and Sects, & *c*.', Proceedings of the Indian History Congress, Millennium (61st) Session, Kolkata, 2000–2001, p. 480. The reference to Rāmānand, as Kabīr's preceptor, in *Dabistān-i Mazāhib*, Bombay edition, is on p. 159. Priyadas' ascription of the connexion with Rāmānand is some 60 years later (1712) (Vaudeville, p. 31). But Rāmānand is a simple iconoclastic monotheist (even scornful of 'the Veds and Purānas') in the only composition ascribed to him in the *Gurū Granth Sāhib*, Basantu Hindolu, Rāmānand, Nagari edition, p. 1195.

40 *Dabistān-i Mazāhib*, p. 159.

41 H. Dwivedi, *Kabīr*, Bombay, n.d.

42 Vaudeville, *Kabīr*, pp. 85–89, 120–148.

43 *Dabistān-i Mazāhib*, pp.131ff. The author ('Mobad') refers to 'numerous works in this field (Vedānta)' by Shankarāchārya, and gives a fairly knowledgeable description of his system.

44 For example, 'Kabīr, Māyā is an enchantress, as sweet as sugar.' (*Kabīr Granthāvalī*, p. 25).

45 Edward Sachau's translation of *Alberuni's India*, London, 1910, Vol. I, pp. 122–23, for monotheism, and pp. 73–74, 76, for pantheism.

46 Tara Chand, *Influence of Islam on Indian Culture*, second edition, Allahabad, 1963, pp. 150–53. One difficulty in dealing with Tara Chand's arguments is that he makes use of a large variety of compositions ascribed to Kabīr, without consideration of their authenticity, even in relative terms.

47 For example: 'When I was, Hari (God) was not;
Now, Hari is, I am not.'
(*Kabīr Granthāvalī*, p. 12).

48 Cf. S. Athar Abbas Rizvi, *Muslim Revivalist Movements in Northern India in the Sixteenth and Seventeenth Centuries*, Agra, 1965, pp. 43ff.

49 *Kabīr Granthāvalī*, p. 42. The verse occurs in the Dādūpanthī version. There is no sanction for Vaudeville's (*Kabīr*, p. 269) reading of the *Sāh* as Destiny: it simply means moneylender or merchant–banker of some status.

[50] *Kabīr Granthāvalī*, p. 62.

[51] *Gurū Granth Sāhib*, Sūhī: Kabīr, Nagari edition, p. 792. In these verses *dūt jam* has been interpreted as 'death's messengers', whereas *jam* here clearly stands for *jama'* and is related to the next word *lenā* (to extract).

[52] Anecdotes about Kabīr already circulated among the people when the *A'īn* was written (*c.* 1595) (*Ain-i Akbarī*, Bib. Ind., I, p. 393).

[53] *Dabistān-i Mazāhib*, pp. 159–60.

# 8 Akbar and the Theologians' Declaration (*Maḥẓar*) of 1579

*Osamu Kondo*

About 80 years ago, in the 1920s, a dispute arose among British historians regarding the nature of the 'Sepoy Mutiny' of 1857. The source of the dispute was a paper published in 1922 by F.W. Buckler (1891–1960), then at Cambridge, titled 'The Political Theory of the Indian Mutiny'.[1]

Buckler argued that the edict issued by the Mughal emperor Shāh 'Ālam II in 1765 was the source of authority of the East India Company itself within India. By this edict, the Mughal emperor had granted the right of *dīwānī* to the Company upon the condition that the land revenue collected by the Company should be periodically transferred to the treasury of the Mughal Empire. The 1857 Revolt was an attempt to prevent the Company from acting arbitrarily and committing a breach of the above condition, and to re-establish the loyalty of the Company as a retainer of the Mughal emperor. Based on these circumstances, Buckler argued that if there was a rebel, it was definitely the East India Company, and thus, the British had no grounds on which to bring the Mughal emperor to trial as a rebel or traitor.

Naturally, Buckler's argument was opposed by other British historians.[2] The focal point of the dispute was the relationship between the British East India Company and the Mughal Empire, and the nature of the 1857 Mutiny. It is interesting that in his paper, Buckler also discussed symbolic ceremonies that indicate the relationship between lords and retainers. According to Buckler, the ceremony took the form of the retainer demonstrating his loyalty by requesting an audience (*nazar*) with the lord, and the lord bestowing upon him the robes of honour (*khil'at* in Arabic, *sar-u-pā* in Persian). The relationship between the East India Company and the Mughal Empire was characterized by this ceremony until the nineteenth century.

On the other hand, the second Mughal Indian emperor, Humāyūn (1530–56) was forced on occasion to assume the position of a governor, and had to accept the robes of honor from the Safavid Emperor Shāh Tahmāsp during his period of exile in Persia. It was Akbar who asserted his own absolute sovereignty within his empire. This, according to Buckler, was essentially proclaimed in the scholars' declaration (*mahzar*) on the authority of the Mughal emperor issued in 1579. Henceforth, the Mughal Emperor was a sovereign fully in his own right, and subject to no one else's lordship.

Recently, in India, focus has shifted to another aspect of Akbar's work. Many people are beginning to realize that the composite culture of India, which has been established over many centuries, is at risk with the rise of Hindu fundamentalism. As a result, the study of Akbar's reign has become a pressing issue due to its significance in the development of an integrated Hindu and Muslim culture. In October 1992, a symposium on 'Akbar and his India' was held at the University of Delhi. Nonetheless, in December of the same year, Hindu extremists committed the atrocious act of destroying the Bābrī Masjid at Ayodhya that had been built during Babur's reign.

At the symposium, in his address, Irfan Habib stated that one of the key conceptual foundations of the empire created by Akbar and his political advisor, Abū'l-Fazl (1551–1602), was the elaboration of the implications of the recognition of the emperor as an agent of God. Habib argued that like God, his Principal, the emperor was expected to be impartial in the benefits conferred on the people, regardless of their religion and other attributes.[3] Indeed, the claim that the emperor was an agent of God is expressly made in the 1579 declaration.

This paper, therefore, will begin with a scrutiny of the 1579 declaration.[4]

### Promulgation of the Declaration (*Maḥẓar*)

According to 'Abd al-Qādir Badā'ūnī, the background of the promulgation of the declaration in September 1579 was as follows:

The declaration was promulgated with the signatures and seals of 'Abdullāh Ansārī Makhdūm al-Mulk, Shaikh 'Abd al-Nabī, the minister of land-grants, Jalāl al-Dīn Multānī, *qāzī al-quzāt,* Ṣadr Jahān, *muftī-yi kull,* and Shaikh Mubārak, all regarded as some of the most knowledgeable *'ulamā* of that age, and Ghāzī Khān Badakhshī, a prominent epistemologist. It defined the absolute supremacy of the righteous leader (*imām-i 'ādil*) over the *mujtahid* (one qualified to exercise *ijtihād* or legal interpretation), and laid out the rationale behind this supremacy. All ambiguities in law were to be eliminated by the exercise of sovereign intervention in case of disagreements among interpreters. The emperor's order once given would become absolute for everyone, regardless of their religious or secular position. There had been a lengthy discussion on this issue. The discussion was around how the term *ijtihād* (deriving rules) should be defined and who should be regarded as entitled to be a *mujtahid*. In addition, discussion ensued on the exact limits of authority of the righteous leader. This leader was held to be positioned above the *mujtahid* and was competent to make fair decisions on secular affairs, to make final rulings on conflicting issues according to the circumstances and the requirements of the time. Finally, as a result of the discussions, all participants, some voluntarily and the others reluctantly, signed or put their seals of endorsement on the document.[5]

Following the above explanation, Badā'ūnī quoted the full text of the declaration as follows:

> India has been a centre of peace and security as well as a place of justice and benevolence, as kings granted justice and enlightenment to the blessed people. Therefore, many people from Arabia and Iran sought immigration and naturalization. This included commoners and nobility, especially scholars with a profound knowledge of Islamic literature, and those acquainted with the details of the tradition. These people were also leaders in the forest of spiritual salvation and the carriers of diverse knowledge in a highly intellectual world.
>
> The leaders and outstanding scholars with extensive knowledge of the Qur'ān and hadīs̱ [issuing this document] are all devout followers of their religion and have capabilities that are respected by all people. In order to reinforce the situation created by the given facts and to understand what this situation implies, they have discussed in earnest and deliberated at length, and have arrived at an answer to a profound question of great significance by consulting the scriptures: 'Obey God, and obey the Apostle and those in authority amongst you' in the Chapter of Women (Qur'ān) and 'On judgment day, the one who is closest to God is the righteous leader. Those who obey the current ruler (*amīr*)

are those who wish to devote themselves to God and those who disobey the current ruler are disbelievers.' This answer has been arrived at based on the true traditions (*hadīs̱*) as well as following the sense of reason. Therefore, the scholars proclaim the following:

Before God, the righteous ruler (*sultān-i 'ādil*) is positioned above those who are qualified to exercise *ijtihād*. The great emperor, Abu'l-Fath Jalāl al-Dīn Muḥammad Akbar, the Islamic monarch and a protector of the people, a leader of the adherents (*amīr al-mu'minīn*) and the reflection of the universal God – may Allāh protect his empire in perpetuity – is the most righteous, sagacious, and pious. Therefore, if there is a difference in opinion among those who are qualified to exercise *ijtihād* on matters of religion, the emperor shall select one from among the differing opinions, using his supreme comprehension and clear judgment. If this decision is deemed by the emperor as beneficial to humanity and positive for the world-order as well as aligned with his views, the emperor's order, based on this decision, must be followed, under all circumstances and without any exceptions, by all people including the emperor's subjects. Similarly, if the emperor prepares an order based on his rational thought and gives the order as bringing benefit to humanity and not conflicting with the sacred scriptures, obedience to it is demanded under all circumstances and without exception. Defiance will lead to conviction in the afterlife and be the cause of suffering in religion and worldly affairs in this life.

This document was written in a truthful spirit as a declaration (*maḥẕar*) by the scholars of theology and Islamic Law who follow the righteous path to declare the glory of God and Islam. This date is the Rajab month in 987 (24 August–22 September 1579).

After quoting the above statements, Badā'ūnī explained that the declaration was drafted by Shaikh Mubārak. Unlike the others who reluctantly signed the document, Shaikh Mubārak signed it without protest and added a sentence to his signature which read, 'This is what I have longed for, for many years.' After this *fatwā* (religious ruling) or declaration was presented to the emperor, he was able to exercise *ijtihād*, and the supremacy of the guide (*imām*) was established, eliminating all opposing factions.[6]

**Significance of the Declaration**

The implications of this declaration can be summarized in the following four points:

First, it officially recognized Akbar as a caliph. This is apparent from the fact that Akbar was given the title of *amīr al-mu'minīn.* Other titles, such as *imām-i 'adil* or *sultān-i 'adil,* can also be interpreted as indicating that Akbar was held to be a caliph. Second, as a matter of course, it definitely placed Akbar, as caliph, above the *mujtahids.* (Some Islamic scholars argued that the door to *ijtihād* has been closed since the tenth century, and the fresh exercise of *ijtihād* itself was prohibited. The Shi'ite *'ulamā,* however, did not take this position.)

Third, as a consequence of the facts mentioned in the first and second points, the declaration specified that Emperor Akbar had the authority to select an opinion in the event of a disagreement among *mujtahids.* Fourth, Akbar was allowed to issue religious rulings (*fatwā*), provided he did not violate the statements in the divine text (*nass*).[7]

With these distinctive features, the 1579 declaration delivered a strong message to the world outside the empire, that the Mughal emperor is qualified as a caliph and demonstrated the empire's inherent authority, independent from the Safavid Empire of Persia, the Ottoman Empire and the Uzbek khanate of central Asia. The purpose of this was to avoid any intervention of these powers. On the other hand, inside the empire, the declaration was intended to restrict the *'ulama's* authority and to establish the emperor's absolute supremacy, not only in the secular field, but also in religious areas, especially over scholars of Islamic law, and to establish the emperor as the supreme authority in both religious and secular matters. This was a significant action in terms of the establishment of the early modern despotic monarchy of the Mughal Empire, as well as in its religious implications.

Buckler also published a paper focusing on this declaration in 1924[8] and reiterated his argument, which is discussed in the beginning of this chapter. Buckler again emphasized that the objective of the declaration was to become independent from the Safavid Persian Empire, for which, according to him an opportunity had been created by conditions in Iran following the death of Shāh Tahmāsp in 1576. Buckler also pointed out that in order to avoid the antipathy of the Shi'ites in the Mughal Empire, by explicitly dismissing loyalty to the

Safavid ruler, the statements in the declaration contained several expressions used by Shi'ites in order to obscure this intent and to make it difficult for the Shi'ites to resist the declaration. Thus Akbar challenged the position of the emperor of the Ottoman Empire as the Sunni caliph by declaring himself as a caliph, and also delivered a clear message that the Empire was free from the Shi'ite leaders of the Safavid Empire by declaring that his position is above that of *mujtahid.*

Buckler's views have not gone unchallenged. Nurul Hassan and Yasuhiro Ona have criticized Buckler's placing of the significance of the 1579 declaration in the context of international developments, especially in Persia.[9]

**Impact of the Declaration**

Although Buckler's argument has been criticized, his papers have brought to our notice an important perspective that cannot be ignored when we examine the significance of the declaration in the light of later history leading to the Khilafat movement in the twentieth century. Though the details are not examined in this paper, the issue of the symbolic ceremonies of the audience with the lord and the bestowing of robes of honor, which Buckler raised in his 1922 paper, was also an important one.

Immediately after the declaration was promulgated in September 1579, Makhdūm al-Mulk and Shaikh 'Abd al-Nabī, who signed the declaration, resiled from their endorsement of the declaration. These two individuals, who had outstanding authority in religious affairs and Islamic law, began to say publicly that they had been forced to put down their signatures on it and, that, therefore, the declaration was invalid. Akbar decided to send these two men into exile, by compelling them to undertake a pilgrimage to Mecca in the beginning of 1580. Their official assignment was to carry gifts from the emperor to the scholars in Hijaz. Soon after their departure for Mecca, a serious revolt broke out in Bengal and Bihar, and Mīrzā Muhammad Hakīm, Akbar's younger half-brother in Kabul, responded to this uprising by launching an invasion, thereby posing a major threat to Akbar.

The immediate cause of the revolt was the fact that the benefits provided to officials and soldiers of the Mughal army in Bengal and Bihar were substantially reduced. However, Muhammad Yazdī, a Shi'ite who had emigrated from Persia and had become the *qāẓī* of Jaunpur, fuelled the revolt by issuing a *fatwā* which explicitly stated that any rebellion against Akbar would be deemed to be a fulfilment of one's religious obligation. Muẕaffar Khān, the governor of Bengal, was killed by the rebels in April 1580, and the Mughal army led by Todar Mal, who succeeded Muẕaffar K͟hān as general of the loyal forces, was surrounded by the rebels at Monghyr.[10]

In February 1581, when the rebellion in Bengal and Bihar was finally under control, Akbar personally led an army against Mirza Hakim. He made a triumphal entry into Kabul in August; and in December, he returned victorious, to the capital, Fatehpur Sikri. Thus, the attempt to attack the Mughal Empire from both sides ended in failure. The news of the rebellion seemed to have reached the two men on their pilgrimage at Mecca, and they returned in haste, expecting a change in the political situation in India. Akbar was naturally enraged at this conduct on their part – Makhdūm al-Mulk was poisoned to death and 'Abd al-Nabī was arrested and murdered in prison.

In 1581, when the rebellion in Bengal and Bihar were still under way, Akbar was strongly influenced by the pantheistic mysticism of Ibn al-'Arabī and became devoted to the creed of *sulh-i kul* (universal harmony), calling for a spiritual unification of human beings. According to Iqtidar Alam Khan, Akbar embraced this creed, and Abū'l-Faẓl elaborated it, to suit the current circumstances. Instead of implying a state of unity with God, through achieving the state of annihilation (*fanā*), the creed was transformed into a principle that promoted social unity in the culturally diverse Indian society. After 1581, Akbar's view of the world, which was inseparable from this creed of 'universal harmony', began to veer considerably away from the Islamic mainstream.[11]

There was a greater shift in Akbar's beliefs with the emergence in early 1582 of the new *silsila* (religious order), which made the Emperor its preceptor (*murshid*). According to Badā'ūnī, the condition for initiation into this *silsila* was through the acceptance of the four steps of allegiance, which required the readiness to sacrifice property (*māl*), life (*jān*), honour (*nāmūs*) and religion (*dīn*). Further, according to Badā'ūnī, Akbar termed its creed *Tauhīd-i Ilāhī* (the [assertion of] the Unity of God).[12]

Light and torch flames were considered sacred, and, above all, honouring of the sun was emphasized in this new *silsila*. With regard to this, it is likely that the order was influenced by Zoroastrianism and Hinduism. However, the influence of Islamic mysticism in the conditions for initiation indicated in Badā'ūnī cannot be ignored. With this new *silsila* that had no sacred scriptures or priests, Akbar attempted to create a type of cult that placed the emperor at the centre and consisted of members from the elite of the Court. Initiation was, therefore, strictly restricted, at least initially. Despite this restriction, the number of people wishing to enter the order appear to have grown rapidly. Abū'l-Faẓl tells us that despite the strict and difficult conditions for initiation, 'thousands of people came from various countries believing the discarding of the robe of the existing religion and entering the new *silsila* to be a lasso to capture all happiness'.[13] The use of the word *silsila*, which means religious order or chain in Islamic mysticism, is noteworthy. Roy Choudhury following H. Blochmann inaccurately, called this a 'Divine Faith' (*Dīn-i Ilāhī*), but suggested that it was similar to a type of *śūfi* order. The similarity to a sufic order was based on the fact that Abū'l-Faẓl used the word *silsila*, as well as on the list of conditions of initiation customary for sufic orders as given by Bada'ūnī.[14]

However, there is no indication that the followers of this new *silsila* continued to increase in number, and it has been suggested that the order faded into oblivion with the end of Akbar's reign. Towards the end of his reign, Akbar became more tolerant as an increasing number of Muslims became dissatisfied with his position. He also no longer showed as much interest in religion as he had in the past. It is assumed that a major cause for this change is the fact that after the promulgation of the 1579 declaration, his supremacy as an absolute ruler in both religious and secular affairs was firmly established. Of course, there were other factors that affected Akbar's precise articulations of his religious views which cannot be ignored, such as the expedition to the Deccan, an attempt at a revolt led by his son, Prince Salim, the later emperor Jāhangīr, and the assassination of Abū'l-Faẓl (1602).

**Notes and References**

1 F.W. Buckler, 'The Political Theory of the Indian Mutiny,' *Transactions of the Royal Historical Society*, fourth series, Vol. 5, 1922, pp. 71–100. This paper has been reprinted in the following collection, which contains other works by Buckler and his critics: M.N. Pearson (ed.), *Legitimacy and Symbols: The South Asian Writings of F.W. Buckler*, Ann Arbor, 1985, pp. 43–84. However, this chapter is based on the original version.

2 S.M. Edwardes, 'A Few Reflections on Buckler's Political Theory of the

Indian Mutiny', *The Indian Antiquary*, Vol. 52, 1923, pp. 198–203; reprinted in *Legitimacy and Symbols*, pp. 75–84; D. Dewar and H.L. Garrett, 'A Reply to Mr. F.W. Buckler's "The Political Theory of the Indian Mutiny"', *Transactions of the Royal Historical Society*, fourth series, Vol. 7, 1924, pp. 131–159, reprinted in *Legitimacy and Symbols*, pp. 85–113.

3 Irfan Habib's speech at the symposium 'Akbar and his Age', held on 17 October 1992 at Delhi University, *Social Scientist*, Vol. 20, Nos 9–10, 1992, pp. 68–72.

4 There are two pioneering papers by Yasuyuki Ona on the religious issues during Akbar's reign: 'Akbar's Mahzar', *Journal of the Historical Society of Japan*, Vol. 84–88, 1975, pp. 1–37; 'The Sulh-i kull by Abū'l-Faẓl, principally from the descriptions in the Akbar-nama,' *The Journal of the Research Department of the Toyo Bunko*, Vol. 58–1/2, 1976, pp. 163–95.

5 'Abd al-Qādir Badā'ūnī, *Muntakhab al-Tawārīkh*, Vol. II, edited by W.N. Lees and Ahmad Ali, Calcutta, 1865, reprint, Osnabrück, 1983, p. 270.

6 Ibid., pp. 271–72.

7 As for the fact that the *nass* includes not only the statements in the Qur' ān but also the hadīs, see Khaliq Ahmad Nizami, *Akbar and Religion*, Delhi, 1989, p. 345. Also see note 7 in the paper by Nurul Hasan indicated in following note 9 of this paper.

8 F.W. Buckler, 'A New Interpretation of Akbar's "Infallibility" Decree of 1579,' *Journal of the Royal Asiatic Society of Great Britain and Ireland*, 1924, pp. 591–608; *Legitimacy and Symbols*, pp. 131–48.

9 Saiyid Nurul Hassan, 'The "Mahzar" of Akbar's Reign', *Journal of the United Provinces Historical Society*, Vol. 16, Part 1, 1943, pp. 125–37; Ona, 'Akbar's Mahzar', pp. 10–11.

10 Yasuyuki Ona, 'The sullh-i kull by Abū'l-Faẓl'; A.L. Srivastava, *Akbar the Great*, Vol. I, Agra, 1962, pp. 268–95; Ishtiaq Husain Qureshi, *Akbar: The Architect of the Mughal Empire*, Karachi, 1978, pp. 93–104.

11 Iqtidar Alam Khan, 'Akbar's Personality Traits and World Outlook: A Critical Reappraisal', *Social Scientist*, Vol. 20, Nos 9–10, 1992, pp. 16–30.

12 Badā'ūnī, op. cit., pp. 304, 325. According to Badā'ūnī, those who wished to enter this new *silsila* took an oath to 'accept the four steps of allegiance consisting of renouncing property, life, honour and religion' upon initiation.

13 Abū'l-Faẓl, *Ā'īn-i Akbarī*, Vol. I, edited by H. Blochmann, Calcutta, 1872, p. 160.

14 M.L. Roy Choudhury, *The Din-i Ilahi or the Religion of Akbar*, second edition, Calcutta, 1952, reprint, New Delhi, 1985, p. 187.

# 9 The Road to Sulḥ-i Kul
## Akbar's Alienation from Theological Islam

*Shireen Moosvi*

The factors behind the formulation of Akbar's religious views and measures of tolerance as they unfolded after the *maḥẓar* or scholars' declaration of his authority in matters of Muslim law in 1579, have long been a subject of debate among historians. As early as about 1653, the author of the *Dabistān*, a remarkable work on contemporary religions, saw in Akbar's espousal of religious tolerance the working of a high degree of political 'foresight', aiming to construct a nobility of diverse religious composition so that no single group might occupy a position of dominance.[1] It has indeed been thought in more recent writing as well that Akbar's principle of *Sulḥ-i Kul*, publicly proclaimed after 1579, was designed essentially to accommodate the Rajputs and Iranis (who were mostly Shi'as) within what upto now had been a largely Sunni nobility.[2]

A practically opposite view stemmed largely from the curious mistranslations by H. Blochmann of two passages in Abū'l-Faẓl's *Ā'īn-i Akbarī*, where the translator repeatedly introduced the words 'Divine Faith', though the Persian text contains no corresponding words to justify this designation of Akbar's religious views. An ordinary person would naturally assume that Blochmann was here rendering a word like *Dīn-i Ilahī* into English.[3] Blochmann bolstered his interpretation by rather liberal translations of passages from Badāūnī's *Muntakhabu't Tawārīkh*; and these led V.A. Smith to suppose that Akbar, in the amplitude of his worldly power, went on to promulgate an 'official religion'.

In other words, Akbar's religious beliefs were, on this view, not intended to further political success, but rather the political success already achieved engendered in him an ambition to be the prophet of a new full-blown religion.[4] This is a perception which still persists in a fairly considerable amount of writing on Akbar. These two opposite interpretations may be judged to form two extremes among the various opinions held. Somewhere in between stands the thesis of Iqtidar A. Khan, who has seen a kind of three-stage evolution of policy mainly shaped by Akbar's changing relations with *zamindars*, notably Rajputs, promoting, in the first stage, conciliation, 1562–66; in the second, a turn to Islamic orthodoxy, 1567–1579; and, finally, in the third stage, the adoption of a policy of tolerance, from 1579 onwards.[5]

In the present paper, I do not intend to take issue with any particular view, but make a fresh effort at elucidating the developments in the light of evidence we are now in possession of.

First of all, let us consider what India, especially northern India, was like when Akbar, on his father's sudden death, occupied the throne in 1556 at the young age of fourteen. It should be appreciated that a consensus on measures of religious co-existence in the political and social sphere had long been accepted since the early days of the Delhi Sultanate. The presence of Hindu officials, in Muhammad Tughluq's administration (1324–1351), for example, is fairly well established.[6]

In the immediately preceding Sūr administration the spectacular status bestowed upon Hemu by 'Ādil Shah Sūr is not to be treated just as an aberration. Todar Mal, also a bureaucrat without any chiefly status, must have held a high position in the Sūr administration; otherwise, it would not have been possible for him to rise to so high a position in Akbar's administration, as early as 1562–1563, as to be able to interpose for Raja Ganesh, the chief of Nandun (Panjab), and to have been granted the title of Raja as well.[7] Beside the individual examples of high-ranking Hindu officials is the well attested fact that Sher Shāh's orders and official endorsements on them were often bilingual, the Persian text being also written in the Devanagari script.[8] There is no prior example of such consideration for the convenience of Hindu officials. It is certainly a strong testimony to the wide presence of Hindus, at least at the level of revenue collectors and petty officials.

The prevailing conditions in north India have been most aptly summed up by 'Abdu'l Qādir Badāūnī who, describing Sharif Amuli's arrival in 'Hindustan' from the Deccan, laments that 'since Hindustan is a vast country the scope here for free conduct is broad, one does not concern oneself with others, and everyone can be as he pleases'.[9]

The accuracy of this description is borne out in the ease with which Chaitanya and his sect obtained space in Brindaban and received protection and encouragement. An incident of the year 1517 is illustrative of the conditions. On his way from Brindaban to Prayag, when Chaitanya went into a swoon by the flute playing of a milkman, a Pathan, Bijli Khan, at the head of ten horsemen arrested Chaitanya's companions on suspicion of having drugged the ascetic for the purpose of robbing him; they were released only when, on coming back to his senses, Chaitanya himself explained the situation. Bijli Khan and his horsemen were reported to have been so impressed by Chaitanya that they joined his sect.[10] The same period witnessed some acts of persecution of the Mahdavi sect of Muslims mainly at the instance of theologians, but the Mahdavis too had their supporters and admirers outside their circle.[11] Even among theologians, a figure like Kabir could elicit admiration. Thus, so orthodox a man as Abdu'l Haq '*Muhaddis*', writes in his collection of biographies of Muslim saints, the *Akhbāru'l Akhyār* of how his grandfather told his father that monotheists like Kabir were a class apart from both Muslims and Hindus, implying that there could be no disapprobation of them.[12]

One must remind oneself that Akbar's childhood was spent practically entirely from infancy to the age of twelve in Kabul in surroundings that were closely attuned to the cosmopolitan cultural traditions inherited from late Timurid Herat. He must surely have been reminded by those who brought him up there of how he had taken birth in the house of a Hindu chief (at Umarkot): his aunt, Gulbadan Bāno, who was with him in Kabul herself gratefully records the support offered to Humayun and the protection provided to Ḥamīda Bāno Begum by Rana Prasad of Umarkot at the time of Akbar's birth.[13] With his keen interest in history, he might have learnt that his father Humayun sought and received help from Shāh Tahmāsp, the Shī'a king of Iran, and, perhaps a little later, that his grandfather Bābur had entertained no qualms about making an alliance against Ibrāhīm Lodi with Rānā Sāngā.[14]

Akbar's early education included lessons in painting including the art of drawing human portraits under the famous artist Khwāja 'Abduṣ Ṣamad,[15] an art that had developed so much in Herat, over which the famous Bihzad had once presided. It hardly mattered that many orthodox Muslims considered painting to be a forbidden art. Bayazid, in his memoirs, reports Akbar's father Humayun's enthusiastic patronage of it.[16] Such cultural heritage must always be borne in mind when we consider Akbar's later catholic attitude towards different cultural streams.

But there were also certain important traits specific to Akbar's person, from a very early period, whose role cannot be overlooked. Akbar had an enormous amount of curiosity, and he wished to know about everything, including what the common people did, and how they lived.

In the sixth Regnal Year (1560–61), he went incognito to a popular festival, 'as was his habit' and was engrossed in observing the various actions and modes of behaviour of the people present, when he came to be recognized by some people. Only by squinting his eyes was he able to conceal his identity, and escape from an embarrassing situation.[17] Rafi'uddin Shirazi, a Persian merchant who visited Agra in the early 1560s, narrated a few other incidents of this kind which occurred during 1562–63. The young emperor at least twice separated himself from the hunting party accompanying him and went alone chasing the prey. Once, by not revealing his identity, he allowed himself be imprisoned in a cattle-pen by the villagers. On another occasion, he went alone to an inn (*sarai*), and, after being fed by a *bhatyaran* (a woman innkeeper), was resting there, when a merchant party arrived and taking him for a disrespectful loafer, gave him a few lashes and drove him away. Rafi'uddin himself saw him moving about in a crowd with some companions without ceremony, and also publicly flying kites from the roof of the palace in casual attire.

It is thus obvious that Akbar mingled freely among both Hindus and Muslims. The *bhatyaran* might well have been a Hindu. If Rafi'uddin is to be believed, he already had a Brahman girl as a mistress, and his order forbidding slave-trade was attributed to this intelligent or humane girl's pleas.[18] It is in such circumstances that we can explain one of Akbar's earliest *farmāns*: this was issued in April 1561 to assign a village in lieu of his salary to *ustād* (master) Rāmdās *rangrez* (dyer). Then, another *farmān* was issued in May 1562 to give him further land in *in'ām*. A third *farmān* in March–April 1569 was issued to assist the same Rāmdās in recovering the sum of Rs 13 which he had lent to a certain person.[19] A mere master dyer, Rāmdās thus held a *jāgīr* assignment well before Akbar's meeting with Raja Bharamal, and his marriage with the latter's daughter in January–February 1562. Contacts with the Rajputs were, therefore, neither the earliest example nor the exclusive sphere of Akbar's growing contacts with Hindus.

Here what the Vrindavan documents tell us is of much interest. In January 1565, Akbar issued a *farmān* to grant *in'ām*-land to the Chaitanya priest Gopāldās, at the recommendation of Raja Bhāramal; in October 1568, at Todar Mal's recommendation, a *farmān* was issued to hand over management (*adhikār*) of the Madan Mohan and Gobind Dev temples to Jīv Gosāin; and, in 1576, a grant was made to Govardhan and other priests, upon the proposal of Shahbāz K͟hān Kambo.[20] From Badāūnī, we learn that, in 1574, Akbar desired that *Singhasan Battīsī* be translated by Badāūnī; and, in 1575–76, he directed a translation of the *Atharvaveda* to be prepared.[21]

We can thus see that the abolition of the pilgrimage tax and, then, the *jizya* in 1563 and 1564 are part of a pattern, which was maintained throughout the 1560s and 1570s. Just as the turn to a tolerance of Hinduism in the early 1560s cannot simply be attributed to a desire to placate the Rajputs, so too Akbar's fierce military campaigning in Rajasthan, beginning with the storming of Chittor in 1568 cannot be made the basis for hypothesizing an 'orthodox' turn in Akbar's policy during the late 1560s and early 1570s.[22]

There is, at the same time, no reason to believe that a general policy of conciliation with his Hindu subjects required Akbar to challenge Muslim orthodoxy. Akbar could pray five times a day, and visit the Ajmer shrine, which he did first of all in 1562.[23] Badāūnī aptly described his beliefs in Islam before the *'ibādatk͟hāna* discussions as those of 'a mere ordinary [believer], a follower of tradition and custom'.[24] Such an attitude could accommodate Timurid culture as well as tolerance towards non-Muslims, and also allow one to issue holy-war *fatḥnāmas* upon capturing Chittor and Ranthambor (1568 and 1569).

Why, then, did the religious crisis of the mid-1570s break out?

It seems to me here that what Badāūnī says has to be given more weight than has hitherto been the case. He argues that by the early 1570s, Akbar had become conscious of the way in which at repeated moments of danger, he had been saved by God, and of how so many kinds of success had come his way through His aid. He began to retire to a cell to meditate on God, which came duly to be called *'ibādatk͟hāna* ('place of prayer'). He wished to make some return to God, for what boons He had granted him; and this ignited in him an intense desire to serve religion in some decisive way.[25]

There is some independent confirmation of how this feeling in Akbar grew. One important index is his extraordinary attachment to the Ajmer shrine displayed in the 1570s. From 1570 onwards, Akbar began to go on pilgrimage to Ajmer every year, sometimes twice a year. In 1574, he went there on foot and, in 1576, partly on foot.[26] His visits to Ajmer ceased only after 1579.

There is, therefore, much plausibility in Badāūnī's suggestion that Akbar turned to the theologians to tell him what he should do to bring into effect the dictates of God, that is, the Sharī'at.[27] This is certainly far more persuasive a thesis than Abū'l Faẓl's that the *'ibādatkhāna* discussions were a deliberate means whereby Akbar, like a coin-tester (*ṣairafī*) sifted the bad from the good, and also himself laid bare divine truths (*ḥaqā'iq*) by his 'sacred' utterances.[28]

What Abū'l Faẓl suggests is obviously unhistorical, arising out of his theory of how Akbar purposely concealed his own wisdom in earlier days. What Abū'l Faẓl held to be Akbar's innate wisdom, itself came to be generated in part by the *ibādatkhāna* deliberations. There came about an immense and sincere disillusionment in Akbar with regard to Islamic theology once its various elements began to be discussed by scholars in front of him. On each point, there arose bitter controversy: 'the differences among the legal schools (*mazāhib*) reached such a point', relates Badauni, 'that one party would accuse the other of infidelity and deviation, and the controversies, going beyond the matters of Sunnī, Shī'a, Ḥanafī, Shafa'ī, jurist and rationalist, entered the core of the principles [of the faith].'[29]

There were also certain difficulties, both personal and political, once Akbar committed himself to the course of implementing the *Sharī'at.* In the Timurid family, up till Babur, there had been no limitation on marriages with free-born women. The senior wives upto four in number were called *begams,* the others *āghā.* Akbar followed the same custom, though the term *āghā* went into disuse. In Muslim law, there is a Quranic limitation to four free-born wives, though none on concubines. Akbar wished to know whether by some device nine or eighteen free-born wives could be permitted! Even with *mut'a* (contractual) marriages, there would be difficulty in permitting more than four such wives at one time.[30] Beside these personal embarrassments, the political implications were still severer. In 1575–76, the orthodox leaders Shaikh 'Abdun' Nabī and Makhdūmu'l Mulk persuaded Akbar to re-impose the *jizya,* though 'like a painting on water it soon disappeared'.[31] The moment Akbar's views altered, the tax was formally withdrawn (1579–80).[32]

Clearly, the difficulty for Akbar lay not only in the manifestations of the huge disagreements among the theologians, but also on what they were agreed on. The former could be disposed of by the *maḥẓar* of 1579, by which the leading scholars at Akbar's court were persuaded into ceding the right of interpretation (subject to many conditions) to Akbar as a just sovereign.[33] The implications on what the orthodox theologians were agreed upon were more troubling, for these could be greatly restrictive as far as Akbar's own sovereign authority was concerned.

It is, therefore, not surprising that Akbar should now turn to those ideas within sufistic thought which seemed to bypass the Sharī'at and establish a direct relationship with God. Shihābu'ddin Maqtūl's 'illuminationist' theory with its suggestion of the great position of the elect of God, and the concepts of *Insān al-Kāmil* (Perfect Man) and *Sulḥ-i Kul* in the Ibn 'Arabī tradition offered important alternatives within Islamic thought, which Akbar would now grasp. *Sulḥ-i Kul* implied that (a) all apparent reality of the world, including religion, was an illusion, so religious differences, as, indeed, all other points of difference lost their significance; and (b) all the different faiths should, therefore, be tolerated to secure mutual amity. But *Sulḥ-i Kul* by no means exhausted Akbar's new ideological position – there was now to be a special position for reason (*'aql*), by whose mediation mutual peace could be maintained among all disputants; and a hugely elevated place was to be provided for the Just Sovereign, who could be seen as the Perfect Man and God's Vicegerent for people of all faiths, to implement, so to speak, the *Sulḥ-i Kul.* There was thus a new ideological foundation laid for the Mughal Empire.[34]

It is now, worth considering how a mild sufic critic, Muhammad Ghauṣī Shattārī, writing in 1613, looked back at the whole process:

> For some time, the circumstances of the day accorded with the Sharī'at [under Akbar]. When the worldly scholars and the traditionally learned, for the purpose of self-aggrandizement, not that of truth-seeking, fell upon each other, diverse kinds of assertions appeared among them. Jurists' disagreements and the controversies of innovation emerged into daylight. The Emperor, failing to

> reach the depth of the differences and the objects of controversy, drove his (hitherto) firm faith into the field of suspicion and speculation. He brought the practice of *Sulh-i kul,* which is the seat of secrets of the seekers of [self-]annihilation, into open view in pubic discourse. But this did not attain acceptance. As a result, he shunned the company of some of the narrow-minded scholars, and, acting on his own opinion, dispersed this tribe away from his court.[35]

This author shares with Badāūnī, to whose work he does not seem to have had access, the view that it was the disagreements among scholars, and not the matters on which they were agreed, that brought Akbar his total disillusionment with Muslim theology. Disagreements were, indeed, a factor that engendered doubts about the reality of the unified facade of Islamic orthodoxy. But the real issue still would seem to be whether Akbar could implement what every theologian was agreed on, without overturning his practical arrangements adopted since his accession. This being impossible, a rejection of Muslim orthodoxy became inescapable. It was now an ideal moment to turn to those elements of sufic thought which, if logically developed, would render Muslim theology more or less secondary, if not irrelevant. G͟hauṣī Shattārī is perceptive in holding that by his recourse to the mystic notion of *Sulḥ-i Kul,* Akbar was clearly bringing esoteric precepts out into the practical field – something no *ṣūfī* had previously thought of or countenanced. Yet, what seemed to the sufic author of *Gulzār-i Abrār,* an act of indiscretion, might today appear to us a bold stroke of genius. It could justify tolerance at every level, and so provide the ideological prop for Akbar's measures to build an empire acceptable to most of his subjects, while clothed in a terminology sufficiently Islamic to overcome the qualms of his Muslim nobles.

**Notes and References**

1 *Dabistān-i Maẕāhib*, published by Qāzī Ibrahim, Bombay, 1292/1875, p. 379.

2 M. Athar Ali, *The Mughal Nobility under Aurangzeb*, Bombay, 1966, p. 16.

3 Abū'l Faẓl 'Allāmī, *The Ā'īn-i Akbarī*, I, translated by H. Blochmann, revised by D.C. Phillott, Bib. Ind., Calcutta, 1927, p. 175. This translation was originally published in 1873. Cf. M. Athar Ali's criticism of Blochmann's renderings in *Mughal India: Studies in Polity, Ideas, Society and Culture*, New Delhi, 2006, p. 163.

4 V.A. Smith, *Akbar the Great Mogul*, second edition, London and Oxford, 1917, pp. 150–60.

5 Iqtidar Alam Khan, 'The Nobility under Akbar and the Development of his Religious Policy, 1560–80', *Journal of Royal Asiatic Society*, 1968, pp. 29–36.

6 See Ẕiyā Baranī, *Tārīkh-i Fīroz Shāhī*, edited by Sayyid Ahmad Khan, W.N. Lees and Kabir al-Din, Bib. Ind., Calcutta, 1862, p. 505. Cf. T.A. Jackson, *The Delhi Sultanate: A Political and Military History*, Cambridge, 1999, pp. 278–95 and M. Athar Ali, *Mughal India, Studies in Polity, Ideas, Society and Culture*, pp. 33–34.

7 Abū'l-Fazl, *Akbarnama*, II, edited by Ahmad Ali, Calcutta, 1873–87, pp. 169–70. The incident is placed prior to the execution of Adham Khan. Blochmann seems to miss this reference and says that Todar Mal first appears in Badāūnī's account in the seventeenth regnal year (1572–73), *Ain-i Akbari*, translated by Blochmann, revised by D.C. Phillott, p. 376.

8 See, for example, Central Record Office, Allahabad, Series I: No. 318 (Shershah's *farmān* of AH 947/AD 1540–41), and Sher Shāh's *farmāns* in *Oriental College Magazine*, Vol. IX, No. 3, May 1933, pp. 121–22, 125–128.

9 'Abdul Qādir Badāūnī, *Muntakhab-ut Tawarikh*, II, edited by Nassau Lees and Ahmad Ali, Calcutta, 1865, II, p. 245.

10 D.C. Sen, *Chaitanya and His Age*, Calcutta, 1922, pp. 228–29.

11 S.A.A. Rizvi, *Muslim Revivalist Movements in Northern India*, Agra, 1965, pp. 68–134.

12 *Akhbār-ul Akhyār* (*Takmila*), Deoband, 1913–14, p. 306.

13 *Humāyūn Nāma*, edited and translated by A.S. Beveridge, *A History of Humayun*, London, 1902, p. 59.

14 *Bāburnāma*, translated by A.S. Beveridge London, 1921, p. 531.

15 Jahāngīr, *Tuzuk-i Jahāngīrī*, edited by Syed Ahmad, Ghazipur and Aligarh, 1863–4, p. 18.

16 Bāyazīd Biyāt, *Tazkira-i Humānyūn o Akbar*, edited by M. Hidayat Hosain, Bib. Ind., Calcutta, 1941, pp. 68, 176–77.

17 *Akbarnāma*, II, pp. 145–46.

18 *Tazkiratu'l Mulūk*, Brit. Lib. Add. 23883, ff.172b–174b. For translations, see Shireen Moosvi, *Episodes in the Life of Akbar*, New Delhi, 1994, pp. 28–31.

19 See Irfan Habib's reproduction and translations of these documents with commentary in *Akbar and his India*, edited by I. Habib, New Delhi, 1997, pp. 270–87.

20 Cf. Tarapada Mukherjee and Irfan Habib, 'Akbar and the Temples of Mathura', *Proceedings of the Indian History Congress*, 48th Goa session, 1987, pp. 234–50.

21 Badāūnī, III, 177–78; and II, p. 213.

22 I realize that here I stand in some disagreement with Professor Iqtidar Alam Khan's views as propounded in his article. 'The Nobility under Akbar and the Development of his Religious Policy, 1560–80', *JRAS*, 1968, pp. 29–36.

[23] *Akbarnāma*, II, p. 157.

[24] Badāūnī, II, p. 255.

[25] Badāūnī, II, p. 200. Badāūnī enters this passage under AH 983 (1575–76), but *Akbarnāma*, III, pp. 112–13 shows that the '*ibādatkhāna* had been established by 1574–75.

[26] *Akbarnāma*, II, 157, 356, 364, 372–3; III, pp. 34, 38, 44, 65, 79–80, 110, 164, 185, 212, 216, 251.

[27] Badāūnī, II, pp. 200–02. The earlier work of 'Ārif Qandahārī, edited by Moinuddin Alvi et al., Rampur, 1962, pp. 40–41, has similar implications.

[28] *Akbarnāma*, III, pp. 112–13.

[29] Badāūnī, II, p. 255.

[30] Ibid., pp. 207–09.

[31] Ibid., p. 210.

[32] Ibid., p. 276.

[33] For the text of the *maḥẓar*, signed in August–September 1579, see Niẓāmu'ddīn Aḥmad, *Ṭabaqāt-i Akbarī*, edited by B.De, Bib. Ind., Calcutta, 1913, Vol. II, pp. 344–46. There are trifling variations between this text and the version given by Badāūnī, II, pp. 344–46.

[34] I summarize here what has been investigated in considerable depth by M. Athar Ali, 'Akbar and Islam', in Milton Israel and N.K. Wagle (eds), *Islamic Society and Culture: Essays in Honour of Professor Aziz Ahmad*, New Delhi, 1983; Iqtidar A. Khan, 'Akbar's Personality Traits and World Outlook', in *Akbar and his India*, edited by Irfan Habib, New Delhi, 1997; and Irfan Habib, 'A Political Theory for the Mughal Empire: A Study of the Ideas of Abu'l Fazl', *Proceedings of the Indian History Congress, 59th session*, Patiala, 1998, pp. 329–40.

[35] Muḥammad Ghauṣī Shattārī, *Gulzār-i Abrār*, edited by Mohammad Zaki, Patna, 1997, p. 277.

# 10 The Philosophy of Mullā Ṣadrā and its Influence in India

*Syed Ali Nadeem Rezavi*

Ṣadruddīn al-Shīrāzī, or Mullā Ṣadrā (1571–1640), is perhaps the singlemost important philosopher in the Muslim world in the last 400 years. The author of over 40 works, he was the central figure of the major revival of philosophy in Iran in the sixteenth and seventeenth centuries. Devoting himself almost exclusively to metaphysics, he constructed a critical philosophy which brought together Peripatetic (*mashshā'i*), Illuminationist (*ishrāqi*) and Gnostic (*'irfān*) philosophy along with Shi'ite theology (*kalām*) within the compass of what he termed a 'metaphilosophy' or Transcendental Wisdom (*al-hikma al-muta'āliya*), the source of which lay in the Islamic revelation and the mystical experience of reality as existence. It was as a result of this philosophy that Mullā Ṣadrā came to be popularly known as *Sadr al-muta'allihīn* (the foremost of the transcendental philosophers).

In this paper an attempt is made to analyse the philosophy of this notable Shi'ite philosopher and the response which it received in India, where he came to be regarded both as a votary of reason and as a logician within the realm of Muslim theology.

Peripatetic (*mashshā'i*) philosophy (*hikma*) in the Islamic world had gained considerable importance between the ninth and twelfth centuries. The peripatetic system which came to have considerable significance within both Islamic and Western philosophy had been established by Ibn Sīna.[1] His book *Mantiq al-mashriqiyyīn* (*Logic of the Orientals*) not only deals with logical differences between him and Aristotle, but also includes a reference to other works of his own in which he claims to have gone in an entirely different direction from that of other peripatetic (*mashshā'i*) thinkers. A highly influential attack on the role of philosophy as part of Islam was subsequently carried out by al-Ghazali in his *Tahāfut al-falāsifa* (*The Incoherence of the*

*Philosophers*). Al-Ghazali argued that the peripatetic philosophers (especially Ibn Sīna) present as truths such theses as are either faith-denying (*kufr*) or innovatory (*bid'a*). In spite of his anti-philosophical leanings, closer inspection of many of his texts reveals that he himself continued to adhere to many of the leading principles of Ibn Sīna's thought. Further, in common with many other opponents of philosophy, he had a high regard for logic (which was regarded as a tool of philosophy rather than as part of it) and insisted on the application of logic to organized thought about religion. Some opponents of philosophy such as Ibn Taymiyya went even so far as to criticize logic itself.[2] As a result of such criticisms, peripatetic philosophy went into a sharp decline in the Sunni world after the twelfth century. But it still continued as part of a variety of philosophical approaches among Shi'ī circles, where it combined with elements of illuminationist (*ishrāqi*) philosophy, and developed into more and more complex theoretical systems.

The *Ishrāqi* school of philosophy originated with Shihabuddin Suhrawardi whose basic premise was that knowledge is available to man not through ratiocination alone, but through illumination resulting from the purification of one's inner being. He founded a school of philosophy which is mystical but not necessarily against logic or a limited use of reason. He criticized Aristotle and the Muslim Peripatetics on logical grounds, before setting out to expound the doctrine of *ishrāq*.[3] This doctrine was based not on the refutation of logic, but on transcending its categories through an illuminationist knowledge based on immediacy and presence, or what Suhrawardi himself called 'knowledge by presence' (*al-'ilm al-huzūri*), in contrast to conceptual knowledge (*al-'ilm al-husūli*) which is the ordinary method of knowing based on concepts.[4]

It was these two trends that Mullā Ṣadrā tried to mix with the Shi'ī *kalām*. Mullā Ṣadrā's metaphilosophy was based on existence (*wujūd*) as the sole constituent of reality; it rejected any role for quiddities (*māhiyya*) or essences in the external world. Existence was for him at once a single unity and an internally articulated, dynamic process, the unique source of both unity and diversity. From this fundamental starting point, Mullā Ṣadrā was able to find original solutions to many of the logical, metaphysical and theological difficulties which he had inherited from his predecessors.

Mullā Ṣadrā, as a student at Isfahan, had been taught by or

came under the influence of such thinkers as Mīr Muhammad Bāqir Astarabādi (Mir Dāmād), Shaikh Bahā'uddin Amuli (Shaikh Bahāi) and Mīr Abul Qāsim Findiriskī.[5] The new school of theosophical Shi'ism founded by Ṣadrā, was partly a continuation of the 'School of Isfahan' founded by these three scholars.

Mir Dāmād, whose poetic *nom de plume* was 'Ishrāq', is also referred to as the 'Third Master' (after Aristotle and al-Fārābi). He was recognized as a jurist, a mystic and a philosopher. However, it was principally as a philosopher that Mīr Dāmād distinguished himself.[6] *Kitāb al-Qabasat* is Mīr Dāmād's most significant philosophical work, and it consists of ten *qabas* ('a spark of fire') and three conclusions.[7] Its central theme is the creation of the world and the possibility of its extension from God.[8] In it, Mīr Dāmād engaged in the age-old debate over the priority of 'essence' (*māhiyya*) over 'existence' (*wujūd*). He ultimately decided on the priority of essence, a position that was later fundamentally disputed by his distinguished pupil Mullā Ṣadrā.

Like Mīr Dāmād, Mīr Abul Qāsim Findiriskī, who had also taught Mullā Ṣadrā, was deeply influenced by the *mashshā'i* philosophy. He also wrote on *'irfān* (gnosticism). He outlined a whole theory of visionary experience, which presupposes the idea of 'spiritual senses', the senses of *'ālam al-misāl* which were later emphasized by Mullā Ṣadrā.[9]

In his major work *al-Hikma al-muta'āliya fi-'l-asfār al-'aqliyya al-arba'a* (*The Transcendent Wisdom Concerning the Four Intellectual Journeys*), known popularly as *Asfār*, Mullā Ṣadrā confesses to the shift from his teachers' position:

> In the earlier days I used to be a passionate defender of the thesis that the quiddities are the primary constituents of reality and existence is conceptual, until my Lord gave me spiritual guidance and let me see His demonstration. All of a sudden my spiritual eyes were opened and I saw with utmost clarity that the truth was just the contrary of what the philosophers in general had held. . . . As a result [I now hold that] the existences (*wujūdāt*) are primary realities, while the quiddities are the 'permanent archetypes' (*a'yān thābita*) that have never smelt the fragrance of existence.[10]

By taking the position of the primacy of existence, Mullā Ṣadrā was able to answer the objections of Ibn Rushd and the illuminationists by pointing out that existence is accidental to quiddity in the mind, in so far as it is not a part of its essence. An implication of Mullā Ṣadrā's theory of reality and existence being identical is that existence is one but graded in intensity; to this he gave the name *tashkīk al-wujūd* (systematic ambiguity).[11]

According to Ṣadrā, existence can be conceived of as a continual unfolding of existence, which is thus a single whole with a constantly evolving internal dynamic. Reality to him is ever-changing. The imagined 'essence' gives things their identities. It is only when crucial points are reached that one perceives this change and new essences are formed in our minds, although change has been continually going on. Due to this 'infinite diversification', the so-called realm of 'immutable essences' does not exist for Mullā Ṣadrā.[12] Time, in his view, is the measure of this process of renewal; it is not an independent entity where events take place. Rather, it is a dimension exactly like the three spatial dimensions – the physical world thus is a spatio-temporal continuum.

This theory permitted Mullā Ṣadrā to give an original solution to the problem of the eternity of the world which had continually pitted philosophers against theologians in Islam. In his system, the world is eternal as a continual process of the unfolding of existence, but since existence is in a constant state of flux due to its continuous substantial changes, every new manifestation of existence in the world emerges in time. The world, that is, every spatio-temporal event from the highest heaven downwards, is thus temporally originated, although, as a whole, the world is also eternal in the sense that it has no beginning or end, since time is not something existing independently within which the world in turn exists. Ṣadrā conceived of *hikma* (wisdom) as 'coming to know the essence of beings as they really are', or as 'a man's becoming an intellectual world corresponding to the objective world'. Philosophy and mysticism, *hikma* and Sufism, are for him two aspects of the same thing. To engage in philosophy without experiencing the truth of its content confines the philosopher to a world of essences and concepts, while mystical experience without the intellectual discipline of philosophy can lead only to an ineffable state of ecstasy. When the two go hand in hand, the mystical experience of reality becomes the intellectual content of philosophy.

The characteristic features, or rather objectives of Mullā Ṣadrā's 'transcendental philosophy' are thus described by James Morris:

> [A] condition of intrinsic finality, completion, fulfillment, and inner peace (compatible with the most intensive activity); a unique sense of unity, wholeness, and communion (with no ultimate separation of subject and object); a distinctive suspension (or warping or extension) of our actual perceptions of time and space; where nature is involved, a vision of all being as essentially alive (in a way quite different from our usual distinction of animate and inanimate entities); a sense of profound inner freedom and liberation (or, negatively stated, the absence of anxiety, guilt or regret); a perception of universal, nonjudgmental love or compassion, extending to all beings; a paradoxical sense of 'ek-stasis', or standing beyond and encompassing the ongoing flow of particular events (including the actions of one's 'own' body).[13]

Ṣadrā appears to be a man 'fundamentally concerned both with the dialectical interplay between experience and transcendence, and a journey towards it, a journey which not just Muslims were making, but the whole of humanity'.[14] He was not only the one who brought about a synthesis of traditional and rational knowledge and so was the most notable among the philosophers of the Shiraz school, but he was, in effect, a reviver of rational sciences. In the words of Nasr:

> [Mullā Ṣadrā], by coordinating philosophy as inherited from the Greeks and interpreted by the Peripatetics and Illuminationists before him with the teachings of Islam in its exoteric and esoteric aspects . . . succeeded in putting Gnostic doctrines of Ibn 'Arabi in logical dress. He made purification of the soul a necessary basis and complement of the study of Hikmat, thereby bestowing on philosophy the practice of ritual and spiritual virtues which it had lost in the period of decadence of classical civilization. Finally, he succeeded in correlating the wisdom of the ancient Greek and Muslim sages and philosophers as interpreted esoterically with the inner meaning of the Qur'an.[15]

Ṣadrā laid the basis for what was effectively a new theosophical school of Shi'ism which combined within it elements of various existing systems to form a synthesis whose influence helped inspire renewed debates within Twelver Shi'ism.[16]

When Mullā Ṣadrā and the earlier generation of Iranian scholars were debating fundamental issues of philosophy in the manner we have outlined, India had already experienced under Akbar (d. 1605), an official shift towards the patronage of the rational sciences at the expense of Muslim theology. It was prescribed that only such sciences as arithmetic, agriculture, household management, rules of governance, medicine, etc., should comprise the educational curriculum.[17] There was a stress on reason (*'aql*) which was to be given precedence over traditionalism (*taqlīd*).[18] This open stress on rationalism was in some respects remarkable for the time. The chief proponent of the rational attitude during this period was Abul Fazl.[19] Among the two important functions which Abul Fazl assigns to a just ruler (*kār giya*), one is that such a sovereign 'shall not seek popular acclaim through opposing reason (*'aql*)'.[20] The large number of Persian Shi'ī emigrants to Akbar's India included physicians like Hakim Abul Fath Gilani along with his two brothers, Hakim Humam and Hakim Lutfullah, Hakim Ali, and a technologist like Shah Fathullah Shirazi, and the turn towards rationalism could probably have also owed a little to their arrival. We have the (admittedly late) testimony of Azad Bilgrami that it was Fathullah Shirazi who introduced the works of Iranian rationalist thinkers like Muhaqqiq Dawwani,[21] Mir Sadruddin, Mir Ghiyasuddin Mansur and Mirza Jan in India. He would not only himself teach these works but under his influence they were introduced in the curriculum of the seminaries of higher education.[22] Most of these Shi'ī migrants, it appears, were the followers of the Akhbari *fiqh* which was the most popular among the Shi'as in North India during the Mughal period.[23] This school rejected the legitimacy of independent legal reasoning and held that in the absence of the twelfth Imam, who was in occultation, state-related functions could not be carried out in his name by the clergy.[24]

Conducive ground for the penetration of Iranian philosophical ideas might also have been prepared by the visit of Mullā Ṣadrā's teacher, Mīr Findiriskī to India during the reign of Shahjahan.[25] Findiriskī (d. 1640–41), during his stay, is said to have been attracted to Indian Yogic practices and to have written *Muntakhab Jog*, an anthology of *Yoga Vashishtha*. He also wrote *Usūl al-fusūl*, a treatise on Hinduism which unfortunately does not survive. He was the most notable intellectual link between the tradition of Islamic philosophy of Iran and the movement for the translation of Sanskrit texts into Persian in India.[26]

The legacy of the *ma'qūlāt* (reason) favoured during the reign of Akbar was carried forward by such noted scholars as Abdus Salam Lahori, Abdus Salam Dewi, Shaikh Daniyal Chaurasi and ultimately, Mulla Qutbuddin Sihalawi, the father of Mulla Nizamuddin, the first rector of the Farangi Mahal seminary.[27] Another rationalist scholar in the Mughal court was Mulla Shafi'ai Yazdi Danishmand Khan, the employer of the famous François Bernier.

The *hikmat* traditions as they developed in Iran appear to have secured easy acceptance in the Mughal Empire during the reign of Shahjahan. An example can be given of Mulla Mahmud Faruqi of Jaunpur, a peripatetic scholar who had been a student of Mīr Dāmād at Shiraz. He was not only invited to the Mughal court but counted Prince Shah Shuja and Shaista Khan amongst his pupils.[28] A contemporary of Mullā Ṣadrā, he joined the Mughal court in 1640. Very soon, we find him taking part in a debate with Mulla Abdul Hakim Siyalkoti, a scholar who had written a number of glosses and commentaries on the works of Mulla Sharif Juzjani, Sa'duddin Taftazani and Mulla Jalaluddin Dawwani.[29]

The author of *Dabistān-i Mazāhib* (*c.* 1653), during the same reign, records the names of two scholars who had obtained training in the philosophical traditions of Iran. Hakim Dastur of Isfahan received training under 'Mir Baqir Damad, Shaikh Bahauddin Muhammad, Mir Abul Qasim Findiriski and other such scholars of Shiraz'.[30] Another was Hakim Kamran who, he says, was addressed by Mir Findiriskī as 'brother'.[31] Settled in the regions of Lahore and Agra respectively, these scholars might have also come into contact with Ṣadrā's views which were creating a stir during the same period in Shiraz. Of the famous Sarmad, who probably arrived in India from Iran in early 1640s, it is distinctly stated by the same author, apparently on the basis of what Sarmad told him himself, that he had studied 'under the sages of Iran, such as Mullā Ṣadrā and Mīr Abu'l Qāsim Findiriskī and others'.[32] How much his turn to mysticism was influenced by their teaching should be an interesting theme to pursue.

Evidence for the transmission of Mullā Ṣadrā's ideas and his 'Transcendental Wisdom' and rationalism to India comes from what we learn about commentaries written on him in India. Mullā Nizamuddin Sihālwi (fl. 1700) of the Farangi Mahal tradition is credited with the formulation of the curriculum for instruction known as *Dars-i Nizāmi*.[33] It was designed to direct the student to the most difficult and comprehensive books on a subject, so that the pupil was forced to think. This curriculum has been criticized for placing too much emphasis on the rational sciences. According to Robinson, it 'stipulates no specific bias and insists on no particular books'.[34]

Mulla Nizamuddin wrote a commentary on Mullā Ṣadrā's *Sharh-i Hidātayat al-Hikma* (a book which expounds his transcendental philosophy) and introduced this work in his syllabus, the *dars-i nizāmi*.[35] This commentary is now popularly known as *Ṣadrā*. Within a few years of the compilation of Nizamuddin's work, Mulla Hasan Farangi Mahali (d. 1794–95), a famous logician of the same school of thought, wrote his own commentary on Mullā Ṣadrā's *Hikmat*, which was also taught in various Indian seminaries of the eighteenth century. Similarly, 'Alim Sandilvi Farangi Mahali, the founder of the Khairabad School, compiled his own commentary of Mullā Ṣadrā's *Hikmat*.[36] Mullā Ṣadrā appears to have been noticed by Shah Abdul Aziz Dihlavi as well. A commentary written by the Shah, *Sharh-i Mulla Sadra*, is preserved in the Maulana Azad Library, Aligarh.[37] The *Ṣadrā* was also introduced in the curriculum of the Shi'ī *madrasas* of Awadh and till as late as the 1960s formed part of the curriculum at *Sultān-ul Madāris*, a well-known Shi'ī seminary at Lucknow. It is, however, quite interesting to note that with the growing influence of the *Usūli fiqh* after Dildar Ali Nasirabadi 'Ghufrānma'āb' (1753–1820), the influence of *Ṣadrā* in the Shi'ī seminaries in North India declined. According to the *Usūlis*, thinkers like Mullā Ṣadrā, who followed a mystical philosophy, were heretics.[38] Presently, Mullā Ṣadrā and his works are hardly known or remembered in either the Shi'ī or the Sunni institutions of North India.

It thus appears that within a few decades of the death of Mullā Ṣadrā (d. 1640), he began to receive notice from the scholarly circles in India and interest in his philosophy continued to be displayed at least up till the second half of the twentieth century. This shows that despite the conventional Shia–Sunni divide, India and Iran yet belonged to a largely common intellectual region. It is difficult, however, to get an answer to the question as to how far Ṣadrā's larger vision was integrated or adopted in Indo–Muslim thought – whether it was just noticed and docketed to be taught, or also endorsed fully in spirit.

**Notes and References**

[1] Oliver Leaman, 'Concept of Philosophy in Islam', *Routledge Encyclopaedia of Philosophy: Islamic Philosophy*, edited by Edward Craig and

O. Leaman, 1998, vol. 5, pp. 5–9. For the online edition see http://www.muslimphilosophy.com/ip/rep/H006.htm

2 Ibid.

3 S. Hosein Nasr, 'Mystical Philosophy of Islam', *Routledge Encyclopaedia of Philosophy*, op. cit., vol. 6, pp. 616–20. For the online version see http://www.muslimphilosophy.com/ip/rep/H004.htm

4 Muhammad Ha'iri Yazdi, *The Principles of Epistemology in Islamic Philosophy: Knowledge by Presence*, Albany, NY, 1992. For Suhrawardi and his philosophy see John Cooper, 'al-Shihab al-din Yahya al-Suhrawardi', *Routledge Encyclopaedia of Philosophy*, op. cit., vol. 9, pp. 219–24. For the online version see http://www.muslimphilosophy.com/ip/rep/H031.htm

5 *The Encyclopaedia of Islam*, new edition: D. MacEoin, 'Mulla Sadra', Leiden, E.J. Brill, 1993, vol. 7, p. 547. For Findiriski, see Ibid., *Supplement*, 2004, pp. 308–09.

6 A. Hadi, *Sharh-i hal-i Mir Damad va Mir Findiriski* (*Commentary on the Thought of Mir Damad and Mir Findiriski*), Isfahan, 1984, p. 134.

7 Mir Damad , *Kitab al-qabasat* (*Book of Embers*), edited by M. Mohaghegh, T. Izutsu, M. Bihbahani and I. Dibaji, Tehran: McGill University, Institute of Islamic Studies, Tehran Branch, 1977.

8 Hamid Dabashi, 'Mir Damad and the Founding of the School of Isfahan', in S.H. Nasr and O. Leaman, eds, *History of Islamic Philosophy*, London, 1996, pp. 597–634. For the online version see http://www.muslimphilosophy.com/ip/rep/H053.htm; see also S.H. Nasr, 'The School of Isfahan', in M.M. Sharif, ed., *A History of Muslim Philosophy*, Wiesbaden, 1966, vol. 2, pp. 904–32.

9 S. Athar Abbas Rizvi, *A Socio-Intellectual History of the Isna 'Ashari Shi'is in India*, vol. II, Canberra, 1986, pp. 219–20.

10 Mulla Sadra, *al-Hikma al-muta'aliya fi-'l-asfar al-'aqliyya al-arba'a* (*The Transcendent Wisdom Concerning the Four Intellectual Journeys*), edited by R. Lutfi *et al.*, Tehran and Qum, Shirkat Dar al-Ma'arif al-Islamiyyah, 1958–69?, 9 vols; vol. 1, Introduction.

11 In discussing the philosophical views of Mulla Sadra, I have followed the writings of Hosein Nasr and John Cooper. See S.H. Nasr, *Sadr al-Din Shirazi and His Transcendent Theosophy: Background, Life and Works*, Tehran, Imperial Academy of Philosophy, 1978; J. Cooper, 'Mulla Sadra (Sadr al-Din Muhammad al-Shirazi) (1571/2–1640)', *Routledge Encyclopaedia of Philosophy*, op. cit., vol. 6, pp. 595–99 (for the online version see http://www.muslimphilosophy.com/ip/rep/H027.htm

12 Nasr, *Sadr al-Din Shirazi*, op. cit., pp. 55–68; see also Fazlur Rahman, *The Philosophy of Mulla Sadra*, Albany, New York, 1976.

13 James Winston Morris, *The Wisdom of the Throne: An Introduction to the Philosophy of Mulla Sadra*, Princeton, 1981, p. 9.

14 Francis Robinson, *The Ulama of Farangi Mahall and Islamic Culture in South Asia*, Delhi, 2001, p. 55.

15 Nasr, 'Sadr al-Din Shirazi (Mulla Sadra)', *A History of Muslim Philosophy*, Wiesbaden, 1966, vol. II, p. 958.

[16] J.W. Morris, *The Wisdom of the Throne: An Introduction to the Philosophy of Mulla Sadra,* Princeton, 1981, p. 49; see also *The Encyclopaedia of Islam,* new edition, D. MacEoin, 'Mulla Sadra', op. cit., vol. 7, p. 547.

[17] *A'in-i Akbari,* edited by H. Blochmann, Calcutta, 1872, vol. I, pp. 201–02.

[18] Ibid., II, p. 229.

[19] See Irfan Habib, 'A Political Theory for the Mughal Empire: A Study of the Ideas of Abu'l Fazl', Proceedings of the Indian History Congress, 1998, Patiala Session, pp. 329–40.

[20] Ibid., I, p. 3.

[21] For al-Dawwani see John Cooper, 'Jalal al-Din Dawani', *Routledge Encyclopaedia of Philosophy,* op. cit., vol. 2, pp. 806–07. For the online version see http://www.muslimphilosophy.com/ip/rep/H038.htm.

[22] Mir Ghulam Ali Azad Bilgrami, *Ma'asir ul Kiram,* Agra, 1910, pp. 236–37.

[23] S.A.A. Rizvi, *Shah Waliullah and his Times,* Canberra, 1980, pp. 190–95; J.R.I. Cole, *Roots of North Indian Shi'ism in Iran and Iraq, Religion and State in Awadh, 1722–1839,* Delhi, 1989, p. 27.

[24] See Norman Calder, 'The Structure of Authority in Imami Shi'i Jurisprudence', Ph.D. dissertation, School of Oriental and African Studies, 1980.

[25] See S.A.A. Rizvi, *History of Isna 'Asharis,* op. cit., pp. 219–20; idem, *Shah Waliullah and his Times,* Canberra, 1980, pp. 64–65.

[26] Ibid. See also *The Encyclopaedia of Islam,* new edition, *Supplement,* 2004, pp. 308–09.

[27] For these scholars, see *Ma'asirul Kiram,* op. cit., pp. 209, 235–36.

[28] S.A.A. Rizvi, *Shah Waliullah and his Times,* op. cit., p. 66.

[29] Shahnawaz Khan, *Ma'asirul Umara,* Calcutta, 1881–91, vol. II, pp. 30–32; see also S.A.A. Rizvi, *History of Isna 'Asharis,* op. cit., II, pp. 224–27.

[30] *Dabistan-i Mazahib,* Lucknow: Nawal Kishore, 1904, p. 364.

[31] Ibid., p. 365.

[32] Ibid.

[33] For the early development of the *dars-i nizami* and the books included in this curriculum, see Muhammad Raza Ansari, *Bani-i dars-i nizami,* Lucknow, 1973; Altafur Rahman, *Qiyam-i Nizam-i Ta'lim,* Lucknow, 1924; G.M.D. Sufi, *al-Minhaj,* op. cit., pp. 89–152.

[34] *The Encyclopaedia of Islam,* new edition, *Supplement,* Leiden, E.J. Brill, 2004, p. 292.

[35] *Ma'asir-ul Kiram,* op. cit., p. 220.

[36] See Maulana Fazl-i Imam Khairabadi, *Tarajim-i Fuzala,* edited and translated by Mufti Intizamullah Shihabi, Karachi, 1956. Cf. Francis Robinson, *The Ulama of Farangi Mahall,* op. cit., p. 52.

[37] Shah 'Abdul' Aziz, *Sharh-i Mulla Sadra,* MS, Firangi Mahal Collection, Maulana Azad Library, Aligarh Muslim University, Aligarh.

[38] Muhammad Faizbakhsh, *Tarikh-i Farahbakhsh,* translated by W. Hoey, *Memoirs of Delhi and Faizabad,* Allahabad, 1888–89, vol. II, pp. iii–iv.

# 11 Women in the Sikh Discourse

## Liberation or Ambivalence?

*Kamlesh Mohan*

In this paper, my objective is twofold. Firstly, I shall try to map out the radical shift in the conceptualization of women in the Sikh religious tradition, and examine how far it has its roots in Brahmanical patriarchy while making some departures from the Hindu religious tradition. This scrutiny is carried down to the tradition's eventual freezing, representing a distinct retrogression, visible in the stereotyping of roles as religious boundaries and identities becoming sealed from the late nineteenth century onwards. Secondly, I wish to underline the negative role of the patriarchal attitudes within the Sikh community, drawing upon the customs of the numerical majority of the high-status Jats, in inhibiting the process of gender equality, not only in demographic terms, but also in terms of social and economic empowerment. I shall examine the implications of the precedence increasingly given to the development of a consciously martial culture over the initial commitment to socio-religious reform in the course of the evolution of the Sikh *panth.*

I divide this paper into three sections. In the first section, the role of socio-historical environment and its interaction with material factors in shaping new religious movements such as the Sikh movement and its agenda will be briefly discussed. I analyse Guru Nanak's perception of contemporary society and polity. The second section aims at pinpointing the essential components in the images and roles of women as envisaged in the hymns of the *Adi Granth.* In the third section, apart from scrutinizing gaps between precept and practice, I shall try to deal with the broad question: what can women do with religion and how can they use religious tradition and values to their advantage in a changing society?

I

Generally speaking, religious protest movements tend to arise in situations of socio-economic dislocation and conflict often caused by changes in political authority and masters. The movements embody attempts to come to terms with these changes, to create new value systems in which they can be accommodated and their oppressive impact lightened. In each movement, the relative strength and specific characteristics of the elements of social protest and accommodation vary. They also tend to change as the movements progress,[1] as is evident from the shift in emphasis from peaceful change to the use of arms in the case of the evolution of the Sikh religion.

In order to understand the birth and growth of Sikhism as a protest movement, and its drive to remove prejudice against women, we must locate its founder Guru Nanak in his socio-historical environment.[2] We must realize that the process of the establishment and consolidation of the Delhi Sultans' political authority from the twelfth century onwards was held to be associated with wars and conquests, plunder and slaughter, not excluding destruction of places of worship and conversion. The process was modified by the policy of a particular Sultan or emperor or their governors and the exigencies of political or economic patronage expected or received in areas inhabited by the Hindus. It may be pointed out that the Punjab bore the brunt of this great socio-political upheaval. Amidst this confusion and conflict, people were forced to redefine reality, political loyalties, economic relationships and their religious beliefs and protect identities by prostration or compromise.

Unlike the ordinary people and the pragmatic social as well as economic elites, non-conformist visionaries articulated their critique of the existing socio-cultural institutions and the practices of both Hinduism and Islam. For example, Kabir's hymns represent the agony of an individual who tries to make a divided society conform to Divine Unity. Guru Nanak, on the other hand, chose to go beyond expressing individual dissatisfaction and discontent with the existing political and socio-religious order.

In the process of discovery of his life's mission, Guru Nanak developed a broad protestant movement based on a threefold critique. The first concerns the several forms of human folly and ignorance; the second is directed against the cruel, unjust and discriminatory conduct of contemporary rulers; and the third is focused upon God's seeming indifference to human predicament.[3] Whether called a critique or response to the contemporary reality, the Sikh Gurus especially Guru Nanak, Guru Arjan and Guru Gobind Singh perceived a close relationship between political abuses and social degradation. The *Gurbani* portrays human beings in a variety of social situations, contexts and roles: householder, thinker, devotee, preacher, ruler, leader, etc.[4] The synoptic vision of the bhagats, sages and gurus, whose hymns have been included in the *Guru Granth*, touches practically all aspects of human life – individual, familial, social, moral, religious and humanistic. On a close analysis from this perspective, the *Guru Granth* can very well be called a social document and a political critique.

How far are these articulations relevant for mapping shifts in the conceptualization of women and their roles? While elaborating his conception of an ideal king and his duties, he has underlined the inherent greatness of woman as a mother. For an illustration, let us read this line: 'Why should we call women 'evil' who give birth to kings.'[5]

Guru Nanak's anguish over the prevalent political chaos and oppression was compounded by his awareness of the use and exploitation of women for sexual gratification through forcible means, prostitution and polygamy. From this was derived his extreme sensitivity to the vulnerability of women (irrespective of their affiliation to any caste, religion or class) under immoral and licentious rulers and in situations of war and social dislocation. As he says in *Babarwani*:

> Babar has descended upon India with
> the wedding-party of lust and forcibly
> demands surrender of the bride.
> Decency and law have hidden themselves.
> Evil is structuring about in triumph.
> Mohammedan and Hindu priests are discarded,
> And Satan is solemnizing the marriages.[6]

Guru Nanak's references to the miseries and degradation of women, sometimes direct and sometimes indirect, are suggestive of their helplessness arising from threats of physical violation and dependent position in the family system. In *Rāg Āsā*, these women–sufferers have been described as *hinduani, turkani, bhattiani* and *thakurani*.[7]

Nanak's moral judgement also extends to the luxurious lives of men and women, their glittering marriage ceremonies and reckless indulgence in conjugal as well as extramarital sex, without any thought of God.[8] The senseless pursuit of pleasure by the rulers and nobles alike is contrasted with their helplessness after loss of

> They had never remembered Ram, now
> They cannot invoke Khuda.[9]

Let me make a brief reference to the social position of Hindu women here and the customs enforcing her subordination from the eleventh to the fifteenth centuries in order to understand the significance of Guru Nanak's call for justice to women. Alberuni noticed that a Hindu woman was inferior and subordinate to man,[10] notwithstanding the respect given to her as a daughter, wife and mother among the Brahmanas, the Rajputs and the Khatris.[11] A respectable Hindu wife was expected to be completely devoted to her husband and prove her fidelity at the cost of her life. The wide prevalence of the custom of *sati*, i.e., self-immolation by the widow on her husband's funeral pyre among the high castes such as Brahmanas, Khatris, and Rajputs, was noticed by Alberuni.[12] Ibn Battuta recorded a case of *sati* in Ajodhan (Pakpatan)[13] in the Punjab. The custom of *sati* continued to be practised in the Punjab as late as the nineteenth century, as Ganesh Das has recorded.[14] The construction of *sati-chauras*,[15] i.e., spots of worship in honour of those who immolated themselves, showed that young widows were humiliated and treated as domestic drudges in case they chose to live.

Similarly, prohibition on the remarriage of widows had been sanctified through several centuries. Child marriage, which was a common practice before AD 1200, required the girls to be married before the age of puberty; infanticide was also widely practised by Brahmanas, Khatris and Rajputs in this region.[16]

As far as the religious milieu in the Punjab was concerned, it was characterized by a variety of religious beliefs and practices originating in Hinduism, Buddhism and Islam. In north India, the growth of several esoteric cults and sects, Tantric practices and rites of *sadhus, jogis* and *fakirs* had facilitated the exploitation of the masses and oppression of women, across religious affiliation. In Punjab, *Nath yogis*, especially Gorakhnath and Puran Bhagat, are thought to represent 'what is left of Buddhism'.[17] The *Nath yogis* advocated renunciation of all worldly ties and pleasures. Their opposition to association with women was based on the belief that a woman is the main temptress in the path of a *yogi*, who aims at suppressing and sublimating all sexual desire. While Kabir shares this antipathy to women, Guru Nanak denounces the *yogīs* or their denigration of women and favours the achievement of salvation by his disciples without neglecting their duties as householders. Guru Nanak's thought on women is largely consistent with the Bhakti trend, where it opposed the traditional monopoly of Hindu priests and the caste system. Katherine Young rightly concedes that the 'popularity of Bhakti resulted in no small measure from its inclusion of such marginal groups as women and sudras. . . . Being female was generally no bar to Bhakti.'[18]

It may be pointed out that the gender dichotomy and tension appears in glaring form in the Bhakti sects. The break is to be seen between a tradition transmitted by word of mouth among women and an elaborate search and evaluative legacy transmitted through written texts among men.[19] In other words, the dichotomy between the oral and the written often reflects the dichotomy of the feminine and the masculine. It is evident in the compilation of Bhakti hymns in the *Adi Granth*. The exclusion of the hymns of women Bhaktas from the *Adi Granth* such as Mirabai,[20] Lal Ded[21] and Akka Maha Devi[22] may thus possibly reflect an unstated gender bias. Such bias could be due to the pressures of multiple patriarchies in the Punjabi society of the time. It is possible though that it was thought in the case of Mira Bai, at any rate, that there were elements of image-worship in her compositions.

## II

How do the multiple patriarchies articulate themselves? Images and symbols are the most often used means of projecting realities of women's lives and positions within a particular milieu. Traditional Sikh approaches to the question of gender, which have presented Sikhism as radically different from other religions on this issue, claim gender equality, primarily, on the basis of selected scriptural passages. By pointing out a variety of feminine images, such as maternal and bridal in the scriptures especially the *Adi Granth* and *Dasam Granth*, as well as grammatically feminine theological concepts, it has been argued in a recent scholarly study that the feminine principle is privileged over the male.[23]

Guru Nanak's philosophy and style have provided a model for

successive Gurus. In his keen awareness of women's degraded position in contemporary society and the idealization of their image and roles and advocacy of social dignity for them, he was followed by Guru Amar Das and Guru Gobind Singh. For the *Tat Khalsa*, in fact for the majority of the Sikhs, every explanation begins with Guru Nanak. Almost always, they cite the following *sloka* from *Āsā di Vār:*

> Fro… women born, shaped in the womb,
> To women betrothed and wed.
> We are bound to woman by ties of
> Affection, on women a man's future
> Depends. If one woman dies he seeks
> Another; with a woman he orders his life.
> Why should one speak evil of women,
> They who give birth to kings?
> Women also are born of women; none
> Takes birth except from a woman.
> Only the true one, Nānak, needs no help from a woman.
> Blessed are they, both men and women.[24]

This *sloka* is regarded as representative of the total attitude of all Sikhs to the ideal place of women, including their access to God's grace. Somewhat contrary to the conventional view of his times, Guru Nanak repudiated the prevalent notions of *stri-swabhava*, i.e., women's inherent nature as 'evil', 'unclean', temptation incarnate, fickle, mean, impure, treacherous, indiscriminate, avaricious, etc.[25] Keen to associate women with his religious message, he protested against their ill-treatment and their social victimization through the inhuman customs of infanticide, *purdah*, child-marriage, *sati* and many other evil practices such as polygamy, adultery and sex crimes.

Guru Nanak's positive views about woman's character, role and position nucleate around maternal images. In the Sikh sacred scripture, motherhood is indeed celebrated. It is replete with images of gestation, giving birth and nurturing. As the woman is valued as an individual and a human being (instead of being worshipped as a goddess in a hidden sanctuary), the structure of her body is prized. Thus, the *Adi Granth* is not reticent about the natural processes of the female body such as menstrual bleeding. Nikky-Guninder Singh regards these scriptural statements about a mother's physical acts of creation, nurturance and sustenance 'as the bold affirmation of the glory of motherhood which is at the heart of contemporary feminist thinking in religion.'[26]

The other recurrent images of the mother in the *Adi Granth* are based on their grammatical usage. For example, *joti* (light), *kudrati* (cosmos) or nature and *mati* (wisdom) have been projected as evidence of the acceptance of not only the concept of harmony between man, woman and cosmos in the Sikh tradition, but also of unity and equality of humankind irrespective of sex, caste or creed. Believing that *joti* is all pervasive and transcendent, a popular couplet from the *Adi Granth* is often cited for its positive social implications:

> Allah first created Light, and from that all were made.
> From that one light came the whole cosmos
> Whom shall we then declare good, whom bad?[27]

Whereas *joti* in the Sikh view is the Divine spirit, *kudrati* is creation itself. Grammatically feminine, *kudrati* is regarded as a manifestation of the transcendent. A Sikh scholar, while analysing the varied connotations of *kudrati*, has argued that it is also vital to the conception of society as the offspring of the 'Mother'.[28] Creativity is the common quality of God and mother; thus, there is no conflict, but harmony.

Further on, the equation between mother and wisdom has been underlined in the *bani* (also cited as evidence of the dominance of the feminine principle in the Sikh vision as the Gurus used the grammatically feminine word 'bani' for their message). The following line from a couplet has been cited for support:

> Mother is wisdom; father contentment.[29]

Let us turn to the argument of abundance of bridal imagery in Guru Nanak's hymns as evidence of gender equality in spiritual and mundane life. It has been suggested that the bridal symbol develops the 'nuances of intimacy and passion in the human relationship with the Divine'.[30] It has also been argued that the bride symbol further confirms the feminine principle which pervades the Sikh vision of the transcendent because the individual's quest for union with God has been presented in terms of bride-and-groom relationship throughout the *Guru Granth*: 'The soul-bride is longing day and night to see him with her own eyes.'[31]

The bride has also been lauded as a 'paradigmatic figure' because she enables the devotees to do away with traditional antithesis and dualism by interconnecting family, society, cosmos, nature and the transcendent.[32] Without going into a detailed discussion about the variety of meanings and values of the bridal finery and ritual embellishments as a preparation for her nuptial union with God, two points must be stressed. Firstly, these signify the bride's good deeds, and secondly, physical and intellectual qualities play a complementary role in the spiritual quest. For example, a few *slokas* in the *Guru Granth* which describe the effect of cosmetics on her eyes, show the interactive relationship between physical eye and mental eye, sight and insight in the pursuit of union with God.

The imagery of the soul–bride in the scriptures has been projected as evidence of 'a more egalitarian and open-minded social structure' among the Sikhs in general.[33] It may be conceded that Guru Nanak's description of mystical experience gained through the senses and his emphasis upon the centrality of household in an individual's religious life raise the concept of conjugal relations to a sacrosanct spiritual level. By dubbing the escapist *siddhas* as runaways from social responsibilities,[34] he rejected the prevalent belief in the value of celibacy and asceticism as facilitators of salvation.

The succeeding Gurus contributed to the clarity and enrichment of Guru Nanak's unconventional ideas about women's roles and images and about a healthy marital relationship. For example, Guru Amar Das says:

> The bride and groom are not those who,
> though together in body, are in spirit alone [separate].
> It is when the two bodies have a single soul
> that they become one.[35]

While taking a clear stand against widow-burning, Nanak gave it a new meaning, though he did not directly call for the abolition of the inhuman practice:

> Do not call her a suttee who burns herself with
> (her husband's) corpse.
> Know her as a suttee, Nanak, who dies
> in the agony of separation.[36]

This couplet condemns the violation of a woman's rights as a widow who is compelled to commit *sati* in times of extreme emotional vulnerability. Another couplet defined *sati* thus:

Know her as a suttee who dwells in purity and peace;
Who serves her husband and calls
Upon him when she awakens.[37]

Undoubtedly, the Sikh Gurus' messages seem radical in the existing patriarchal set-up which saw nothing wrong in the husbands' desertion of wives, in polygamy, adultery and prostitution. Apart from creating awareness about the social victimization of women, the Sikh Gurus gave women the right to initiation into the Sikh religion and participation in religious gatherings without being veiled. Their views were upheld by the Sikh *Rahit Maryada.*

Some scholars, who have dealt with the gender perspective in the sacred writings of their religion, laud it as an emancipatory tool without taking into account the problems either with the idealistic view or its misogynistic tendencies. For example, Harbans Singh,[38] Nikky-Guninder Singh[39] and J.S. Grewal[40] have focused upon the positive aspects of maternal and bridal images. It may be pointed out that these traits and images have been used for essentializing notions of ideal womanhood and gender roles in society. These stereotypes have also been manipulated as tools of social control of women – their dress code, behaviour patterns, self-images and world-view.

I wish to argue that the existing social ethics and ideological dominance of Brahmanical patriarchy continued to influence some of the Sikh Gurus' notions of ideal womanhood despite their critical temper. Abundance of feminine images within the Sikh scriptures as well as the use of grammatically feminine form in theological concepts are not sure evidence of the full dilution of gender bias or of the myriad forms of patriarchy. Nikky-Guninder Singh has contended that the 'Sikh word is not a masculine logos, it is the beautiful and formless *bani.*'[41] Such 'feminine' usage goes back to the Vedic texts wherein the notion of sacred speech is deified as a goddess.[42] It is not definite whether their articulation of sacred speech is simply indicative of the influence of the surrounding milieu or of the actual intent of the Gurus to honour women.

As opposed to the assertion made regarding the domination of the feminine over the male in Sikh scriptures, Harjot Oberoi has pointed out: 'In the early Sikh traditions God was almost exclusively conceived in masculine terms (*Akal Purukh, Karta Purukh*) and metaphors. The devotee was a bride yearning for God as bride-groom.'[43]

Even the epithets used for God in the verses in the female devotional voice are masculine, such as *Prabh, Ram* and *Rangila.* The 'relationship' of the soul–bride, i.e., woman with God, is that of *prem* or *preet.* It is in this context that the woman is depicted in several states metaphorically, including her girlhood (*balari*), wifehood (*sohagan*), bad woman (*dohagan*) and lovelorn (*birhan*).

In the Sikh scriptures, the two dominant images of mother and bride contain some elements of misogyny. Despite the celebration of motherhood, there are indications of ambivalence. For example:

> As does the mother cherish her pregnancy, in her
> son pinning her hope;
> That grown up, would give her wherewithal,
> And bring joy and pleasure.
> Even such is the love of God's devotee to the Lord.[44]

This verse reflects the preference for a boy in the patriarchal value system of contemporary Punjabi society through the metaphor of the dependence of the devotee on God.

A similar kind of ambivalence runs through the images of 'bride' and 'wife'. On the one hand, feminine traits are glorified, while on the other, the woman is projected as placed in a subordinate position – it is her qualities of submissiveness, self-abnegation, obedience to the male master that have been glorified. Although the language of the *Adi Granth* is allegorical, it reflects the popular social perception of the ideal woman:

> Possessed of thirty-two merits, holy truth
> is her progeny.
> Obedient, of noble mien,
> to her husband's wishes compliant.[45]
> The lord is my husband, I His wife.
> The Lord is immensely great, I so small.[46]
> A wife faithful to Lord must devote
> Herself body and soul to him
> And must behave in all respects
> As the faithful wedded wife.[47]

The following verse upbraids husbands for obedience and subservience to women:

Men obedient to their women-folk
Are impure, filthy, stupid;
Men lustful, impure follow their
Women-folk's counsel.[48]

There are numerous passages which show that the duality of body and mind, opposition between sensual and spiritual[49] and a stereotyped image of woman as inferior or even evil have not been negated. It is evident from couplets quoted below that all the bad qualities and *Maya* have been associated with women:

The egoist is like a loose woman,
A bad woman, given to casting spells.[50]
Attachment with Maya is like a loose woman
A bad woman given to casting spells.[51]
Maya afflicts one who by egoistic thinking is intoxicated,
It afflicts one attached with progeny and wife,
It afflicts one attached to elephants,
Horses and material objects.[52]

The bridal imagery reflects not only ambivalence, but also feudal mentality. In the *Adi Granth*, the relationship between God and the soul–bride has been valorized in terms of the relationship between man and woman in a feudal society. The relationship is not of equality but of inequality, where the husband is treated as the Lord and the wife exists merely to serve him and yearn for his grace:

Blessed is the Bride who knows her true Lord,
And submits to the command of her Master and sheds her Ego:
And imbued with her Lord revels in his love.
O my loved Mate, know thou the signs of the union with the Lord;
That, she alone is united who dedicates her
body and soul to her Lord, and cares not
for what the world says.
I, the Lord's Bride, have now assumed
Full control of my [mind's] Household, by the Guru's Grace,
and, through my Lord's Mercy, my ten
sense-organs slave for me.[53]

It may also be pointed out that the principle of monogamy

was not conformed to by the sixth and the tenth Gurus. Later on, Maharaja Ranjit Singh and other Sikh rulers also had many wives.

Now let us examine the issue of the influence of Brahmanical patriarchy on the Sikh religion. Sikh thought, which was surrounded by an androcentric society, could not shake off the overwhelming Brahmanic influence. Despite Guru Nanak's endeavour to break free from the existing socio-cultural ethos, his teachings and exhortations to his followers to practise gender justice failed to change the negative attitude of his followers towards women. It is reflected in two essential points: normative models for women and social practices and customs.

Firstly, the normative models and roles prescribed for women in Sikh sacred literature are very much in line with Brahmanical patriarchy. Not only is the Sikh history of five hundred years a record mainly of the activities of men, Sikh society and institutions have tended to be mainly male-centred. As the Sikh Gurus, scribes and historical writers were invariably male, their symbols and images reveal their perceptions about what should be the ideal behaviour of women. The images utilized in the Sikh sacred writings invariably focus upon women's important functions in the domestic arena and not in the public arena. Thus, the *Adi Granth* contains many images of mother, bride and feminine roles, as has been discussed already.

The influence of Brahmanical culture is also evident in Guru Gobind Singh's writings. His incorporation of the powerful Hindu goddess Durga as a literary figure into the *Dasam Granth*, has been projected as a tribute to the positive Sikh attitude towards feminine power.[54] But this needs to be evaluated in a socio-historical context. Considering the fact that Gobind Singh's formative years were spent in the Shivalik Hills, the stronghold of the Shakti and Durga cults, his choice of the latter goddess out of the large pantheon is understandable. Instead of being a proof of the 'feminine-affirming' mentality, it was a spontaneous assimilation of the contemporary hill culture and its later penetration into the Sikh culture of the plains. Its real significance should be seen in the growing complexity of patriarchal patterns wherein ambivalence may often be mistaken for positive intent.[55]

The valorization of these very images has been naturally instrumental in the essentialization of notions of womanhood and feminine roles in society. For example, the theological concept of service (*seva*) makes no distinction between 'male' and 'female' tasks, but experience shows the gap between the ideal and the practice.[56] Firstly, rooted prejudices regarding the sexual division of labour are accepted as a norm in Sikh as well as Hindu households. The majority of Sikh men who cook, clean and serve food happily in the gurdwara, look down upon similar domestic chores at home. Brahmanical patriarchy survives, though in a more liberal form, yet with its inherent contradictions intact.

Secondly, Brahmanical influence is also reflected in the sociological patterns of Sikh society and its practice of gender discrimination. Despite their condemnation of the evils of the caste system, the Sikh Gurus neither expressly rejected it nor tried to organize their followers into a casteless order. Converts to Sikhism from lower castes, who were attracted by its egalitarian message, often failed to get rid of their inferior status in the ritual hierarchy even after the baptism ceremony. Disabilities for women did get compounded as they were subject to the prejudices and stereotypes associated with caste and gender. This is evident from the exclusively male and high-caste status of the Guru lineage. The Gurus certainly conferred 'equal opportunity of access to spiritual liberation. It was not equality in the sense that women might do everything that might be open to men.'[57] While elaborating this point, W.H. McLeod goes on to say that it is

> misleading to see in his [Guru Nanak's] teachings or those of his successors a reordering of society wherein organization and control of vital and long-term decisions were exclusively in male hands. Despite many emancipatory elements in their teachings, the Gurus indirectly upheld the existing order which was shorn of its authoritarian aspect to some extent without dismantling the core structures.

The current stereotypes and prejudices against women have remained strong because the socialization process in the family could not be reoriented by the radical beliefs of the Sikh Gurus alone. The institution of family continued to legitimate the low value of daughters through the inhuman practice of female infanticide by a number of social groups, namely Bedis[58] and Mohyal Brahmans in nineteenth-century Punjab. The widespread social custom of dowry payment (as a maintenance fee for the daughter) to the groom's parents and transfer of property to male heirs among the followers of Sikhism, especially the land-owning castes, reflect the mentality of son-preference. Ironsically, patriarchal society in north India, including the Punjab, devalues women but valorizes them as the guardians of family honour, purity of lineage and cultural traditions, including religious values and practices, exclusively formulated by men.

The Singh Sabha movement, described as 'the greatest social reform movement of the Sikhs'[59] held a view of public morality with visibly dominant patriarchal content. Its vigorous drive to construct a 'separatist' Sikh history, distinct for the followers of the *panth* (whose cultural ties with the other social groups had been denied and cut off), was matched by its persistent efforts to establish distinct *rites de passage* through well-planned propaganda and widely circulated printed literature.[60] That the entire reform-agenda, especially the life cycle ceremonies nucleated around the universal patriarchal precept 'society must be ordered and controlled by men', is best illustrated by the Anand wedding ceremony. Codified on 22 October 1909, after over three hundred mass meetings and a number of petitions,[61] the Sikh marriage ritual enjoins the bridegroom to be 'the protector of the [bride's] person and her honour'. Then, the officiant [*granthi*] counsels the bride to accept her husband as a 'master of all love and respect'. Its real implication was that women needed protection, provided the woman complied with modernized forms of competent domesticity.

The ritual changes introduced by the new cultural elite among the Sikhs called *Tat Khalsa* were ultimately inserted in the manuals of conduct, whose latest version has been published under the title *Sikh Rahit Maryada* in 1950. Exemplifying the *modus operandi* of the 'invention of tradition', to use Hobsbawm's phrase, these *rites de passage* continue to have special bearing in the reconstitution of the personhood of Sikh men and women and their perceptions of identity, communal solidarity and vision of history. It had far-reaching implications in the crucial positioning of women in the process of transmission and conservation of the new cultural tradition. Entrusted with the responsibility of socializing the girl child to internalize the male-constructed symbols, images, codes of behaviour, dress and other values conducive to the patriarchal control of social and economic structures, institutions and resources, women had to be co-opted to defend the religious tradition and perform their prescribed roles as nurturers of family, community and nation. While 'inventing' the Sikh tradition, the Singh Sabha reformers made few departures from the essentials of

Hindu patriarchy. For example, a rigid perception of feminine and masculine traits and functions, roles and spaces was integrated into their ideology. It is not surprising that the reproductive potential of women rather than their productive capacity in economic and intellectual terms continued to be prized.

The leading ideologues of the Singh Sabha movement, namely Bhai Takht Singh, Bhai Mohan Singh Vaid and Bhai Vir Singh perceived the crucial role of the ideal woman in the moral uplift of the Sikh people. That was why they focused upon writing, publishing and circulating a wide variety of didactic literature including tracts, short stories and novels as well as school-magazines for students in Sikh Kanya Mahavidyalaya (Ferozepur),[62] for potential wives and mothers. For example, Bhai Vir Singh crafted superwomen of the ideal mould in his novels *Sundari* (1898), *Baba Naudh Singh* (1921), *Satwant Kaur* and other literary writings.[63] Sensitive to the inspirational value of historical novels in mobilizing support for socio-religious reforms, Bhai Vir Singh permitted his fictional heroines to cross over from domestic to the neutral territory of jungles, which symbolized public space. Portrayal of his model women as responsible for community meals (*langar*), serving and nursing the sick as well as wounded soldiers, reinforced the legitimacy of their traditional functions. Their rare appearance in a skirmish and subsequent capture by the enemy indirectly emphasized a woman's inherent vulnerability, rather than acceptance of her engagement with unconventional activities and roles.

It is, therefore, possible to argue that some misogynistic elements continued to exist within the broadly emancipatory and egalitarian content of the teachings of the Sikh Gurus and in the Singh Sabha reformers' agenda. These scriptural messages, when translated into an operative value system in the context of women, show many nuances. The gap between precept and practice is fairly visible in the actual life of Sikh women whom male-dominated society, polity and economy have forced to accept double standards on crucial matters – the variation in their status, their roles as women and choices in education, health, marriage, access to economic resources including property rights, codes of behaviour and dress. It has led to gender inequalities and injustices, which assume a complex form owing to the long process of interpenetration with caste patriarchies, as Sikhism has historically expanded.

## III

In the preceding analysis of the conceptualization of women in the Sikh religious tradition from the early sixteenth century onwards, I have tried to show that misogynistic tendencies, rather than Sikhism's own emancipatory potential, have increasingly influenced male perceptions and images of women, and its prescription of a code of conduct for women in domestic as well as public spaces. Hence, the Sikh tradition has turned into a discourse of ambivalence rather than of liberation.

In the nineteenth century, the Singh Sabha leadership, while defining a separate identity for the Sikh community through the demarcation of religious boundaries and life-cycle ceremonies, as distinct from those of the Hindus, endorsed the ideal of 'competent domesticity' floated in the parallel movement by the Arya reformers. In effect, a selective bonding of components of Brahmanical, bourgeois and tribal cultures in relation to women was crafted. In the reformed Sikh and Hindu traditions, women have been subordinated to the husband, family, kinship networks and the religious community. Since the Jats have continued to form a dominant part of the *panth*, women are often seen as subjected to tribal patriarchy, sometimes enforced through polygamy with a view to retaining power and property in the male line – fathers, uncles and brothers. The inevitability of the ordained transfer of a girl from the parental to the marital home has continued to deprive her of authority and individual autonomy in exercising her choice on a number of crucial issues, like education, marriage, spacing of children, residence, employment, and claim to share in parental and husband's property. It is supported by demographic data, which show a decline in sex ratio, higher female infant mortality, continuing incidence of child-marriage, rising rate of reported dowry-deaths and bride-burning in the Punjab as well as a lower level of female literacy and work-force participation.

Despite emancipatory directions from Guru Nanak and his successors, Sikh women are still subjected to multiple patriarchies of caste, tribe, family and religion. The persistent demand for a separate personal law for Sikhs is a blatant example of an obsession with the patriarchal agenda, i.e., perpetuation of women's disabilities with regard to marriage, maintenance, inheritance and guardianship, though the legislation of such a separate code has been linked with the cause of their autonomy as a religious community. In fact, a firm regulation of women's lives and bodies in male hands has remained an objective for men, despite their willingness or even enthusiasm to modernize their homes, sacred places and agricultural economy through the use of latest technologies. The Punjab was the first state to commercialize amniocentesis as early as 1979, 'a development that has favoured' the birth of male babies and elimination of female foetuses.[64] Despite protests by press and women activists against the 1982 newspaper advertisements, featuring New Bhandari Ante-natal sex-determination Clinic at Amritsar, the State Government refrained from ordering any prohibition of amniocentesis.[65] It is difficult to say whether the growing popularity of these practices in the Punjab (having the highest number of abortions of female foetuses) will at last ignite a feminist movement and its active intervention in preventing the abuse of medical technologies.

It is naturally relevant to identify the factors which have frozen the process of social change, specifically relating to women. Firstly, for the Sikh Gurus, who contributed to a positive change in the socio-religious milieu from the sixteenth century onwards, it was religious reform, not social change, that was the major objective. The condemnation of oppressive social customs such as infanticide, sati and polygamy and their injunctions to followers to treat women honourably flowed from their own broad humanist perspective. Guru Nanak's teachings initially moulded his disciples' attitude towards gender relations perceiving women as essentially virtuous rather than evil. However, the transformation of the very character of the *panth* from a religious movement into a religio-political movement necessarily brought a shift in the priorities of the Gurus.[66] For example, Guru Hargobind's call to arms as a measure of self-defence in the seventeenth century took precedence over their concern for the removal of social customs oppressive of women. In fact, their religious commitment to securing and protecting their autonomy against the authority of the Mughal government in the eighteenth century diverted attention from women's plight in society. As a result, the positive orientation towards women found in the teachings of the earlier Gurus was not further developed or even sustained. It is likely that some Gurus even endorsed some of the norms of the contemporary male-dominated ethos. Thus, a gap came to exist between the ideal Sikh view, and the social patterns actually prevailing, especially as concern women.

Nikky-Guninder Singh has noted various reasons for this

dichotomy between the 'empowering' messages of the Sikh scripture and actual practice. She has drawn attention to the negative role of the patriarchal exegetes such as translators, commentators and teachers who have been 'excising female symbolism and imagery [and] replacing it with a male one. Because the sacred text has not been meaningfully read, Sikh women do not enjoy the status that Guru Nanak wanted them to have.'[67] Another explanation for the inability of the comparatively young Sikh tradition to break the stranglehold of the existing, male-centred culture was the overwhelming presence of the Hindu and the Islamic traditions in the region.[68] It is even possible that the beliefs and attitudes of the Jats, who form the dominant component of the *panth*, may have exercised more influence on the patterns of Punjabi society, particularly its Sikh segment, than have Brahmanical and Islamic values.

It must be conceded that there is a close relationship between religion and social change. On the one hand, religious traditions have played a seminal role in the transformation of various societies. On the other hand, these have often been used as an instrument for the subjugation and oppression of women in the domestic space. In the hands of many socio-religious reformers, religion has provided and continues to provide an effective means of standardizing the patriarchal agenda, norms and practices for regulating women's behaviour and activities not only within the four walls of homes, but also within the expanding public space comprising school, colleges, offices, factories, market place, etc.

In the present times, many radical-minded women have raised a variety of questions regarding values, norms and code of conduct prescribed for them by Hindu, Sikh and Islamic religious scriptures. One of these questions is: what should women do with religion? Should they reject it or reinterpret it for recasting gender relations and societies in which they live? Devaki Jain has provided answers to this question while discussing Gandhi's effective and creative use of the Hindu religious traditions for mobilizing the Indian masses, particularly women, for social and political struggles.[69] Through his imaginative approach, Gandhi was able to elucidate linkages between the feminine qualities of compassion, caring and tolerance (valued by Hindu, Christian, Islamic and Sikh religious traditions), and strategies for social change.

Punjabi women, having the advantages of being exposed to

the composite culture of this region, are in the happy position to identify more creatively the positive messages and directions in their religious traditions. These can be used for formulating a gender-sensitive, broad-based ethic. For example, two essential teachings of the Sikh Gurus, *Kirat Kar* and *Vand Chhak*, may be used effectively for legitimizing women's right to work and access to economic resources. Similarly, Guru Nanak's emphasis on the desirability of marriages and family life for procreation may be positively interpreted to project the criticality of the joint contribution of men and women in ensuring a just economic life. Recognition of women's contribution to productivity and intellectual growth can be facilitated through the creative mediation of religion, which continues to mould thinking, values and behaviour of a large number of Indians.

**Notes and References**

1 David N. Lorenzen, 'Kabir Panth and Social Protest', in Karin Schomer and W.H. McLeod, eds, *The Sants: Studies in a Devotional Tradition of India*, Delhi, 1887, p. 293.

2 I have based my observations regarding socio-environment on a number of works, such as K.M. Ashraf, *Life and Conditions of the People of Hindustan*, Delhi, 1959, 1969; Aziz Ahmad, *Studies in Islamic Culture in the Indian Environment*, Delhi, 1964; V. Upadhayay, *Socio-Religious Conditions of North India*, 700–1200 AD, Varanasi, 1964; Tapan Raychaudhuri and Irfan Habib, *The Cambridge Economic History of India*, Vol. I (2 volumes), *c.* 1200–1750, Delhi, 1982, 1984.

3 For an interesting discussion on this aspect see Wazir Singh, 'Social Protest in Sikh Gurbani', in the *Journal of Medieval Indian Literature*, Vol. 2, No. 162, March–September, 1978, pp. 34–36.

4 Ibid., p. 31.

5 Gopal Singh (translator), *Sri Guru Sahib*, 4 Vols, Delhi, 1978, p. 467. Hereafter, the English version of quotations cited from the *Adi Granth*, unless otherwise noted, shall be excerpted from Gopal Singh's translation.

6 Ibid., Guru Nanak, p. 722.

7 Ibid., pp. 1382–84.

8 Ibid., p. 4.

9 For a translation of this couplet, see Manmohan Singh (translator), *Sri Guru Granth Sahib*, 6 Vols, Amritsar: S.G.P.C. 1964, 1965, pp. 382–84; Gopal Singh's translation, pp. 414–15.

10 K.M. Ashraf, *Life and Conditions of the People of Hindustan*, pp. 166–67; A.B. Pandey, *Society and Government in Medieval India*, Allahabad, 1965, pp. 203–04.

11 *Alberuni's India*, translated by Edward C. Sachau, London, 1926, I, pp. 179–81.

[12] Ibid., p. 155. Romila Thapar, *A History of India*, London, 1967, p. 152. She has pointed out that *sati* was literally equated with a 'virtuous' woman.

[13] *Ibn Battuta: Travels in Asia and Africa*, translated and edited by H.A.R. Gibb, London, 1953, p. 191.

[14] Ganesh Das, *Char-Bagh-i Panjab*, edited by Kirpal Singh, Amritsar, 1965, pp. 188–200.

[15] Ibid., p. 252, Ganesh Das has given an interesting description of a case of *sati*.

[16] V. Upadhayay, *Socio-Religious Conditions of North India, (700–1200 AD)*, Varanasi, 1964, pp. 153–54; Kiran Davendra, 'Position of Women in Punjabi Society', in Mohinder Singh, ed., *Prof. Harbans Singh Commemoration Volume*, 1988, p. 238; McLeod, *Sikhism*, London, 1977. McLeod (p. 246) has argued that 'the *rahit-namas* of the eighteenth and early nineteenth centuries contain implicit prohibitions of female infanticide, thereby testifying to the practice among some members of the Panth.' The Bedis offered a prominent example.

[17] Bhai Mohan Singh, cited in Charlotte Vaudeville, *A Weaver Named Kabir*, Delhi, 1993, 1997, p. 77.

[18] Katherine K. Young, 'Hinduism', in Arvind Sharma, ed., *Women in World Religions*, Albany, 1987, pp. 76–77.

[19] Guy Poitevin and Hem Prabha Pairkar, *Stone-mill and Bhakti: From the Devotion of Peasant Women to the Philosophy of Swamis*, Delhi, 1996, p. 260.

[20] Mirabai, a rebel Bhakta, is believed to have been born towards the end of the fifteenth century, within the Rathor Rajput family who held control over Merta (in the present-day Rajasthan). Married to the heir-apparent to the throne of Chittor (ruled by Sisodiyas), she refused to consummate the relationship and declared her love and allegiance for Lord Krishna. Her *bhajans* are sung with great fervour in Rajasthan, Gujarat and Saurashtra. For an unconventional study of this historical Bhakta, see Parita Mukta, *Upholding the Common Life: The Community of Mirabai*, Delhi, 1997.

[21] Popularly known as Lal Ded, she was born sometime between 1317 and 1320 in a Kashmiri Brahman family and died in 1372. After 12 years of married life, she became a wandering ascetic. She composed verses in her own genre *Vaakh*. For more details, regarding her life and times, see Jaya Lal Kaul, *Lal Ded*, Delhi, 1973.

[22] Akkamahadevi, one of the greatest Kannada poets of the twelfth century, began her life as a spiritual seeker and a poet after her departure from the palace of her royal husband in Uduthalli. She spent the rest of her life as a naked *sanyasin*, until she reached her destination Kadali, a sacred grove in the hills. Srisaila was the home of her *Isht-devta* – Lord Chennamalikarjuna. The most dramatic part of her journey was her visit to Kalyana, the great centre of the twelfth-century philosophical debates with her peers like Basvana, Allama and Chenna Basvana. The most memorable products of her spiritual journey were her poems, popularly called *vachannas*. These

lyrical poems have been described as a sacred journey through the profane world.

23 Nikky-Guninder Kaur Singh, *The Feminine Principle in the Sikh Vision of the Transcendent*, Cambridge, 1993, p. 3, 7.

24 Gurcharan Singh Talib (translator), *Asa di Var*.

25 J. Leslie, *Strisvabhava: The Inherent Nature of Women*, Vol. I, Part 11. N.J. Allen, R.F. Gombrich, T. Ray Chaudhary, eds, Delhi, 1986. This is a commentary on Tryambakajavan's *Stree Dharampadhiti*, an eighteenth-century document.

26 Nikki-Guninder Singh, p. 56.

27 Gurcharan Singh Talib (translation), p. 1349.

28 Nikky-Guninder Singh, p. 67.

29 Quoted in ibid., p. 69.

30 Nikky-Guninder Singh, p. 90.

31 *Adi Granth*, pp. 703–05.

32 Nikky-Guninder Singh, p. 91.

33 Ibid., p. 98.

34 *Adi Granth*, p. 1013.

35 *Adi Granth*, pp. 748, 788.

36 Ibid., p. 787.

37 Ibid., p. 788.

38 Harbans Singh, 'Place of Women in Sikhism', *Journal of Religious Understanding*, Vol. X, No. 3, July–September, 1990.

39 Nikky-Guninder Kaur Singh, *The Feminine Principle in the Sikh Vision of the Transcendent*, op. cit.

40 J.S. Grewal, 'Gender Perspective on Guru Nanak', in Kiran Pawer (ed.), *Women in Indian History: Social, Economic, Political and Cultural Perspectives*, New Delhi, 1996, pp. 141–57.

41 Nikky-Guninder Singh, p. 252.

42 Thomas J. Hopkins, *The Hindu Religious Tradition*, Belmont, CA, 1971, pp. 19–20.

43 Harjot Oberoi, *The Construction of Religious Boundaries: Culture, Identity and Diversity in the Sikh Tradition*, Delhi, 1994, p. 97. This may be contrasted to the sufic discourse where God is often envisioned as a female Beloved, and the seeker as a male lover.

44 *Adi Granth*, p. 165.

45 Ibid., p. 371.

46 Ibid., p. 483.

47 Ibid., p. 31.

48 Ibid., p. 304.

49 Ibid.

50 Ibid., p. 639.

51 Ibid., p. 182.

52 Ibid.

53 Ibid., p. 737.

[54] Nikky-Guninder Singh, p. 121.

[55] It must be pointed out that the powerful and autonomous goddess Durga draws her power from male gods. Thus, her omnipotence has at best an ambiguous status. Turning from mythical to actual perception of danger and awe of divine female figures of Kali/Durga, whether by the illiterate villagers or the urban-educated middle classes, the overall attitude towards women can be characterized as ambivalent, rather than positive. This indication is available in the contradictory signals in a number of verses in the *Guru Granth* which reject the goddess: 'He who worships Maha-Maya falls from the pedestal of man to be reborn a "woman"' (*Adi Granth*, p. 871).

[56] Kanwaljit Kaur, 'Sikh Women', in Gobind Singh Mansukhani and Jasbir Singh Mann, eds, *Fundamental Issues in Sikh Studies*, Chandigarh: Institute of Sikh Studies, 1992, p. 103.

[57] W.H. McLeod, *Sikhism*, London, 1997, pp. 243–44.

[58] In *Sikhism*, McLeod has treated explicit prohibitions against female infanticide in the *Rahit-namas*, i.e., manuals of conduct of the eighteenth and early nineteenth centuries as a definite proof of the existence of these customs among some followers of the Sikh *panth*. In his view, the practice of hypergamy for the marriage of daughters and inheritance patterns in favour of sons were the two major causes of female infanticide in the peasant society of this region.

[59] Gurdarshan Singh Dhillon, 'Character and Impact of the Singh Sabha Movement on the History of the Panjab', unpublished Ph.D. thesis, Punjabi University, Patiala, 1973, p. 39.

[60] For an incisive discussion of the construction of *rites de passage*, see Harjot S. Oberoi, 'From Ritual to Counter-Ritual: Rethinking the Hindu–Sikh Question, 1884–1915', in T.O'Connel, Milton Israel, Willard G. Oxtoby *et al.*, *Sikh History and Religion in the Twentieth Century*, Delhi, 1990, pp. 1236–58. Its appendix contains the list of 24 manuals on *rites de passage*, written between 1884–1915.

[61] Details regarding its legislation have been discussed in I.S. Talwar, 'The Anand Marriage Act', *The Punjab Past and Present*, Vol. II, Part 2, October, 1968, pp. 400–10. See also Ajmer Singh, *Anand Vivah Par Vichar Ka Khandan*, Amritsar, 1908. It contains a strong defence of the Anand Marriage ritual.

[62] For a detailed account of Bhai Takht Singh's struggle for establishing the Sikh Kanya Mahavidyalya, see *Zinda Shaheed Bhai Takht Singh* (in Punjabi), Patiala, 1980.

[63] For a complete list of his works see Harbans Singh, *Bhai Vir Singh*, Delhi, 1972, 1984.

[64] W.H. McLeod, *Sikhism*, p. 245.

[65] Renuka Dagar, 'Women's Rights in Punjab: Interventionists' Perspective', in Kiran Pawar, ed., *Women in Indian History*, pp. 227, 233.

[66] J.S. Grewal, 'A Perspective on Early Sikh History', in Mark Juergensmeyer and N. Gerald Barrier, eds, *Sikh Studies: Comparative Perspectives on a Changing Tradition*, Berkeley, 1979, p. 34. While discussing the changes in

the focus of the Sikh community with the passage of time, he explores the historical and logical connections between the activity and ideas of various phases.

67 Nikky-Guninder Singh, p. 253.

68 Ibid., p. 255.

69 Devaki Jain, 'Gandhian Contribution towards a Feminist Ethic', in Dian L. Eck and Devaki Jain, eds, *Speaking of Faith: Cross-Cultural Perspectives on Women*, New Delhi, 1986, pp. 256–70.

# 12 Constructing the Hindu Identity

*Dwijendra Narayan Jha*

## I

The quest for India's national identity through the route of Hindu religious nationalism began in the nineteenth century and has continued ever since. In recent years, however, it has received an unprecedented boost from those communal forces which have brought a virulent version of Hindu cultural chauvinism to the centre stage of contemporary politics and produced a warped perception of India's past. This is evident from the indigenist and propagandist writings which support the myth of Aryan autochthony, demonize Muslims and Christians, and propagate the idea that India and Hinduism are eternal. In an effort to prove the indigenous origin of Indian culture and civilization, it has been argued, though vacuously, that the people who composed the Vedas called themselves Aryans and were the original inhabitants of India.[1] They are further described as the authors of the Harappan civilization, which the xenophobes and communalists insist on rechristening after the Vedic Saraswatī. Such views have received strong support from archaeologists whose writings abound in paralogisms;[2] and from their followers, whose work is dotted with fakes and frauds. A notable instance was the attempt to convert a Harappan 'unicorn bull' into a Vedic horse so as to push the clock back on the date of the Vedas and thereby identify the Vedic people with the authors of the Harappan civilization.[3] This obsession with pushing back the chronology of Indian cultural traits and with denying the elements of change in them[4] has taken the form of a frenzied hunt for antiquity. We see a stubborn determination to 'prove' that the Indian ('Hindu' is the synonym in the communal lexicon) civilization is older than all others and was, therefore, free from any possible contamination in its formative phase.

In this historiographical format India, i.e., Bhārata, is timeless. The first man was born here. Its people were the authors of the first human civilization, the Vedic, which is the same as the 'Indus–Saraswatī'. The authors of this civilization had reached the highest peak of achievement in all arts and sciences, and they were conscious of belonging to the Indian nation, which has existed eternally. This obsession with the antiquity of the Indian identity, civilization and nationalism has justifiably prompted several scholars, in recent years, to study and analyze the development of the idea of India.[5] Most of them have rightly argued that India as a country evolved over a long period, that the formation of its identity had much to do with the perceptions of the people who migrated into the subcontinent at different times, and that Indian nationalism developed mostly as a response to Western imperialism. But not all of them have succeeded in rising above the tendency to trace Indian national identity back to ancient times. For instance, a respected historian of ancient India tells us that 'the inhabitants of the subcontinent were considered by the Purānic authors as forming a nation', and 'could be called by a common name – Bhāratī'.[6] Assertions like this are very close to the Hindu jingoism which attributes all major modern cultural, scientific and political developments, including the idea of nationalism, to the ancient Indians. Although their detailed refutation may amount to a réchauffé of what has already been written on the historical development of the idea of India, I propose to argue against the fantastic antiquity assigned to Bhārata and Hinduism, as well as against the historically invalid stereotypes about the latter, and thus to show the lack of substance behind the ideas which have fed the monster of Hindu cultural nationalism in recent years.

## II

The geographical horizon of the early Aryans, as we know, was limited to the north-western part of the Indian subcontinent, referred to as *Saptasindhava*,[7] and the word Bhàrata in the sense of a country is absent from the entire Vedic literature, though the Bharata tribe is mentioned at several places in different contexts. In the *Aṣṭādhyāyī* of Pāṇini (500 BC) we find a reference to Prācya Bhàrata in the sense of a territory (*janapada*) which lay between *Udīcya* (north) and *Prācya* (east).[8] It must have been a small region occupied by the Bharatas and cannot be equated with the Akhaṇḍabhārata or Bhārata of the Hindutva camp. The earliest reference to Bhāratavarṣa (Prākrit *Bharadhavasa*) is found in the inscription of Kharavela (first century BC),[9] which lists it among the territories he invaded – but it did not include Magadha, which is mentioned separately in the record. The word may refer here in a general way to northern India, but its precise territorial connotation is vague. A much larger geographical region is visualized by the use of the word in the *Mahābhārata* (composed over the period *c.* 200 BC to AD 300), which provides a good deal of geographical information about the subcontinent, although a large part of the Deccan and the far south does not find any place in it. Among the five divisions of Bhāratavarṣa named, Madhyadeśa finds frequent mention in ancient Indian texts; in the *Amarakośa* (also known as the *Nāmalingānuśāsana*), a work of the fourth–fifth centuries, it is used synonymously with Bhārata and Āryāvarta;[10] the latter, according to its eleventh-century commentator Kṣīrasvāmin, being the same as Manu's holy land situated between the Himalayas and the Vindhya range.[11] But in Bāṇa's *Kādambarī* (seventh century), at one place Bhāratavarṣa is said to have been ruled by Tārāpīḍa, who 'set his seal on the four oceans' (*dattacatuḥsamudramudraḥ*);[12] and at another, Ujjainī is indicated as being outside Bhāratavarṣa,[13] which leaves its location far from clear. Similarly, in the *Nītivākyamṛta* of Somadeva (tenth century), the word *bhāratīyāḥ* cannot be taken to mean anything more than the inhabitants of Bhàrata, which itself remains undefined.[14]

Bhāratavarṣa figures prominently in the Purāṇas, but they describe its shape variously. In some passages it is likened to a half-moon, in others it is said to resemble a triangle; in yet others, it appears as a rhomboid or an unequal quadrilateral or a drawn bow.[15] The *Mārkaṇḍeya Purāṇa* compares the shape of the country with that of a tortoise floating on water and facing east.[16] Most of the Purāṇas describe Bhāratavarṣa as being divided into nine *dvīpas* or *khaṇḍas*, which, being separated by seas, are mutually inaccessible. The Purāṇic conception of Bhāratavarṣa has much correspondence with the ideas of ancient Indian astronomers like Varāhamihira (sixth century AD) and Bhāskarācārya (eleventh century). However, judging from their identifications of the rivers, mountains, regions and places mentioned in the Purāṇas, as well as from their rare references to areas south of the Vindhyas, their idea of Bhāratavarṣa does not seem to have included southern India. Although a few inscriptions of the tenth and eleventh centuries indicate that Kuntala (Karnataka) was situated in the land of

Bhārata,[17] which is described in a fourteenth-century record as extending from the Himalayas to the southern sea,[18] by and large the available textual and epigraphic references to it do not indicate that the term stood for India as we know it today.

An ambiguous notion of Bhārata is also found in the *Abhidhānacintāmaṇi* of the Jaina scholar Hemacandra (twelfth century), who describes it as the land of *karma* (*karmabhūmi*), as opposed to that of *phala* (*phalabhūmi*).[19] Although he does not clarify what is meant by the two, his definition of âryàvarta (which may correspond with Bhārata) is the same as that found in Manu.[20] In fact, Āryāvarta figures more frequently than Bhārata in the geo-historical discourses found in early Indian texts. It was only from the 1860s that the name Bhāratavarṣa, in the sense of the whole subcontinent, found its way into the popular vocabulary. Its visual evocation came perhaps not earlier than 1905 in a painting by Abanindranath Tagore, who conceived of the image as one of Bangamātā, but later, 'almost as an act of generosity towards the larger cause of Indian nationalism, decided to title it "Bhāratmātā"'.[21] Thus, it was only from the second half of the nineteenth century that the notion of Bhārata was 'forged by the self-conscious appropriation and transposition of discourse at once British-colonial, historical, geographical and ethnological, as well as received Puranic chronotopes'.[22]

In many texts Bhārata is said to have been a part of Jambūdvīpa, which itself had an uncertain geographical connotation. The Vedic texts do not mention it; nor does Pāṇini, though he refers to the *jambū* (the roseapple tree).[23] The early Buddhist canonical works provide the earliest reference to the continent called Jambūdvīpa (Jambūdīpa),[24] its name being derived from the *jambū* tree which grew there, having a height of one hundred *yojanas*, a trunk fifteen *yojanas* in girth and outspreading branches fifty *yojanas* in length, whose shade extended to one hundred *yojanas*.[25] It was one of the four *mahādīpas* (*mahādvīpas*) ruled by a Cakkavattī. We are told that Buddhas and Cakkavattās were born only in Jambūdīpa, whose people were more courageous, mindful and religious than the inhabitants of Uttarakuru.[26] Going by the descriptions of Jambūdīpa and Uttarakuru in the early Buddhist literature, they both appear to be mythical regions. However, juxtaposed with Sihaladāpa (Siṃhaladvīpa or Sri Lanka), Jambūdīpa stands for India.[27] Aśoka thus uses the word to mean the whole of his empire, which covered nearly the entire Indian subcontinent, excluding the far southern part of its peninsula.[28]

Ambiguity about the territorial connotation of Jambūdvīpa continued during subsequent centuries in both epigraphic and literary sources. In a sixth-century inscription of Toramāṇa, for instance, Jambūdvīpa occurs without any precise territorial connotation.[29] Similarly, the identification of Jambūdvīpa remains uncertain in the Purāṇic cosmological schema, where it appears more as a mythical region, than as a geographical entity. The world, according to the Purāṇas, 'consists of seven concentric dvīpas or islands, each of which is encircled by a sea, the central island called Jambūdvīpa'.[30] This is similar to the cosmological imaginings of the Jainas who, however, placed Jambūdvīpa at the centre of the central land (*madhyaloka*) of the three-tiered structure of the universe.[31] According to another Purāṇic conception, which is similar to the Buddhist cosmological ideas, the earth is divided into four *mahādvīpas*, Jambūdvīpa being larger than the others.[32] In both these conceptions of the world, Bhāratavarṣa is at some places said to be a part of Jambūdvīpa, but at others the two are treated as identical.[33]

Since these differently imagined geographical conceptions of Bhārata and Jambūdvīpa are factitious and of questionable value, to insist that their inhabitants formed a nation in ancient times is sophistry. It legitimates the Hindutva perception of Indian national identity as located in remote antiquity, accords centrality to the supposed primordiality of Hinduism, and thus spawns Hindu cultural nationalism.[34] All this draws sustenance from, among other things, a systematic abuse of archaeology by a number of scholars, notably B.B. Lal. The *Pañcatantra* stories, Lal tells us, are narrated on the pots found in the digs at Lothal,[35] and the people in Kalibangan cooked their food on clay *tandurs* which anticipated their use in modern times.[36] The Harappans, his sciolism goes on, practised the modern 'Hindu way of greeting' (*namaskāramudrā*); their women, like many married ones of our own times, applied vermilion (*sindūr*) in the parting of their hair and wore small and large bangles, identical to those in use nowadays, up to their upper arms. They are said to have practised fire worship (which is attested through the Vedic texts and not by Harappan archaeology!) and to have worshipped the *linga* and *yoni*, the later Śaivism being pushed back to Harappan times. An attempt is thus made to bolster an archaic and ill-founded view – supported and recently revived by several scholars[37] – that the Harappan religion, which, according to the Hindu cultural nationalists was in fact 'Vedic–Hindu', was 'the linear progenitor' of modern Hinduism.[38]

## III

Those, including some supposed scholars, with an *idée fixe* about the incredible antiquity of the Indian nation and Hinduism have created several stereotypes about Hinduism over the years, especially recently, and these have percolated down to textbooks. A few sample statements from two books randomly chosen adequately illustrate the point: 'Hinduism [is] a *very* old religion . . . sanatana dharma i.e. the Eternal Spiritual Tradition of India.'[39] 'The Vedas are . . . recognized . . . as the most ancient literature in the world. The term 'sanatana' is often used to highlight this quality[40] . . . freedom of thought and form of worship is unique to Hinduism. . . .[41] In Hindu history no example of coercion or conversion can be found[42] . . . there is no conflict [in Hinduism] between science and religion.'[43]

The above passage contains several cliches which lend support to militant Hindu cultural nationalism. One of these – the imagined 'oldness' of what has come to be known as Hinduism – has been an obsession with Hindu rightist groups, and needs to be examined in the light of historical evidence. It is not necessary to go into the etymological peregrinations of the word 'Hindu', derived from 'Sindhu', on which much has been written. It would suffice here to state that the earliest use of the word, as is well known, can be traced back to the *Zend Avesta*, which speaks of Hapta Hindu (identical with the Ṛgvedic *Saptasindhava*) as one of the 16 regions created by Ahur Mazda. The word retained its territorial connotation for a long time and did not acquire any religious dimensions. According to one scholar,[44] the earliest use of the word 'Hindu' in a religious sense is found in the account of Hsṃan Tsang, who tells us that the bright light of 'holy men and sages, guiding the world as the shining of the moon, have made this country eminent and so it is called In-tu' (the Chinese name for India being *Indu*, moon).[45] But the religious affiliation, if any, of these 'holy men and sages' remains unknown, which hardly supports the view that Hsüan Tsang used the word *In-tu* (Hindu) in a specifically religious sense – indeed, the later Chinese pilgrim I-tsing questioned the veracity of the statement that it was a common name for the country.[46]

Similarly, the suggestion that the use of the word 'Hindu' in a religious sense began immediately after the conquest of Sind by

Muhammad ibn Qāsim in 712 is hardly tenable. It has been asserted that the 'Hindu' was 'now identified on a religious basis' and that 'conversion from this Hindu religion' was now possible.[47] The sources bearing on eighth-century Sind indicate the existence of several non-Islamic religions and sects of Brāhmaṇism and Buddhism, denoted by the Arabic compound *barhimah-samaniyah* used by the classical Muslim writers. But the word 'Hindu' in their writings had a geographic, linguistic, or ethnic connotation. In the *Chachnāma*, for example, *hinduvān* means Indians in general and *hindavī* stands for the Indian language.[48] The first use of 'Hindu' in the religious sense is found in the *Kitāb-ul-Hind* of Alberuni (AD 1030),[49] who at one place distinguishes Hindus from Buddhists, but at another holds the distinction to be between *śramanas* (Buddhists) and brāhmaṇas.[50] He states that 'they [Hindus] totally differ from us in religion'.[51] Alberuni's understanding was limited to Brāhmaṇical religious beliefs and practices, and his use of the word 'Hindu' was far from clear and coherent.[52] It is, therefore, not possible to credit him with any definite or essentialist view of a Hindu religion,[53] much less treat his perception as a landmark in the development of Hindu religious identity. The ambivalence surrounding the word 'Hindu' continued for a long time, so that even three centuries after Alberuni we find Ziyāuddīn Baranī, the first Muslim to write the history of India (known as the *Tārīkh-i-Fīrūzshāhī*), making frequent references to Hindus (*Hunūd* and *Hindu'ān*), either as a religious category or as a political one and sometimes as both.[54] In the sixteenth century, despite Akbar's familiarity with and patronage of non-Islamic religions of India, Abū'-l Faẓl could do no better than 'merely give resumes of Brahmanism . . . presumably because this was the most prestigious',[55] and these are nowhere near the notion of a Hindu religion. Half a century after his death, the anonymous author[56] of the *Dabistān-i-Mazāhib*, who claimed to present a survey of all religions and sects, devoted one full chapter to the religion of the Hindus and other Indian sects, but failed to provide a clear understanding of what was intended by the use of the term 'Hindu'. In his work, the word means the orthodox Brāhmaṇical groups (*smartians*) as well as the non-Islamic belief systems of various schools, sects, castes and religions of India. At some places, the rubric 'Hindu' includes Jainas and at others it excludes them, along with the Yogīs, Sanyāsīs, Tapasīs and Chārvakas.[57] A similar vagueness in the connotation of the word is seen more than a hundred years later in the history of Gujarat called the *Mirat-i-Ahmadi*, authored by 'Ali Muhammad Khan (1761), who uses it 'as a term of reference for people of all religions, castes, sub-castes, and professions who can be classified as a group different from the Muslims' and 'reckons the Jain clergy (Shevra) and the laity (Shravak) as Hindus even though he is aware of the difference in the religious persuasions of, as well as the antagonism between, the Jains and the Vaishnavites (Maishris)'.[58] The fuzziness of definitions of 'Hindu' and 'Hinduism' is thus unquestionable. This is rooted, to a large extent, in the fact that Arabic and Persian scholarship describes all non-Muslim Indians as 'Hindus'.

What possibly added to the ambiguity surrounding the word is the fact that Indians did not describe themselves as Hindus before the fourteenth century. The earliest use of the word in the Sanskrit language occurs in a 1352 inscription of Bukka, the second ruler of Vijayanagara's first dynasty, who described himself with a series of titles, one of them being *hindurāya suratrāna* (Sultan among Hindu kings). His successors continued to use this title for 250 years, 'until as late as the opening years of the seventeenth century'.[59] In North India, Rāṇà Kumbha was the first to style himself as *hindusuratrāṇa*, in an inscription dated 1439.[60] Despite the use of the title by royalty, the word 'Hindu' does not occur in the mainstream Sanskrit literature until the early nineteenth century, with the rare exceptions of Jonarāja's *Rājataraṅgiṇī* (1455–59),[61] which uses the word as part of the compound *hindughoṣa*, and Śrīvara's *Jain Rājataraṅgiṇī* (1459–77), which refers to the social customs of the Hindus (*hindukasamācāra*)[62] and their language (*hindsthānavācā*),[63] as distinct from the Persian language (*pārasībhāsayā*) and also mentions a place called Hinduvāḍā[64] (modern Hindubata, 15 miles north of Sopore). The three Sanskrit texts of the Gauḍīya Vaiśṇava tradition, ranging from the early sixteenth to the late eighteenth centuries, do not mention the word 'Hindu' at all,[65] nor does it occur in the *Brahmasūtra* commentary written by the famous Gauḍīya Vaiśṇava *ācārya* Baladeva Vidyābhūṣaṇa (1750), who tried to 'affiliate the Krishna Chaitanya tradition with "official" Advaita Vedanta'.[66] It was not before the first half of the nineteenth century that the word 'Hindu' begins to appear in the Sanskrit texts produced as a result of Christianity's encounters with Brāhmaṇical religion. Among the religious debates and disputations of the early nineteenth century, centring round the alleged superiority of Christianity vis-à-vis Brāhmaṇism, an important controversy was generated by John Muir's evangelist critique published as *Mataparīkṣā* (in Sanskrit) in 1839, which provoked three Indian pandits to defend their religion.[67] One of them, Haracandra Tarkapancānana, in his reply to Muir, impugned him as *hindudharmātivairin* (Hinduism's great foe)[68] and laid down conditions for becoming 'eligible [*adhikārin*] for [Vedic] *dharma*', 'having become Hindus [*hindutvam prāpya*] in a subsequent birth'.[69] But the occurrence of the word 'Hindu' in Sanskrit texts remained rare, and the two nineteenth-century Bengali encyclopedists, Rādhākānta Deb (1783–1867)[70] and Tārānatha Tarkavācaspati (1811–1885)[71] could not cite any text other than the obscure and very late *Merutantra* (eighteenth century),[72] providing an extremely specious etymology of the word based on it.[73]

The word 'Hindu' is rarely seen in the medieval vernacular *bhakti* literature as well. Ten Gauḍīya Vaiśṇava texts in Bengali, their dates ranging from the sixteenth to the eighteenth centuries, were examined. The word 'Hindu' was found 41 times, and *Hindudharma* 7 times, in the 80,000 couplets of only 5 of the 10 texts. Apart from the small number of occurrences, the interesting aspect of the evidence is that there is no explicit discussion of what 'Hindu' or *Hindudharma* means.[74] The word 'Hindu' is also used in different contexts by Vidyāpati (early fifteenth century), Kabīr (1450–1520), Ekanāth (1533–1599) and Anantadās (sixteenth century). On this basis a scholar has argued that a Hindu religious identity defined itself primarily in opposition to Muslims and Islam and had a continuous existence through the medieval period.[75] This argument is seriously flawed because it is based on the patently wrong assumption that all non-Muslims were part of the postulated Hindu identity, and ignores the basic fact that the medieval *sants* and *bhakti* poets used the term 'Hindu' with reference to adherents of the caste-centric Brāhmaṇical religion, against which they raised their voices.[76] The general absence of the words 'Hindu' and 'Hindudharma' in the precolonial Sanskrit texts and their limited connotation in the not-too-frequent occurrences in the *bhakti* literature clearly indicate that Indians did not create a Hindu religious identity for themselves, as is argued by some. Of course the word was in use in precolonial India, but it was not before the late eighteenth or early nineteenth centuries that it was appropriated by Western, especially British, scholars,[77] whose writings helped the imperial administration to formulate and create the notion of Hinduism in the sense in which we understand it today. The British borrowed the word

'Hindu' from India, gave it a new meaning and significance, reimported it into India as a reified phenomenon called Hinduism.[78] They used it in censuses and gazetteers as a category in their classification of the Indian people, paving the way for the global Hindu religious identity – a process perceptively equated with the 'pizza effect', based on how the Neapolitan hot baked bread exported to America returned with all its embellishments to become Italy's national dish.[79] Given this background, Hinduism was a creation of the colonial period and cannot lay claim to any great antiquity.[80] Although some echo the views of B.B. Lal and his followers to proclaim that its origins lay in the Indus valley civilization and in what they call Aryan culture,[81] Hinduism may yet be held the youngest of all religions, a nineteenth-century neologism popularized by the British.[82] That it has come to stay, despite the endless ambiguities of connotation in it, is a different matter.[83]

**IV**

Just as Hinduism as a religious category acquired much visibility in Christian missionary writings and in British administrative records,[84] so also it was not until the nineteenth century did it come to be labelled *sanātanadharma.* The term can be translated in a variety of ways: 'eternal religion' or 'eternal law',[85] 'unshakeable, venerable order',[86] 'ancient and continuing guideline'[87] or 'the eternal order or way of life'.[88] It has been used by a variety of representatives of modern Hinduism, ranging from neo-Hindus like Vivekananda and Radhakrishnan to the leaders and followers of reform movements as well as their opponents. Although some scholars have tried to project it as having a 'dynamic character', *sanātanadharma*[89] was basically an orthodox resistance to reform movements[90] and drew on references to itself in ancient Indian literature. The earliest occurrence of the term is found in the Buddhist canonical work *Dhammapada,* according to which the eternal law (*esa dhamma sanātano*)[91] is that hatred and enmities cease through love alone; but it is mentioned frequently in the Brāhmaṇical texts as well. The *Mahābhārata* often uses the expression *eṣa dharmaḥ sanātanaḥ* 'as a sanctioning formula intended to emphasize the obligatory nature of social and religious rules',[92] but its use to justify Śvetaketu's mother's being snatched away by a Brāhmaṇa would be far from palatable to modern sanātanists.[93] The *Gītā* uses the term in the plural to mean the 'venerable norms for the families' (*kuladharmāḥ sanātanaḥ*)[94] and describes Kṛṣṇa as 'protector of the established norms' (*śāśvatadharmagoptā sanātanaḥ*).[95] Similarly, in the law book of Manu, *sanātanadharma* stands for established 'customs and statutes of the countries, castes and families',[96] though the Purāṇas use the term in various senses. According to the *Matsyapurāṇa*, it is rooted in virtues like the absence of greed and attachment, the practice of celibacy, forgiveness, compassion for living beings, etc.[97] The *Varāhapurāṇa* at one place refers to the eternal *dharma* promulgated by Varāha,[98] and at another, states that according to the eternal law one should not sink into grief on seeing the fortunes of others and one's own distress (*eṣa dharmaḥ sanātanaḥ*).[99] In another Purāṇa, Śiva defines his eternal *dharma* (*dharmaḥ sanātanaḥ*)[100] as consisting of *jñāna, kriyā, caryā* and *yoga*, though in several epic and Purāṇic passages *sanātana* is used as an epithet for divinities like Kṛṣṇa, or for Dharma, who himself is thought of as a deity. The *Uttararāmacarita* of Bhavabhūti (eighth century), the earliest secular work to refer to *sanātanadharma*, mentions it in the sense of fixed laws and customs; and the Khanapur plates (sixth century), which contain the earliest epigraphic reference to it, use it in speaking of rites and rituals prescribed by *śruti* and *smṛti* (*śrutismṛtivihitasanātanadharmakarmaniratāya*). Although these textual references provide different connotations of the term *sanātanadharma*, it has generally been understood in the sense of traditionally established customs and duties of countries, castes and families, in texts as late as the *Mahānirvāṇatantra* (eighteenth century), by an unknown author, and the *Śāstratattvavinirṇaya* (1844) of Nilakaṇṭha (Nehemia) Goreh.

It was in the nineteenth century, that *sanātanadharma* emerged as a key concept in traditionalist self-assertion against Christianity, as well as in the reform movements (Brahmo Samaj and Arya Samaj), it came to be stereotyped as a venerable, 'eternal', 'all encompassing' and 'inclusive' (*sarvavyapaka*) religion, 'with no temporal beginning, no historical founding figure', one which needed no innovations or reforms.[101] This added to the conceptual opacity and vagueness of the 'timeless religion', which had to wait for its first codification by the Englishwoman Annie Besant who, in collaboration with Indian scholars like Bhagwan Das, drew up a textbook[102] on *sanātanadharma* for use at the Central Hindu College, Benares, whose establishment in 1898 owed much to her initiative.

## V

Hinduism has often been viewed not only as eternal (*sanātana-dharma*), but also as a monolithic religion in which there is 'agreement about some static universal doctrine'.[103] This stereotype has received support not only from Hindu right-wing political groups, but also from serious scholars of religion who define Hinduism as 'the religion of those humans who create, perpetuate, and transform traditions with legitimizing reference to the authority of the Vedas'.[104] An early, though indirect, endorsement of the legitimizing authority of the Vedas comes from Yāska (fifth century BC), who describes Vedic 'seers' as 'having attained a direct experience of *dharma*' (*sākṣātkṛtadharma*).[105] Later, Manu categorically states that 'the root of religion is the entire Veda' (*vedo'khilo dharmamūlam*),[106] and that the authority of the *śruti* and the *smṛti* is not to be questioned or reasoned about (*amimāṃsya*).[107] His assertion has received much support over time from the different philosophical systems, though their apologetic patterns have varied considerably. Nyāya and Vaiśeṣika, though not affiliated to the Veda, recognized it as a 'source of knowledge' (*pramāṇa*), and their leading early medieval thinkers (Uddyotakara, Vācaspatimiśra and Udayana) defended it, sometimes even by developing new arguments.[108] Much stronger support for the Vedic texts, however, came from the Mimāṃsā, whose 'genuine affiliation with, and commitment to, the Veda are generally accepted'.[109] Mimāṃsā thinkers like Kumārila, Prabhākara and Maṇḍanamiśra (all of the eighth century) laid great emphasis on the principle that *dharma* is justified by the Veda alone (*vedamūlatva*).[110] Similarly, Śaṇkara (eighth century) treated all the declarations of the Veda as authoritative,[111] and defiance of it (*vedavirodha*) as heresy.[112] Indeed, the acceptance of the authority of the Vedas is an important feature of Brāhmaṇical orthodoxy, but their number being only four, an amorphous category of the 'fifth Veda' came into being as early as the later Vedic period.[113] This led to an open-endedness in the Vedic corpus, a phenomenon also in keeping with the general absence of and aversion to writing and the Brāhmaṇical preference for the oral transmission of all knowledge.[114] The *Mahābhārata*,[115] the Purāṇas[116] and the *Tantras*[117] are called the 'fifth Veda', just as the large body of Tamil devotional hymns in the Śaiva and Vaiśṇava traditions, ranging in date from the sixth to the ninth centuries AD, claimed Vedic status.[118] Many religious teachers holding different opinions sought to legitimize their teachings with reference to the Vedas during the medieval period. Acceptance of the authority of the Vedas is, in fact, an important feature even of modern Hindu revivalist movements like the Arya Samaj of Dayananda, who is sometimes called the Luther of India.[119] But all this cannot be construed to mean that Hinduism acquired a monolithic character, for it has rightly been pointed out that allegiance to the Vedas was very often a fiction, nothing more than a 'raising of the hat, in passing, to an idol by which one no longer intends to be encumbered later on'.[120]

There is substantial evidence to show that the Vedas did not always enjoy a pre-eminent position even in Brāhmaṇical Hinduism.[121] Anti-Vedic ideas, in fact, began to find expression in the *Ṛgveda* itself. The famous Ṛgvedic passage which equated Brāhmaṇas with croaking frogs was an early attempt to ridicule the Vedas and their reciters.[122] In addition to the satirization of the Brāhmaṇas, there is also evidence of the questioning of Vedic knowledge: 'Whence this creation developed is known only by him who witnesses this world in the highest heaven – or perhaps even he does not know.'[123] At several places in the *Ṛgveda*, Indra is abused and his very existence is questioned.[124] Thus, in a hymn to Indra it is said: 'to Indra, if Indra exists' (*RV*, VIII.100.3), and in another the question is asked (*RV*, II.12.5): 'about whom they ask, where is he? . . . And they say about him, "he is not" . . . '. Scepticism about the Vedic sacrifice was expressed by reviling it at the end of the *mahāvrata* Soma festival, as is evident from several Ṛgvedic passages.[125] The sanctity of the Vedas was questioned soon after their composition. The Upaniṣads contain several passages which deprecate the Vedas. The *Muṇḍaka Upaniṣad*, for example, regards the four Vedas as 'lower knowledge' (*aparāvidyā*).[126] Similarly, in the *Nirukta*, Yāska (sixth–fifth centuries BC) describes Kautsa as saying that 'the Vedic stanzas have no meaning' and that 'their meaning is contradictory'.[127] Indications of the undermining of Vedic rituals are also found in the Dharmaśāstra texts, which have been the main vehicle of Vedic thought. Baudhāyana, for instance, cites the view that non-Vedic local practices may be allowed in their own territory, though his own opinion is that 'one must never follow practices opposed to the tradition of learned authorities'.[128]

An unwillingness to concede a legitimizing role to the Veda manifested itself in many texts representing the various strands of Brāhmaõical thought. For example, in the *Bhagavadgītā*, which has been the most popular Hindu religious text through the centuries, Kṛṣṇa tells Arjuna in unambiguous terms that those who delight in the eulogistic statements of the Vedas (*vedavādaratāḥ*) are full of worldly desires (*kāmātmānaḥ*),[129] and that the desire-ridden followers (*kāmakāmāḥ*) of the Vedic sacrificial rites stagnate in the world.[130] The Purāṇas often undermine the supremacy of the Vedas despite their general allegiance to them. While one Purāṇic text tells us that God thought of the Purāṇas before he spoke the Vedas, others state that the Vedas are 'established' on the Purāṇas.[131] 'There is no higher essence or truth than this', the *Agnipurāṇa* tells us, and 'there is no better book, . . . there is no better *śāstra*, or *śruti* or . . . *smṛti* . . . for this Purāṇa is supreme.'[132] The *Bhāgavatapurāṇa* was similarly said to have superseded and transcended the Vedas, and Jīva Goswmī (sixteenth century) of the Gauīya Vaiśṇava school vehemently denied that this text was based on the Vedas at all.[133] Despite the fact that the authors of the Tantric texts tried to base their doctrines on the Vedas, they also undermined their authority. For example, the *Mahānirvāṇatantra*, an eighteenth-century work, states that the Vedas, Purāṇas and Śāstras are of no use in the *kaliyuga*[134] and 'declares that all of the other religious traditions are encompassed by and disappear within the Tantric *kuladharma*, just as the tracks of all other animals disappear within the tracks of the elephant.'[135] All this may not amount to a repudiation of the Vedas, but it certainly indicates that all post-Vedic Brāhmaṇical religious traditions did not look to them for legitimacy.

Several religious movements, within the fold of what is now known as Hinduism, in fact, rejected the authority both of the Brāhmaṇas and that of the Vedas. Vīraśaivism, a Śaivite sect whose followers are also called Lingāyats and which gained prominence in Karnataka in the twelfth century, is a case in point. Its hagiographical texts bear ample testimony to the fact that, at least in the early phase, the Vīraśaivas ridiculed the Vedas and unequivocally rejected them. The *Bāsavapurāṇa* speaks of a Vedāntist who was humiliated by Bāsava at the court of Bijjala, and the *Cennabāsavapurāṇa* narrates how a Vedic scholar was ridiculed by the Lingāyats, who had the Vedas recited by dogs.[136] Similarly, the adherents of the south Indian Śrāvaiśṇava sect of Tenkalai rejected the Vedas and composed their own Veda, called the *Nālāyiraprabandham*.[137] This rejection of Vedic authority seems to have been a feature of other medieval religious movements as well. The Mahānubhāvas in Maharashtra and the Sahajiyās in

Bengal also renounced the Vedas. So did individual medieval *bhakti* saints like Kabīr (fifteenth–sixteenth centuries) and Tukārām (seventeenth century).[138] As recently as the nineteenth century, precisely at the time when Dayananda Saraswati was busy spreading the word that the Vedas are the repository of all knowledge, they were rejected by Ramakrishna, who said: 'the truth is not in the Vedas; one should act according to the Tantras, not according to the Vedas, the latter are impure from the very fact of their being pronounced.'[139] Evidently, thus, different religious sects have not had the same attitude towards the Vedic corpus, and even the texts of specific sectarian affiliations often express contradictory views about it. This being so, the stereotype of a monolithic Hinduism based on the Vedas must be seen as a myth deliberately propagated both by some scholars as well as by right-wing Hindu groups, all of whom not only ignore the plurality of religious beliefs and practices covered by the umbrella term 'Hinduism', invented in the colonial period, but who also deny the centuries-long process of their evolution.

**VI**

The stereotyping of Hinduism as eternal, monolithic, tolerant and non-proselytizing began soon after its invention in the nineteenth century, and the effort to present it as different from all the other religions of the world has gathered momentum over the years. Not content with imagining their religion to be unique, the Hindu cultural nationalists persist in noisily proclaiming its imagined uniqueness. The clichés about it receive inspiration and support from the writings of scholars of religion based at universities in the West, where departments of religious studies or comparative religion have mushroomed after the Second World War, their number having come to exceed 1,200 in the United States alone.[140]

Most of the scholars affiliated to these departments and a few of their Indian disciples[141] are inspired by Joachim Wach and Mircea Eliade,[142] and speak of the science of religion (*religionswissenschaft*); but, in reality, they study Hinduism as a socio-historically autonomous phenomenon, thus supporting the claim that religion is *sui generis*. Opposed to the scientific analysis of religious data and to any kind of reductionism, they have studied religion by prioritizing 'interior and generally inaccessible personal experiences and religious convictions at the expense of observable and documentable data',[143] focusing on the 'transhistorical religious meaning of any given hierophany'.[144] The influence of these scholars is reflected in the anti-historical attitude of the bulk of writing on Hinduism produced by Western scholars and their Indian followers. For example, one of the leading Western scholars of religion, and possibly the most influential, Wendy Doniger, has studied many neglected aspects of Hinduism (e.g., myths, symbols, metaphors) on the basis of an extensive use of Sanskrit texts, and has provided interesting and provocative interpretations of the early Indian myths and religions, often rousing the Hindu diaspora's ire. But she has generally shied away from examining their changing social contexts. The same may be said of several recent publications on Hinduism which do not view religion as a multifactoral historical and cultural process, but as a decontextualized phenomenon, not linked to material realities on the ground.[145]

There are a few exceptions from India,[146] but most Western scholars writing on various aspects of early Indian religions, especially Hinduism, describe them merely as systems of faith and salvation and 'prioritize their abstract essences and homogeneity over their socio-political context'.[147] In their works, phenomenology takes precedence over rational historical enquiry and a subtle defence of Hinduism masquerades as serious academic enterprise. Naturally, stereotypes about it tend to become deep-rooted and their grip on the masses strong.

The study of religion in academia needs to be rescued from those 'scholars of religion', who accept premises that strengthen the stereotypes which feed religious fundamentalism and who unnecessarily take upon themselves the task of defending 'the religiosity of religion', a task which the sybaritic sadhus, despite their questionable personal track records, can discharge with greater efficiency. Historians cannot be the custodians of religion; their task is to critically examine it.

**Notes and References**

1 N. Prinja, *Explaining Hindu Dharma: A Guide for Teachers*, Norfolk, 1996, p. 10, cited in Sudeshna Guha, 'Negotiating Evidence: History, Archaeology and the Indus Civilization', *Modern Asian Studies*, Vol. 39, No. 2, 2005, p. 399.

2 S.P. Gupta, *The Indus-Saraswati Civilization: Origins, Problems and Issues*, Delhi, 1996, p. 142; B.B. Lal, 'Rigvedic Aryans: The Debate Must Go On', *East and West*, Vol. 48, Nos 3–4, December 1998, pp. 439–48. For a rebuttal

of Lal, see Ram Sharan Sharma, 'Identity of the Indus Culture', *East and West*, Vol. 49, Nos 1–4, December 1999, pp. 35–45; Irfan Habib, 'Imagining River Saraswati – A Defence of Common Sense', *Proceedings*, Indian History Congress, 61st session, Kolkata, 2001, pp. 65–92.

3 For an assessment of the 'evidence' of the horse in the Harappan context, see R.S. Sharma, *Looking for the Aryans*, Hyderabad, 1994, pp. 14–34; idem, *Advent of the Aryans in India*, Delhi, 1999, pp. 12–21; Asko Parpola, *Deciphering the Indus Script*, Cambridge, 1994, pp. 155–59. For the debate centring on the forged evidence of the horse, see Michael Witzel and Steve Farmer, 'Horseplay at Harappa: The Indus Valley Decipherment Hoax', *Frontline*, 13 October and 24 November 2000.

4 For detailed comments on the views of Lal and his followers, see Sudeshna Guha, op. cit., pp. 399–426. In keeping with his indigenist approach, B.B. Lal speaks of the resemblance between the graffiti on megalithic and chalcolithic pottery on the one hand, and Harappan script characters and Brāhmī letters on the other, in 'From the Megalithic to the Harappa: Tracing Back the Graffiti on the Pottery', *Ancient India*, 16, 1960, pp. 4–24. More recently he has made a tongue-in-cheek endorsement of the view that the Harappan script was the precursor of the later Brāhmī (*The Saraswatī Flows On*, Delhi, 2002, pp. 132–35), though not long ago he was of the view that the Harappan script was read from right to left. The most recent view, however, is that the Harappans may not have been a literate people at all (Steve Farmer and Michael Witzel, 'The Collapse of the Indus-Script Thesis: The Myth of a Literate Harappan Civilization', *Electronic Journal of Vedic Studies*, Vol. 11, No. 2, 2004, pp. 19–57.

5 B.N. Mukherjee, *Nationhood and Statehood in India: A Historical Survey*, New Delhi, 2001; Irfan Habib, 'The Envisioning of a Nation: A Defence of the Idea of India', *Social Scientist*, Vol. 27, Nos 9–10, 1999, pp. 18–29; idem, ed., *India: Studies in the History of an Idea*, Delhi, 2005; Rajat Kanta Ray, *The Felt Community: Commonality and Mentality before the Emergence of Indian Nationalism*, New Delhi, 2004; Manu Goswami, *Producing India*, Delhi, 2004.

6 B.N. Mukherjee, op. cit., p. 6; Rajat Kanta Ray, op. cit., pp. 49, 55; and p. 180, notes 33, 34.

7 *Ṛgveda*, VIII, 24, 27. This is the only Ṛgvedic passage where the word *saptasindhava* is used in the sense of territory; at all other places in the *Ṛgveda* it is used to mean the seven rivers (*Vedic Index*, II, p. 324).

8 *Aṣṭādhyāyī*, IV.2.113.

9 D.C. Sircar, *Select Inscriptions Bearing on Indian History and Civilization*, I, no. 91, line 10.

10 *Amarako÷a*, II.6, 8. Krishnaji Govind Oka, ed., *The Nāmalingānuśāsana: Amarakośa of Amarasiṃha* (with the commentary of Kṣīrasvāmin), Delhi, 1981, p. 47.

11 *Manusmṛti*, II.22. According to the *Kauṣītaki Upaniṣad* (II.13), Āryāvarta was bounded on the west by Adarsana near Kurukṣetra, and on the east by Kālakavana near Allahabad.

[12] *Kādambarī*, edited and translated by M.R. Kale, Delhi, 1968, p. 290; V.S. Agrawal, *Kādambarī: Ek Sāṃskritik Adhyayan*, Varanasi, 1958, p. 188.

[13] *Kādambarī*, p. 311; V.S. Agrawal, op. cit., 1958, p. 205.

[14] *Nītivākyamṛtam* of Somadeva Sūri, *Prakīrṇaka*, 78.

[15] S.M. Ali, *The Geography of the Purāṇas*, New Delhi, 1966, p. 109.

[16] Ibid.

[17] For references, see Ishrat Alam, 'Names for India in Ancient Indian Texts and Inscriptions', in Irfan Habib, ed., *India: Studies in the History of an Idea*, p. 43.

[18] *EI*, XIV, no. 3, lines 5–6.

[19] IV.12. *Abhidhānacintāmaṇi*, edited with an introduction by Nemichandra Sastri, with the Hindi commentary *Maṇiprabhā* by Haragovind Sastri, Varanasi, 1964, p. 235.

[20] Ibid., IV.14.

[21] Sugata Bose, 'Nation as Mother: Representations and Contestations of "India" in Bengali Literature,' in Sugata Bose and Ayesha Jalal, eds, *Nationalism, Democracy and Development: State and Politics in India*, Delhi, 1997, pp. 53–54. For a discussion of the Tamil mother and Bhāratmātā, see Sumathi Ramaswamy, 'The Goddess and the Nation: Subterfuges of Antiquity, the Cunning of Modernity', in Gavin Flood, ed., *The Blackwell Companion to Hinduism*, Indian reprint, Delhi, 2003, pp. 551–68.

[22] Manu Goswami, op. cit., chapters 5 and 6.

[23] *Aṣṭādhyāyī*, IV.3.165.

[24] G.P. Malalasekera, *Dictionary of Pāli Proper Names*, II, pp. 941–42, s.v. Jambūdīpa.

[25] Malalasekera, op. cit., p. 941.

[26] Ibid., p. 942.

[27] *Mahāvaṃsa*, V. 13; *Cūlavaṃsa*, XXXVII.216, 246; Malalasekera, op. cit., p. 942.

[28] D.C. Sircar, *Select Inscriptions Bearing on Indian History and Civilization*, Calcutta, 1965, I, no. 2, line 2.

[29] Ibid., no. 56, line 9.

[30] D.C. Sircar, *Studies in the Geography of Ancient and Medieval India*, Delhi, 1960, pp. 8–9.

[31] Pravin Chandra Jain and Darbarilal Kothia, eds, *Jaina Purāṇa Kośa* (in Hindi), Jain Vidya Samsthan, Srimahavirji, Rajasthan, 1993, pp. 256, 259. *Harivaṃśa Purāṇa*, 5.2–13. According to some, it is divided into six parts (*khaṇḍas*), of which one is *āryakhaṇḍa* and is the same as Bhārata, the remaining five being *mlecchakhaṇḍas*. Among the Jaina texts, the *Jambūdvīpaprajñapti* provides the most detailed account of Jambådvāpa and Bhàrata. See *Jambūddivpaññattisuttam*, edited by Kanhailalji Kamal *et al.*, Shri Agam Prakashan Samiti, Vyavara, Rajasthan, 1986. The Jaina texts had several geographical categories in common with the Purāṇic ones, but they had many unique spatio-temporal conceptions too.

[32] Ibid., p. 9, note 1.

[33] D.C. Sircar, *Studies in the Geography of Ancient and Medieval India*, pp. 6, 8.

[34] Historians who locate Indian nationalism in the distant past are, to a certain extent, inspired by the champions of the notion of a Greater India in ancient times. An organization called the Greater India Society was founded in Calcutta in 1926, with the objective of organizing the study of the history and culture of Asian countries in which ancient Indians supposedly established colonies. Rabindranath Tagore was its *purodha* (spiritual head), but scholars who extended active support to the Society included P.C. Bagchi , Suniti Kumar Chatterji, Phanindra Nath Bose, Kalidas Nag, U.N. Ghoshal, Nalinaksha Datta and R.C. Majumdar. See Susan Bayly, 'Imagining "Greater India": French and Indian Visions of Colonialism in the Indic Mode', *Modern Asian Studies*, Vol. 38, No. 3, 2004, pp. 703–44. It is to the writings of the last named historian (R.C. Majumdar) that Hindu supremacists and cultural nationalists often turn for legitimacy even today. Moreover, there were and still are scholars in different parts of the country who feed into the 'Greater India' dialectic. One of them, Raghuvira made the following statement: 'Our ignorant journalists and governmental papers call Indonesia 'Hindesia', as though the term were to be divided into 'India' and 'Asia' (Hind+Asia). The fools! The correct translation of Indonesia is *bharatadvipa*, for *nesia* derives from the Greek *nesos*, island' (A. Bharati, 'The Hindu Renaissance and Its Apologetic Patterns', *Journal of Asian Studies*, 29, 1970, p. 276).

[35] B.B. Lal, *The Earliest Civilization of South Asia: Rise, Maturity and Decline*, Delhi,1997, p. 175.

[36] B.B. Lal, *The Saraswati Flows On*, p. 95.

[37] Among those who, directly or indirectly, support the idea of the Harappan religion as being the 'progenitor' of modern 'Hinduism', mention must be made of Asko Parpola, op. cit., D.K. Chakravarti (*India: An Archaeological History*, New Delhi, 1999) and B.B. Lal (*The Earliest Civilisation of South Asia* and *The Saraswati Flows On*). S.P. Gupta, in a book review, makes the following fantastic assertion: 'the culture of the Indus-Saraswati . . . continues to live in India even today' (*Puratattva*, Vol. 31, 2000–01, p. 190). For a reasoned critique of their views, see K.M. Shrimali, 'Constructing an Identity: Forging Hinduism into Harappan Religions', *Social Science Probings*, Vol. 15, Nos 1–2, 2003, pp. 1–59; Sudeshna Guha, op. cit., pp. 399–426.

[38] S.P. Gupta, *The Indus-Saraswati Civilization: Origins, Problems and Issues*, p. 147.

[39] Makhan Lal *et al.*, *India and the World for Class VI*, National Council of Educational Research and Training, New Delhi, September 2002, p. 133.

[40] Nawal K. Prinja, *Explaining Hindu Dharma: A Guide for Teachers*, Norwich, 1996, p. 7. The book was produced by the Vishwa Hindu Parishad. The history textbooks used in the RSS-run Shishu Mandirs and other schools abound in similar pearls of wisdom about Hinduism.

[41] Ibid., p. 13.

[42] Ibid., p. 54.

[43] Ibid., p. 153.

44 Arvind Sharma, 'Of Hindu, Hindustān, Hinduism and Hindutva', *Numen*, Vol. 49, 2002, pp. 3–4.

45 Samuel Beal, *Si-Yu-Ki: Buddhist Records of the Western World*, Delhi, 1969, p. 69.

46 *A Record of Buddhist Religion as Practised in India and the Malay Archipelago (AD 671–695) by I-tsing*, translated by J.Takakusu, Delhi, 1966, p. 118.

47 Arvind Sharma, op. cit., p. 6, points out that Muhammad ibn Qāsim appointed his adversary Dahir's minister Siakar as his advisor after the latter's acceptance of Islam. Since conversion from what he calls 'Hindu religion' became possible, he implies that a Hindu identity had already emerged. Similarly, the Brāhmana princes of Sind, Jaysiyah (b. Dahir) and his brother Sassah, converted to Islam at the invitation of the Caliph 'Umar b. 'Abd al-Aziz (Derryl N. Maclean, *Religion and Society in Arab Sind*, Leiden, 1989, pp. 33, 48). But mere acceptance of Islam by certain Sindis does not justify a reified perception of Hinduism as early as the eighth century.

48 Maclean, op. cit., pp. 12–13; Irfan Habib, *Linguistic Materials from Eighth-Century Sind: An Exploration of the Chachnama*, Symposia Papers 11, Indian History Congress, Aligarh, 1994, pp. 8–9.

49 Alberuni's reference to Hindu religion has been treated as a landmark in the 'religious semantic journey' of the word 'Hindu', just as the raid on Somanātha by Mahmåd has been blown out of proportion by some scholars, e.g., Arvind Sharma, op. cit., pp. 6–7. Cf. Narayani Gupta's statement that 'it is fashionable to criticize Mill, but to most Indians precolonial India has two pasts (Mill's "Hindu" and "Islamic" civilizations), and the attack on Somanath by Mahmud in 1025 has the same emotive significance as the Turks' conquest of Constantinople in 1453 had for conventional European history' ('Stereotypes versus History', *India International Centre Quarterly*, Summer, 1999, p. 169).

50 *Alberuni's India*, translated by Edward C. Sachau, London, 1910, I, pp. 7, 21; cited in Irfan Habib, 'India: Country and Nation – An Introductory Essay', in idem, ed., *India: Studies in the History of an Idea*, p. 5, note 14.

51 *Alberuni's India*, p. 19.

52 For a detailed, though biased, view of Alberuni's perception of Brahmanical religion, see Arvind Sharma, *Studies in 'Alberuni's India'*, Wiesbaden, 1983.

53 The general absence of an essentialist view of the religion of the Hindus may be inferred from the many inscriptions, including the one from Veraval, discussed by Anwar Hussain ('The "Foreigners" and the Indian Society: *c.* Eighth Century to Thirteenth Century', unpublished MPhil dissertation, Jawaharlal Nehru University, 1993, chapter IV). B.D. Chattopadhyaya (*Representing the Other: Sanskrit Sources and the Muslims*, Delhi, 1998, p. 78) rightly points out that whatever essentialism may be there in Alberuni's description is contradicted by many records including the Veraval inscription, which speaks of the reconstruction of a demolished mosque by Jayasimha Siddharaja.

[54] Baranī mentions Hindus 40 times in his *Tārīkh-i-Fīrūzshāhī*. See Qeyamuddin Ahmad, 'Baranī's References to the Hindus in the *Tārīkh-i-Fīrūzshāhī* – Territorial and Other Dimensions', *Islamic Culture*, 56, 1982, pp. 295–302. The Moroccan traveller Ibn Battūtah, a contemporary of Baranã, interpreted the name Hindu Kush as 'Hindu killer' because the Indian slaves passing through its mountainous terrain perished in the snows. This has been given a communal slant (Arvind Sharma, op. cit., p. 9), but see footnote 61.

[55] Romila Thapar, 'Syndicated Hinduism', in Günther-Dietz Sontheimer and Hermann Kulke, eds., *Hinduism Reconsidered*, Delhi, 1997, p. 73.

[56] The author of the *Dabistān* has been variously identified, e.g., as 'Mobad', Muhsin Fani, Mirza Zulfiqar Beg and Kaikhusrau Isfandyar.

[57] Manisha Mishra, 'Perception of the Hindus and their Religious Systems as Described in the *Dabistan-i-Mazahib*', unpublished MPhil dissertation, Department of History, University of Delhi, 2003.

[58] Najaf Haider, 'A "Holi Riot" of 1714: Versions from Ahmadabad and Delhi', in Mushirul Hasan and Asim Roy, eds, *Living Together Separately: Cultural India in History and Politics*, Delhi, 2005.

[59] Philip B. Wagoner, 'Sultan among Hindu Kings: Dress, Titles, and the Islamicization of Hindu Culture at Vijayanagara', *Journal of Asian Studies*, Vol. 55, No. 4, November 1996, p. 862. Cf. Hermann Kulke, *Kings and Cults: State Formation and Legitimation in India and Southeast Asia*, Delhi, 1993, pp. 208–39.

[60] B.D. Chattopadhyaya, op. cit., p. 54.

[61] *Hindughoṣa* may be taken to mean the Hindukush mountain (*Rājataraṅgiṇī* of Jonarāja, edited and translated by Raghunath Singh, Chowkhamba, Varanasi, 1972, verse 381). Also see footnote 54 above.

[62] *Jaina Rājataraṅgiṇī* of Śrīvara, with translation, critical introduction and geographical notes by Raghunath Singh, Varanasi, 1977, 3.218.

[63] Ibid., 2.215.

[64] Ibid., 2.51.

[65] Joseph T. O'Connell, 'The word "Hindu" in Gaudiya Vaisnava Texts', *Journal of the American Oriental Society*, Vol. 93, No. 3, 1973, pp. 340–43.

[66] Wilhelm Halbfass, *India and Europe: An Essay in Philosophical Understanding*, Delhi, 1990, p. 193.

[67] The pandits were Somanātha (Subāji Bāpu), Haracandra Tarkapancānana and Nilakaṇṭha Goreh, the last of whom ultimately converted to Christianity and was baptized as Nehemiah Goreh. For a discussion of the material produced in the context of the controversy, see Richard Fox Young, *Resistant Hinduism: Sanskrit Sources on Anti-Christian Apologetics in Early Nineteenth Century India*, Vienna, 1981.

[68] Haracandra Tarkapancānana, *Matapariksottaram*, Calcutta, 1940, p. 1; cited in Richard Fox Young, op. cit., p. 93.

[69] Richard Fox Young, op. cit., p. 150.

[70] The multi-volume lexicon *Śabdakalpadruma* appeared between 1819 and 1858.

71 *Vācaspatyam.*

72 The crucial passage is given by V.S. Apte (*Practical Sanskrit–English Dictionary*, s.v. *hindu*): *hindudharmapraloptāro jāyante cakravarttinaḥ/hīnam ca dūṣayatyeka hinduritiucyate priye.* Apte dates the text to the eighth century AD, but one is intrigued by its reference to *Tantriks* born in London who will become lords of the earth!

73 *Hīnam dūṣayati iti hindu*: the Hindu 'spoils' (*dūṣayati*) what is 'inferior' (*hīnam*). Halbfass, *India and Europe*, p. 515, note 96. The twentieth-century text *Dharmapradīpa*, written by three leading pandits in the 1930s (Calcutta, 1937), discusses in detail the rules laid down for the purification of those Hindus who joined or were forced to join other religions: *atra kevalaṃ balād eva mlecchadharmaṃ svīkāritānāṃ hindūnām . . . vividhāḥ prāyaścittavidhayo nirdiṣṭ dṛśyante*, p. 219; cited in Halbfass, *India and Europe*, p. 534, note 66. The word also occurs in the *Dharmatattvavinirṃaya* by Vāsudeva Śāstrin Abhyaṇkara, Poona, 1929.

74 Joseph T. O'Connel, op. cit., pp. 340–44.

75 David N. Lorenzen, 'Who Invented Hinduism', *Comparative Studies in Society and History*, Vol. 41, No. 4, October, 1999, pp. 630–59. Also see 'Introduction', in Lorenzen, ed., *Bhakti Religion in North India: Community, Identity and Political Action*, Delhi, 1996.

76 R.P. Bahuguna, 'Recent Western Writings on Medieval Indian Sant Movement', ICHR Seminar on 'Dialogue with the Past: Trends in Historical Writings in India', Bangalore, 14–16 February, 2003; idem, 'Symbols of Resistance: Non-Brahmanical Sants as Religious Heroes in Late Medieval India', in Biswamoy Pati *et al.*, eds, *Negotiating India's Past: Essays in Memory of Partha Sarathi Gupta*, Delhi, 2003. Also see idem, 'Some Aspects of Popular Movements: Beliefs and Sects in Northern India during the Seventeenth and Eighteenth Centuries', unpublished Ph.D. thesis, Department of History, University of Delhi, 1999.

77 Charles Grant used the term 'Hindooism' first in a letter to John Thomas in 1787, and subsequently, in his *Observations on the State of Society among the Subjects of Great Britain*, written in 1792 (Will Sweetman, *Mapping Hinduism: Hinduism and the Study of Indian Religions 1600–1776*, Halle, 2003, p. 56, note 12). William Jones also used the term 'Hindu' in the religious sense in 1787 (S.N. Mukherjee, *Sir William Jones and British Attitudes to India*, Cambridge, 1968, p. 119; Dermot Killingley, 'Modernity, Reform, and Revival', in Gavin Flood, ed., *The Blackwell Companion to Hinduism*, p. 513). Rammohun Roy was, however, perhaps 'the first Hindu' to use the word 'Hindooism' in 1816 (Dermot Killingley, *Rammohun Roy in Hindu and Christian Traditions: The Teape Lectures 1990*, Newcastle-upon-Tyne, 1993, p. 60; cited in Richard King, *Orientalism and Religion*, Delhi, 1999, p. 100).

78 Several scholars have argued that Hinduism was a colonial construct which finally took shape when the imperial administration engaged in the classification into categories of the Indian people through the mechanism of the census. Important among them are: Vasudha Dalmia ('The Only Real

Religion of the Hindus: Vaisnava Self-Representation in the Late Nineteenth Century', in Vasudha Dalmia and Heinrich von Stietencron, eds, *Representing Hinduism: The Construction of Religious Traditions and National Identity*, New Delhi, 1995, pp. 176–210); Robert Frykenberg ('The Emergence of Modern "Hinduism" as a Concept and as an Institution', in Günther-Dietz Sontheimer and Hermann Kulke, eds, *Hinduism Reconsidered*, Delhi, 1997, pp. 82–107); John Stratton Hawley ('Naming Hinduism', *Wilson Quarterly*, Summer, 1991, pp. 20–32); Harjot Oberoi (*The Construction of Religious Boundaries: Culture, Identity and Diversity in the Sikh Tradition*, Delhi, 1994, pp. 16–17); and Heinrich von Stietencron ('Hinduism: On the Proper Use of a Deceptive Term', in Sontheimer and Kulke, op. cit., pp. 32–53). Their views have been contested by quite a few scholars in recent years, e.g., Will Sweetman, op. cit., and Brian K. Pennington, *Was Hinduism Invented?: Britons, Indians and the Colonial Construction of Religion*, New York, 2005. Their main source of inspiration is David Lorenzen ('Who Invented Hinduism?', *Comparative Studies in Society and History*, Vol. 41, No. 4, October, 1999, pp. 630–59), who has argued that 'a Hindu religion . . . acquired a much sharper self-conscious identity through the rivalry between Muslims and Hindus in the period between 1200 and 1500, and was firmly established before 1800' (p. 631). While he thus assigns primary agency to 'rivalry between Muslims and Hindus' in the construction of Hinduism, he also pronounces: 'Hinduism wasn't invented by anyone, European or Indian. Like Topsy, it just grow'd' (ibid., p. 655). One wonders if this recourse to escapism is not a mere muddying of the waters of history!

79 Agehananda Bharati, 'The Hindu Renaissance and Its Apologetic Patterns', *Journal of Asian Studies*, 29, 1970, pp. 267–87.

80 Recently Brian K. Pennington (*Was Hinduism Invented?: Britons, Indians, and the Colonial Construction of Religion*, New York, 2005) has vehemently opposed the view that Britain invented Hinduism on the grounds, first, that that argument 'grants . . . too much power to colonialism' and, second, that denying the existence of Hinduism prior to the arrival of the British 'introduces an almost irreparable disruption in Indian traditions that can only alienate contemporary Indians from their own traditions' (p. 5). He seems to forget that colonialisms everywhere have manipulated facts to suit their interests. And worse, must historians cease to work because their reasoned conclusions show that 'traditions', held to be crucial to the psychic welfare of today's people, are concocted?

81 Gavin Flood, *An Introduction to Hinduism*, first South Asian edition, Delhi, 2004, p. 50.

82 Richard H. Davis, 'A Brief History of Religions in India', Introduction, in Donald S. Lopez, Jr, ed., *Religions of India in Practice*, Indian reprint, Delhi, 1998, p. 5. Also see John Stratton Hawley, 'Naming Hinduism', *Wilson Quarterly*, Summer 1991, pp. 20–23; and Wendy Doniger, 'Hinduism by Any Other Name', ibid., 35–41.

83 The only clarity about Hinduism is that it is used as a catch-all category for

all non-Abrahamic religions (Islam, Judaism, Christianity), and is thus a negative appellation. In the Hindu Marriage Act (1955), 'Hindu' includes not only Buddhists, Jainas and Sikhs, but also all those who are not Muslims, Christians, Parsis or Jews. There is, therefore, much substance in Frits Staal's view that no meaningful notion of Hinduism can be obtained except by exclusion, and in his argument, it fails to qualify both as a religion and as 'a meaningful unit of discourse' (*Rules Without Meaning: Ritual, Mantras and the Human Sciences*, New York, 1989, p. 397).

84 Bernard S. Cohn, *An Anthropologist among the Historians and Other Essays*, Delhi,1987, pp. 224–54.

85 Klaus Klostermaier, *A Survey of Hinduism*, Albany, 1989, pp. 31, 531.

86 Halbfass, *India and Europe*, p. 344.

87 Julius Lipner, *Hindus: Their Religious Beliefs and Practices*, London, 1994, p. 221.

88 Julius Lipner, 'On Hinduism and Hinduisms: The Way of the Banyan', in Sushil Mittal and Gene Thursby, eds, *The Hindu World*, New York, 2004, Indian reprint, Chennai, 2005, p. 19.

89 John Zavos, 'Defending Hindu Tradition: Sanatana Dharma as a Symbol of Orthodoxy in Colonial India', *Religion*, 31, 2001, pp. 109–23. Also, see Vasudha Dalmia, *Nationalization of Hindu Traditions: Bharatendu Harischandra and Nineteenth-Century Benaras*, Delhi, 1997, pp. 2–4, note 5.

90 It is not surprising that early twentieth-century pandits like V.S. Abhyaṇkara, Anantakrṣṇa Śāstri, Sītārām Śāstri and Śrīvijaya Bhattācharya were against the introduction of 'new sectarian traditions' (*nūtanasampradāya*, *Dharmapradīpa*, p. 64) and described themselves as 'followers of eternal religion' (*sanātanadharmīya, sanātanadharmāvalambin, Dharmapradīpa*, pp. 207, 219; *Dharmatattvavinirṇaya*, pp. 39ff).

91 *Dhammapada*, I.5. It has been suggested the word *sanātana* may have some connection with *sanatā*, which occurs in the Vedic literature only twice. At one place it occurs along with *dharma* (*RV* 3.3.1d ) and at another, without it (*RV* 2.3.6ab). In both cases, the word *sanatā*means 'from old times' or 'always'. I am thankful to Professor Shingo Einoo, who drew my attention to these references.

92 *Mahābhārata*, xii.96.13; 128.30; 131.2; xiii.44.32; 96.46; xiv.50.37; cited in Halbfass, *India and Europe*, p. 558, note 56.

93 According to the story, when his mother was being led away by a Brāhmaṇa, he flew into a rage and was calmed down by his father, who told him not to get angry because this was the eternal law (*eṣa dharmaḥ sanātanaḥ*), *Mahābhārata*, I.113, verses 11–14.

94 *Gītā*, I.40.

95 Ibid., XI.18.

96 *Manu*, I.118; VII.98; IX.64, 325.

97 *Matsyapurāõa*, 143.32, Ānandāśramagranthāvali, 1981, p. 269. Cf. *Brahamāṇḍapurāṇa*, II.31.36–38; 91.30–32.

98 *Varāhapurāṇa*, 126.7.

99 Ibid., 126.43.

[100] *Śivapurāṇa*, 7.2.10.30–72.

[101] Halbfass, *India and Europe*, p. 343.

[102] *Sanātanadharma: An Elementary Text-book of Hindu Religion and Ethics*, Central Hindu College, Benares, 1910. This was followed by several works on the *sanātanadharma*, e.g., *Sanātanadharmadīpikā* by Hamsayogin, Madras,1917; Ganga Prasad, *The Fountainhead of Religion*, 1909; Shri Bhārat Dharma Mahamandala, ed., *The World's Eternal Religion*, Benares, 1920.

[103] Julius Lipner, *Hindus: Their Religious Beliefs and Practices*, p. 221.

[104] Brian K. Smith, *Reflections on Resemblance, Ritual and Religion*, Oxford University Press, 1989, pp. 13–14.

[105] *Nirukta*, I.20.

[106] *Manu*, II.6. Cf. *Manu*, XII.95–96.

[107] Ibid., II.10.

[108] Wilhelm Halbfass, *Tradition and Reflection: Exploration in Indian Thought*, Albany,1991, pp. 24–27.

[109] Ibid., p. 33.

[110] Brian K. Smith, op. cit., p. 18; Halbfass, *India and Europe*, pp. 326–29, 359. Cf. Louis Renou, *The Destiny of the Veda in India* (English translated by Dev Raj Chanana), Delhi,1965, pp. 40–46.

[111] Renou, op. cit., p. 37.

[112] Brian K. Smith, op. cit., p. 18.

[113] *Itihāsapurāṇaṃ pañcamaṃ vedānāṃ vedam, Chandogya Upaniṣad*, 7.2, *The Principal Upanisads*, edited and translated by S. Radhakrishnan, Delhi, 1991, p. 470. For a discussion of the claim of the *Mahābhārata* to be the 'fifth Veda', see John Brockington, *The Sanskrit Epics*, Leiden, 1998, p. 7. According to some scholars, even the *Atharvaveda* did not belong to the 'revealed' Vedic corpus and its followers invented legends and allegories to prove the superiority of the text and earn for it the status of a 'divine revelation' (Lakshman Sarup, *The Nighaṇṭu and the Nirukta*, Indian edition, Delhi, 1984, Part 1, pp. 72–73).

[114] Frits Staal, 'The Concept of Scripture in the Indian Tradition', in Mark Juergensmeyer and Gerald Barrier, eds, *Sikh Studies: Comparative Perspectives on a Changing Tradition*, Berkeley, 1979, pp. 121–24. For a different point of view, see C. Mackenzie Brown, 'Puranas as Scripture: From Sound to Image of the Holy Word in the Hindu Tradition', *History of Religions*, 26, 1986, pp. 68–86.

[115] The *Mahābhārata* (I.56.33) claims: *Yad ihāsti tad anyatra, yan nehāsti na tat kvacid* ('That which is found herein exists elsewhere; that which is not here, is nowhere').

[116] The Purāṇas often claim to be the essence of all the Vedas (*sarvavedasāra, akhilaśrutisāra, sarvavedārthasāra*), or the soul of the Vedas; *Bhāgavata Purāṇa* 1.2.3, 1.3.42, 12.13.15; *Nāradīya Purāṇa* 1.1.36, 1.9.97; *Skanda Purāṇa* 5.3.1.22; cited in Brian K. Smith, op. cit., p. 26.

[117] Halbfass, *India and Europe*, p. 366.

[118] Brian K. Smith, op. cit., pp. 20–29. The tradition of extending the use of the word *veda* is seen in the description of Nammalvar's *Tiruvaymoli* as

*Draviḍaveda*. It was in keeping with this old practice that the 'Tranquebar Bible' was entitled *Vedapustagam* and B. Ziegenbalg described the Bible and the Christian religion as *satyavedam* or 'the true Veda' (Halbfass, *India and Europe*, p. 340).

119 J.E. Llewellyn, *The Arya Samaj as a Fundamentalist Movement*, Delhi, 1993, chapter 2. Also see J.T.F. Jordens, *Dayanand Saraswati: His Life and Causes*, Delhi, 1981.

120 Louis Renou, *The Destiny of the Veda in India*, p. 2.

121 Although this is not a discussion of the various forms and levels of atheism and heresies in India, it is necessary to recall that among those who repudiated the authority of the Vedas outside the Brāhmaṇical fold and earned the epithets *pāṣandas* (heretics) and *nāstikas* (non-believers in the Vedas), the important ones are the Jainas, the Buddhists and the *Cārvākas*, the followers of Cārvāka also being known as *lokāyatikas*. The Vedas, according to the Jainas, were *anāryavedas*, which they replaced with their own scriptures, calling them *āryavedas*. They also describe the Vedas as *mithyāsūtras* (*micchāsūya*) (Renou, op. cit., p. 87). Gautama Buddha is equally unsparing in his denunciation of the Vedas and says that '. . . the talk of the Brāhmaṇas versed in the three Vedas turns out to be ridiculous, mere words, a vain and empty thing' (*Dīghanikāya*, London, 1967, Vol. I, p. 240, *Tevijjasutta* 15). Further, he describes the three Vedas as 'foolish talk', 'a waterless desert', and their threefold wisdom as 'a pathless jungle' and 'a perdition' (ibid., p. 248, *Tevijjasutta*). The strongest condemnation of the Vedic texts, however, came from the Cārvākas. According to them, the Veda is 'tainted with the three faults of untruth, self-contradiction, and tautology . . . the incoherent rhapsodies of knaves (*dhurtapralāpa*)', *Sarva-darśaṇa-saṇgraha*, translated by E.B. Cowell and A.E. Gough, London, 1914, p. 4.

122 *Ṛgveda*, VII.103.

123 *Ṛgveda*, 10.129.7.

124 J.C. Heesterman, *The Inner Conflict of Tradition*, Delhi, 1985, p. 77.

125 J.C. Heesterman, op. cit., p. 75; *RV*, V.30.1, VI.18.3, VI.27.3, VIII.64.7, VIII.100.3, X.22.1 (cited in ibid., p. 225). Also see Wendy Doniger O'Flaherty, 'The Origin of Heresy in Hindu Mythology', *History of Religions*, 10, May, 1971, p. 284, note 83.

126 *Muṇḍaka Upaniṣad*, I.1.4–5. Lakshman Sarup (*The Nighaṇṭu and the Nirukta*, Indian edition, Delhi, 1984, pp. 74–75) lists several anti-Vedic Upaniṣadic passages: *Muṇḍaka Upaniṣad*, III.2.3; *Kaṭha Upaniṣad*, I.2.23; *Bṛh. Upaniṣad*, I.5.23; *Kauṣītaki Upaniṣad*, II.5; *Chāndogya Upaniṣad*, V.11–24; *Taittirīya Upaniṣad*, II.5.

127 Lakshman Sarup, op. cit., I.15.

128 Wendy Doniger O'Flaherty, 'The Origin of Heresy in Hindu Mythology', p. 286.

129 *Bhagavadgītā*, II.41–46.

130 Ibid., IX.21. Cf. XI.48, 53.

131 *Matsyapurāṇa*, 53.3.20, 5.3.1.20; *Nāradīyapurāṇa*, 2.24.16; cited in Brian K. Smith, op. cit., p. 26.

132 *Agnipurāṇa*, 383, 47–50; cited in C. Mackenzie Brown, op. cit., pp. 70–71.

133 Halbfass, *India and Europe*, p. 366.

134 N.N. Bhattacharyya, *History of Tantric Religion*, Delhi, 1982, p. 75.

135 Halbfass, *India and Europe*, p. 366. The *Mahānirvāṇatantra* is 'probably the most widely known' and the most recent of the Tantras. Written in the second half of the eighteenth century, it contains much material on such varied themes as marriage, conjugal ethics, inheritance, caste rules and slavery, though it has been described by J.D.M. Derrett as a 'well-intentioned fraud'. For a useful discussion of the work, see Teun Goudriaan and Sanjukta Gupta, *Hindu Tantric and Sakta Literature*, Wiesbaden, 1981, pp. 98–101; J.D.M. Derrett, *Essays in Classical and Modern Hindu Law*, Leiden, 1977, vol. 2, pp. 197–242; N.N. Bhattacharyya, *History of the Tantric Religion*, pp. 74–75.

136 R.N. Nandi, 'Origin of the Vīraśaiva Movement', in D.N. Jha, ed., *The Feudal Order*, Delhi, 2000, p. 485, note 47. The *smārtas*, who joined the Vīraśaiva movement in large numbers, retained their superiority, undermined its fraternalism and paved the way for the growth of the Brāhmaṇical caste system among its followers. Not surprisingly, the Vīraśaivas, in the later phase of their movement, preached loyalty to the *varṇāśramadharma*, as is evident from the works of Bhīmakavi and Śrīpati Paṇḍita (both of the fourteenth century). The latter even said that only the performance of caste duties and Vedic rites could purify a person and prepare him for final liberation (ibid., p. 477; Suvira Jaiswal, 'Semitising Hinduism: Changing Paradigms of Brahmanical Integration', *Social Scientist*, Vol. 19, No. 12, 1991, p. 22.). The Vīraśaiva emphasis on the observance of caste duties, as well as on the necessity of seeking legitimation from the Vedas is evident from one of their basic texts, the *Liṇgadhāranacandrikā*; Louis Renou, op. cit., p. 61, note 1.

137 Louis Renou, op. cit., p. 2.

138 Ibid., p. 2.

139 Cited in ibid., p. 3.

140 Kwagsu Lee, 'Resisting Analysis, Persisting Interpretation: A Historiography of Some Recent Studies of Hinduism in the United States', *Social Science Probings*, Vol. 15, Nos 3–4, Winter 2003, p. 28.

141 Among the younger Indian scholars advocating the idea of *sui generis* religion, mention may be made of Kunal Chakrabarti, according to whom, 'religion as man's response to the ultimate reality has an autonomy and a dynamic of its own,' 'Recent Approaches to the Study of Religion in Ancient India', in Romila Thapar, ed., *Recent Perspectives on Early Indian History*, Bombay, 1995, p. 189.

142 Kwangsu Lee, op. cit., p. 28.

143 Russell T. McCutcheon, *Manufacturing Religion: The Discourse on Sui Generis Religion and the Politics of Nostalgia*, New York, 2003, p. 128.

144 Kwangsu Lee, op. cit., pp. 12–13.

145 Constraints of space do not permit us to list and discuss all the recent writings on Hinduism, but a few of the most recent ones may be men-

tioned: Gavin Flood, ed., *The Blackwell Companion to Hinduism*, first Indian reprint, Delhi, 2003; idem, *Introduction to Hinduism*, Cambridge, 2004; Arvind Sharma, ed., *The Study of Hinduism*, Columbia, 2003; Sushil Mittal and Gene Thursby, eds, *The Hindu World*, London and New York, 2004, first Indian reprint, 2005; Axel Michaels, *Hinduism: Past and Present*, Princeton, 2004, Indian edition, Delhi, 2005.

146 Unlike most scholars of religion, there are a few who have looked at early Indian religious developments against the backdrop of social change. Examples are Debiprasad Chattopadhyaya (*Lokāyata*), D.D. Kosambi (*Myth and Reality*), Suvira Jaiswal (*Origin and Development of Vaiṣṇavism*), R.S. Sharma (*Tantricism*), R.N. Nandi (*Social Roots of Religion in Ancient India*). For comments on their relevant writings, see Kunal Chakrabarti, op. cit., pp. 182–89.

147 Russell T. McCutcheon, op. cit., p. 3.

# 13 From Religious and Social Reform to Economic Nationalism

## The Nineteenth-Century Reformers of Andhra

*V. Ramakrishna*

In this paper, we propose to discuss the economic ideas of nineteenth-century reformers in the Andhra region of the erstwhile Madras Presidency. The present Telangana region of Andhra, which then formed part of Hyderabad state under the Nizam, was an independent princely state. It took considerable time for Hyderabad state to catch up with changes that were taking place in the British ruled territories, and hence our discourse is confined to coastal Andhra.

Nineteenth century social reform movements were inevitably religious movements as well, since many of the customs and practices the reformers wished to eradicate had, in the eyes of the practitioners, hallowed religious sanction. We take this relationship for granted; many, if not all, the reformers discussed below could invoke principles attributed to Hinduism to bolster their case for social reforms. Yet as they turned from social to economic matters, the religious veneer practically disappeared and modern secular ideas took over, as we will presently see throughout their economic discourse.

It would seem that the reformers were initially concerned exclusively with social problems even though a shift in their focus towards economic issues was visible by the turn of the century. In exploring their economic ideas, we have relied upon speeches, writings, memoranda and a few contemporary tracts. We have also gone through native news papers wherever original files are available and, in their absence, official native newspaper reports. Based on these, we will endeavour to make a few formulations. While doing so, we would like to keep in mind the situation obtaining in different parts of the country and also at the all-India level. Viewing the problem from a wider pan-Indian perspective will help us to know whether or not the filtering of ideas from national to regional levels was taking place and, conversely, how Andhra reformers were responding to the inflow of such ideas.

The second half of the nineteenth century (after the Revolt of 1857), witnessed a spurt of political consciousness in India. This found expression in the establishment of several associations primarily in the Presidency towns[1] and also, in a few instances, in mofussil towns[2] which focussed attention on contemporary issues. Furthermore, the starting of a number of vernacular journals throughout the country helped in the organisation of public opinion. They often acted as the carriers of ideas to the general population.[3] These attempts at the mobilization of public consciousness were obviously due to an important social development during this period, namely, the rise of professional middle classes.[4] Consisting mainly of the educated sections of society, this intelligentsia owed its rise to several factors of which the most significant was British colonial policies themselves.

Changes that followed in social and educational spheres ushered in an era of enlightenment in the realm of ideas. Though social reform was their main concern, earlier religious and social reformers were not oblivious to developments taking place around them.[5] This trend, among them, became more pronounced during the last two or three decades of the nineteenth century. Their writings and reform activities made people appreciate, more in the later period, the pernicious effects of colonial rule over India. To start with, their efforts took the forms of constitutional agitation for a voice in the administration of the country. The chief means of agitation adopted by them was the printing press. Prior to or even during the early phase of the Indian National Congress, when people were not mobilized in large gatherings and demonstrations, the press was the only medium through which nationalist ideas were disseminated. More often than not, they managed the press as a non-profit enterprise, sometimes even running at a loss.

It did not take much time for early nationalists to realize the limitations inherent in the mere rhetoric of pressing for constitutional development leading to the increasing participation of Indians in framing state policies and securing their implementation. Neither did it seriously affect and influence the government, nor did it arouse the masses to whom the constitutional advance and Indianization of services made much meaning. What mattered to them most was their economic plight. Heavy taxation, coupled with unemployment and recurrent famines made their lives miserable. It was in this context that the economic ideas of Indian national movement had their origin. The need to motivate masses into an active segment of the national movement by championing their economic distress and its analysis engaged the attention of the early nationalists. This was the sure way of enlisting the active support of people without whose participation the movement would have remained an upper-class affair.

Dadabhai Naoroji, the Grand Old Man of Indian Nationalism, was the progenitor of this trend at the national level. It was soon followed by eminent nationalist economists like R.C. Dutt, G.V. Joshi, D.E. Wacha, Subrahmanya Iyer and Ranade.[6] The mainstay of Naoroji's economic critique of colonial rule in India was the Drain Theory. It stated that there was a perennial flow of wealth from India to Great Britain. He declared that 'India is suffering seriously in several ways and is sinking in poverty.'[7] He wrote in 1886: 'The short of the whole matter is that under the present evil and unrighteous administration of Indian expenditure, romance is the beneficience of the British rule, the reality is the bleeding of the British rule.'[8] Other prominent Indian leaders who saw the evils of the Drain were Ranade, Bholanath Chandra and R.C. Dutt. Ranade stated that 'of the national income of India, more than one-third was taken away by the British in some form or the other'.[9] Bholanath Chandra asserted that the 'yawning gulf' of the Drain was widening every year.[10] Dutt observed the Drain from India to be 'unexampled in any country on earth at the present day'.[11] Many other leaders like G.V. Joshi, D.E. Wacha, G.K. Gokhale, Subrahmanya Iyer and others spoke of the evil effects of the drain of wealth from India to England.

Naoroji developed an argument that since enormous wealth was flowing out of India, indigenous capital formation was being prevented, which permanently crippled industrial growth. It greatly hurt the national interests as it would facilitate the 'penetration and exploitation of India by foreign capital'.[12] The political implications that flowed out of this theory are much more important. It brought into clear focus the contradiction between Indian people and British imperialism. The realization that India is ruled by a foreign power became a powerful plank on which the slogan of 'self-government' was considered a panacea for all problems faced by India.

However significant and comprehensive the Drain Theory might be, the economic ideas of nationalists were not confined to it alone. Equally, they attacked the economic exploitation of colonial rule in the spheres of agriculture, trade, industry and finance. The native industries, especially textiles, were already ruined. R.C. Dutt successfully put forward his argument that the oppressive land revenue policies of the British resulted in the extreme poverty of peasants and repeated famines. To promote native industrial enterprise, they popularized the idea of Swaraj and, by 1896, a powerful swadeshi campaign was started in some parts of the country, like Maharashtra.

The growth of public consciousness in South India took the same form and pattern as the all-India level. The earliest public association established in Madras in the 1830s was the Hindu Literary Society. It concentrated mainly on educational activities and arranged public lectures to generate political consciousness. Its attitude towards social problems was progressive as it condemned social evils and undertook programmes such as the promotion of widow remarriage, female education and the uplift of depressed classes.[13] The Hindu Literary Society was a forerunner of the Madras Native Association (MNA), established in 1844. Its founder was Gajula Lakshminarasu Chetty (1806–1869), a Telugu-speaking leading tradesman of Madras city whose forefathers had migrated from Andhra.[14] The MNA was, in fact, the forerunner of Madras Mahajana Sabha (1884) which adopted a clear nationalist agenda and preceded the establishment of Indian National Congress founded in 1885.

Being located in Madras, the MNA had branches in various parts of the Presidency, including some towns such as Guntur in the Andhra region. The MNA drew the attention of the British Parliament, through a memorial in 1852, to the questions of over-assessment, lack of proper roads, neglect of public works, the disabilities of the peasants on account of police atrocities and expensive judicial arrangements, the employment of torture in the collection of revenue, and the policy of discrimination against educated Indians in the matter of employment in the civil service.[15] This famous petition was not only an indictment of the colonial rule in the Madras Presidency, but also reads like a charter of rights for the amelioration of the conditions of peasants. No other leader of South India had made such a thorough study of the consequences of the agrarian measures introduced by the colonial rulers in the wake of the Permanent Settlement and the Ryotwari system. The petitioners brought to the notice of Parliament 'an idea of the cruelties under which Ryotwari system can be and is actually exercised by the government servants'.[16] The petitioners argued that the village system which prevailed in the North-Western Provinces (U.P.) was more advantageous. They further referred to the imposition of several other vexatious taxes including *moturpha* (profession tax), salt tax, etc. They complained about the negligence in the repair of roads, lack of irrigation facilities, *abkari* tax etc. The petitioners stated that the poverty of peasants 'renders them too poor to purchase Company's salt for their miserable food of boiled rice and vegetables, the latter too frequently wild herbs; . . . unable to supply themselves with clothes beyond a piece of coarse cotton fabric worth 2 annas in twelve months.'[17] They appealed to the British Parliament 'to spend far larger portions of the revenues upon the improvement of the country where they are derived.'[18] The petition of 1852 was a document of historical importance and set out a veritable charter of rights and reasoned criticism of colonial administration while the petition warned the rulers against the consequences of Christian proselytization and indoctrination in educational institutions under governmental patronage, anticipating one of the causes of the Revolt of 1857. The MNA submitted yet another petition to the government in 1854 with further evidence about the employment of torture in the collection of taxes.

A significant aspect of the post-1857 period was the publication of a number of Telugu journals and periodicals.[19] They dealt with topics of current interest and the conditions of the people. Edited and managed by members of the new intelligentsia, they reflected the grievances of the general populace. They generally criticized government measures such as the Arms Act, Ilbert Bill and, more significantly, the changes introduced by the land settlements resulting in heavy taxation. To the latter changes, public reaction was sharp, as reflected in the press as well as in the resolutions of associations.[20] But other matters too were taken up. As far back as 1859, the MNA protested against the total Europeanization of civil services.[21] *Vivekavardhani*, a journal edited and published by the leading reformer of the times, Kandukuri Veeresalingam, wrote about poverty in India. This journal, which undertook the pursuit of a whole social reform agenda, remarked that 'intelligent, hard working natives are to be content with posts worth below a hundred, while good-for-nothing Europeans are placed above them drawing some hundreds of rupees'.[22] Their criticism was essentially twofold, namely, over exclusion of Indians from services and increasing civil expenditure.

The growing impoverishment of India was the most significant aspect which recurred continuously in the columns of Telugu papers during this period. In an elementary form, at least, the theory of Drain came to be articulated in the columns of the contemporary journals. *Vivekavardhani*, in April 1880, wrote:

> Almost all the clothes worn by the rich as well as poor are manufactured in England. It is much cheaper than the cloth that our weavers produce here. It is manufactured by machines and hence cheaper. Hence everyone has given up buying Swadeshi cloth; they are all buying clothes manufactured in Europe. Crores of rupees that are spent every year in the purchase of foreign cloth are thus flowing out of our country into foreign lands impoverishing further a country which is already poor. If on the other hand, textiles mills are set up in our country, all that money will remain here.[23]

The same journal (*Vivekavardhani*) in January 1881, published a leading article 'Poverty of India'. It categorically declared that the Indian poverty was due to the annual remittance of a sum of twenty crores to England and the decay of indigenous industries due to the unfair competition with machine-made goods from England. For the first time, the author of the article (perhaps Veeresalingam) came out boldly stating that even during the 'despotic Mughal Government the country was not so poor'.[24] The author stated that heavy taxation was only one of the reasons. The flow of wealth out of India (which did not occur, according to the article, during the Mughal rule) was the other important reason. In 1885, the same journal (*Vivekavardhani*) criticized the government for the heavy expenditure incurred on the army and hence the burden of taxation.

Similar views were expressed by other journals such as the *Vartalahari* (October 1883) and *Sujanaranjani* (July 1885).[25] The latter stated that 'no one of the former rulers of India has taken its wealth to other countries . . . the English spent Indian money on subjects as wars, etc., which do not concern India . . . in short, all Englishmen plunder India'.[26] In 1875, *Loka Ranjani* protested against the exorbitant price of salt which was selling at Rs 240 per *garce*.[27] It further stated: 'Heavy taxation oppresses the people much, that while they are totally unable to pay *kist* [instalment] on cultivated lands from want of rains and the consequent failure of the crop, they are taxed for lands not cultivated. In fact, it is believed that the people were better-off before the transfer of the country to the Crown.'[28] The editor found fault

> with the Viceroy for having passed the new Tariff Act, because the cotton imported into India is heavily taxed, while thread and cloths of foreign manufacture imported here are much more lightly taxed; this cramps trade in India, as, it is believed, this is done at the instance of the Manchester merchants. . . .[29]

The revenue settlements introduced by the British in the Andhra region led to the serious deterioration of economic condition of the peasantry due to the imposition of heavy land tax resulting in severe famines and migration of the poor abroad. *Lok Ranjani* (1875) complained of this to the government. This view was endorsed by Srinivasa Raghava Iyengar who spoke about the poverty of people and their hand-to-mouth existence.[30] The *Andhra Prakasika* (1887) and *Suryodaya Prakasika* (1904) wrote about the increasing rural indebtedness, high interest rates and the corrupt practices of officials during *Jamabandy* when people were subjected to several illegal exactions.[31] Several other journals of the period such as the *Vrittanta Chintamani* (1901), the *Krishnapatrika* (1905) and others emphasized India's growing poverty and its causes and heavy expenditure of the government towards wars, bureaucracy and the consequent drain of wealth.

Drawing their inspiration from the Indian National Congress and its annual sessions, district associations were formed in Andhra. Conferences were regularly organized by them.[32] Topics of public interest, ranging from education to land revenue, to appointment of Indians in services and the corruption of officials were discussed and appropriate resolutions passed. What the press was doing at the level of the spread of ideas and criticism of government policies was followed up by organizing people at the district level. Prominent people in public life–teachers, vakils (advocates), writers, editors of journals, social reformers, rich peasants and traders – that constituted the emerging middle classes, participated in them.

The leading reformers and intellectuals of the period were Kandukuri Veeresalingam, Gurajada Appa Rao, Chilakamarti Lakshminarasimham, Panappakam Anandacharlu, B.N. Sarma, Mocharla Ramachandra Rao, to mention only a few. Not all of them were nationalists. Some of them could be classified as moderates and others were liberals or, at best, could be described as moderates among moderates. Veeresalingam even extolled the virtues of British rule and described it as 'God-given'. While, on the one hand, admitting the defects of the British rule, he wanted people to rely upon the British to introduce constitutional reforms to ensure peace, justice and good government. In fact, he belonged to that section of reformers of the period who strongly believed that social reforms should precede political changes and, if it did not happen, feared that political freedom would be of no real value to people. Veeresalingam feared that if the British rule were to end, India would again plunge into anarchy and disorder and prayed 'God to ensure the British rule over us for ever'.[33] However, Veeresalingam still voiced his protest against the growing impoverishment of India and the drain of wealth to England. Also, though in very general terms, Veeresalingam evinced enthusiasm for Swadeshi and the manufacture of Indian products. In this, one could see the conflict of views among the early reformers. On one hand, they pinned their hopes for support on local British officials in their reform activities, and, in general, they saw the colonial masters as the facilitators of social changes in India. Nevertheless, they had also some understanding of destructive economic consequences of colonial rule. Later reformers and nationalist leaders like Unnava Lakshminarayana, Konda Venkatappaiah, Jonnavittula Gurunatham, Bhogaraju Pattabhiseetharamaiah and others are not being considered in this paper as they became more active only after the Vande Mataram movement (1905).

Of the earlier period, the writings of two reformers deserve our attention. Chilakamarti Lakshminarasimham, a contemporary and close follower of Veeresalingam in Rajahmundry, was a creative writer, a poet, playwright and a novelist. He participated in the annual session of the Indian National Congress held at Madras in 1894 and displayed more awareness regarding the evil effects of British rule. He took part in the first Godavari district Conference held at Kakinada in 1895.[34] He composed and read fourteen stanzas (in Telugu) about British rule in India which received much acclaim from the delegates.[35] Chilakamarti here highlighted the plight of cultivating peasants by enumerating the countless taxes that the British imposed on people and also various types of illegal extractions that the officials, from village to the district level, forcibly took from people. In a graphic manner, the poet depicted, in an easy and popular idiom, the hardships encountered by the people and their increasing burden of debt. He exhorted different sections of people affected by the British rule to organize conferences regularly and represent their grievances to the government.[36] These poems, the writer claimed in his autobiography, became so popular that they were recited in public meetings and *kalakshepams.* More importantly, Chilakamarti Lakshminarasimham, while translating the speech of Bipin Chandra Pal during the Swadeshi movement tour of Andhra, at Rajahmundry, recited extempore a poem which became well-known throughout Andhra. It summarized in brief the Drain theory and the exploitative nature of the British rule. The English version of the poem in part is as follows:

> India is a gentle milch cow
> And the starved calves are Indians
> The subtle cowherds muzzle them
> To snatch the entire store of milk.[37]

The other reformer who directly commented on the economic effects of British rule was Attili Suryanarayana, a patriot and a lecturer in Pithapuram Rajah's college, Kakinada. He authored a small tract in Telugu, *Hindudesa Daridryamu* ('Poverty of India').[38] It contains five chapters titled as follows:

> Administration of the early rulers
> Famines
> Our income
> Taxes
> Flow of wealth

The author, in a brief introduction, says that India, once a land of plenty and prosperity, is now ravaged by famines. He acknowledged that he had read the writings of Naoroji, Digby, R.C. Dutt and Subrahmanya Iyer.

It is clear from the contents of the tract that the author borrowed ideas from the contemporary writings of nationalist economists and incorporated them in his book. The author displayed remarkable clarity in his arguments by briefly outlining the history of India from the earliest times and drawing a contrast with the modern period when India experienced a number of famines. Quoting extensively from the writings of Digby, Samuel Smith (Member, British Parliament), Subrahmanya Iyer, Naoroji, Sir George Campbell and other leading writers, he convincingly established the fact that the British rule was economically ruinous to India. What is unique about the book is that it is replete with statistics drawn from government records and the writings of British officials. The chapter on 'Flow of Wealth' brings out the illusion of the benevolence of British rule by quoting Lord Martin that despite the rich natural sources that the country possessed, the general populace were poverty-stricken due to the drain of large sums of money annually in the name of Home Charges and other items of expenditure.[39] Also, the author laid out facts about the tariff measures of the Government which resulted in the flow of wealth out of the country.[40] The book concludes by declaring that there was no use in placing faith in the fairness of the British rulers and, therefore, it would be better if people could rely upon themselves and explore ways and means of eradicating the scourge of poverty. The author's views, as seen from the date of publication, 1907, were definitely much more advanced than the early reformers' and also followed a rational approach by adopting the empirical method of reliance upon statistics in arriving at appropriate conclusions.

The reformers of the nineteenth century (and early twentieth century) in Andhra played a historic role in exposing the true nature of British rule in India. They brought out the significant point that India was ruled by a foreign country for economic exploitation. During this formative stage, the myth that British rule showered innumerable benefits on India was exploded. Keeping in view the general tenor of the writings of reformers of the period in Andhra on economic ideas, a few conclusions can be drawn. First, in the exposure of the economic policies of the British, the reformers of the nineteenth century, compared to their counterparts at the national level, did not reveal the same rigour and depth. Except for one theoretical tract, all other writings were in the shape of either articles in journals or comments or speeches in public meetings. Serious writings on economic topics perhaps started only in the post-Swadeshi phase of the national movement. That the Andhra region did not produce a serious economic thinker was perhaps due to the fact that the region lacked a major metropolis. The Presidency headquarters were located away in Madras. The lack of effective communication with leaders and ideologues of the country during the early phase of the national movement was yet another reason. Even then, the tract that we mentioned (published in 1907) dealt comprehensively with the Drain theory and its negative effects on capital formation in India and hence the space created for subsequent flow of foreign capital into India. However, the political implications of Drain theory that only self-government would end economic exploitation were not effectively worked out. Nevertheless, the writings of reformers in Andhra did not lag behind the other parts of the country in grasping the exploitative nature of colonial rule in India.

**Notes and References**

1 For details about these associations see Tarachand, *History of Freedom Movement in India*, Vol. II, New Delhi, 1974, pp. 525–27.

2 For example, the Kakinada Literary Association (in coastal Andhra) established in 1877 of which further particulars are furnished in this paper.

3 *Kesari* (Maharashtra), *The Bengalee, Indian Mirror, Amrit Bazar Patrika* (Bengal), *Crescent, Native Public Opinion* (Madras) are some of the journals and newspapers started during the period. In the Andhra region, journals like *Purusharthapradayini, Vivekavardhani*, and *Sasilekha, Savithri*, about 20 Telugu journals in all were in circulation. See, for details, K.R. Seshagiri Rao, *Studies in the History of Telugu Journalism*, New Delhi, 1968.

4 For a lucid analysis of this development and the role of middle classes in modern Indian history, see B.B. Misra, The *Indian Middle Classes*, Cambridge, 1978.

5 See, for example, 'Economic Thought of Rammohan Roy', in Susobhan Sarkar, *Bengal Renaissance and other Essays*, New Delhi, 1970.

6 Ranade's *Essays on Indian Economics* and *Miscellaneous Writings*, G.V. Joshi's *Writings and Speeches*, Gokhale's *Speeches*, Subrahmanya Iyer's *Some Economic Aspects of British Rule in India*, Wacha's *Speeches and Writings* and Ramesh Chunder Dutt's two volumes of *Economic History of India* are particularly worth mentioning.

7 Dadabhai Naoroji, *Poverty and Un-British Rule in India*, London, 1901, p. 31. He further stated, 'The fact was that Indian natives were mere helots. They were worse than American slaves for the latter were at least taken care of by their masters whose property they were'. Ibid., p. 652.

8 Dadabhai Naoroji, *Speeches and Writings*, second edition, Madras, n.d, p. 329, cited in Bipan Chandra, *The Rise and Growth of Economic Nationalism in India*, New Delhi, 1977, second edition, p. 640.

9 Ibid., pp. 640–41.

10 Ibid.

11 Ibid.

12 Bipan Chandra, op. cit., p. 666.

13 R. Suntharalingam, *Politics and National Awakening in South India (1852–1891)*, Tucson, Arizona, 1974, pp. 45–46.

14 See for a biographical account of Lakshminarasu Chetty, G. Parameswaran Pillai, *Representative Men of Southern India*, Madras, 1896; see for a com-

prehensive account of Madras Native Association, M.P.R. Reddy and A. Jagannadham, *Gajula Lakshminarasu Chetty: Life and Times, 1806–1866*, Kavali, n.d.

[15] See for full text of the petition, M. Venkatarangaianh, *The Freedom Struggle in Andhra Pradesh*, Vol. I, *1800–1905*, Hyderabad, 1965, Document No. 10, pp. 120–27.

[16] Ibid.

[17] Ibid.

[18] Ibid. In response to the representations of MNA, Mr Danby Seymour, a member of the British Parliament, came to Madras in 1852 to ascertain the truth of the Memorials. He made a tour of South India, accompanied by Lakshminarasu Chetty. Seymour, after witnessing the methods of torture employed by the government officials, submitted his report and apprised the members of the House of Commons of its contents. A commission was appointed in 1854 to go into the matter and, based on its report, torture was abolished.

[23] K. Veeresalingam, *Complete Works*, Vol. VIII, Rajahmundry, 1951, pp. 24–25. The article was originally published in *Vivekavardhani.*

[24] M. Venkatarangaiya, op. cit., Document No. 70, pp. 224–25.

[25] Ibid., Documents No. 77 and 82, pp. 228–29, 231.

[26] Ibid.

[27] Ibid., pp. 219–20.

[28] Ibid.

[29] Ibid.

[30] S. Srinivasa Raghavaiyangar, *Memorandum on the Progress of Madras Presidency*, Madras, 1893, p. 97.

[31] M. Venkatarangaiah, op. cit., Documents nos 100 and 128, pp. 259–60, 274–75.

[32] The Krishna District Conference was the first (also perhaps the first in India) to be organized in 1892. Other District 'social' conferences followed. See V. Ramakrishna, *Social Reform in Andhra (1848–1919)*, New Delhi, 1983, especially Chapter 7, pp. 189–204.

[33] This invocation occurred in a lecture by Veeresalingam at Rajahmundry, 10 November 1889. See Veeresalingam's *Collected Works*, Vol. VIII, op. cit., p. 9.

[34] Chalakamarti Lakshminarasimham, *Sweeyacharitamu* (autobiography in Telugu), Visakhapatnam, 1957, pp. 129–31. Nyapati Subba Rao, who later became the Secretary, Indian National Congress, presided over this conference.

[35] Ibid.

[36] Ibid. That Chilakamarti held loyal sentiments towards British rule is borne out by the fact that during the Diamond Jubilee celebrations of Queen Victoria, he wrote fifteen stanzas extolling her virtues and glorifying her rule.

[37] The poem is translated by a poet, Amarendra (Guntur), cited in M. Venkatarangaiah, op. cit., Vol. II, *1906–1920*, p. 19. Chilakamarti

translated all the speeches of Bipin Chandra Pal at Rajahmundry and he recited this poem during the last lecture.

38 This rare tract has 33 pages. It was first serialized in the journal, *Manorama*, published from Rajahmundry. It is not referred to by any scholar so far. It was printed and published by S. Gunneswara Rao Brothers' Chintamani printing press and priced at 2 annas.

39 Ibid., pp. 26–27.

40 Ibid.

# 14 Reason and Faith

## A Defence of Foucault's Critique of Post-Enlightenment Modernity

*Farhat Hasan*

'Globalization' is a complex phenomenon, hard to describe, and almost impossible to define. It imbibes deeply contradictory forces, and eludes all attempts to pigeonhole it into a straightjacket. It is, of course, true that globalization tends to homogenize cultures along the lines of the modern Western world. Since globalization is itself an outcome of the triumph of Western capitalism, the two can with justification be conflated together; a large number of contemporary theorists see globalization and Westernization as synonyms, or as two sides of the same coin. The picture becomes convincing once we look at the obvious shifts in consumer lifestyles in the third-world countries, something that is often described as 'the Macdonaldization of the third world'. For several Western scholars, particularly those subscribing to the 'convergence theory', the Western homogenization of the world is both irreversible and inexorable; it is also equally welcome, for modern Western culture represents the culmination of human achievement. The religious, regional and local forces that are resisting it can do so for the time being, but it would ultimately be engulfed by the emerging world order inevitably modelled after the image of the West. It is within this framework that Fukuyama, for example, propounds his theory of the 'end of history' which unabashedly proclaims the global triumph of capitalism (Fukuyama 1992). The same frame of reference informs Huntington's 'clash of civilization' thesis where Islam, engaged in a losing battle, is projected as the last bastion to be conquered by the global forces of modernity (Huntington 1993).[1]

The actual situation is far less simple, for, while certain fundamental modern Western values enjoy a worldwide ascendancy, cultural encounters of the West with the rest of the world have substantially changed their very nature and meaning, making them more complex and multifarious. Modernization is not a homogenous and uniform process, but includes diverse, even conflicting tendencies. The cultural flows in the contemporary world are not unidirectional, proceeding from a 'hegemonic cultural centre' to the world's peripheries, but reciprocal and multi-directional, influencing and reshaping all members of the global community, though unequally. Furthermore, no society ever receives cultural products from the outside passively, without engagement; these are usually modified and moulded by the recipients to suit their local needs, values and aspirations (Featherstone 1990: 10).

The point we seek to make here is not that a 'global culture' does not exist, but that it is marked 'by an organization of diversity rather than by a replication of uniformity' (Hannerz 1990: 237). The revolution in information and communications technology has indeed accelerated the exchanges of cultural resources, breaking down insular normative structures and belief systems. This has not left the West unaffected, but the impact of these developments has been felt rather differently by the West when compared with the rest of the world. It has been shown by Edward Said that Europeans' perception and experience of the colonial world shaped their sense of self-identity; the 'other' was as much a part of the 'self' as the 'self' itself. In his words, 'European culture gained in strength and identity by setting itself off against the Orient as a surrogate and even underground self' (Said 1991: 3).

The process, in fact, had deeply paradoxical consequences. On the one hand, the orientalist discourse was employed in the West, along with other discourses of power, to further marginalize oppressed social groups, reinforcing and refashioning ideological dominance over women, workers, sexual 'deviants', blacks and the destitute. But on the other, encounters with the supposedly exotic and alien civilizations undermined the universalist and hegemonic claims of European modernity, based on post-Enlightenment epistemic and normative thought, and revealed its particularity, exclusions, contradictions and silences. Michel Foucault, along with several other postmodernist thinkers, is a product of this development.

However, Foucault's critique of post-enlightenment science and rationality should not be construed as amounting to a negation of modernity. Unfortunately, most critics project 'modernism' and 'postmodernism' as antithetical to each other, and emphasize the differences between them through pairs of contrasting types – form: antiform; purpose: play; hierarchy: anarchy; centring: dispersal; transcendence: immanence; signified: signifier, etc. (Swingwood 1998: 164). This makes it easier to attack the postmodernists, because they can be shown to be against everything that modernity has achieved; but the perspective is neither appropriate, nor particularly fruitful. Foucault repeatedly insisted on describing his work as situated within the post-Enlightenment tradition. It is not the achievements of modernity that he attacks, but its failures, its inconsistencies and its silences. Foucault's project should not be seen as amounting to a rejection of modernity, but instead as an effort to enlarge and broaden its frame of references, so as to make it richer, more inclusive, and above all, more equitable and just. Foucault even described his mission as that of a 'political moralist'.

In the well-integrated, but unequal world we live in, there is a real threat that globalization might become an instrument of Western hegemony, and, losing its emanicipatory potential inherent in the mutual sharing of cultural capital, serve instead the forces of cultural homogeneity. Indeed, globalization has continually minimized the space for local diversities, and alternate normative frameworks. Equally, there is a danger of the local communities themselves becoming insular and homogenous, transforming themselves into sites of social injustice and intolerance. This is a particularly noticeable development in India where communal–fascist groups for some time not only captured the centre stage of national politics, but have also produced a framework, under the garb of 'cultural nationalism', for the multiplication and qualitative expansion of fanaticism and intolerance in our society. It is ironic that these groups, and their ideological advocates, rely on postmodernism, and the Foucaultian critique of rationality in particular, to legitimize their political outlook. Indian social theorists critical of postmodernism have also accepted their premises uncritically, if only to demonstrate the futility and hazards of the theory. Aijaz Ahmad has, for example, argued that Foucault's position on religion is 'astonishingly traditionalist', so traditionalist indeed, that it would be acceptable to even the most blatant communal organization (Ahmad 2000: 469–70).

Ahmad's complaint is based on an interview in which Foucault praised the Iranian Islamic revolution, describing it as 'the uprising of a whole nation against a power that oppresses it' (Foucault 1990: 212). However, he defended the revolution not because of its religious character, but because it expressed 'the collective will' (ibid.: 215), it being a moment in history 'in which one cannot situate the internal contradictions of a society, and in which one cannot point out a vanguard either' (ibid.: 213). This 'collective will', as he said, did not reflect religious zeal, but a shared experience of political and economic subordination of the nation: 'the rejection of submission to foreigners, disgust at the looting of natural resources, the rejection of a dependent foreign policy, American interference . . . ' (ibid.: 215). Ahmad, perhaps, in a rather enthusiastic projection of Foucaultian postmodernism as amounting to a return to the 'pre-modern' (Ahmad 2000: 470), reads Foucault's interview in bits and pieces, ignoring the thrust of his argument, in order to be able to place his thought alongside the contemporary anti-modern and conservative social movements. Foucault's enthusiasm for the Iranian revolution is a guarded one; his apprehensions emerge precisely from the constraints and limitations on individual subjectivity that follow from the coming together of religion and politics. As he pertinently asks: 'will this unitary movement, which, for a year now has stirred up a people faced with machine guns, have the strength to cross its own frontiers and go beyond the things on which, for a time, it has based itself?' (Foucault 1990: 224). Furthermore, if we leave his controversial interview aside, Ahmad's position becomes even more untenable for it is not borne out from the overall implications of Foucault's main, and more substantial, writings. Freedom is actually at the core of Foucault's thought, but he defines 'freedom' not negatively as mere absence of restraints, but instead as a state of social existence where individual differences, identities and subjectivities are accepted and appreciated.

Foucault is both a philosopher and a historian. His philosophy interrogates practice; it is not concerned with questions of 'truth' and laws of nature. His history is not about past, but a 'history of the present': 'History [is] the depths from which all beings emerge into their precarious, glittering existence' (Foucault 1970: 219). He creatively combines the two disciplines to develop his critique of the modern civilization, based on what he calls the 'ontology of the present', that is, through an analysis of the conditions for the emergence of the modern human subject.

In order to better appreciate Foucault, it would, perhaps, be a good idea to place his critique by the side of orthodox Marxism. He shares with the Marxists a sensitive awareness of the inequities of capitalism, but unlike them, prefers to situate their origins not in the forces of production ('base'), but in the domain of politics and culture ('superstructure'). Foucault also does not believe that these inequities can be encompassed within the economic framework of class alone, but class is deeply entangled with other forms of oppression, based on gender, race, sexuality, etc., all of which are products of bourgeois domination. In the May 1968 issue of *Esprit*, a left journal, Foucault argued against the privileging of class war in comparison to other movements of resistance. The fight of 'women, prisoners, conscripted soldiers, hospital patients and homosexuals' was, according to him, as radical and revolutionary as 'the revolutionary movement of the proletariat' (cited from Merquior 1991: 155). It was actually not a question of hierarchizing oppression that was important, but the realization that all these forms of oppression emerge from 'the same system of power'. In Foucaultian theory, the effort is to subvert the system through a multiplicity of social, economic and cultural struggles, for, unless that was achieved, political struggles, however radical and revolutionary, would not succeed in establishing a free and just society. They would merely relocate domination from one social arena to another. One does notice in all this the obvious influence of the critical theorists of the Frankfurt School, but it should be emphasized that the critical theorists saw themselves as working within a Marxist framework, relying on Marx's early writings when he was not yet drawn to materialist determinism. Foucault's critique of modern, bourgeois culture transcends both Marxism and critical theory in that he saw this culture as constituted by the triangular relationship of discourse–knowledge–power.

In a major departure from structuralism, Foucault presents 'discourse' as bereft of any 'deep' or 'hidden' structure, and, further, by collapsing the signifier–signified dyad, equates 'discourse' with 'knowledge'. Discourse, according to Foucault, does not represent 'truth', but is integral to the whole process of truth-formation that is knowledge. He sees modern, bourgeois discourses not in terms of language, but as bodies or disciplines of knowledge (Foucault 1970; 1972). The political significance of his discourse theory becomes manifest when he takes the next step of arguing that discourse, particularly modern discourse, is a product of power relations. Since discourse both enables and constrains our thought, speech and writing, all systems of knowledge are deeply implicated in relations of power:

> We should admit . . . power produces knowledge (and not simply by encouraging it because it serves power or by applying it because it is useful); that power and knowledge directly imply one another; that there is no power relation without the correlative constitution of a field of knowledge, nor any knowledge that does not presuppose and constitute at the same time power relations. (Foucault 1977: 27)

Similarly, at another place, he says:

> In a society such as ours, but basically in any society, there are manifold relations of power which permeate, characterize and constitute the social body, and these relations of power cannot themselves be established, consolidated nor implemented without the production, accumulation, circulation and functioning of a discourse. There can be no possible exercise of power without a certain economy of discourses of truth which operates through and on the basis of this association. We are subjected to the production of truth through power and we cannot exercise power except through the production of truth. (Foucault 1980: 93)

Modern disciplinary knowledge functions within and is a part of the 'episteme' of science and rationality. Rejecting the progressivist and constructivist views of science, Foucault sees it as an instrument of power, serving the interests, and codifying the experiences, of dominant bourgeois, Western culture. At the same time, Foucault argues, science is able to conceal the interests it defends and the power relations it perpetuates by insulating itself from self-reflection, thwarting under its sovereign regime the possibilities for the development of its own critique.

But, through what processes does knowledge 'constitute' power? In three ways, argues Foucault, which could broadly be categorized as *exclusion, subjection* and *normalization.* Modern knowledge is based on a systemic exclusion of the interests and experiences of the oppressed and subjugated peoples. It is based on the interests and experiences of a particular kind of subject: the male, bourgeois, white, heterosexual subject. Secondly, modern knowledge, based on science and rationality, by setting limits to what can and cannot be said, written and thought, subjects people to ideological conformism and uncritical submission to the prevailing order of power. 'Subjection', therefore, refers to those concepts, ideas and epistemic structures that constitute the modern human subject, enabling it to 'tell the truth about itself' (Foucault 1990: 38) and preventing it from exploring, even envisaging, other possibilities and alternatives external to the dominant 'episteme'. Thirdly, modern science and rationality act as instruments of normalization by introducing supposedly 'correct' and 'functional' forms of thinking and behaviour. Modern knowledge draws a rigid distinction between 'normal'/ 'correct' behaviour and an 'abnormal'/'delinquent'/ 'pathological' one, with the result that the individual uncritically comes to accept the dominant bourgeois culture as necessary for social order and development. The other consequence of 'normalization' is that the experiences and beliefs of the oppressed and marginal peoples are peripheralized, and are increasingly seen as irrelevant, even injurious to the well-being of society. It is as instruments of normalization, for example, that the modern discourses on madness (Foucault 1967) and sexuality (Foucault 1979) reveal their complicity with power.

Foucault's intervention on modern knowledge adds certain fresh dimensions to our understanding of globalization. For one, it shows that Western hegemony is not only a product of political and economic developments, but also – and perhaps more significantly – of the changes in the discursive field. The Western 'episteme', based on modern science and rationality, enjoys a universal status in global culture, and claims for itself the sovereign right to re-arrange hierarchies and even obliterate other 'discourses' emerging from outside the Western world, in accordance with their distance from its epistemic and normative claims. Modern science, therefore, has become the instrument through which modern West reproduces the conditions for its global dominance at the level of ideology and culture.

The more important point here is that Foucault's critique not only resists and challenges Western global hegemony, but all forms of hegemony. His condemnation of modern science and rationality should not be seen as legitimizing the reactionary, conservative and consciously anti-modern movements, such as Islamic fundamentalism and the 'cultural nationalism' of the Sangh *parivar*. The political morality within which Foucault's critique is situated is not confined to Western disciplinary knowledge, but extends to all discourses and practices that restrain and inhibit the freedom of the human subject, through techniques of exclusion, subjection and normalization. Indeed, there is no scope in Foucault's thought for justification of political discourses that are exclusive, insular and intolerant of diversity and critical reflection. Foucault repeatedly emphasized that the chief concern of his discourse ethics is to recover 'subjugated' or 'marginal' knowledges, disqualified and excluded from 'official discourse' (Foucault 1978). 'Subjugated' knowledges are 'a whole set of knowledges that have been disqualified as inadequate to their task or insufficiently elaborated: naïve knowledges, located low down on the hierarchy, beneath the required level of cognition or scientificity.' The main purpose of his critical, 'archaeological' method is to reveal these knowledges: 'It is through the reappearance of this knowledge, of these popular knowledges, these disqualified knowledges that criticism performs its work' (Foucault 1980: 81–82).

Foucaultian criticism is not concerned with the question of which discursive system is closer to 'truth' or/and better suited to society. This question, in the Foucaultian perspective, is itself coercive and disciplinary, a product of power relations, for it suppresses diversity in perspective and equal co-existence of a multiplicity of 'truths'. The main concern in Foucault's writings is not to describe or create a proper, ideal 'discourse', but to investigate conditions under which a discourse becomes hegemonic, the sole repository of truth, and intolerant of diversity, criticism and freedom.

Within this framework, of course, the charge of relativism against Foucault seems mistaken. If, as the critics argue, science and rationality are incapable of objective knowledge by virtue of their entanglement with power, how can one verify the validity claims of different epistemic and normative structures? How can one authenticate the truth-claims of one statement against another? And, how can one hold one kind of political practice better than another? Several feminist and left-oriented thinkers have found Foucault's attack on orthodox notions of science, rationality and the unified subject as providing an important dimension to sources of gender-and class-based oppression. However, the difficulty in Foucault for them lies in the fact that once all value judgments and truth-claims are rejected, emancipatory political projects lose their own significance. The point is succinctly made by Eric Hobsbawm, the distinguished Marxist historian:

> 'Postmodernist' intellectual fashions imply that all facts claiming objective existence are simply intellectual constructions. In short, that there is no clear difference between fact and fiction. But there is, and for historians, even for the most militantly antipositivist ones among us, the ability to distinguish between the two is absolutely fundamental. We cannot invent our facts – either the present Turkish government, which denies the attempted genocide of the Armenians, is right or it is not (Hobsbawm 1993: 63).

Another historian, George Fredrickson, in a similar vein, writes:

> The postmodernists question the existence of a reality or set of objective facts external to the historian's 'discourse' [because for them] history is increasingly viewed as a form of fiction – [But] if we cannot prove that the Holocaust revisionists are wrong in some inarguable way, we are clearly in deep trouble. (Cited from Spiro 1996: 775).

Though the charge is not without some justification, my point is that Foucault is not against science, but a particular kind of science: a narrow, positivist science that is exclusively concerned with domination over nature and people. He is also not an 'anti-rationalist', but what he attacks is the instrumental and purposive rationality of the Enlightenment period that is deeply fused with modern, bourgeois aims of domination and control. Foucault is a believer in a multiplicity of 'truths' and 'rationalities', but within his political–moral perspective, it is important (a) that these multiple rationalities should not be absorbed into an exclusive, dominant discourse, and (b) that 'discourses' should be extricated from power relations, for until that is achieved, knowledge would not provide freedom, but would continue to impose newer and improved forms of subjection on the human subject. In the contemporary world, when the space for mutual disagreement, dissent and tolerance is being progressively reduced, one may feel Foucault's interrogation of modernity is quite valuable in allowing us to arrive at a fresh ethical/normative framework for the global community, based on a better appreciation of diversity and difference.

Foucault is conscious of the fact that human subjection is not only a product of modern discourse, but is also a result of the political forces. In *Discipline and Punish*, therefore, he shifts his attention to the institutions of social control – prisons, schools, hospitals, military centres, psychiatric institutions, etc. – and the role they play in the reproduction of power relations in society. He argues that modern, bourgeois dominance is not explicable exclusively in terms of the mode of production, but is also crucially related to changes in the configuration of power relations. These changes have made power far more diffused, regular, widespread and impersonal but have, above all, extended the domain of its activity to include control and administration of life:

> For the first time in history, no doubt, biological existence was reflected in political existence; the fact of living was no longer an inaccessible substrate that only emerged from time to time, amid the randomness of death and its finality; part of it passed into knowledge's control over power's sphere of intervention. Power would no longer be dealing simply with legal subjects over whom the ultimate domination was death, but with living beings, and the mastery it would be able to exercise over them would have to be applied at the level of life itself; it was the taking charge of life, more than the threat of death, that gave power its access even to the body. (Foucault 1979: 143)

Power manages and modifies 'life' through institutions of social control which have together established a disciplined society that exercises on its people continuous control, policing and surveillance. Disciplinary power, with its techniques of normalizing judgement and hierarchical surveillance (or 'panopticism'), seizes the human 'body', and through the 'body', the 'soul' (Foucault 1977: 29, 201, 217), rendering it obedient, docile and productive. Discipline 'increases the forces of the body [in terms of economic utility] and diminishes these same forces [in political terms of obedience]' (Foucault 1977: 138). It is this that explains the triumph of industrial capitalism, for capitalism not only requires productive bodies, but also docile 'souls' (Foucault 1980: 105).

Foucault's views on disciplinary institutions makes us sensitive to the diversity of power relations, and its presence in routine, everyday encounters of social life. It also draws our attention to the need to preserve civil societies in our global age, from where individual freedom can be preserved, protected and enhanced. Critics have accused Foucault of being a 'neo-anarchist' (Merquior 1991: 141–60), but, in actual fact, his work envisaged a global order that is marked by a multiplicity of perspectives, ensuring to each individual freedom and justice, irrespective of gender, class, race and belief systems. That is why he refers to his ethics variously as representing an 'aesthetics of existence' or 'stylization of the self' (Foucault, 1984a: 4; 1984b: 350–51). The choice of words – 'aesthetics' and 'stylization' – is deliberate; it marks an attempt to relocate ethics from the insular regime of 'truth' to a diverse, heterogeneous, freedom-imbibing domain of 'art'. At another place, he describes his ethics as 'care of the self' (Foucault 1988a), which he makes clear, is not possible without care for others:

> The risk of dominating others and exercising over them a tyrannical power only comes from the fact that one did not care for one's self and that one has become a slave to his desires. But if you care for yourself correctly, i.e. if you know ontologically what you are, if you also know of what you are capable, if you know what it means to be a citizen in a city . . . If you know what things you must fear and those you should not fear . . . if you know, finally, that you should not fear death, well, then, you cannot abuse your power over others. (Foucault, 1988b: 8)

The repeated use of 'know' in the above passage makes it clear that Foucault does after all believe in certain 'truths' and considers them to be essential for a progressive ethical behaviour and political practice. One such 'truth' is that 'self-care' is not possible without the care for others. The other is that freedom promotes more freedom, repression augments repression. That, in a sense, is the essence of Foucault's political thought and moral outlook.

This paper, originally entitled 'Globalization and Post-modernism: Re-assessing Foucault's Interrogation of Modernity', was presented at a seminar on 'Globalization, Language, Culture and Media', organized by the Department of Humanities and Social Sciences, IIT, Kanpur, 30 January–1 February 2001.

**Note**

1 Huntington's thesis has been critically examined from various perspectives by several scholars of political Islam; but, particularly, see Esposito (1992) and Halliday (1994: 91).

**A Select Bibliography**

Adorno, T., 1973, *Negative Dialectics*, New York: Seabury Press.

Adorno, T. and Horkheimer, M., 1972, *Dialectic of Enlightenment*, translated by J. Cunning, New York: Herder and Herder.

Ahmad, Aijaz, 2000, 'Postmodernism in History', in K.N. Panikkar, T.J. Byres and Utsa Patnaik (eds) *The Making of History: Essays Presented to Irfan Habib*, New Delhi: Tulika.

Esposito, J., 1992, *The Islamic Threat: Myth or Reality?*, Oxford: Oxford University Press.

Featherstone, M., 1990, 'Global Culture: An Introduction', in M. Featherstone, ed., *Consumer Culture and Postmodernism*, London: Sage.

Foucault, M., 1967, *Madness and Civilization: A History of Insanity in the Age of Reason*, London: Tavistock.

———, 1970, *The Order of Things: An Archaeology of the Human Sciences*, London: Routledge.

———, 1972, *The Archaeology of Knowledge*, London: Tavistock.

———, 1977, *Discipline and Punish: The Birth of the Prison*, London: Allen Lane.

———, 1978, 'Politics and the Study of Discourse', *Ideology and Consciousness*, 3.

———, 1979, *The History of Sexuality, Volume One: An Introduction*, London: Allen Lane.

———, 1980, *Power/Knowledge: Selected Interviews and Other Writings 1972–1977*, London: Harvester Press.

———, 1984a, 'What is Enlightenment?', in P. Rabinow, ed., *The Foucault Reader*, Harmondsworth: Penguin.

———, 1988a, *The Care of the Self: The History of Sexuality, Volume Three*, London: Penguin Press.

———, 1988b, 'The Care of the Self as a Practice of Freedom', in J. Bernaver and D. Rasmussen, eds, *The Final Foucault*, Cambridge, Mass.: MIT Press.

———, 1990, *Politics Philosophy Culture: Interviews and Other Writings 1977–1984*, New York: Routledge.

Fukuyama, F., 1992, *The End of History and the Last Man*, New York: Free Press/ Maxwell Macmillan.

Halliday, F., 1994, 'The Politics of Islamic Fundamentalism: Iran, Tunisia and the Challenge to the Secular State', in Akbar S. Ahmad and Hastings Donnan, eds, *Islam, Globalization and Postmodernity*, London and New York: Routledge.

Held, D., 1980, *Introduction to Critical Theory: Horkheimer to Habermas*, London: Hutchinson.

Hobsbawm, E.J., 1993, 'The New Threat to History', *The New York Review*, 16 December.

Horkheimer, M., 1974, *Critique of Instrumental Reason*, New York: Seabury Press.

Jay, M.,1973, *The Dialectical Imagination: A History of the Frankfurt School and the Institute of Social Research, 1923–1950*, Boston: Little Brown.

Marcuse, H., 1956, *Eros and Civilization*, London: Routledge.

Melford, E. Spiro, 1996, 'Postmodernist Anthropology, Subjectivity and Science', *Comparative Studies in Society and History*, 38, 4 October.

Merquior, J.G., 1991, *Foucault*, London: Fontana Press.

Swingwood, A., 1998, *Cultural Theory and the Problem of Modernity*, New York: St. Martin's Press.

# 15 Contemporary Communalism

## Textuality and Mass Culture

*Nirmalangshu Mukherji*

At least since the 1990s, there has been a phenomenal rise in the numbers and the political clout of communal forces in India to the point where they were actually able to capture state power at the centre for the first time in independent India, albeit in 'coalition' with smaller forces who played a minor role in the regime anyway. Furthermore, they were able to form governments in a number of major states in the northern and western parts of the country. In that, they not only exercised prolonged control over vast masses of people, they did so with legitimate electoral approval. What explains this phenomenon?

It is implausible that this vast socio-political phenomenon can be traced to a single and decisive feature of Indian society – social theory is no physics. Hence, the phenomenon has to be understood from a variety of directions, and in terms of interactions between them. Following one of the possible directions in this exploratory paper, we suggest two interrelated theses:

(a) Distinguished between a textual culture and a mass culture, the role of religion as *mass culture* is a significant dimension of the overall picture.

(b) Religious mass culture may turn into regressive mass political action *in the absence of* classical, secular platforms for the expression of the democratic aspirations of people.

### The Character of Communal Fascism

A fair amount of preparatory work is needed before we develop the suggested theses. Unlike syncategorematic expressions such as 'real money', the adjective 'communal' in the expression 'communal fascist' is genuinely attributive;[1] that is, communal fascism is a specific version of fascism, not the general one. In fact, we will suggest that the specific form of communal fascism witnessed in contemporary India may be a rare phenomenon.

Characterizations of fascism vary over a large historical and ideological spectrum. For the limited purposes of this paper, we assume that emergence of fascism in a political order is characterized by the following features, among others: (i) growing concentration of wealth and the accompanying impoverishment of masses, (ii) growing attack on the democratic and economic rights of working people, (iii) aggressive promotion of a fundamentalist-supremacist view of history and culture, and (iv) constructing external enemies to unite people under the threat of war.

We emphasize that these four conditions need to be simultaneously satisfied for a regime to be counted as fascist. In that sense, fascist regimes are to be distinguished from plain authoritarian regimes, including most dictatorial regimes, without denying that a fascist regime is also authoritarian and, eventually, dictatorial. Non-fascist authoritarian regimes certainly satisfy the first two conditions, but unless they satisfy the other two conditions as well, they will not be counted as fascist regimes.

Turning to the first two conditions for fascism, the characterization implies that a fertile ground for fascism obtains at a stage of capitalist development in a country where increased concentration of wealth requires not only greater exploitation of domestic population, but imperialist adventures as well. In other words, the ruling classes have imperialist ambitions that have not yet been realized. Further, the second condition suggests that the condition of the working masses needs to be in disarray both in terms of their economic and political impoverishment – a condition that is typically created by defeats in large-scale wars, but could also be created by attacks from external imperialism. Hence, both the ruling and the working classes are in a decisive stage of transition. That is, the working masses desire a radical change in their economic conditions without being able to do so in terms of democratic organizations. The absence of democratic organizations and institutions sets the material conditions for fascism. If the stage of transition was supported by organizations of the working masses themselves, the radical change would have led to a revolutionary upsurge, as in Russia in 1917.

The preceding characterization of fascism also suggests – a point often missed – that the growth of fascism is predicated on *mass support*, though once authoritarian rule has been successfully imposed and the imperialist ambitions launched, the continuation of such support may not be required; as a consequence, all democratic institutions will be systematically smashed. But in the early periods of growth, fascism requires a popular basis that can only arise in political systems where the general public had been turned to some semblance of democratic order typically based on universal franchise. So, in some sense, the consent of the people is needed. However, the very fact that substantial sections of people actually vote for a looming fascist regime with the consequent dismantling of all democratic institutions, suggests that the democratic order which paves the way for fascism must be 'fragile' in character.[2]

Once the first two conditions are simultaneously met, the characterization leaves much room for variations in how the last two are satisfied. For example, most fascist regimes target indigenous minority communities in order to strike fear in the majority community and to marshal their obedience for the regime. But targeting of minority communities by itself is neither a necessary nor a sufficient condition for fascism. European settlers targeted – in fact exterminated, like in North America – indigenous populations by sheer power of the gun to establish the rule of the white race. These were massive racist acts, but they will not count as fascism under the definition adopted.

In the other direction, fascism can arise in a society with almost spontaneous support from the general public without targeting any specific minority community to create the basis for that support. A typical example was the rise of fascism in Italy in which, no doubt, working-class organizations and progressive groups were systematically smashed, but fascism did not have an overt racist formulation. Mussolini, who did hold a supremacist view of history and culture, was opposed to National Socialism in Germany because it was 'one hundred percent racism: against everything and everyone; yesterday against Christian civilization, today against Latin civilization.'[3] Similar remarks apply to fascism in Japan and Spain.

This variety supports Georgi Dimitrov's well-known observation:

> No general characterization of fascism, however correct in itself, can relieve us of the need to study and take into account the special features of the development of fascism and the various

> forms of fascist dictatorship in the individual countries and at its various stages. It is necessary in each country to investigate, study and ascertain the national peculiar ties, the specific national features of fascism and to map out accordingly effective methods and forms of struggle against fascism.[4]

*Communal* fascism arises at a very specific moment in the social history of a country. It is restricted to the form of fascism that satisfies conditions (iii) and (iv) by targeting a minority community as the source of all malaise affecting the economic and cultural supremacy of the country. Even within this restricted category, it is debatable whether a fascist regime that targets domestic minorities needs to have an overtly *religious* dimension to it.

Nazi Germany is a case in point. That specific form of fascism targeted the Jews, but it is unclear if the Jews were targeted because of their Judaic religion, or simply because they could be characterized as belonging to an inferior – semitic – race. Moreover, it is also unclear if the supremacist view of history promoted by Nazism was itself based on a conception of a superior religion such as Christianity; as noted, Nazism is often characterized as un-Christian. It is also unclear how far the targeting of minorities was needed to garner mass support. Although Nazism did exploit the historical fallout of anti-semitism in the general culture, the actual campaign of extermination was mostly carried out in secret; in any case, these campaigns were not ratified in terms of electoral support, because by then all democratic institutions had been smashed. The present point is that the religious dimension of German fascism is at best ambiguous.

In contrast, the Muslims in India do not belong to a separate race; thus, targeting the Muslim minority – including open, state-sponsored attempts at extermination – can only be based unambiguously on religious identity.[5] It follows that the religious identity of the *majority community* was somehow marshalled to construct a supremacist view of history that viewed Islam as a threat. In other words, in the Indian case, conditions (iii) and (iv) were satisfied, at least in part, specifically in religious terms. The task is to explain what those terms are.

**Insufficient explanations**

Given the focus of this paper, we will attempt only a cursory review of the politico-economic environment – conditions (i) and (ii)

– that prevailed in India during the recent growth of communal fascism. We hope to show that a study of the politico-economic dimension by itself falls short of explaining the phenomenon of communal fascism; thus, the argument reinforces the specific need to study the religious dimension noted above.

The aspects of concentration of wealth and the impoverishment of the masses during the period under consideration may be summarized as follows. Although the GDP growth had indeed increased to about 6.7 per cent per annum during the 1990s, employment growth rate had actually fallen from 2 per cent in mid-1980s to 0.98 per cent in 2000.[6] Turning to other indicators, there is clear evidence that there has been a drastic fall in the off-take of subsidized grain by the poor from the Public Distribution System, and, between 1995–96 and 1998–99, a total of 60.84 lakh subscribers have ceased to be members of the national Provident Fund scheme.[7]

So, who grew? During the same period, 'the MNCs increased their sales by 322 per cent and gross profit by 369 per cent', and the 'Indian corporates garnered an increase in gross profit of 336 per cent and net sales by 303 per cent,' while their excise duty obligations increased by less than half of these figures.[8] While per capita income, boosted by the rising GDP, showed substantial growth by Indian standards, massive poverty in rural India culminated in large-scale suicides by farmers across the country. It is not difficult to understand how the effect of growth was distributed. During this period of aggressive implementation of the neoliberal agenda which saw a number of Indian corporations enter the 'Fortune 500' club and a relatively affluent middle class – roughly, 20 per cent of the population – emerge, the rest of India essentially turned into what the noted economist Utsa Patnaik has called the 'republic of hunger.'[9]

Interestingly, Utsa Patnaik traces the rise of communal-fascist forces in the country during the same period to this massive attack on agriculture. Our contention is that although the near-collapse of the agricultural sector did create the necessary material basis, via condition (i), for these forces to acquire strength, this condition by itself does not explain the specific form of fascism that emerged. For example, a very similar collapse of rural economy was witnessed in the late 1950s to early 1960s with the telling features of shrinkage in cultivated area, massive fall in productivity, exponential increase in unemployment, near-famine conditions, etc. But that period, instead of giving rise to fascism, led to one of the most impressive phases of people's movement in India that ultimately led to the consolidation of the public distribution system, rural credit, state control of agricultural pricing, and the like. An explanation of the current scene therefore needs some additional dimension apart from the economic dimension alone.

As hinted, part of that additional dimension, in sharp contrast to the 1960s, was the failure of people's movements to launch progressive political action. Democratic movements seem to have suffered a downward trend after reaching a peak around the mid-1970s. Since then, basic livelihood issues such as land reform, prices, health care, education, and human rights, among others, have ceased to dominate the agenda of electoral politics, not to speak of the stark absence of nation-wide movements on these issues. At least for the last two decades, there has been no large-scale working-class movement, no significant uprising, nothing comparable to the food movements of the 1960s. This is not because there has been any amelioration on these counts – just the opposite in fact – but because the very democratic basis for these movements has lost the power to develop. Given the fractured and uncertain nature of governance in these decades, it would have been difficult for the state, other things being equal, to repress any large-scale democratic movement such as the rail strike of 1974. Yet there is a strong feeling that other things are not equal, that the conditions are such that movements like this cannot even be contemplated.[10] Needless to say, a study of this complex phenomenon is beyond the scope of this essay.[11]

But, there as well, it is unlikely that the specific explanation can be reached in terms of general politico-economic conditions alone. Consider some of the suggestions of Prabhat Patnaik on related issues.[12] Patnaik traces some aspects of the phenomenon, with the consequent rise of communal fascism, to the loss of 'socialist vision' after the collapse of the socialist bloc. Again, without denying the international significance of this event, it is unclear if the rise of communal fascism is necessarily linked to the collapse of 'socialist vision'. Two related phenomena immediately come to mind: the massive anti-war movements witnessed across the globe since '9/11', and the formation of the World Social Forum in 2001. Noticeably, much of the groundwork for these large movements was conducted over the last few decades independently of the socialist bloc – some would say, *in spite* of it, since the 'socialist bloc' had ceased to inspire the 'socialist vision' decades ago. In any case, these movements took their current shapes at least a decade after the collapse of the bloc.

In fairness, Patnaik is careful to note both that 'the triumph of the inegalitarian ideology predates the collapse of the Soviet Union and hence requires a separate explanation', and that 'the collapse of socialism does not per se explain the growth of communal fascism that has occurred.' According to him, one of the basic factors for 'the emergence of the inegalitarian ideology and the growth of fascism worldwide, including in our own country', is the emergence of 'international finance capital, based on the "globalization of finance"', that 'undermines the capacity of the nation-state to play any agency role, such as is enjoined upon it by all socialist and redistributivist visions.' While we agree that much of the impoverishment of the concentration of wealth can be linked to the new form of international finance capital that gave rise to the current neoliberal economic agenda,[13] it is unclear if it necessarily leads to the loss of socialist vision on a grand scale, much as the rulers of the neoliberal regime want it to be so. No other region of the world has been subjected more than Latin America to decades of direct enforcement of neoliberal order, often backed by the power of the gun. Except for Cuba, no country in that region can be viewed as belonging to the erstwhile socialist bloc. Yet in recent elections in country after country in Latin America, the neoliberal order has been directly challenged by people's movements geared to a 'redistributivist vision'.

In India, despite the smaller (but growing) presence of neoliberalism and 50 years of pluralist democracy, nothing comparable to the people's movements just mentioned has been seen for some decades; for example, the anti-war demonstrations in the major metropolitan centres of India fell far short of what was achieved in small university campuses in the West.[14]

These disturbing concerns took an ominous shape in Gujarat. In early 2002, the simmering power of communal fascism launched on open attack on the Muslim minority in Gujarat in perhaps the most savage communal pogrom in contemporary India.[15] As Patnaik rightly observes in his article, 'informed by honesty, integrity and a humaneness', and 'with rare unanimity', the mainstream secular media 'exposed the complicit role played by the State government in the attacks on the minority community and demanded the removal of the State Chief Minister.' Despite the extensive coverage by the media, the pogroms went on for several days while the rest of the country watched. In fact, as observed at the beginning of this essay, while the communal-fascist BJP had lost most of the elections after coming to power in 1999, the BJP won handsomely in the elections that *followed* the pogroms in some major states. Subsequently, elections were also held in Gujarat itself, where the BJP was returned to power with an overwhelming majority.

Part of the explanation for this phenomenon, no doubt, can be traced to 'Islamic terror', rather than to Islam itself. As Basharat Peer observes, the victory of the communal-fascist forces in Gujarat 'lengthened the shadow of Hindu religious violence and Islamic terror attacks that loomed over India throughout 2002. In Gujarat, the fear of Muslim-sponsored terrorism consolidated effectively the Hindu nationalist votes.'[16] In the post-'9/11' scenario, in the name of assisting the civilized world in its fight against terrorism, the Government of India sided with the US military and economic interests with a straight face. Having thus appeased the United States and its neoliberal supporters in India,[17] the NDA Government returned to its basic communal–fundamentalist agenda in the atmosphere of unconcealed Islamophobia that engulfed much of the non-Muslim world after '9/11'.[18] What the US aggression and the accompanying propaganda machine enabled the Sangh Parivar to do was to claim not only moral legitimacy, but also some form of international solidarity for its attacks on minorities, especially the Muslims.[19] Exploitation of this 'window of opportunity' paid handsome dividends for both the right-wing, jingoist governments in India and the United States.[20]

However, the explanation essentially places the cart before the horse. The massive propaganda around 'Islamic terror' could be launched and acted upon by the BJP-led governments both at the Centre and in Gujarat precisely because people had already voted them to power. The Gujarat phenomenon, which includes the electoral successes, demonstrates the peak of that power; we need to explain how the communal-fascist forces reached that peak. In other words, the ability of these forces to exploit the opportunity provided by '9/11' required that the popular ground was already covered. The development of this popular ground for the communal-fascist forces is the major concern here.

In the article, we have referred to Prabhat Patnaik's suggestion that 'what is true of the present situation is that people no longer have clear notions of "right" and "wrong"' such that 'a degree of confusion, uncertainty and fuzziness has got introduced into the moral conceptions of the people'. As noted, Patnaik traces this state of moral confusion to 'the collapse, for the time being at any rate, of all dreams of building a society that is not based on private aggrandizement.' Further, 'the recent inegalitarian thrust of social analysis, which has acquired credibility and hegemony, associated inter alia with the collapse of the socialist project, has altered these long-held notions without substituting anything in its place.' It is natural therefore that the moral void 'forecloses the possibility of going beyond the existing "authority class".'

It is at least debatable if the fairly definitive electoral verdicts across Northern and Western India and, more specifically, in such large states as Gujarat, Rajasthan and Madhya Pradesh, can be explained in terms of a moral vacuum, rather than as an expression of a specific regressive moral choice. Furthermore, the case for the (recent) collapse of the 'socialist vision' seems overstated since the left had no penetration in the regions of the country under consideration; hence it is difficult to understand what 'social vision' engaged the people in those regions prior to the rise of communal fascism. If anything, explanation is needed as to why the left movement with its 'socialist vision' failed to penetrate the greater part of India. In any case, Patnaik's suggestion explains at best the tilt towards authoritarianism – a phenomenon visible in the Indian scene long before the current advent of communal fascism. The explanation requires an additional dimension to link the general rise of authoritarianism to one specifically of the communal-fascist kind.

### The Religious Dimension

The preceding considerations lead – inexorably, in my view – to the significance of the religious dimension as a factor in explaining the spectacular growth of communal fascism. In addition, taking clues from Patnaik's suggestion, it seems that this religious dimension enabled large masses of people of the majority (Hindu) community to endorse the programme of communal fascism, albeit with 'a degree of confusion, uncertainty and fuzziness'. In particular, the vote in Gujarat suggests a massive moral failure of a substantial section of the general public.

It is difficult to admit that a moral failure of the masses, especially at the grass roots, is the standing basis for a progressive social analysis. Even with examples of Nazi Germany in hand, we ought to adopt the null hypothesis that people are essentially rational and non-communal such that we are asked to proceed to a deeper understanding of an apparently conflicting phenomenon. This is not to deny either that large sections of people may hold false beliefs, or that they can be temporarily driven to frenzy. But to explain a sustained mass political action of the kind under discussion here, we are obliged to search for rational grounds based on sustainable historical practices, even if those grounds and practices sometimes lead to large-scale false beliefs, and regressive political forms. Ascription of moral failure to whole peoples can only be a last resort in social analysis, if at all. This is all the more pertinent in the recent Indian case since the same people voted the communal-fascist forces out of power in the stunning elections of May 2004. We cannot have it both ways.

To that end, it is instructive to state explicitly the argument that ascribes moral failure to people as a conclusion. With the argument in hand, we can proceed to examine each premise carefully to see if the argument can be blocked. It seems to me that the following argument underlies the discussion of morality in the last section.

It is undeniable that a vast majority of people engage in religious practices; we will presently see the extent of this phenomenon. These practices are religious, rather than something else, because they are typically prescribed by religious texts. Religious texts are bodies of beliefs that have been enshrined in a literary form, including the oral. The textual content of these beliefs is largely false, irrational, and often communal. The communal aspect of religions ensues from the fact that, proclamations of universal brotherhood and the equality of all religions notwithstanding, every religion embodies at least subliminal – often explicit – claims of exclusivity and supremacy of lineage. Most major religions contain a sharp category of the 'other' as essentially suspect and inferior – pagan, heretic, *kafir*, *mlechha*, to name a few. It is also undeniable, as we saw, that masses had voted for the communal-fascist forces in particular regions consistently for over a decade.

Schematically, we set out our premises as follows:-

i. Religious beliefs are largely false, irrational and communal in character.

ii. Religious beliefs are largely enshrined in texts including folk-texts.
iii. Masses participate widely in religious practices.
iv. Masses have voted for communal forces, especially in Gujarat.

It follows that, other things being equal, masses are or have become communal, irrational and agents of false beliefs. The argument is not strictly deductive; which interesting argument ever is? Nonetheless, with the insertion of suitable missing premises, the general negative message seems to follow.

### *Valid Premises*

It seems, even on cursory inspection, that the steps of the argument just stated are individually valid; or, more cautiously, it can be maintained that these steps are at least *prima facie* plausible such that it is not irrational to hold them together consistently. If so, then the disturbing conclusion sketched above becomes plausible as well. The only way to defeat the argument, if at all, is to show that other things are *not* equal; that is, the premises allow an interpretation in which the conclusion does not follow even if the premises are individually true. This move, we shall see, leads to the distinction between textuality and mass culture.

### *Steps I and II: The 'Inverted World'*

The argument can be challenged at various points. For example, one could challenge Step I by simply denying the irrationality of religious beliefs. In effect, this challenge amounts to placing religious beliefs at least on par with secular, scientific beliefs that are typically held to be the prime examples of rationality. In fact, it is not uncommon to hear these days that religious beliefs are *superior* to scientific beliefs, and only a Euro-centrically warped notion of 'rationality' prevents us from realizing this. For the purposes of this paper, we wish to stay away from this debate, and will simply adopt, without further argument, Karl Marx's classic view that 'Religion is the sigh of the oppressed creature, the heart of a heartless world, just as it is the spirit of a spiritless conditions. It is the *opium* of the people.'[21] The challenge is to block the argument while admitting the truth of Premise I.

According to Marx, then, religions enable people to escape the heartless world and its spiritless conditions because 'this state, this society produce religion, an *inverted world-consciousness*' giving shape to an '*inverted world*'. The point to note is that Marx identifies religions with a certain world-view, namely, an 'inverted' one. World-views are nothing but systems of belief; in the case of religion, these systems of belief are centred around concepts of divinity, afterlife, migration of the soul, liberation from material conditions, hell, heaven, and the like. Together, they help in the construction of an inverted world since none of them arise from the empirical conditions of the 'heartless world' itself.

Due to their non-empirical basis, the fundamental concepts of religion are only of 'philosophical' interest in so far as they do not directly link up with the material conditions of people, just as the system of concepts is useless for 'this state, this society'. The canonical structure of religions therefore is far more complex. There are analogies from common experience, often mixed with little allegories involving real and fictitious characters, that generate an abiding, *memorable* interest in the conceptual system. There are logical claims, typically supplemented with metaphysical argumentation, to rule out alternative conceptions, or to show the superiority of the current conception. Moreover, there are complex attempts to derive specific guidances or goals – for example, significance of attaining *moksha* – from the conceptions so reached. Finally, there are recommended practices – often elaborate and tied with massive dosages of symbolism – whose successful renditions are supposed to satisfy the guidances.

We call this total canonical system, the *textuality* of religions. Typically, the noted textuality is enshrined in actual texts phrased in a complex technical vocabulary internal to the textual tradition – hence the need for preachers, *pandits*, evangelists, and the like. It is important to understand just which aspect(s) of this complex structure fall under Marx's conception of religion. *Inter alia*, it is also important to see just where the common people enter this complex system.

For now, if religions are viewed primarily as belief-systems, then it is difficult to assign rationality to the textual forms which enshrine such beliefs. In that sense, religious beliefs can well be harnessed, under suitable historical conditions, to give rise to a communal-fascist state of mind, even if religious texts by themselves may not have a unique fascist interpretation.[22]

### *Steps III and IV: Extent of Religious Practices*

These steps of the argument are empirical in character. Step III is amply supported by facts. Keeping to the religious practices of the Hindu community, several million people take a dip in the cold waters of the Ganges every day during the Kumbha Mela; millions throng the annual religious celebrations at Gangasagar, Puri and Dwarka; hundreds of thousands of people travel long distances to visit the temple at Tirupati; despite heavy odds, several thousands travel to the shrines at Amarnath, Kedarnath, and Badarinath every year.[23] These are some of the more publicized events carried by the newspapers. Beyond these, there are thousands of temples and other shrines scattered across the country – Tarapith in Bengal, for one – which attract massive crowds for several days every year. Apart from these, there are local temples, gurus, assemblies, *akharas*, yoga centres, and the like, where thousands of people gather on a daily basis. We should also mention more community-based folk festivals with a pronounced religious dimension such as the Durga Puja, Dussera, and Ram Navami. Once we take a cumulative view of the total phenomenon, it is hard to see any significant section of the population – except some of the urban, western-educated, well-off sections of the intelligentsia – not taking part in some practice or the other. The left has largely ignored this massive fact.

As noted, Step IV – vote for communal-fascist forces – is also well accounted for by facts. Even if we factor out the effects of clever political alliances, electoral malpractices, and the winner-take-all system of election, we simply cannot deny the phenomenal rise in the popular support for the BJP and the Shiv Sena since the 1990s.[24] A tiny part of the support that came from the wealthy sections of the population was, no doubt, based on explicit endorsement of the communal-fascist agenda of these parties. With the eclipse of the strong, authoritarian base of the Congress and the rise of the neoliberal agenda, the class interests of these sections coincided with the politico-economic goals of the BJP and Shiv Sena.

But the support of this section, though significant for marshalling state policy, is not sufficient for winning nearly 200 seats in Parliament and capturing power alone or in coalition in such major states as Maharashtra, Gujarat, Madhya Pradesh, Uttar Pradesh and Rajasthan. Despite its unconcealed neoliberal and pro-imperialist agenda, how did the BJP manage to secure the votes of vast masses of urban poor, landless peasants, labourers and tribals, none of whom is likely to have a fascination for the stated agenda? The only explanation, it would seem, is that impoverished masses have turned communal.

As far as we can see, this uneasy conclusion can be blocked only by severing the link between steps II and III. In other words, the argument assumes that the widespread religious practices of the masses is causally linked to the religious beliefs enshrined in the texts. If, therefore, there is a separation between religious *texts* and religious *practices* of the masses, then the conclusion will not follow. I will argue that on empirical evidence this separation seems to be the case.

**Texts and Practices**

Religious thought as enshrined in religious texts can be separated from religious practices engaged in by common people on the following grounds, among others.

First, as Rajat K. Ray and Nupur Chaudhuri (in this volume) explain with a specific example, religious texts are often coded with many-layered meanings. The primary layer, open to common interpretation, conceals much of the secondary metaphorical meaning that can be reached by a more discerning audience with knowledge of the specific religious tradition. Moreover, the secondary meaning may conceal a tertiary meaning that is essentially maintained as a secret and is made available, under specific instructions from the guru, to the most devout members of the sect. A very similar account of religious texts was offered by Robert Nozick.[25] Working through a number of religious texts in the Hindu tradition, Nozick argued that, on the surface, expressions such as 'supreme ecstasy', 'self-revelation' and 'universe unfolding onto itself' are literary devices for describing religious experience. Below the surface, however, the specific expressions might well indicate intricate sexual practices that help the practitioner attain the suggested state; needless to say, those practices are a closely guarded secret and are never made available to the common devotee.

Second, even with respect to the primary, 'popular', level of meaning, it is common knowledge that the religious practices of the masses have little to do with the religious texts themselves. In an underdeveloped set-up such as India, the high rate of illiteracy is a clear impediment to an access to texts. Even within the literate sections of the population, formal literacy is essentially insufficient for marshalling the intricate and abstract character of religious texts. In many cases, the masses are excluded from an access to religious texts by conscious design. In the Indian case, the use of Sanskrit, for example, is designed to create an elite, male, and Brahmanical audience from which other castes, tribals, and women have been systematically excluded. Even within the favoured group, listening to Sanskrit *slokas* – often rendered by ill-equipped *purohits* who have little knowledge of the language themselves – is a matter of ritualistic obedience rather than of comprehension. In most cases, such rituals are the *only* link between a text and the practices that are supposed to follow from it. In effect, Marx missed the empirical point that, even if religions offer an 'inverted world', it is hard to see that the masses live in it with a full understanding of that world.

Third, a clear division between the practice of rendering the texts and *other* practices has evolved over centuries. As noted, women have been largely excluded from the sanctum sanctorum of religious textuality in the Hindu tradition, yet most of the preparatory work for the solemn events is done by women themselves – cleaning up the place, collecting and arranging flowers, looking after the comforts of the *purohit* or the guru, and the like. Not surprisingly, women themselves do not view these practices as additional domestic labour, but as privileged *religious* practices. The scene repeats itself in other religions as well. Anecdotally, it is well-known that poor, illiterate Muslims eagerly travel long distances with enthusiasm to reach a mosque for the Friday prayers much before the prayers begin. Their task is to clean up the place, organize the prayer area, control the crowds, etc. Just before the prayers begin, they recede to the background, and the elite walk in to occupy the area from where the sermons are delivered.

Fourth, as a result, what comes to the masses as expressions of religious textuality at best are folklore, adventures of gurus, anecdotes of miracles, and a large dosage of sermons on health, morality, sexuality, values of patriarchy and other social hierarchies. Although it is obvious, it is important to emphasize that these emerge from the class-divided society itself, and have little to do with the specificity of religious texts. For example, these sermons are perfectly consistent within an atheistic set up or a tradition, such as Buddhism, which makes no specific textual appeal to divinity and the metaphysical order in which it is embedded. In fact, in the case of most tribal religions, the entirety of religious practices may be viewed as closed around these moral guidances that do not seem to be based on any overarching metaphysical concern. However, the distance between the textuality of religions and the religious practices of the masses is neither sharp nor absolute. It comes in grades depending on the organizational character and the historical spread of the concerned religion – less for Islam and Christianity, more for Hinduism and the rich variety of individual-based sects allowed there. New religions such as Sikhism seem to occupy intermediate positions.

**'Festival of the Masses'**

What then explains the sustained historical fascination of the masses with religion? How are religious systems able to work as the 'sigh of the oppressed' and as 'opium of the people?' If the analysis sketched above is even partially valid, then it is hard to ascribe the historical fascination to the intellectual content of religions, which appears to be the basis of Marx's critique of them. In other words, there must be some other way of describing the sustainability of religions that remains invariant across the explicit articulation and changes of their scholastic narratives. Given the separation between texts and the practices engaged in by the masses, it follows that those sustaining features could be located in the internal properties of religious practices themselves.

It also follows that those practices can be viewed as largely independent of textuality despite the professed link between them. Practices, especially those with a massive symbolic character, need some or other system of thought to anchor them. In the absence of any other system of thought, it is not surprising that those practices attached themselves, tenuously, to the available religious ideologies; they could have attached themselves to something else if that were historically available. What could be the features of such sustainable practices? I will briefly mention six dimensions that seem to me to be immediately relevant for the purposes at hand; surely, there are others.

*Solidarity:* Religious occasions bind people under a common cause shared by the members of the gathering. Successful performance of complex religious rituals requires co-operative gestures which foster a sense of community spirit among the participants.

*Altruism:* Most religions contain a clause devoted to the welfare of others, especially underprivileged members of the same community. It could take the form of collecting donations, organizing community meals, health care, and the like.

*Egalitarianism:* Notwithstanding the lifestyles and locations of top religious leaders and their cohorts, most religions advocate on paper a disapproval of extreme concentration of wealth and recommend a redistributive vision of society. In effect, religions advocate a 'simple life' that most people are compelled to lead anyway by dint of their material condition. A religious point of view in that sense renders value to the otherwise difficult lives led by the masses.

*Pacifism:* Although religious wars have been at least as frequent as purely territorial ones in history, religions also recommend, other things being equal, a peaceful vision of the world that includes the notion of universal brotherhood.

*Domesticism:* Although religions such as Christianity, Islam, and, growingly, Hinduism aim for universal coverage, all religions typically embed themselves in local cultures to attain a variety of ethnic identities. In that sense, religious institutions are common grounds for the preservation of local cultures in the face of cultural onslaught from outside. When the cultural onslaught is accompanied by imperialist programmes, these institutions can, in fact, play a limited anti-imperialist role.

*Spirituality:* The preceding factors, along with the subliminal expectation that religions offer a coherent perspective to the complex problem of living, make participation in religious activity a meaningful preoccupation that every human being yearns for – religion is a spirit of a spiritless condition.

*Festivity:* Religious events are typically marked with colour displayed amidst general whiteness, flowers, cleanliness, joyful participation, and music. In fact, the structure, content and the delivery of religious music gives a coherent unity to each of the factors just listed. Most religious music, without failing to be essentially good music, is accessible to the common people so that they can actively engage in it.

One does not have to be communal to feel attracted to such a system of practices if religions provide them, especially when this is the *only* source available in an otherwise degrading human condition. It also explains why the elite, intellectual sections of the people feel less attracted to religion. They have other secular resources in which these universal human dimensions are satisfied – access to high culture, for example.

More significantly for our purposes, each of these practices is very much a part of progressive mass organizations. Those who have some acquaintance with people's movements – peasants, workers, teachers, youth, etc. – can amply testify to the festive character that almost spontaneously ensues when people gather under a cause. By parity of reason, the absence of broad, sustainable, and democratic movements geared to the basic livelihood issues of the people has left a wide vacuum in *political* practice of the masses. It is not surprising that masses have found those practices within religious systems since they are historically available in any case. In the last two decades – precisely the period of democratic deficit under consideration – the Sangh Parivar has been able to enter and fill that political space by adding an explicit religious dimension to their communal-fascist agenda. It is worth noting that the phenomenal growth of the Vishwa Hindu Parishad and Bajrang Dal are more recent dimensions of the Parivar. By joining and thereby co-opting the religious lives of the masses, they have been able to marshal much of their religious energy towards the *political* agenda.

It is a well-known fact of human life that when the penchant for the values of solidarity, altruism, and the like, are satisfied, a certain sense of loyalty to institutions that order them develops. As a result, the participants may in fact ignore or downplay the negative features often associated with these institutions, especially when their act of participation can be viewed as essentially separated from the fallout of such negative aspects. When the negative aspects begin to dominate, values of solidarity and domesticity tend to restrain the ability of the participants to voice protest, generating thereby moral confusion among the masses and allowing the insidious forces to pursue their agenda.

The phenomenon is not restricted to communal-fascist programmes alone. The chequered, and often problematic, history of the communist movement in the last century provides enough examples. Given the loyalty to 'infant socialism' and the values associated in defending it, people essentially downplayed the outrages committed by the ruling oligarchies in 'socialist' countries. When facts about wide-scale repression and secret operations began to attain a public face, people either recoiled in disbelief or lapsed into silence, while continuing to lend support to the regimes out of their historical loyalty to the basic cause.

In the Indian case, the absence of the left – and, hence, of people's movements – across vast stretches of the country allowed the Sangh Parivar not only to fill the political space, as noted, but also to implement a massive propaganda almost at will since the loyalty of the people had already been secured through their entrenchment in the religious machinery.

However, as with every repressive order, people ultimately withdraw their support when material conditions override the binds of loyalty and an alternative political space begins to open up. The general elections of 2004 testify in part to this phenomenon – class concerns supersede cultural loyalties.[26] We must note though that the salvaging of the body politic from the clutches of communal fascism was achieved only in part. Given the massive historical presence of religions in the consciousness of the people, religious platforms can always be used by communal-fascist forces if secular alternatives fail to ameliorate the material conditions of the masses.

This is a revised version of a paper presented at the panel discussion on 'Religion and Material Life' organized under the auspices of the Aligarh Historians Society at Mysore in December 2003. I am indebted to the distinguished audience present on that occasion for a very lively discussion.

**Notes and References**

1 See W.V.O. Quine, *World and Object*, Cambridge: MIT Press, 1960, p. 103, for the relevant distinction.

2 Noam Chomsky, 'Manipulation of Fear', foreword essay in N. Mukherji, *December 13: Terror over Democracy*, Bibliophile South Asia, New Delhi, 2005, p. xvii.

3 Benito Mussolini, 'Doctrine of fascism,' cited in *Encyclopaedia Britannica, Macropaedia*, Volume 7, p. 185. It is a different issue that Mussolini joined Hitler later on for the conquest of Africa and other regions.

4 Georgi Dimitrov, 'Unity of the Working Class against Fascism', in *Selected Works*, volume 2, Sofia Press, 1972, pp. 86–119.

5 This point needs some qualification in view of the current Islamophobia.

6 Planning Commission figures, released 21 May 2001.

7 'Union pick up reforms gauntlet', Government Business, p. viii, *The Times of India*, 25 May 2001.

8 Ibid.

9 Utsa Patnaik, *The Republic of Hunger*, Sahmat, 2004.

10 The official leader of the impressive struggle of the railway workers, George Fernandes, has turned into a leading collaborator with the communal-fascist forces.

[11] See my 'On reasons for the state', *Indian Social Science Review*, Volume 1, No. 2, 1999, pp. 311–28, for some preliminary effort at explanation. Unfortunately, I have not been able to locate any full-length study of this crucial issue.

[12] Prabhat Patnaik, 'Markets, morals and the media', *Frontline*, Volume 19, Issue 15, 20 July–2 August 2002.

[13] See Prabhat Patnaik's illuminating introduction to a new edition of V.I. Lenin's *Imperialism: The Highest Stage of Capitalism*, New Delhi: Leftword, 2001.

[14] In contrast to the massive, nationwide protests against the presence of Robert McNamara witnessed in the 1960s, the captains of the neoliberal world order, including their representatives in the US government, are given red-carpet treatment in their increasingly frequent visits to India – the list includes Bill Gates, James Baker, Bill Clinton, Condoleezza Rice, Donald Rumsfeld, Colin Powell, Richard Armitage, among others.

[15] See *Crime Against Humanity: An Inquiry into the Carnage in Gujarat*, Concerned Citizens' Tribunal, published by Anil Dharkar for Citizens for Peace and Justice, 2002. Also, *State Sponsored Genocide: Factsheet Gujarat 2002*, CPI(M) Publications, 2002.

[16] Basharat Peer, 'Victims of December 13', *The Guardian Weekend*, 5 July 2003.

[17] Within months after the carnage in Gujarat, the same media turned around and vigorously supported the regime in its 'India shining' campaign. Events in Gujarat, though condemnable, were systematically projected as an aberration.

[18] Vaskar Nandy, 'War against Terrorism: Perspective on Protests', *Economic and Political Weekly*, 27 October 2001. Also, Mahmood Mamdani, *Good Muslim, Bad Muslim: America, the Cold War and the Roots of Terror*, Pantheon Books, 2003. For the Australian scene, see Iain Lygo, 'Who will be charged under terrorism laws?', *Znet*, 23 October 2004.

[19] See my 'Gujarat and the world order', *Znet South Asia*, June 2002.

[20] See Vidya Subramaniam, 'Two gods, one message', *The Hindu*, 11 November 2004. The topic is discussed in some detail in my *December 13: Terror over Democracy*, Bibliophile South Asia, New Delhi, 2005, Chapter 1.

[21] Karl Marx, 'Contribution to the critique of Hegel's Philosophy of Law', in K. Marx and F. Engels, *Collected Works*, Vol. III, Moscow: Progress Publishers, 1975, p. 175.

[22] As hinted, I doubt if religious beliefs can fail to have a communal character. In saying this, I am obviously identifying genuine secularism with principled atheism. I am also questioning the widely-held view – often aligned with secularism – that religious beliefs may be viewed as essentially 'personal' in character. These stronger theses are not needed for the purpose at hand.

Moreover, as noted, textuality of religions are complex bodies of doctrines; hence, it is unlikely that every item in those systems strictly qualifies as a 'religious' item. Those non-religious items of the texts then may well supply an edifice for genuinely secular thought. In *Problem of False Beliefs* (MPhil dissertation, University of Delhi, 2004), Mitsu Jain made a preliminary attempt to study this issue.

23 It is well documented that millions of pilgrims have been visiting these shrines for centuries travelling by foot for months over dangerous mountain roads, often infested with man-eating animals; thousands perished along the way. More recently, the crowds for the annual pilgrimage to Amarnath had to be stopped by force at Jammu and Pathankot; while the rich generally stayed away, poor people with scant resources, kept on gathering despite the terrible situation in Kashmir.

24 Political compulsion seems to be the only reason why parties such as the AIADMK are not generally counted as communal-fascist.

25 Robert Nozick, *Philosophical Explanations*, Chapter 3: 'Why is there something rather than nothing', see especially the final section on mysticism, Harvard University Press, 1978.

26 See my '2004 Elections and after', *Revolutionary Democracy*, Vol. 10, No. 2, 2004.

# Contributors

The late M. ATHAR ALI was Professor of History, Aligarh Muslim University.

D.P. CHATTOPADHYAYA is Chairman, Centre for Studies in Civilizations, New Delhi, and General Editor, Project of History of Indian Science, Philosophy and Culture.

NUPUR CHAUDHURI is Lecturer in the Department of History, Presidency College, Kolkata.

BARUN DE is former Director, Centre for Studies in Social Sciences, Kolkata.

IRFAN HABIB is Professor of History (retd.), Aligarh Muslim University.

FARHAT HASAN is Reader in History, Aligarh Muslim University.

SUVIRA JAISWAL is Professor of History (retd.), Jawaharlal Nehru University, New Delhi.

DWIJENDRA NARAYAN JHA is Professor of History (retd.), University of Delhi.

OSAMU KONDO is Professor of History in Osaka, Japan.

KAMLESH MOHAN is Professor of History, Panjab University, Chandigarh.

SHIREEN MOOSVI is Professor of History, Aligarh Muslim University.

## *Contributors*

NIRMALANGSHU MUKHERJI is Professor of Philosophy, University of Delhi.

V. RAMAKRISHNA is Professor of History (retd.), University of Hyderabad.

RAJAT KANTA RAY is Vice Chancellor, Visva Bharati, Santiniketan.

SYED ALI NADEEM REZAVI is Reader in History, Aligarh Muslim University.

K.M. SHRIMALI is Professor of History, University of Delhi.

# Index

# *Index*

Vindhyaśakti, 84
Viṣṇudāsa, 88
Vishwa Hindu Parishad, 280
Vivekananda, Swami, 128, 219
*Vivekavardhini*, 243

Wach, Joachim, 224
Wacha, D.E., 240
Watt, Montgomery, 135
Weber, Max, xiii
Wellhausen, J., 138
Whaling, Frank, 86
women, in prehistory, xvi; marriage practice, xix–xxi, 172; *sati*, xxviii; inheritance rights, xxx, xxxiii; and Sikhism, xxxiv, 187–209
World Social Forum, 268

Xenophanes, 17

Yadava, B.N.S., 52
Yang Chu, 15
Yazdī, Muhammad, 163
Yi-Jing (I-tsing), xxiii
Yoga, Yogis, 108–09; and Tantra, 114; Nāth-, 150
*Yoga Vāsiṣṭha*, 85

Zeno, 18
Zvelebil, Kamil, 74